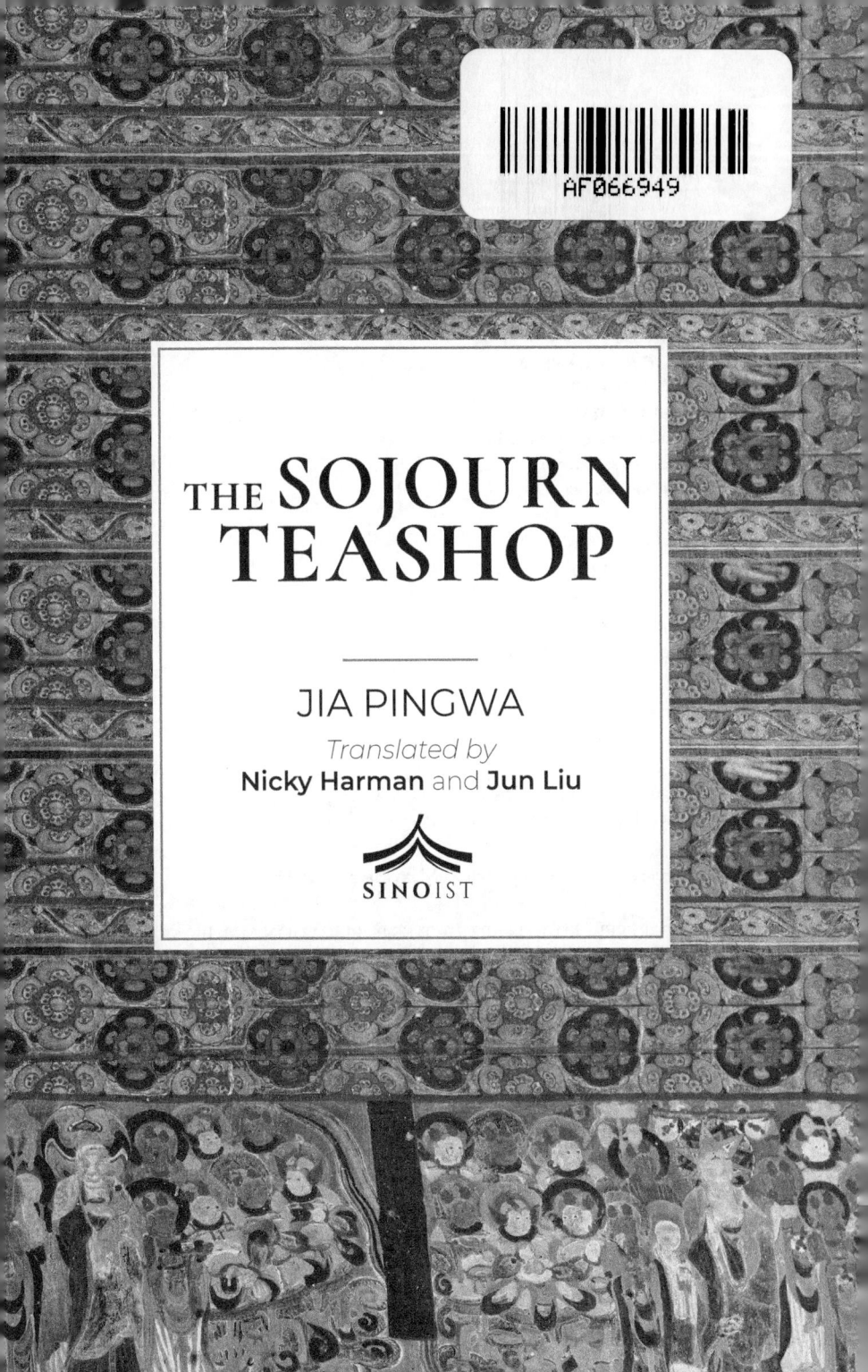

ACA Publishing Ltd
University House
11-13 Lower Grosvenor Place
London SW1W 0EX, UK
Tel: +44 (0)20 3289 3885
E-mail: info@alaincharlesasia.com
www.alaincharlesasia.com
www.sinoistbooks.com

Beijing Office
Tel: +86 (0)10 8472 1250

Author: Jia Pingwa
Translators: Nicky Harman & Jun Liu

English Translated Edition published by Sinoist Books
(an imprint of ACA Publishing Ltd)

Chinese language copyright © 暂坐 (Zan Zuo) 2020,
by The Writers Publishing House Co., Ltd, Beijing, China

English language translation copyright © Nicky Harman, 2022

ALL RIGHTS RESERVED. NO PART OF THIS PUBLICATION MAY BE REPRODUCED IN MATERIAL FORM, BY ANY MEANS, WHETHER GRAPHIC, ELECTRONIC, MECHANICAL OR OTHER, INCLUDING PHOTOCOPYING OR INFORMATION STORAGE, IN WHOLE OR IN PART, AND MAY NOT BE USED TO PREPARE OTHER PUBLICATIONS WITHOUT WRITTEN PERMISSION FROM THE PUBLISHER.

This novel is entirely a work of fiction. The names, characters and incidents portrayed in it are the work of the author's imagination. Any resemblance to actual persons, living or dead, events or localities is entirely coincidental.

Hardback ISBN: 978-1-83890-540-8
Paperback ISBN: 978-1-83890-530-9
eBook ISBN: 978-1-83890-531-6

A catalogue record for *The Sojourn Teashop* is available from the National Bibliographic Service of the British Library.

THE SOJOURN TEASHOP

JIA PINGWA

Translated by
NICKY HARMAN & JUN LIU

SINOIST BOOKS

LIST OF CHARACTERS

Hai Ruo, owner of the Sojourn Teashop

The Sisterhood

Lu Yike, runs an advertising agency, Hai Ruo's closest friend
Yan Nianchu, sells medical equipment
Feng Ying, painter
Xia Zihua, former model
Xiang Qiyu, runs the Terahertz Energy Tank
Xi Lishui, owns a car dealership
Si Yinan, owns a furniture shop
Xu Qi, Yinan's lover, comes from a TCM family
Yu Benwen, runs a hotpot restaurant, amateur photographer
Ying Lihou, rents out street-front properties, lost money through Yan Nianchu

TRANSLATOR'S NOTE

In the lively scene of contemporary Chinese literature, Jia Pingwa (1952-) stands with Mo Yan and Yu Hua as one of the biggest names. Jia Pingwa's fiction focuses on the lives of common people, particularly in his home province of Shaanxi, and has hitherto been largely set in the countryside (*Shaanxi Opera*, forthcoming, and *Broken Wings*, 2019) or in the lives of workers from the countryside who have moved to the big city (*Happy Dreams*, 2017). Jia's most recent novel, *The Sojourn Teashop*, is very different: it focuses on a dozen women in the city and their struggles to run their businesses, battle with bureaucracy and corruption, and find personal happiness.

Hai Ruo, the centre of the sisterhood, shows the author's increased understanding of the opposite gender from previous female protagonists in his books. Like the Russian matryoshka doll Eva gives her, Hai Ruo is many things: a successful teashop owner who attracts a group of like-minded business women, the single mother of a wayward son and a woman with deep longings. Her name 海若 literally means "ocean-like", which encapsulates the depth of the female characters, echoing the author's praise in the Afterword of the real-life teashop owner and her friends.

Alongside Hai Ruo is another fascinating character, Yi Guang. The author placed a prism in front of this man and leaves ample space for our imagination to work. Of particular interest is Yi Guang's quote of an ancient classic towards the middle of the book: "But this is 'nourishing the bird with my own food, not with what the bird needs for its sustenance'." This comes from Zhuangzi, the great Taoist philosopher of the third century BCE. It is said the Duke of Lu had a rare visitor, a beautiful seabird. Delighted, the duke plied the bird with his favourite food accompanied by court music. The bird sulked, touched nothing and died in three days.

According to the author, Yi Guang is lamenting that he will never reach the highest level in writing and painting because he must work within official boundaries, instead of following the true nature of arts and literature. It's important to note this as a crucial turning point in shaping this complex character.

Another interesting feature is the analogy between plants and the women in the sisterhood. Some comparisons are obvious, Si Yinan is upright and tough like the *nanmu* tree, as her name suggests; Yan Nianchu curries favour with men in power for her own gain, like an asparagus fern. Yi Guang's couplet of birds chattering happily amid intermingled tree branches laden with flowers comes from a poem by the Song dynasty poet Shi Yannian. This captures the genial friendship of the sisterhood.

In April 2021, I joined the project upon Nicky's invitation. The initial aim was for me to simply translate the draft of Chapter Seven until the end. Eventually I also worked on the entire book with Nicky and Sinoist Books' editor David Lammie in many rounds of editing.

Our method: I translated the draft from Chinese into English, Nicky did the first and second checks as I moved on to the next chapter. In this initial stage, our attention was focused on faithfully capturing every nuance of meaning in the Chinese text. When the Afterword was done, we went through the entire book with the Chinese text alongside the translation. With a much deeper understanding of the book's plot, character relations and the author's intention, we were able to spot many issues. In the all-English read-throughs, we aspired to reach a higher literary standard in the target language, and made special efforts to identify and pin down the voice appropriate to each character as much of the book is delivered in dialogue.

Throughout this process, I researched the meanings, sources and contexts of cultural or historical terms to help Nicky find the most appropriate and natural expressions. As Nicky points out in her Asian

Books Blog posts, we had a "push-pull" factor in the co-translation: me on getting all details right, Nicky on ensuring its literary quality. Eventually, what readers find here is just the tip of the iceberg – the huge amount of work we did remains unseen, but without it a faithful translation would have been out of reach.

A big decision we made was how to name the characters. Chinese society hinges upon relationships in order to function. How people address each other clearly indicates the formality or intimacy of their relationship.

From the very beginning, we decided to keep two-character names such as Hai Ruo throughout the book, but for three-character names like Ying Lihou, we only mention the full name once in each chapter, then use the given name thereafter, even though the Chinese generally uses the full name. By doing so, we made the narrator, and readers, closer to the characters, which is more engaging for English readers. In dialogues and narrations from a character's perspective, we used full names to indicate a formality as befitting the occasion.

Besides the actual names, there are several terms of address that we debated among ourselves before arriving at the present solution.

Hai Ruo is the heart of the sisterhood and probably the eldest, so most of her friends and staff call her "Hai-jie". "Jie" means elder sister and signifies a close relationship. We followed the Chinese text to use the term "-jie" wherever it appears in the original.

When Yi Guang appears in this book, most people call him Yi Guang-laoshi, or Yi-laoshi. "Laoshi" means teacher, but it's an honorific title for people of great knowledge and prestige. It's worthy of note that Yi Guang and Hai Ruo never use "jie" or "laoshi" to each other, because of their intimacy and similar age.

As an indication of the complex relations in this book, we adopted another term of address for the shop assistants working for Hai Ruo. Most of them only have a family name, and are known in the original simply as xiao-Fang or xiao-Su. "*xiao*" (小), meaning small, or little, is a term of endearment for younger people, as opposed to "*lao*", or old, in *laoshi* (teacher), *laowai* (foreigner). We rejected the option of Little Fang as being misleading, and similarly decided against only calling these assistants Fang or Su with no prefix. This would sound very formal, completely losing the note of friendliness in the Chinese. It just so happens that Xiao (肖) is a common family name in Chinese, so to

TRANSLATOR'S NOTE

avoid confusion, we not only use the prefix but always keep it in the lower case, xiao-Fang, even when it appears at the beginning of a sentence.

We also took steps to name several characters to establish clearer images in English. In the early *chuanqi* stories of the Tang and Song dynasties more than a millennium ago, the characters' names were rarely used. A typical story would refer to the protagonists as *sheng* (the young man) or *nü* (the young woman). Two characters in this novel are treated the same way. Xi Lishui's new boyfriend Wang Beixing and Xin Qi's husband Tian Chengbin are just identified as "the man". Another tradition in ancient Chinese writing was referring to a person by their official title or place of origin. The author only mentions briefly the surname of the general secretary of Xijing's Party committee, who remains in the dark on a chair of power. By using their names more often, we hope they will be more memorable.

There is another character, Xia Zihua's mother, who doesn't have a name at all. She appears in many chapters and plays an important role, as Hai Ruo and the sisterhood take meticulous care of them. Calling her Zihua's mother, the old woman/lady, or Xia Lei's grandma/granny feels tedious and even disrespectful. So we discussed the issue with the author, and he kindly supplied us with a family name, Qi. There is already a Mr Qi in the book, an entrepreneur connected to Mr Ning the general secretary. He never appears directly and is easily distinguishable from Mrs Qi.

Throughout our translation, the author has shown tremendous patience with our carefully chosen questions. His assistant Ma Li and editors in China relayed the questions and answers back and forth tirelessly. Literary and academic translator Jack Hargreaves took precious time to help us check the particularly challenging passage on the Buddhist mural in Chapter Two. My family in Xi'an provided invaluable insight into the local cuisine, culture and history. At one point, they even tracked down mutton *paomo* restaurant owners for advice on how to prepare and eat the iconic soup. And finally, I'd like to thank Nicky for inviting me onto such a fulfilling project, and always being understanding and supportive.

Jun Liu
March 2022

1. EVA • XIJING CITY

THERE IS A MOUNTAIN TEMPLE outside Hangzhou with couplets hung at the gate. They read:

> North to south, south to north, people hurry back and forth.
> Climbing high, climbing low, why not sojourn before you go?

What for? Why, to drink tea, of course. Teashops have sprung up all over China. There's one right here in Xijing City, called the Sojourn Teashop.

In 2016, a Russian woman called Eva returns to Xijing. She is surprised to find the city enveloped in a pall of smog, even though it is the beginning of spring.

There was smog when she was here five years ago, but it was nothing much, and no one took it seriously. It was common for dark clouds to hang over the Qinling Mountains to the south of the city. People used to joke, "Beijing's sent us some smog!" But the haze was gauzy thin and dissipated quickly. This time is different: the air is the colour of smoke, with cream and brown patches, at first dimming the light, then becoming so dense that you cannot tell how far away things are. You feel as if it hides a monster. Cars and buses seem to sink into it. The road markings are no longer visible, and the buildings become weightless and appear to float in the murk.

But still the streets and alleys teem with people.

Let us imagine the earth as a mountain. Wild beasts – from lions, tigers and bears to goats, badgers, foxes and hedgehogs – lurk in every gully. Hideous fish drift in rock pools, bizarre birds inhabit deep ravines. The Chinese are much like birds. There are vast numbers of them, they take flight and cover the sky, they dive down and fill the tree branches, they shriek madly, they parrot each other, filling the air with a tremendous uproar. When speech becomes so clamorous, it loses all sense and rhythm and begins to sound like nothing so much as a million people cracking sunflower seeds between their teeth.

The noise wakes Eva up. She pushes open the window, to find that it is dawn. In the pale light, crowds of people churn along the smoggy street. It is a strange and terrifying scene.

She hears a cough at the door, and the landlady comes in, carrying a net bag of Chinese chives, courgettes, long chilli peppers and spring onions, and a box of eggs. Eva arrived without warning late the night before, and the landlady complained that she would have made some mushy pancakes for her, if only she'd known she was coming. Mushy pancakes are a kind of *jianbing* where the batter is mixed with eggs and chopped vegetables. They are much tastier than ordinary *jianbing*, and Eva loves them. Grateful to her landlady for remembering how much she likes them, she had said casually, "Let's have them tomorrow, then," without thinking that the woman would actually go out and buy the ingredients.

"Why don't you sleep a bit longer?" her landlady suggests.

Eva takes the shopping bag and the box of eggs from her, and gives her a pat on the back. "You must have gone to the market very early!"

"Time's getting on, the streets are full of people."

"Really? In so much smog?"

"They're swarming like ants out there!"

Eva smiles and looks out the window again, thinking, Why do people feel the need to move around so much? What are they up to? The air's so bad but the streets are still bustling. Have they got nothing better to do than wander around in search of somewhere to fill their bellies? The miasma from the smog smells like a mixture of hot stove fumes and rubbish bins.

Her landlady is asking, "When you've eaten, are you going to the Sojourn Teashop?"

"That's right," says Eva. "I have to see Hai Ruo." She is faintly embarrassed to be joining the throngs who crisscross the city in every direction. She has just arrived from St Petersburg and here she is, staying in the old city and about to set off for Quhu New District, adding yet one more body to the crowds, just like them.

Eva is indeed just like them. In the five years she spent studying here, she became a Xijinger, one who could name all the streets: Capital Road, Hanyang Road, Fuyou Street, and Imperial Examination Street, Academy Alley, Vermilion Bird Street, Black Turtle Road, East Market, West Market, Charcoal Fair Alley, Candy Shop Alley, Dust-Down Gate... As she talks about Xijing and its history as the capital of thirteen dynasties, she becomes flushed and animated, which emphasises the freckles on the bridge of her nose. She feels she knows the cityscape and people's way of doing things inside out. She knows their temperament, the clothes they wear and what they eat. Even her Mandarin Chinese smacks strongly of Xijing dialect.

Five years ago, she completed her studies here and went back to St Petersburg. But her mother died and she broke up with her boyfriend. Night after night, she used to dream of Xijing: she walked its distinctive grid-shaped streets, flew kites from the top of the city wall and listened to the age-old sounds of urban life. Or she sat at a stall in the night market and guzzled stir-fried noodles and barbecued meat, ordered sheep-fries and talked loudly to the stall owner in the harsh local dialect, munching on the testicles in full view of the passers-by, her lips smeared with their oil. Or she squeezed through the crowds on the banks of the moat to watch the amateur singers practising their local opera. Lean, be-rouged men and women belted out their songs, mouths so wide you could plug a fist into them. Every time she walked down the street in her dreams, she picked up a discarded empty plastic water bottle, and put it into the rubbish bin. Or if she came across a newly-planted osmanthus tilting precariously, she trod it firmly into the ground. Each time, she woke up unable to ignore how deeply Xijing had got under her skin. Yes, Xijing is her second home. She went back to St Petersburg, and now she has returned to Xijing. She calls them both "my home".

Eva eats and goes downstairs. In the yard, a wisteria has grown up a trellis and overhangs the stone table, its branches and leaves so entangled that they drape all four sides, like curtains. Once upon a time, Eva used to sit with her books at the table. A cat always kept her company, lying in the shade as she read. Is the cat still here? The moment the thought comes to her, she hears a long-drawn-out screech. Eva looks around, and the old gatekeeper comes hurrying over, broom in hand. His belly is even bigger than before, his shirt is too tight and the buttons are done up wrong, as usual.

"Good morning!" Eva greets him politely.

He grunts, and bangs the trellis with his broom, shouting, "What are you caterwauling like that for in broad daylight?" Suddenly, he seems to recognise Eva but by that time, she is on her way out of the gate of the compound. Behind her, she hears him say, "Oh! Eva, is that you?"

The cat screeches again from the roof of the carport. The Chinese love dogs, but they don't like cats very much. Dogs are pets. Cats are strays, roaming the compounds and annoying the hell out of everyone with their yowling.

There are half-a-dozen elderly women sitting on park benches outside, each with assorted shopping bags beside them, resting their aching feet, one leg crooked on the other knee so they can knead their soles and heels. They are all residents of the compound, familiar faces to Eva though she cannot put a name to them. The fat one has a ground-floor flat on the same staircase as her landlady. She has bought bean curd, celery and a big-head catfish. It must have been gutted just now in the market because drops of bright red blood drip from its tail. She also has a freshly-killed and plucked cockerel, its head and wattle still attached, the stiff feet sticking out of the plastic bag.

Eva greets her, and she responds in English, "Hello!"

"Is it Sunday today?" asks Eva.

"No, tomorrow."

"Oh, no wonder you're buying such a lot!" Eva laughs.

The old woman laughs too, and her slack flesh quivers. These old folk are not well off and count every cent when they go shopping, bargaining fiercely over a handful of spring onions in the market.

They peel the skin off every spring onion and pinch off the hairy roots before the bunch goes on the scales, and just before they leave, they sneak a garlic root in too. But at the weekend, those who can afford it buy a bit more, and on Saturday evening they get on the phone to their children and invite them for lunch. Come Sunday, the compound is at its most cheerful and lively, full of families from all corners of the city. As evening draws in, the young ones depart, and the old ladies pack up the tables, chairs and benches, wash the pots and pans, and then sit down, exhausted but happy.

The compound folk were always very welcoming to Eva, but she never got used to their ways, nor to living in such cramped conditions. That was what first led her to the Sojourn Teashop and Hai Ruo.

It is rush hour and Eva cannot get a taxi, so she has to go on foot. She follows the crowds that flow along South Avenue through the old city, then out through the city gate and down the avenue alongside the moat to the east. There she turns south. The sun has come out. She can see it in the slit of sky between two skyscrapers, its bare outline – no rays are visible – looking like a monkey's bum, or a gob of blood seeping through a gauze dressing on an injured leg. Progress is slow because there is so much foot and vehicle traffic. Eva finds herself squeezed to the edge of the pavement, where she takes a breather while the cars pass by, slicing through the murk. She feels as if she can reach out and grab hold of the smog – but frustratingly it always slips through her fingers.

Stop being so jittery, try to appreciate it, Eva tells herself. She imagines the streets as rivers, and the smog as waves cresting along them. She is swimming through it. Then another image comes to her: the water in the sky and the water on the ground have the same pattern. If a fish jumps out of the river, it is a bird. If a bird dives into the water, it turns into a fish.

There has been an accident at the third T-junction in the southbound lane. The car in front braked suddenly, and the one behind ran into it. The two drivers are arguing.

"Your car's got no brake lights, don't you know how to drive?" one driver accuses the other.

The other says, "Your car's a brown-nose, driving up my car's arse like that!"

"In your dreams! Why would a Merc touch up a Xiali?"

A big crowd has gathered and a traffic jam builds up. The Chinese love to gawp and gloat over someone else's misfortune. There is a lot of pushing and shoving. Some wear masks, others hang their masks under their chins. They cough as they yell encouragement, "Yay! Go for it! Let him have it!" A policeman arrives, blowing his whistle. Eva leaves. Luckily, she knows her way around, and she ducks down a side alley.

There are fewer cars in the alleys but more motorbikes and electric bicycles, their riders weaving expertly in and out of the crowds, whistling by with passengers riding pillion behind them or sacks or crates tied to the back seat. Sometimes you hear the squeal of brakes, but just as it looks as if they are going to hit another bike or a pedestrian, they miss them by a whisker. Eva has the feeling she is being followed, and overhears two men talking.

"That chick has such long legs, why don't they bend when she walks? Hasn't she got any knees?"

"She's amazingly tall, but look at her big feet, they must be a size forty!"

"If we had money, we could get a bit of foreign flesh!"

"Keep your voice down, she might hear you!"

"Don't worry, *laowai* don't understand Chinese."

Eva turns around and asks, "What the hell are you talking about?"

There are two men behind her with long unkempt hair, their clothes spattered with paint spots, probably villagers who have come to town to pick up a bit of work. They exclaim in alarm and make a quick get-away.

Eva passes a small hotel where it looks like the opening ceremony has just finished. The gongs, drums and firecrackers have stopped, but the speakers by the garlanded doorway are blasting out rock-and-roll. Passers-by scuff firecracker cases underfoot, and bits of red paper drift through the smog like flower petals.

On the other side of the alley, Hou's Buckwheat Noodles is full of men who ogle Eva as she passes. The manager comes out with a bowl of slops. As she empties the dirty water down the roadside drain, she tells them off, "Look what you're doing or you'll be feeding those noodles up your nose!"

The drain is full of flies, which fly up and land on people's faces. She hears grumbling, "Hey, can't you keep your flies under control?"

"These flies are not Hou's!" says the manager.

"The old city's full of flies…"

"You're right! Xijing's so ancient, these flies have come down in a straight line from the Han and Tang dynasties!"

There is general laughter, though Eva does not find it very funny. An old man does not laugh either. He is walking by, head bent, his dog on his heels. Man and dog look very alike, except that the dog is too near the ground to see up high. It can only follow the old man's cloth shoes as it trots happily behind.

During her five years here, Eva saw many such old men walking around the city. They are sparely-built and have a certain dignity, having once been government officials, professors, bankers or engineers. But now they are retirees, and growing frail and lonely. No matter how bustling the street, they waft along like dead leaves, ignored by all and sundry. The old man is standing by a street light reading an advertisement pasted on it. There is a contact number offering a prescription for diabetes and prostatitis, and he gets out his notebook to jot it down in case it slips his mind.

In the meantime, the dog has run off to have a pee. It needs to be a place where passers-by will not make the smell fade, but it does not want to forget where it has marked its territory, so it sprinkles under a tree and then at the foot of a low brick wall. It runs back, but follows the wrong pair of cloth shoes out of the alley. Just then a motorbike shoots across the intersection. The man dodges, but the dog does not. It is thrown high into the air, and lands in the middle of the road.

The old man finishes copying down the phone number, turns and realises that his dog has disappeared. He looks up and down the alley. That is when he hears the yelping.

海若

2. HAI RUO • THE TEASHOP

THE WIND HAS GOT UP. It gusts and rackets this way and that, the leaves on the trees clatter and thrum, and many fall to the ground, but gradually the smog thins. Sparrows, dark grey, small as pebbles, hop along the benches outside the park fence, while overhead, a plane crosses the sky. People like watching the sparrows but, perhaps from envy, pay no heed to the plane. Even if they do look up, the plane soon gets smaller and there is nothing to see.

Eva has arrived in the middle section of Lotus Road in Quhu New District. In among the forest of office buildings and shops, a large shopping centre stands out. The first six floors are occupied by shops selling clothes, shoes, hats, bags, cosmetics and electrical appliances, not top of the range but a decent selection, all the same. The seventh floor houses a cinema, a karaoke club, a bar and a cafe. From the eighth to the twelfth floor, eateries serve every sort of snack from all over the province: mutton *paomo* soup, *hulutou* chitterlings with flatbread, *bangbang* pork, *youta* and *mipi* noodles, *ciba* rice cakes and *roujiamo* pork buns. The shopping centre is run on the most up-to-date lines and the customers stream in. One-third go shopping, one-third eat and drink and one-third window-shop.

To the right of the shopping centre, there are five star-shaped residential blocks, each thirty storeys high. Behind these is an antiques market. The stalls are set up before five in the morning, and the market is soon thronged with people picking over the bric-a-brac and looking for bargains, until seven o'clock, when they disappear as suddenly as they have come. For the rest of the day, this pop-up market is deserted, hence its name, the Ghost Fair.

To the left of the shopping centre is the western edge of a park. In fact, it is not really a park, but a long narrow strip of land planted with Chinese red pine. It is fenced off and no one is allowed in, so that three or four stranded kites hanging from the treetops cannot be retrieved. On the other side of the fence, there are newly-planted cherry blossom trees, dozens of them all in a row, their branches and leaves intertwined, their red, yellow and white blossom perfuming the air and full of twittering birds. If you follow the trees, you come to a small square with a wooden bench against the fence, occupied by shoppers from the Ghost Fair. They look disappointed, as if they have failed to land a bargain, and are unsure whether to go home or to the shopping centre to eat. They nod off, or stare vacantly at a two-storey building in front of them.

A magnet ignores wood, earth and bits of paper, but never fails to attract nails, nuts and steel wire. Eva is looking at the building too, and her heart leaps. It used to be the exhibition space for the star-shaped blocks. After the developer sold all the flats, the upper floor of this building was used as storage for the estate management office, and the ground floor was leased, housing two shops at first. Within two years, both shops had a change of use, and were combined into a teashop. Five years on, the walls outside are still painted terracotta red, the beehive under the window on the upper floor at the west end is still there, and even the four pots of roses on the steps at the entrance are still placed symmetrically, two on either side. But there are changes: the entrance is much bigger, and is flanked by floor-to-ceiling glass windows, and the shop sign over the door has been repainted green, with eye-catching gold calligraphy that reads "Sojourn Teashop".

The wind has got up again, and Eva holds her flying hair back from her face. She remembers a sentence she has read somewhere: A wave is the wind of water, and the wind is a wave of the sky.

A pickup is parked outside the teashop. People are carrying stuff out – metal shelving, wooden battens, ladders, paint buckets, large bowls, plastic sheets, as well as bamboo baskets and sacks full of bricks and sand. They move silently in and out.

Suddenly there is a bang, followed by a shrill cry, "Who broke that? Who was it?" A young woman in a green work tunic emerges. It is xiao-Tang. She is plumper than before, and her knee-length tunic fits snugly over her firm buttocks. She holds a large bundle of flowers in her arms.

The workman says, "It's nothing, the rubbish bag broke and the burnt pot fell out."

The broken pot is lying on the steps. xiao-Tang looks at it, and gives it a kick so that it lands in front of the van's wheel. She is going to throw the big bunch of flowers into the pickup too, but the driver objects, "The sunflowers and hawthorn blossoms are still fresh."

"They're over!" xiao-Tang insists, standing on tiptoe and angling the other leg in the air.

"Watch it," says the driver, "or you'll throw yourself in too!"

xiao-Tang smiles and glances across the square. At the corner where the square joins the street, there is a newspaper and magazines kiosk, and a woman standing next to it. xiao-Tang turns to walk up the steps, where the roses in one pot are just coming into bloom. Then she looks back and yells, "Eva? Hey, Eva!"

They run past the car park on the left-hand side of the square towards each other, and embrace warmly, before settling against one of the cars to talk. They are disconcerted when the window of the car rolls down, and there is the driver, still sitting inside. All three of them laugh in embarrassment.

The two women go back to the teashop. Its layout has changed: the long, narrow table against the wall facing the front door is now dedicated to the Tang dynasty tea master, Lu Yu. There are more cabinets, filled with an assortment of boxes of tea and other tea paraphernalia. The cash register has moved from the left-hand side of the door to the northwest corner. And now there is a fridge and a packaging machine, and two round tables as well. The cubicle in the northeast corner is still partitioned off, although the curtain has been replaced by a sliding door. Through the open door, Eva can see a stove, a gas bottle, a kettle and a small cupboard. An exhausted-looking old woman sits inside, her trouser legs rolled up, rubbing her knees. She looks up, then pushes the door so it slides shut. There is a new staircase next to the cubicle, and a toilet discreetly positioned underneath. Opposite the stairs to the right, a middle-aged man in a jacket is sitting at a square table, probably making a purchase of tea. He is teasing a little lad, who is poking him with his fluffy toy dog, pretending to make it bite him.

The teashop staff have not changed. xiao-Su sits at the table at the back, the tea leaves spread out in front of her, picking out stalks, concentrating so hard she might be doing embroidery. She still has lovely long hair. It hangs in a curtain over her face, and she pushes it back, bends her head and scatters more leaves. Her hair falls forward again and, without looking up, she gathers it and twists it into a knot on top of her head, terracotta warrior-style. xiao-Fang seems taller than before, as she stands at the western end of the counter, filling small bags with tea. xiao-Zhen is balanced on top of a stool, placing cakes of tea on the shelves of a cabinet. Dozens of cakes are already displayed there, with names on the wrapping paper like Mangfei, Mangzhi, Xigui, Banzhang, Manzhuan and Yiwu Zhengshan. She is muttering to herself, "Look at those labels, didn't I write them well?"

As Eva walks in, the staff all drop what they are doing and greet her with cries of joy. Eva hugs them all, then digs into her backpack for the lipsticks she has brought and hands them out. The women accept them eagerly, get out their hand mirrors and begin to paint their lips. The kaleidoscope of colours causes a lot of amusement, and even the customer waiting for his tea exclaims, "Someone's poked the magpie's nest!"

Eva brings out some chocolates, and gives the boy a packet too.

"How do you eat this when you've got lipstick on?" xiao-Su and xiao-Zhen exclaim. But they do not wait for an answer, just open their mouths wide, pop a chocolate in, then press their lips together as they chew.

"Where's Hai-jie?" Eva asks. She gives the "jie" a rising tone, which the others find endearing.

"Hai-jie went out early this morning," says xiao-Tang, imitating Eva's pronunciation. "She has stuff to do, I expect she'll be back soon."

"You're making fun of my accent!" Eva accuses her.

"Because your dialect's gone rusty! You know Xijing dialect only has two tones, and the last word in a sentence always falls."

Eva is embarrassed. She shrugs and pulls a face.

"Now don't spoil that pretty face by grimacing," says xiao-Tang. She shouts upstairs, "Mrs Zhang, have you finished clearing up?"

"Yes!"

xiao-Tang takes Eva up the stairs. They meet Mrs Zhang halfway up, holding a mop. She looks at Eva and asks xiao-Tang, "Shall I make a pot of tea?"

"This is a friend of the boss, get some of the Dancong," xiao-Tang instructs her.

Just like the ground floor, the room upstairs is open-plan. It is furnished with replica Ming-style cabinets and an assortment of tables and chairs, all brand-new. There is a display of jade pots, plum vases, porcelain plates, a *guqin* zither, a *ruyi* wand, pieces of agate, coral and turquoise, and flower arrangements.

On a long table against the north wall of the room sits a white marble Buddha statuette with a pronounced ushnisha on the crown of its head, a broad forehead, and large, slanting eyes. Each foot is placed on the opposite thigh in the lotus position, and the left hand lies over the right, palms up, with both thumbs touching, in the meditative Dhyana mudra. Three sticks of sandalwood incense, burned down half way, glow in front of it, their smoke rising straight into the air before dissolving into a tangle of filaments.

On the south side of the room is an arhat couch, with stacks of books and an enamel box divided into a dozen compartments, full of stringed or half-stringed bracelets, balls of coloured cord and beads – pearls, bodhi stones, crystal, red sandalwood and jade – that catch the light. Eva smiles. She remembers these objects so well. They used to be on the ground floor.

"Wow, business must be good, the teashop's expanded!" she exclaims.

"Hai-jie says she's not going to sell tea up here," says xiao-Tang.

"Not sell tea?" Eva is puzzled. "So is this a private room? It's a lovely space for her to get some peace and quiet." Standing in front of the couch, Eva admires the paintings on the wall.

Everywhere in the world, people like to decorate their homes with images from nature: Persian carpets portray the grasslands, Italian slate is like the ocean, and Chinese ink-wash paintings depict landscapes, forests, trees, fish, insects, flowers and birds. Xijing houses are no different. Walls are often covered with paintings in ink-wash or oils. In this room, all four walls are covered with murals:

On either side of the west wall window are paintings of a muscular warrior standing on a lotus pedestal. Short and stocky, he has staring eyes, black hair tied in a topknot, a collar-necklace around his neck, and bare chest and legs. The lotus pedestal is flat-topped, with thin lotus stems and petals pointing downwards, some long, some short.

The north wall has mountains and forests at both ends, within which you can just discern tigers, deer, foxes and golden-tailed birds. Within the forest to the right stands a gatekeeper and a tree of the same height. Its foliage is lush and there are clouds overhead. The gatekeeper has his hair in a topknot crowned with a headpiece. He wears a vest over a wide-sleeved tunic and trousers with a broad waistband, and holds a ceremonial sword.

In the centre of the image is a clearing, with a magnificent stupa on the left and Shakyamuni on the right. The tower sits on a square Sumeru pedestal whose upper layer protrudes over the lower layer, supported by corbels. The stupa's chatra parasol has five layers edged with petals, and a peach-shaped cintamani rimmed in flames tops the tower. Shakyamuni sits in the lotus position, with two auspicious beasts lying beneath his feet, and two bodhisattvas standing on each side.

Around Shakyamuni's halo, three tiers of apsara images are painted on either side. In the lowest tier, the pair of apsaras drift horizontally overhead, their long sleeves and robes floating. Each has one hand pointing down, and a plate of flowers in the other hand. Above them the two apsaras in the second tier undulate, holding a plate of flowers over their heads, their long sashes billowing upwards. In the highest tier, the reclining apsaras face each other, their feet sideways on, hands in front of the body, their sashes floating in rings above them. In front of Shakyamuni, ten monks of smaller stature stand in a line, each holding a lotus flower, with the collars of their kasayas open at the chest.

The east wall is divided by a small window. The far left side is painted with simple outlines of forested hills, and to the right are elephants, argali sheep, hares and monkeys, sitting, walking or running. Beside them are two monks, one kneeling on a wide chair with a netted rope seat and back. To the right of the chair is a long, slender-stalked lotus flower, while underneath it is a kalasa bottle with a narrow mouth and neck and high ring-feet supporting the base. The kneeling monk faces slightly towards the right, and the other monk stands in front of the chair.

In between the chair and the animals in the wooded hills are patterns of clouds and the sun. The sun is painted white, and inside it is the black outline of a three-legged bird also facing right, its wings outspread and its tail cocked.

To the right of the window, the wall has mountains and forests. At its centre is a high platform on which stands a structure with a saddle roof. Curving pointed beaks of owls decorate the tips of the main ridge and sloping ridges. Above this is the outline of a full moon with a toad inside it.

The southern wall is divided into four parts running left to right. Against the backdrop of mountains and forests are kneeling monks, galloping lions, hovering birds of prey, a guide and gatekeepers holding ceremonial swords. The guide leans forward slightly as if walking. He wears a loose robe with broad sleeves and diagonally-crossed collars, and holds a lotus flower with a short, curving stalk.

Eva is entranced and finds herself pressing her palms respectfully together. Mrs Zhang comes in with tea and xiao-Tang gets two teacups out of a cabinet.

"Look, here's the Big Dipper cup," says xiao-Tang, holding a small, hand-painted porcelain cup. "Hai-jie has been keeping it for you."

When Eva was there the first time, Hai Ruo bought some tea porcelain from Jingdezhen, but when they unpacked the case, they found three cups were broken. xiao-Tang wanted to return them and get new ones, but Hai Ruo found someone to repair them with tiny silver staples. One cup needed three staples, another two and the third seven, which happened to be arranged in a Big Dipper pattern. In the past, when people were poor, mending porcelain with staples was looked down on, but nowadays stapling is considered to be adding artistry, like painting a beauty spot on a young woman's flawless face. Eva loved the Big Dipper cup, and Hai Ruo told her, "This is yours from now on!" All the same, she is astonished that Hai Ruo has kept it for her through all these years.

"Did Hai-jie know I was coming back?" she asks.

"She never doubted it. None of us did," says xiao-Tang firmly. Eva is overcome with emotion, and she shivers, like a dewdrop on a grass stem.

xiao-Tang and Eva drink their tea. After three cups, Eva's face is blotchy and beaded with sweat, and she scrapes her hair away from it. Just then, they hear steps on the stairs and put their cups down.

"She's back!" says xiao-Tang.

Before Eva can get to her feet, they hear a voice, "Well, I never! It's Eva, she's beaten the Living Buddha to it!" And Hai Ruo appears at the top of the stairs. She is dressed in a long, wine-red tunic over black trousers and shoes. She still wears the white jade pendant and the jadeite pendant earrings that Eva remembers, but her long hair has been cut short, and she looks thinner. Before Eva can speak, Hai Ruo exclaims, "You must have got to Xijing yesterday. Why didn't you call me?"

Eva suddenly feels very small, even though she is taller than Hai Ruo. She flings her arms around the other woman, buries her head in Hai Ruo's chest and weeps. xiao-Tang quietly retreats downstairs.

Hai Ruo strokes Eva's corn-coloured hair, then tips her chin up and says, "Let me see, have you got fatter or thinner?"

"As you see," says Eva meekly.

"You haven't changed a bit. What time did you get here?"

"Late. It was after dark."

"The night has a way of covering up everything that's shabby and dirty. I bet you thought what a thriving, fashionable city it is now, with all the bright lights!"

"I didn't expect such terrible smog when I got up this morning."

"Yes, the smog's bad, it'll give you a sore throat. Wear a mask when you go out and drink plenty of water. Do you have any lozenges?" And she takes a packet of throat lozenges from her pocket, but Eva stops her.

"I have presents for you!" She opens her bag and takes out a Russian shawl, an antique silver bracelet and finally a matryoshka.

Hai Ruo exclaims in delight at the gifts. She begins to take the doll apart: inside it is another, and another and another. "Amazing! One woman turns into five!"

"That's you," says Eva. "Wife, mother, teashop owner, head of the family, the sisterhood's big sister."

"But I've got no husband now, I'm not anyone's wife!" objects Hai Ruo.

Eva is embarrassed. She does not dare question Hai Ruo and simply says, "Sorry."

"What's there to be sorry about? I have another role – looking after my foreign sister. So what brought you back to Xijing this time?"

"I missed you," says Eva.

Hai Ruo looks at her, and Eva's lips tilt upwards, like petals. "You do say nice things!"

Eva goes on, "I just wanted to see you all. If possible, I'd like to learn how to sell tea. One day I might open a teashop in St Petersburg."

"Fine, this room has just been cleaned up, so you can come and work here, and I'll pay you a salary."

"Really?" Eva is delighted.

"Of course." Eva gives Hai Ruo a kiss on the cheek. "What do you think of the décor?" asks Hai Ruo.

"It's like a Buddhist shrine."

"That's exactly what it is," says Hai Ruo. "I used to worship at Mr Wu's shrine. Mr Wu has been in touch with a Living Buddha from Tibet. He invited him to Xijing and arranged for him to spend a few days with me too, so I rented this room for him to stay in. When the Living Buddha leaves, I figure I can use this room for myself, any time I need some downtime. Besides, the sisterhood can't spend all their time on the ground floor. There's no room for them *and* the customers. They can come up here and be as rowdy as they like."

"I've only met three or four of the sisterhood. I'd like to meet all ten of them this time."

As they talk, Eva suddenly hears a buzzing, like a copper wire vibrating.

"It's the bees," says Hai Ruo.

"You're still keeping bees?"

"You saw the old lady in the cubicle downstairs? Her rheumatism has been giving her a lot of trouble, so every few days, she comes and we get a bee to sting her knees."

Hai Ruo looks round and calls for xiao-Zhen. xiao-Zhen comes up the stairs. Her lips are blood-red, and when she smiles, her teeth are stained red too.

"Why are you wearing that gaudy lipstick to work?" Hai Ruo reprimands her.

"I was trying one of the lipsticks Eva gave us," says xiao-Zhen, and she pulls a tissue from the drawer to wipe her mouth.

"Don't wipe it off then! And what present are you giving Eva in return?"

"I'm taking her out to lunch today," says xiao-Zhen. "There's a place in the shopping centre that braises noodles to a secret recipe. Eva won't have tried that."

"You promised to take me there a month ago. I'm still waiting!" says Hai Ruo.

"Come with Eva then," says xiao-Zhen. Eva laughs.

"Eva will be working here from tomorrow," Hai Ruo tells xiao-Zhen. "I expect you to give her a helping hand."

"Really? You mean I'll have a foreign apprentice!"

Eva cups her hands with respect. "*Shifu!*" she intones.

xiao-Zhen grabs Eva round the waist. "Say '*Shifu*' louder, so everyone downstairs can hear!"

"Stop making her suck up to you!" says Hai Ruo.

Eva goes downstairs with xiao-Zhen, who says to the others, "Have you heard?"

The other assistants look at her. "Heard what? The wind whistling outside?"

"Eva's starting work here tomorrow, and Hai-jie has asked me to take her on. Eva, tell them, it's true, isn't it?"

"Yes. You'll all have to make allowances for me!" says Eva.

"Eva, bring that stool," says xiao-Zhen. "I need a rest. I don't know why, but my feet are killing me today."

Before Eva can obey, xiao-Tang says, "If Eva's going to work with us, xiao-Zhen, give her a copy of the Thirteen Homilies so she can have a good look at it."

xiao-Zhen pulls a face, but goes to the drawer, takes out a sheet of paper in a plastic sleeve and gives it to Eva. xiao-Su smiles, but says nothing, and bends over her work sorting the tea stems.

Eva looks at the sheet of paper. It reads:

1. *Eat in moderation*
2. *Mind what you say*

3. *Be principled*
4. *Be determined*
5. *Be frugal, but generous when others need help*
6. *Work diligently*
7. *Be sincere*
8. *Maintain your integrity*
9. *Adhere to the Golden Mean*
10. *Keep your home clean and tidy*
11. *Cultivate inner peace*
12. *Keep your desires under control*
13. *Treat others with humility*

"Wow, are these rules or ideals?" asks Eva.

"They're traditional feminine virtues," says xiao-Tang. "Hai-jie found them when she was reading and wrote them up as rules for us." Eva looks suitably impressed.

Hai Ruo comes down the stairs. She has changed into a long blue gown, and wears the Russian shawl, Eva's gift, around her shoulders. She tells xiao-Fang to fill a canister with white tea.

"Who's it for?" asks xiao-Fang.

"Lu Yike."

xiao-Fang packs the tea and says to xiao-Tang, "Better note that down: Lu Yike, one canister of Anji white tea, one thousand yuan."

xiao-Tang gets out the accounts book but Hai Ruo says, "No need, it's a present."

"We're a small business," objects xiao-Tang. "If you keep giving tea away, that wipes out a whole day's profit."

"She's one of the sisterhood," says Hai Ruo. "They always buy their tea, but this time it's a gift. I want her to try this new-season tea."

xiao-Su smiles.

"What are you laughing at?" xiao-Tang challenges her.

"Nothing."

Their customer has been standing in front of a cabinet looking at the tea utensils. Now he gets a silver teapot out and asks xiao-Su, "How much is this?"

xiao-Su jerks her chin at xiao-Tang, "Our deputy manager can tell you."

"Twenty thousand, five hundred and fifty yuan," says xiao-Tang. "If you really like it, I'll give you a fifty-yuan discount."

"That's a lot!" the man exclaims.

"You get what you pay for," xiao-Tang tells him. "It's pure silver, imported from Japan."

"I'll buy it if you give me a better discount."

"Then you should take the iron pot next to it, five hundred and thirty yuan."

But the man puts down the silver teapot, collects his tea and leaves.

"He was just trying to hit on you," xiao-Tang tells xiao-Su in a low voice. "He was never going to buy a pot. And why were you calling me 'deputy manager'?"

"Because that's what you are, to my mind."

"Go and see if the old lady's feeling better. If she needs a few more stings, get more bees." xiao-Tang glances at Hai Ruo, but Hai Ruo pretends not to hear and carries on talking to Eva.

"Hai-jie, I'm not sure I can follow all these rules!" Eva is saying.

"Well, if you can't, you can't. You're a temporary employee and a foreigner too."

"Are you off out again?" Eva asks.

"I need to see Lu Yike urgently, but I'll be back soon, and xiao-Zhen's taking us to the braised noodles restaurant."

"Oy-oy!" xiao-Fang shouts. "Are you inviting the boss for a meal?"

"I'm not bribing the boss, if that's what you mean," xiao-Zhen says. "You never asked Eva for lunch but I did, and I just asked the boss to tag along."

"You're making me cry!" says Hai Ruo. "Am I not as good as Eva?"

There is laughter, and cries of, "Then let's all tag along!"

"Huh," says xiao-Zhen. "The first commandment is 'Eat in moderation'. But so long as you don't mind getting fat, let's go!"

"I've met Yike before, can I join you?" Eva asks Hai Ruo.

"The boss didn't invite you, it's not your place to ask!" xiao-Zhen reprimands her.

"I don't start work till tomorrow, *shifu*!" says Eva.

Hai Ruo smiles. "Aren't you tired?"

"No."

So Hai Ruo picks up the tea canister and leaves with Eva.

It is still windy outside, but the smog is gone and they can see everything unusually clearly across the street. A bus stops to let passengers on, and the doors flap close as if they are two hands with the palms turned outward. Nearby, the car park attendant is having another argument with one of the drivers. With his uncombed hair and his creased blue uniform, he is not an impressive figure. The drivers either won't park where they are told to or refuse to pay the parking fee. The attendant loses this particular argument, so he takes out his annoyance on some hawkers who have laid out their goods on the pavement by the kiosk. He spits and shouts abuse in an attempt to get rid of them until Hai Ruo calls him over.

"Best not to spit," she advises him. "And keep out of this wind, and leave those poor people alone. Are you a car park attendant or a fly-swatter?" She notices his chapped lips, and the empty cup hanging at his waist. "Why don't you go to the teashop and get yourself a nice cup of tea?"

She sighs as she leads Eva towards her red Toyota. "The wind is the best thing in China nowadays," she remarks. "The smog in Beijing is even worse than here, but Beijing is blessed with strong winds that blow the smog away. People always say Xijing has perfect feng shui: it lies between the river and the mountain, in a sunny spot sheltered from the north wind. But it's just this sheltered position that is Xijing's undoing."

"Maybe it's time to revise the feng shui theories?" Eva jokes.

Then they hear someone calling, "Mrs Hai Ruo!" To their right, a man hurries across the car park towards them. He is a chubby fellow, bald and bull-necked.

"That rolling gait makes him look like a trotting dog, or is he a shambling bear?" says Eva.

"A bear, for sure," says Hai Ruo and they burst out laughing.

The stranger reaches them and they hurriedly pull themselves together.

"Zhang Huai," he introduces himself. "The Surfing Company."

"Surfing?" Hai Ruo queries. "Xijing's thousands of miles away from the sea!"

"You don't remember me? When the shopping centre was built, we pulled down the village on the site and moved the inhabitants."

"I'm sorry," says Hai Ruo, "we get so many people coming to the teashop."

"Yan Nianchu. I'm her cousin. I drove her the last time she visited your shop. And I know some of your sisterhood."

"Right! Your hair looks different."

Zhang Huai laughs and scratches his head, leaving red marks.

"I have to go out now," says Hai Ruo. "Why don't you go in and have some tea."

"I thought you only sold the tea leaves," Zhang Huai says.

"You're right about that, but you're Nianchu's cousin. Of course, we'll serve you a pot of tea!"

"Nah, it's fine, I'm here because Feng Ying asked me to pass on a message, so I can tell you now."

"Oh?"

"I ran into Feng Ying yesterday on Vermilion Bird Street. She said to be sure to tell you this: someone called Yi Guang owes her a hundred and fifty thousand yuan, and she's borrowed two hundred thousand from Xia someone or another."

"Xia Zihua?"

"That's the one. Feng Ying said Yi Guang should give the hundred and fifty thousand direct to Xia Zihua, and she'll ask her sister to pay the remaining fifty thousand she owes."

Hai Ruo goes pale. "You saw Feng Ying yesterday?"

"Yesterday morning."

"It's not possible! Feng Ying went to the Philippines with an artists' delegation ten days ago. She can't have come back so soon. Even if she has, she'd come to see me herself, not send you with a message! Did you really see Feng Ying in person?"

"Yes, it was definitely her, I'd know her even if she was burnt to a crisp!"

"What a terrible thing to say!"

Zhang Huai looks taken aback. "It's just the way we talk, back where I come from. I just mean I definitely recognised her. She has a mole on her left cheek. She was wearing a white suit jacket and a pale, patterned skirt. That's her, isn't it?"

"It's true she was wearing a white suit and pastel skirt when she left," Hai Ruo says.

"And is she talking about the right people and things?"

"The names are right, but I don't know about any loan."

"Anyway, I've passed on the message now." He steals a glance at Eva. "This *laowai*'s face is as white as a steamed bun!"

"You can't compare fair skin with steamed buns," snaps Hai Ruo. Zhang Huai is reaching out to touch Eva's face, but Hai Ruo smacks his hand away with the tea canister. "Get off her with your dirty hands!" And she shoos him away.

"Who's Feng Ying?" asks Eva when he has gone.

"Feng Ying, Xia Zihua and Yan Nianchu, they're all in the sisterhood," says Hai Ruo. "Feng Ying likes to paint. The mural upstairs in the teashop was done by a painter she introduced me to."

They get into the car, and Hai Ruo calls Feng Ying's mobile. It is switched off. "What's going on?" she says. "He can't have seen Feng Ying, but it sounds like he did."

A gust of wind catches the cherry blossoms, and petals whirl in the air, completely obscuring the rear-view mirror. Tissue of petals, tissue of lies, Eva thinks to herself, but she looks at Hai Ruo and keeps her doubts to herself.

3. LU YIKE • XILAOLI

陆以可

XILAOLI, "WEST BOG", is a shanty town in the old part of the city, full of cramped alleys and tumbledown houses. Bundles of electrical wires snake through the rows of plane trees. The trees were planted in the 1950s and should have grown tall and mature by now. But they have been pollarded repeatedly in order to make way for the cables, and have turned into stumpy specimens with an ugly tangle of branches thrusting out sideways. There is only one building of any significance, standing on its own in the open space at the north end of the alleys.

A fountain is situated in front of the building, coated in thick dust and dry as a bone. Nearby is some outdoor gym equipment. Two people are hanging motionless from the horizontal bars, looking corpse-like. A woman is banging her spine against the iron post of the basketball hoop, and a startled pigeon flaps away without landing. They hear the sound of an *erhu* and spot a man sitting on a brick ledge in the distance, his head bent so low that they cannot see his eyebrows. As he draws the bow back and forth, the music is as sorrowful as the wind, as though he never has an audience for his playing.

"Yike's Capability Advertising Company is on the thirteenth floor," says Hai Ruo.

The lift doors are open and they can see that the cabin is halfway up inside the shaft. Two workers in grease-stained overalls squat underneath, banging noisily.

"Is the lift broken?" asks Hai Ruo.

No answer.

"How long will it take to fix?"

There is still no answer. The two workers stare at the women, the whites of their eyes gleaming in the semi-darkness. Hai Ruo takes Eva back outside and they peer upwards but lose count before they reach the thirteenth floor.

"It doesn't seem to be a very nice neighbourhood," observes Eva.

"It's mixed-use, some residential, some commercial, so you get all sorts of people," says Hai Ruo, and she taps in a number on her phone.

They hear Lu Yike's voice, "Well, I never! I was just thinking of you, and here you are. We're telepathic!"

"Don't flatter yourself," says Hai Ruo.

Yike chuckles and asks, "Where are you?"

"Downstairs."

"Come on up! I just bought a case of Château Lafite Rothschild!"

"The lift's broken."

"It was fine when I came back an hour ago. How come it broke? Hey, you know what, you'll just have to crawl up thirteen floors to see me... like imperial officials had to walk all the way to the palace when they had an audience with the emperor."

"No way! You come down to us!"

"But I've been running around all morning in these heels, and they're killing me!"

"You come down," Hai Ruo insists.

Eva is sniggering. "We've come to see her," she says. "Why's she coming down to us?"

"You think I'm bossy?"

"You certainly are."

Hai Ruo laughs. "Of all my women friends, we're the closest and we don't stand on ceremony with each other. We're like family. Family don't shake hands when they meet."

Soon enough, Yike limps out of the doorway in a haze of perfume. She is wearing designer jeans and a white shirt, with a jade pendant around her neck. She is heavily made-up and has drawn her eyebrows too long, almost into her temples.

"What's that perfume you're wearing?" exclaims Eva.

"I'm just naturally fragrant!" says Yike. Then she realises it's Eva, gives a cry of joy and throws her arms around her. "When did you get to Xijing? It's the first time you've been to my office. What a shame you can't come upstairs."

"Look at you," Hai Ruo says. "Your make-up's enough to scare off Eva!"

"Really? I don't usually wear make-up and I'm no good at it, but I was going to the city hall this morning, so I had to get dressed up. Hey, guess what, I got a compliment from the bureau chief!"

Hai Ruo purses her lips. "He's probably an old man, so any young woman counts as pretty."

"No, this one, Liu, he's new, he's only forty."

"Yeah, anyone who says flowers are pretty is only thinking of plucking them!"

"Well, he didn't pluck me. I was the one in control!" says Yike.

"How many billboards did you get?"

"One, on the airport road."

"Only one billboard and you bought yourself a whole case of Lafite?"

"It's hard going nowadays! Anyway, once it's up, I can run an ad for your teashop before I attract any business. For free."

"There's no point. I only do business with repeat customers."

Yike glances at Eva. "See how different we are?"

Eva laughs.

"If you're not coming upstairs, let me take you to lunch," Yike goes on. "There's a restaurant called The Shrimp Pond inside the West Gate."

But Hai Ruo says, "I didn't come for lunch!" And she pulls Yike aside.

Eva can see they are having a serious talk. She takes her phone out and goes to take a picture of the man playing the *erhu*. The people who were working out are gone, but there is an old lady sitting under the basketball hoop. Another one, not far away, is taking walnuts from her pocket, smashing them and feeding them to the kid she has with her. Then she pinches the kid's nose, first one side, then the other, and says, "Blow! Blow hard!" The kid obediently snorts snot into her hand, and she flicks it away onto the ground. The other old woman moves closer and starts to chat: where is she from, what department does her son work in, has he brought her from the village to live here, or is it her daughter who has a job in the city, and is she here to look after the grandson? The kid is getting bored. He gets another walnut from his granny's pocket and tries to smash it. But it bounces out of his reach and rolls merrily away, stopping at Eva's feet. You wouldn't be so cheerful if you knew you were going to be smashed, thinks Eva.

Hai Ruo is saying, "You know that thing I asked you to do? I feel like you're so wrapped up in your business, you've just dropped it."

"I know it's important," Yike protests. "But even though I've got nearly a dozen young men working for me, when I asked them, only three were willing to donate blood platelets. Anyway, one of the three is a match, so hopefully that'll cure Zihua! He's called Gao Wenlai. He's good-looking."

"This is medical treatment, what does it matter whether he's handsome or not?"

"Zihua's very particular. The greens and the fish she eats, they all have to look good. If Gao Wenlai were ugly, I wouldn't want his blood. Anyway, it's been sorted out. When are we going to the hospital?"

"Did you settle the fee?"

"He'll do it for six thousand. He gets half that every month, so that's two months' salary. I'll cover it."

"No, I'm not letting you pay, we'll split it among all of us, that way everyone can show they're thinking about her. Where's Gao from?"

"From the mountains in southern Shaanxi. He's been working in Xijing for three years but he's had four jobs in that time. He's always late for work in the morning since he started with me. Everyone's annoyed and wants me to fire him, but I had a word with him and found out that he loves poetry. He stays up all night writing poems. He hasn't been able to find a publisher, but that hasn't put him off. I was touched, and kept him on. And now it turns out he's crucial to Zihua's treatment!"

"We owe him big time in that case," Hai Ruo says. "And all this outdoor work he's doing for you won't be good for him. Why don't I offer him a job at the teashop? I'll pay him four thousand yuan. If he really wants to write, he can come an hour later in the morning and he might get a chance to meet Yi Guang-laoshi too."

Hai Ruo makes a call and says, "A platelets donor has been found. It's going to be OK. God willing, she'll get better." Then she makes another call, to ask them to tell the doctor, and to talk to the hospital about getting Xia Zihua a single room. Apparently, she needs to talk to the hospital director for that. She becomes anxious, and her voice rises.

The man is still sawing away at the *erhu*, making ear-piercing sounds. Eva stops taking pictures. She goes up to him and asks very politely if he could stop. "My friend's on the phone over there, it's a really important call. She won't be able to hear herself think if you keep playing like this."

The man doesn't stop. He just stares at her.

"Have I said something wrong?" says Eva. "Why are you staring at me?"

Yike comes over and pulls Eva away. "He's not staring. He's got a glass eye, didn't you notice?"

Eva is still annoyed. After a moment, she asks Yike, "Is someone in Hai Ruo's family sick?"

"No, it's Xia Zihua, from the sisterhood. Have you met her?"

"No, I only ever met three or four of you. I don't remember one called Xia Zihua. Is she very sick?"

"It's leukaemia. She's so weak now, she can hardly get out of bed. The hospital wants to give her a platelet transfusion, but very few people are willing to donate platelets, so they told her family to find a donor. But Zihua only has a mother and a kid. Her mother, Mrs Qi, has bad rheumatism in her legs, and the kid's only two or three years old."

Eva is dismayed. Then she remembers the old lady and the little boy she saw at the teashop. "Does Mrs Qi have white hair? Is the kid quite naughty? And his ears stick out?" she asks.

"Yes, you've met them?"

"I saw them at the teashop this morning."

"The teashop? Then it must be them. Mrs Qi's been using a folk remedy. Every three or four days, she goes there for the bees to sting her legs."

"I wondered why the teashop was still keeping bees."

"Beekeeping's not normally allowed in Xijing," says Yike. "The teashop was originally two shops. One of them belonged to Xia Zihua and sold tobacco and liquor. It was she who applied to the subdistrict office for a special permit. They said yes, but only if the hive was high enough off the ground, so they fixed it under a window on the upper floor. When Hai Ruo took over both shops and turned them into a teashop, the beehive stayed." Yike sighs and adds, "Zihua is supposed to be looking after her mother, but now it's the other way around, her poor sick mum has to take care of her and the kid."

"How sad," Eva says. "Where's the boy's father?"

Yike says nothing.

Eva is taken aback. Maybe the father has died, or divorced Zihua. "Did I say something I shouldn't have?"

"No, it's OK," says Yike. "It's just that I've never seen the father. Zihua never mentions him, and I don't feel like I can ask." She smiles at Eva. "Maybe Hai Ruo knows."

"Hmm," says Eva and changes the subject. "Your pumps are pretty."

Hai Ruo is still talking. Everyone with a mobile is a slave to it, a willing slave. Every time Hai Ruo makes a phone call, she starts in a rather high-pitched voice, as if she is telling them off, then softens her voice and starts pacing back and forth, and finally walks in circles. She looks like an ox turning a millstone, wearing blinkers to keep it from getting dizzy. After a lot of walking around, Hai Ruo looks up at the sky.

"Why does she have so many calls?" asks Eva.

"Trying to get Zihua a single room, maybe?"

"Then why does she sound so bossy, when she's asking for a favour?"

"You have no idea!" says Yike. "Even with me, if she's sending work my way, even if she wants me to help her, she makes it clear who's boss before she tells me about it. The day before yesterday, the teashop was short-staffed, and she asked me to send over some workers. But first she called me and asked, 'Have I done anything to hurt your feelings? Is my business doing better than yours? Are you jealous that I'm prettier than you?' I said, 'No, I have no problem with you or your business.' She said, 'Then why haven't you liked my WeChat posts? And you haven't been to the teashop for ten days!' I said I hadn't got around to looking at her WeChat posts yet, but I was thinking about going to the teashop that very day. You know what, she said, 'Then hurry up, come now, and bring four workers with you.'"

"And did you?" asks Eva.

"I did. It would have been wrong not to." They both laugh.

Hai Ruo is still on the phone. She looks in their direction, as if the call is about to end, but then stops by the holly hedge and carries on talking, idly pulling off leaves with her other hand. Three minutes go by, and she has stripped a branch of its leaves.

Eva goes up to her and says, "Ouch! Poor holly!"

Hai Ruo looks surprised at what she has been doing, but in any case, the phone call is finally over. She heaves a long sigh, then points to Yike. "You've been bad-mouthing me with Eva?"

"Yes! I said you should smash your phone!"

"Right, and you'll get a bang on the head if you don't watch out!" Hai Ruo says and throws something at her. It turns out to be the tea canister she has had in her pocket.

Yike catches it. "Is it a present for me?"

"It's white tea."

"Then I hope it's White Peony. Brewed with a little salt, it tastes superb!"

"Fine," says Hai Ruo. "If you don't want it, I'll have it back!" But as she reaches out for the canister, Yike hugs it tightly to her chest.

"Let me take you to The Shrimp Pond at West Gate," she suggests.

"Is this a welcome-back meal for Eva?" asks Hai Ruo. "If it is, we should go to a big restaurant and get everyone along."

"There's plenty of time to throw a banquet," says Yike. "Today, you're with me and we're having shrimps."

It is not far to the restaurant and there is no parking, so they walk. They pass by a cross-alley, with white circles painted on the walls on both sides, and a large 拆, "For demolition", written inside each circle. There are large, multi-occupancy courtyards with no gates, and they can see single-storey brick buildings with tiled roofs and a jumble of sheds. A few of the sheds have cement roofs, others have walls of plastic panels or sheets of linoleum, all weighed down by wooden slats and stones. Inside the sheds are tricycles, bicycles, bricks, discarded door frames, old televisions and flowerpots full of cockscombs, orchids and ball cacti. Eva peers inside a yard, and realises someone is looking back at her. She shifts her gaze to a persimmon tree with a slender trunk, imagining its last fruit hanging at the end of a branch in winter for the crows to eat.

"Hai-jie," says Yike, "these courtyards have lovely carved gate piers. Someone should photograph them and publish a book. It would be a record of the city's past."

Hai Ruo is about to answer when her phone rings again. Then the screen goes black. "My battery's dead, give me your phone," she commands. Yike hands it over, and Hai Ruo goes a little ahead to call back.

"Is this place going to be demolished?" asks Eva.

"Yup."

"It's about time." Eva looks back at the tall building in the distance. Yike guesses what Eva is thinking. "Hey, Eva, do you want to hear a story about this place?"

"I'm all ears!" And Eva pulls at her ears with a mischievous smile.

"This happened many years ago," Yike begins.

A crowd is gathered under that very persimmon tree. A young woman passes by. She isn't interested in whatever the crowd are looking at, until she hears a voice saying, "Come on in, come on in!" The voice seems to be coming from the middle of the crowd, and there is a peculiar quality of its sound that draws her in. There she sees a cobbler, bending over a shoe he is mending. He finishes nailing the sole on, lays the shoe on a packing case beside him and looks up. Their eyes lock.

Her father! She is rooted to the spot.

His bushy hair is combed backwards (it suits his low forehead), and he has a big nose, long and flat at the tip, with fleshy lips slightly drooping at the corners. It is her father, exactly as she remembers him from her childhood. She does not call out to him, just stands with her eyes fixed on him. He seems aware of her. He reaches out and rearranges the shoes on the box, his head still raised as if allowing her more time to examine him. Then he bends over again to repair the other shoe.

Her father died more than thirty years ago, and yet here he is. Can there be someone else in the world who looks just like her father in his thirties? Has he been reborn and reached the same age?

The young woman backs out of the crowd and returns to the hotel where she is staying. For the rest of the day and all night, she keeps on thinking about it. Whether he was a look-alike or her father reborn, what does it mean to run into him in Xijing? Neither of them spoke at the time, although the look on his face told her that he felt the connection too. The cobbler must be there on a regular basis, she assumes. She plans to see him again, but is struck down by a strange bug, and when she recovers and goes back three days later, he is gone. She is even more convinced that it was her father trying to show her something, so she stays on and eventually buys a house in this block.

Eva shivers as she listens to this bizarre tale. She stares at Yike and asks, "Well? What about the girl, who is she?"

"Me," Yike says.

"Why are you telling me the story, Lu-jie? It's scary. And it's sad."

"You were wondering why I live here in Xilaoli?"

Eva puts her arms around Yike all of a sudden, resting her head on her shoulders. Her cheeks are burning red.

Hai Ruo turns to look at them, and they pull apart, but Hai Ruo says nothing and takes another phone call. "Xiang Qiyu, Xiang Qiyu!" she greets the caller loudly. "Don't mess me around!" Then her voice softens and she seems to be advising the other person. "Got that?" she finally demands. "Repeat it back to me."

"What's going on with Xiang Qiyu?" Yike whispers.

"Who's that?" Eva asks. "Another one of your sisterhood?"

"Uh-huh," says Yike. "I was originally from Wuhan. My mother died when I was one and it was my father who brought me up. In my second year of high school, I rebelled and dropped out, and set up a small business. I didn't settle anywhere for ages, I drifted around Beijing, Shanghai, Shenzhen and Chengdu. Then I came to Xijing on a trip and there was the incident I told you about. So I settled down here. Business was good, I was running my own company and later I met Hai-jie."

At the West Gate, they come to a large square which extends into a triangle at the south end, filled with restaurants. Their frontages are small but the signboards are huge. One of them reads "The Shrimp Pond".

"Get us a private room and order," Hai Ruo tells Yike. "Eva and I are off to the art shop here."

"It's a tiny place, has something there caught your eye?" asks Yike.

"Last month, I went in there and spotted a 'gallery fish' from

Taiwan. I mentioned it to Yi-laoshi and he's interested, so I'm going to take a picture for him."

Yike purses her lips. "Well, don't be long."

"When you're done ordering, call Eva's number."

Eva tells Yike her mobile number and follows Hai Ruo cheerfully into the art shop.

The owner greets them with a nod, and carries on talking to a customer. The conversation seems to be about the geography of Xijing and the wind direction.

"It's not surprising we're prone to smog in such a big city with no way for the wind to blow through," Eva hears.

Then there is grumbling about the city government: the experts proposed building three large wind paths, but only one has been completed. Before the other two were started, a tycoon from Hong Kong had chosen the site, and the plans were turned down on the grounds of economic development.

"Damn it, urban development has already blighted the lives of a generation of farmers, do they have to pay the price of environmental pollution as well?" says the owner.

Hai Ruo is hunting through the shop but cannot find the fish. She asks the shop owner and the answer is that it was sold yesterday. Does he have another? No, it is a rare item. They won't be getting any more in. Hai Ruo is disappointed.

Outside the shop, Eva asks, "Why are these shop owners so keen to talk about local government issues?"

"Even at the *liangfen* noodle stall you get people arguing furiously over UN resolutions!" says Hai Ruo.

"People in this city are an odd bunch!" says Eva.

"Cities like this with run-down economies are full of eateries, and all these men struggling to get by are political commentators."

"Men? Don't women care about politics?"

Hai Ruo is surprised, then says with a laugh, "Everything in China is political."

"Why were you looking for a fish in an art shop?" asks Eva.

"It's not a real fish, it's carved out of pomelo wood. They hang them in the galleries outside temple halls. When pilgrims come to offer incense, they knock on the wooden fish to alert the monks."

"Why fish? Wouldn't a drum be better?" But Hai Ruo cannot answer that one.

Yike calls, and Hai Ruo and Eva go to the restaurant, and upstairs to room number eleven. As soon as they push open the door, they see a man sitting inside. He is tall, with a small head and greasy hair tied back in a thin braid, and wears traditional Chinese clothes: loose white trousers and a cross-buttoned jacket, both of hand-woven cloth and very crumpled. Hai Ruo hurriedly backs out and shuts the door again.

Sotto voce, Eva says, "What kind of gear is that?"

"He must be a painter or a musician. They think they look arty!"

"Scruffy, more like," Eva says.

Then the door behind them opens, and Yike is saying, "Here we are, come in."

"I thought we were in the wrong room," says Hai Ruo.

"I was just in the toilet. This is Mr Fan Bosheng, from the Xijing Painting and Calligraphy Research Association. He knows Yi-laoshi and Feng Ying. We first met at Feng Ying's. We bumped into each other just now and I said, let's eat together."

"Sorry to barge in," says the man. "But when I heard Mrs Hai Ruo was coming, I wanted the chance to meet this lovely lady!"

"What an odd sort of compliment," says Hai Ruo.

"But you are lovely!" Bosheng smiles, revealing stained teeth.

"If only I was as lovely as Lu Yike or this Russian beauty, Eva."

"You're all beautiful. And you have marvellous bone structure," he tells her.

Then Hai Ruo remembers something. "So you also know Feng Ying? Did you know she's gone to the Philippines?"

"I was one of the tour group organisers. But I couldn't go because my mother was suddenly taken ill."

"They're not back yet, right?"

"No, they've extended their trip."

"Nonsense, all nonsense!" Hai Ruo exclaims.

"Me? But it's the truth!" Bosheng protests.

"No, no, not you. I was thinking of something else." And she shows him to his seat. She asks Eva to sit next to him but Eva pops out for a moment and when she comes back, she sits down between Hai Ruo and Yike.

"This restaurant must be really famous if Mr Fan's here," says Hai Ruo.

"It's my first time. Yi Guang-laoshi asked me to come over and look at a carved gallery fish in the art shop opposite, but they've sold it. So I came here for lunch and bumped into Lu Yike."

Hai Ruo smiles. "I went there for the same reason, but it wasn't meant to be."

"Some things aren't meant to be," agrees Bosheng. "Last month, I had a visit from a serious collector, a tycoon from Zhejiang. I specially recommended Yi-laoshi's work to him and he wanted to buy twenty pieces of calligraphy, all in one go. Only it turned out that Yi-laoshi was on his way to the northern Shaanxi plateau to collect folk art. A big fat piece of pork dangled in front of him and he let it drop in the dirt!"

"So you've been bringing him customers," Hai Ruo says.

"I get him five million in profit every year. I know a lot of entrepreneurs, and I've introduced them to almost all the calligraphers and painters in our city."

"So they must have given you a lot of their work by way of a thank you!"

"Yes, quite a few. But I'm not selling. Not one. Works of art gain value the longer you keep them. If you're in too much of a hurry to cash them in, they go for peanuts!"

It is hot in the room and Hai Ruo takes off her jacket, puts it on the hanger and goes to the toilet to touch up her make-up. Eva follows. "Do you understand what we're saying?" asks Hai Ruo.

"The words, yes, but not what you're talking about. That man's such a boaster."

"He's just a wind bag," says Hai Ruo, and she uses the pencil on her eyebrows. "If I don't do my eyebrows for a day, I feel like I don't have them."

"Are you going to make them go up at the ends?" asks Eva.

"That would be over the top! I'd look like Yike!"

They carry on chatting, in no hurry to leave.

Meanwhile, Yike is asking Bosheng, "If you know so many entrepreneurs, can you introduce a few to me?"

"What business did you say you're in?"

"I've got a billboard on the airport road."

"Some of my friends spend a fortune on advertising every year. The airport road is a good location, why only one billboard?"

"It's not easy to get permission."

"You know a deputy director of the Bureau of Industry and Commerce comes from my township? We often play mahjong together. When we next meet, I'll get you over so you can get to know each other. Human beings are emotional animals, after all!"

"Then let me add you to my WeChat," Yike says. Bosheng holds his mobile out for her to scan his QR code. Her fingers are long and slender, delicate as spring onion stems, and her nails are not varnished, just oiled, so they gleam a translucent pink.

"Beautiful!" exclaims Bosheng.

"You mean, my hand?"

"You could be a hand model. These are the most beautiful hands I've ever seen!"

"People say that every beauty has a single flaw, but I'm an ugly person with a single point of beauty." She goes back to her seat and the dishes start arriving. "Hey, you two, come and eat, why such a fuss about make-up over lunch?"

The first dish is crispy pork, followed by stewed bean curd, roast goose and stir-fried lily bulb. Then come ten portions of shrimp: sweet and sour, salt and pepper, spicy, braised, stewed, steamed and boiled, each with a different colour and flavour. It is too bad Bosheng is such a noisy eater. Eva looks up at Hai Ruo, who smiles quietly but says nothing. Between them they polish off all the shrimps, but leave much of the rest untouched. They finish, and Bosheng gets up to settle the bill.

Yike protests, "It's my treat."

"You invited us but I'll pay. How can I not pay for lunch with three such lovely ladies? Yi-laoshi put it so well, admiring women ennobles a man!"

Outside the restaurant, the wind has dropped, but the sky is much darker. Someone is flying a kite in the square – a huge paper centipede hovers in the air.

Eva is so excited that she rushes over to the man holding the kite string and begs, "Please, let me have a go!" He is happy to hand the string roller to the foreign girl and the kite hauls her along. "I'm flying! I'm flying!" cries Eva shrilly.

"Look at her!" says Bosheng. "She reminds me of Feng Ying. We were flying a kite on the banks of the Weihe River a year or so ago. Feng Ying shouted the same way, and the kite dragged her into the water!"

Hai Ruo calls Eva, and the four of them walk back to Yike's office building. Bosheng is going to Yi Guang's studio, in the same direction as Hai Ruo and Eva, so Hai Ruo gives him a lift. Yike says her goodbyes. Her hands resting on the half-open window, she says to Bosheng, "Thank you for treating us, Mr Fan!"

昇
光

4. YI GUANG • THE CLOUD-GATHERING HALL

FAN BOSHENG THINKS he heard voices and rings the doorbell, but immediately all goes quiet. He presses the doorbell again, but hears nothing more.

"Busy, eh?" he mutters. And he takes the lift downstairs and sits on the edge of the flower bed for a cigarette.

A group of pigeons fly into the air from the building opposite, scattering like confetti. Down below, someone is unloading cement, sand and tiles from a three-wheeler. Deliveries come and go: online orders and takeaway food. The boy with the takeaways cannot figure out whether Unit Three is the third door to the right or the left, and asks Bosheng. Not an easy question to ask because he has a bad stammer. Bosheng does not respond.

"I... I asked you... you a question. Why... why don't you a... answer?" says the boy.

"Be... because I... I st... stammer too," says Bosheng. "And you... you'd think I... I was copying you." He still refuses to tell him which doorway is Unit Three.

Some of the residents come down to walk their dogs, first a dalmatian, then a tan-coloured mutt. The tan mutt is so excited when it sees the dalmatian that it rushes over to smell its behind. The dalmatian owner stands between the two dogs and issues a stern reprimand. The mutt's owner is not annoyed because, after all, his dog is a mongrel and has no business messing with the dalmatian's bloodline. He calls it back, clamps it tightly between his legs and comments instead on the pile of cement, sand and tiles. "Who's decorating?" he asks.

Ms Dalmatian grumbles, "That'll be a couple of weeks of crashing and banging, and the corridors full of rubbish and dust!"

"I can understand international condemnation of environmental pollution in China!" Mr Tan-Mutt declares. "This is like doing up a house. People in developed countries did up their houses a long time ago, and obviously, they're quiet and clean now. China is a developing country, just like when someone moves house and renovates, right?" He looks pleased with himself, but Ms Dalmatian says nothing. Mr Tan-Mutt looks around for someone else to back him up and spots Bosheng on the flower bed wall. But he has never seen Bosheng before, and looks dubious. Bosheng takes his sunglasses from his pocket and puts them on. He holds his head high and says nothing.

About an hour later, a woman in her early twenties emerges from the building. She is slim, with long legs, silver hair and red lipstick, and looks like a model from the way she carries herself. Probably visiting Yi Guang, Bosheng thinks, and he smiles. He calls out, "Yi-laoshi!" The woman does not look at him, though her high heels pivot a fraction, before she hurries out of the courtyard.

Bosheng goes in and presses the lift button. Just before the lift takes off upwards, someone shouts, "Wait!" A young man staggers in after him, clutching two large bundles of books.

"Are you getting Yi-laoshi to sign books?" Bosheng asks.

"You've come to see him too?"

Bosheng hands over his business card. The young man looks at it. "I thought you were an artist, and so you are!"

"You're quite right. I see you're a book lover."

"These are to give as gifts."

"Yi-laoshi's calligraphy and paintings certainly make good gifts!"

"Giving a signed book is a better way of building connections than inviting someone for a meal. But I only have a small company, I won't be buying his calligraphy unless I get a really big deal."

When they ring the doorbell this time, the door opens straight away. The curtains are drawn inside, and the lights are on. Yi Guang is standing in the door, without his glasses on. His eyes are puffy, and his hair clings damply to his forehead as if he has just come out of the bathroom. Bosheng tucks himself behind the young man.

"Are you here to get books signed?" says Yi Guang. "You should have made an appointment first if you're bringing me that many to sign!"

"But everyone loves your books!" protests the young man. Yi Guang turns and goes back to the living room, and the young man follows behind. He takes a carton of cigarettes from his backpack and puts it on the low table. "When the taxi driver saw your books, he said, 'Are you going to see Mr Yi Guang to get him to sign them?' 'Do you know him?' I asked, and he said, 'Of course I do, he's a Xijing icon!' He knew you live in this area, because lots of his passengers bring packages of books to get them signed."

Yi Guang puts on his glasses, sits down and bends over the books, muttering, "People come every single day. Just seeing them with books in their hands gives me a headache. I never get time to myself!"

He looks up and sees Bosheng for the first time. "Did you bring him?" he asks.

"No, we've never met. I went to the art store but the gallery fish has been sold. I met this guy in the lift when I came to tell you."

"Sold!" exclaims Yi Guang. "Well, sit down."

But Bosheng remains standing. "You've got even more stuff in this room than before!"

That is certainly true. The shelves that line the four walls are filled with books, and every inch of space – on the tables and the cabinets, and between the sofas – is cluttered with antiques: terracotta tiles, jars, eave tiles, painted figurines; stone lions, mythical beasts like *pixiu* and *qilin*; odd-looking stones and lumps of wood and crystal, lacquerware, as well as framed thangkas, embroidery pieces, papercuts and shadow puppets. A tree trunk the diameter of a serving bowl and reaching right up to the ceiling has been erected in front of the window, its wood smooth and shiny.

The young man is looking around him open-mouthed. This room is like a museum. "What's the wooden pillar?" he asks.

"It's a *tongtianzhu*," Bosheng explains. "It's made of Hainan *huanghuali* wood. The markings look like clouds soaring to the heavens. A symbol of rising power and success."

"Wow, Hainan *huanghuali*! You can't even buy a bracelet in *huanghuali* for less than thirty thousand yuan. I can't imagine how much this great tree trunk costs!"

"He has a dozen lumps of raw Hetian jade, three on his bed alone," Bosheng tells him.

"Yi-laoshi sleeps with stones?" The young man is astonished.

Yi Guang calls through, "Bosheng, come and tie up the signed books for me!" Bosheng stops talking and does as he is told.

When the young man has been sent on his way with his signed books, Bosheng goes to draw the curtains to let some light in. A moth flies out of the folds. The young man comes back and says that he has forgotten to get a picture. He cannot leave without a photograph of such a celebrity. Yi Guang stands, expressionless, as the picture is taken. The young man shakes his hand and leaves with a grin.

"The gallery fish is sold?" Yi Guang says. "I got one a year ago. I wanted this one so I could make a pair – and it's gone!"

"Then let's hope you get lucky," says Bosheng.

"You don't understand. Look at that pair of stone lions, they're almost the same size. I got the first in August last year, and the other one in November. One draws the other along."

"It's not that one draws the other, it's you, your energy, that brings them to you."

Yi Guang grunts. He strokes the stone beasts, a long, skinny sheep and a flattened tortoise. "Once they're carved, they acquire souls."

"You mean they know what you're doing?"

Yi Guang stares. "What do you mean?"

Bosheng laughs. "They see how you make a name with your books, rake in the money with your calligraphy, and how you grant audiences to good-looking women!"

"And when did you ever introduce me to one of those?"

"The day before yesterday, a woman wanted an introduction. She was lovely except for one thing – she'd dyed her hair silver. Weird in a young woman! She isn't good enough for you, so I said no."

"Didn't you know, it's called granny grey. It's the height of fashion!"

"Granny grey? You learn something new every day!" Bosheng says with a wry smile.

"You're a sly one, you know that?" says Yi Guang.

"Absolutely not!" protests Bosheng as Yi Guang steers him towards the bedroom. Flanking the doorway, there are a pair of stone sculptures, each of a boy riding on a lion, one covering his ears, the other covering his mouth.

"They're called the deaf and the dumb, meaning, mind what you listen to, and mind what you say," says Yi Guang.

Bosheng is about to go in, but Yi Guang stops him. Someone is ringing the doorbell again.

This time, it is a fat man, sweating profusely and apologising, "I'm sorry, Yi-laoshi, there was a traffic jam. I'm a bit late."

"Then let's go straight up!" Yi Guang says. Bosheng follows them up the stairs. There are more small stone lions on both sides of each step. At the top, a plaque reads, "Cloud-Gathering Hall". The "Hall" turns out to be a small room of fifteen square metres, with a large desk, a sofa, calligraphy and paintings on the walls, and antique ceramics scattered everywhere.

Standing behind his desk, Yi Guang spreads out a large sheet of rice paper and takes the lid off the inkstone. He loads his calligraphy brush heavily with ink, and asks, "Did you bring the money?"

"I brought ninety thousand," the fat man says, putting a paper bag on the desk and pushing it towards Yi Guang.

Yi Guang puts down his brush. "No, no, that's no good. We agreed to round it up! Sort the money out."

The fat man is sweating more than ever and keeps wiping his head with his hands.

"Yi-laoshi never bargains over his calligraphy," Bosheng says. "Why are you sweating so much?"

"It's because I'm poor!" the fat man says. "The rich have oil but the poor only have their sweat. I know how valuable Yi-laoshi's calligraphy is, I know he doesn't bargain."

Yi Guang puts the lid on the inkstone, gets out a cigarette and gives it to the fat man. "I'll do it later. Have a smoke."

The fat man looks awkward, then takes another 10,000 yuan from his pocket. He holds it in his hand. "A hundred thousand is too much, can you make it less? I had to borrow this off three cousins to make it up to a hundred thousand."

"OK, OK, I'll knock off two thousand."

The fat man licks his finger and counts 2,000 and puts it away, then adds the 8,000 yuan to the 90,000.

"I'll make a note of it," Bosheng offers, but Yi Guang opens the bureau drawer and tosses the money in. "No need." He takes the lid off the inkstone again and dips his brush in ink. "Of course it's expensive. You can use this calligraphy to get a promotion, bag a big project or get a loan."

"True," says the fat man. "Your name opens many doors."

"Right," Yi Guang says. "And you eat the meat while I get the broth." He writes a Tang poem on the paper in flamboyant calligraphy, presses the seal on it, and says, "OK!"

"That's quick!" exclaims the fat man. "You print money!"

"Banknotes have to be printed on both sides, this one's only one side," Bosheng says.

Yi Guang looks at him. "You can write it then!" Bosheng laughs. "My calligraphy is Heaven's reward," says Yi Guang. The fat man looks puzzled. Yi Guang explains, "Books just earn you a reputation, they don't earn you enough to support a family." And he puts the lid back on the inkstone again.

Bosheng grabs a scrap of paper and spreads it out. "Write me something small," he says.

"Next time, when you bring me an album to write in."

"I'd rather have a copper coin now than be promised a silver ingot in the never-never. Just write me four characters," Bosheng wheedles.

But Yi Guang does not budge.

"Two characters then! One!"

"You're taking unfair advantage of me."

"In *Animal World* on TV, elephants, rhinos and even crocodiles have birds to perch on them and peck off the bugs. I'm your bird."

Yi Guang laughs out loud. "All big animals have parasites. You're a parasite but so am I!" With a smile, he writes the character 福, "fortune", on the paper, and throws his brush out of the window.

Yi Guang sees the fat man to the door and comes back inside. Bosheng has made himself a cup of tea and says, "Let me take you to a lamb restaurant tonight. There's one from northern Shaanxi on Vermilion Bird Street that specialises in lamb stews."

"I can't, I'm trying to lose weight," says Yi Guang. "I've already fasted for three days, skipping all meals from noon till the next morning. Have you got any city news?"

"A new karaoke hall's opened in Nanqi Alley, and the girls are great."

"Political news, I mean."

"Political? You know so many city bigwigs, you'd know better than me!" Bosheng pauses. "Let me ask you something. Why can't great artists resist the lure of an official position?"

"In China, art has no power to speak of."

"If you say so. I understand that when it's time for a new chair of the Federation of Literary and Art Circles, Wang Ji was asked to stand, and he agreed."

"The chair of the FLAC has always been someone who's a professional, a real standard bearer. Wang Ji is the right man for it, he's a great painter."

"But did you know that, as soon as the news came out, there were articles libelling Wang Ji on the internet?"

"Jealousy!" Yi Guang says. "Jealousy is the ugliest thing in human nature. Once it develops into hatred, it can lead to anything. When you see Wang Ji, tell him not to be angry about it. If someone has a go at him, they're just getting rid of bad karma for him."

"Do you know who wrote this stuff?"

"Who?"

"The FLAC used some fancy new digital technology to find out. It's Jiao Xiaowen."

"A fellow artist!" says Yi Guang.

"I just can't figure it out. Even if Wang Ji didn't get the job, it was never going to go to Jiao, was it? And to think I got him onto the Philippines delegation."

"He's a creep."

"When the delegation comes back, the Federation's going to send someone to pick him up."

"When will they be back?" asks Yi Guang.

"Didn't Feng Ying call you?"

"No."

"How come? I thought you were close to her."

"I'm close to all of the sisterhood."

Bosheng looks at Yi Guang, who shrugs and gives a big smile.

5. XI LISHUI • XIMING HOSPITAL

XIA ZIHUA duly receives her platelets transfusion, and Hai Ruo and Lu Yike stay with her for a couple of days. Then Hai Ruo calls Xi Lishui to come and take over. Lishui has been going to the gym every afternoon for almost a year and it shows: she has clearly lost weight, her body is toned and she has V-cut abs. When she gets Hai Ruo's call, she hurries home to take a shower, change and put on some make-up, and goes to the hospital. There, she finds that Hai Ruo and Yike have gone, and Zihua's mother and son, Mrs Qi and Xia Lei, are with her.

Xia Lei doesn't seem scared or anxious, just bored; soon after they arrive in the ward, he demands to go downstairs to play. His granny takes him into the corridor, where he peers into one sickroom, then another. In one, the doctor is examining the patient and the quilt is pulled back. The doctor is pressing the stethoscope against her belly, saying, "Breathe in, hold it, breathe out." The kid does the same, sniffing through bunged-up nostrils. One of the patient's family members closes the door on him. Some of the patients get out of bed and shuffle down the corridor. The boy shuffles along behind them until they get to the patients' toilet, then he hares off down the corridor. Mrs Qi is sitting on a bench, rubbing her painful knees and wiping tears from her eyes.

"You really must keep that kid under control!" the nurse

admonishes Lishui. "He's disturbing the other patients running around like that. And he'll spread germs, getting into everything."

"I'll stay," Lishui says to the old woman. "You take Xia Lei home." As soon as they have gone, she makes up a bowl of lotus root powder for Zihua, and then gives her the medicines to take with two sips of water. When the drip has run through, she takes her out for a walk down the corridor, and to the toilet at the far end.

One can see the east wall of the old city from the toilet window. The bricks are badly weathered and pitted with holes. There is one long crack which looks like a dead tree that has fallen over. But in the cracks between the bricks right down the bottom, weeds are growing out, and she can see tiny white flowers, like grains of rice. Someone on top of the wall is playing a sad tune on a *xun*, a traditional terracotta ocarina.

"Lishui, you must be exhausted!" says Zihua. "You go home and eat and take a rest. I'm fine here."

"I don't need any dinner, I'll stay with you tonight. Xu Qi will take over tomorrow morning, and then I'll go home to sleep."

Zihua turns away from her and begins to cry. When they are in the toilet, Zihua asks Lishui to leave her alone, but Lishui refuses and stands waiting with the toilet paper. When Zihua gets off the toilet, she appears dizzy and Lishui supports her, and bends to see the colour of her stool, but Zihua quickly flushes it away. "It's fine, it's normal," she says, fighting for breath.

Back in the ward, she rests and her breathing gradually returns to normal. Lishui combs her hair and takes out a make-up bag to powder her face.

"Do I look worn out?" asks Zihua.

"You've got thinner, but you've got more delicate too."

"Delicate? What's that about?" says Zihua. She goes on, "When people used to talk about qi-and-blood, I thought it was just an expression. I had no idea there's a real connection. If the qi energy is weak, the blood won't flow freely, and vice versa."

"It's the same with me," Lishui says. "If my stomach doesn't hurt, I have no real idea what my stomach is. I sprained a muscle in my lower back last month and now I know where my lower back is." She bends down and pats herself to show Zihua what she means, but Zihua says nothing. There is a strange light in her eyes.

"Do you think I'm being flippant again?" Lishui asks.

"Not at all, Lishui. I used to be the abrasive one. I was always having a go at someone in our sisterhood, especially you and Xu Qi. You have every reason to feel annoyed with me, please forgive me."

"You fight the ones you love, isn't that right? Do you remember when we went to buy a birthday cake for Hai-jie after we ate some leek pasties? There were bits of leek stuck between my teeth. I talked to so many people in the teashop but no one said anything. It was so embarrassing. You were the only person to pull me aside and tell me. I'm only annoyed with you for keeping everything under covers. Like your illness. You should have told us and come to the hospital for treatment much sooner, instead of putting it off."

Zihua smiles through her tears.

"What are you crying about? You look so pretty when you smile!"

"OK, I won't cry any more." Zihua wipes her tears, and changes the subject. "How's business lately?"

"The car showroom? So-so… there is a manager who's in charge. I don't go in much."

"You live such a free and easy life! How's things with Hu Sheng?"

"Nothing doing in that direction."

"He came to see me once to ask if I could put in a good word for him, but before I had time, I got sick."

"He came to see you? He wants you to have a word with me?"

"He says he wants to get back together with you, he says… he says he'll change…"

"Yeah, like a dog stops eating shit!" Then she realises that Zihua is so short of breath that she cannot get the words out, and has gone deathly pale. She helps her lie down.

"It's OK to marry the same man twice…" Zihua manages.

"The water's been poured away, you can't get it back," says Lishui. "Now I understand why Hai-jie, Qiyu, Lihou and Feng Ying have stayed single!"

"You're staying single?"

Lishui laughs. "I don't know if I could stand it."

Zihua attempts to wag an admonishing finger at Lishui, but is overcome with a fit of coughing. As Lishui pats her on the back, Zihua coughs up some phlegm. Her face is beaded with sweat.

"That's enough chit-chat, close your eyes and rest," says Lishui.

Zihua closes her eyes. "You too. Rest on the edge of the bed and have a snooze."

But Lishui does not nap. She spots a book under the pillow, a collection of essays by Yi Guang, and says, "I'll read you an essay." She reads, turns the page, reads some more, and Zihua falls asleep. Lishui sits there quietly looking at her. Her friend's face is gaunt, her cheeks sunken, the cheekbones prominent. Her long, slender "phoenix" eyes, tilted slightly upwards at the corners, are closed. How young Zihua looks. She has always been in good health and looked after herself well. She used to instruct Lishui too, "When you get up in the morning, swill your saliva around your mouth with your tongue, then swallow it. Good for the digestion and good for the teeth too. Squatting exercises and regulating your breathing is good for your reproductive organs." It seems impossible that she is suffering from such a horrible disease. Lishui sighs. Good health and keeping fit have little to do with how long you live. The same way you can end up in a car accident no matter how good your driving skills. She hurriedly pulls herself together. Zihua is going to live a long life, the platelet treatment will cure her, she thinks firmly. She stands up and goes to do some stretches in the corridor.

The lights in the rooms are all off, and the nurse on duty is napping at the nurses' desk. Lishui stands, gazing vacantly into the distance. Then she suddenly remembers something, goes to the stairs at the end of the corridor with her mobile and taps in a number.

Yi Guang answers. He is playing mahjong with friends, and smiles into the phone. "You're calling late! Do you miss me?"

"Sure I miss you, do you miss me?"

"Last night I had a dream that I was giving all of you piggybacks up the mountain, and the first one I gave a ride to was you."

"Why wasn't I alone with you?"

"Because you wouldn't be separated," Yi Guang says.

"If you were piggybacking all ten of us, it must have been exhausting!" Both of them laugh.

"No more joking," says Lishui. "I've got something serious to talk about. Is this a convenient moment?"

"These are all my friends, talk away," says Yi Guang.

Lishui can hear shouting and the clattering of mahjong tiles. "Am I interrupting your game?" she asks.

"I can multitask! What's the matter?"

"I know you're still worried about me being single! You brought a man the last time we all met. Everyone was saying we should get together, and you said you'd be willing to make the introductions."

"Oh, Wang Beixing, he says he likes you."

"Well, I'm wary. I mean, I've been through two men already. What I want to know is, why is he still single at his age?"

"He was married, but it only lasted three months, so he's still practically a virgin."

"Why did they get divorced? He didn't like her or the other way around? Temperament, money problems or physical problems?" asks Lishui.

"Why do you care? You need feelings to fall in love. It happens when your eyes meet. Stop being so rational. It's like you're going shopping."

"I just don't want to jump out of the frying pan into the fire. Besides, I want to know what qualifications he has and what kind of job he does. If he's on a fixed salary, he won't have much savings, but does he have a house? Does he live alone, or with his parents?"

"I'll find out," says Yi Guang. "All I know is that he's a good person. But it takes time to get to know him. He doesn't say much, but what he does say is considered."

"Why do I always end up with men who don't talk a lot?"

"How many people are there in this world with the gift of the gab like you?"

Lishui smiles. "But I'm a pain in the neck, aren't I! And one more thing, do you know his star sign?"

"Are you into fortune-telling? I don't understand anything about astrology, but I heard him say his birthday is the third or fourth week of December."

"Oh, Capricorn!" Lishui says. "I won't keep you any longer now, I'll call you later."

Just then she hears one of the mahjong players say, "Who's that interrogating you? The Party Disciplinary Committee? Nuts!"

Nuts? Lishui cuts the call. Is she nuts? Love is kind of nutty, but so what? And the only medicine for it is finding the right partner! Lishui's lips twitch in a smile.

The stairs are deserted, and the ceiling light in the landing is dim.

The hospital is a place where people come to die. Their ghosts can be anywhere. One might even appear silently on the stairs. But Lishui is not afraid of ghosts. She is confidently healthy, and especially now she is looking for love, she has a yang aura hovering above her head, and that will keep the ghosts away. She starts to flip through her mobile phone. She has a star signs empathy map on it: twelve human bodies with little hearts on them. Aries, with a heart on the right-hand side of the chest. Taurus, with three hearts in the middle and left of the chest. Gemini, a heart-shaped mouth. Cancer, with a heart on the right chest. Leo with a heart-shaped head. Virgo, with two hearts on the right-hand side of the chest. Libra, four hearts around the head. Scorpio, with a heart in the groin. Sagittarius, with a heart in the middle of the chest. Pisces, hearts all over. Aquarius and Capricorn, no hearts at all.

Suddenly Lishui's forehead beads with sweat, and she presses Yi Guang's number again.

Yi Guang picks up but he seems to be talking to someone about the mahjong game.

"I'm sorry to bother you again," Lishui says. "I checked, and Capricorn isn't interested in romance."

"Rubbish! Wang Beixing throws himself into everything he does."

"But in my picture, he's got no heart."

"What picture are you looking at?"

"A star signs empathy map. I downloaded it from the internet."

"It's just one of those dating apps. They're rubbish!"

"Are you Pisces?" Lishui asks.

"My birthday's March fifteenth."

"You *are* Pisces! Pisces is covered in hearts, and that's just what you're like. If it's accurate for you, how can it be rubbish for him?"

Yi Guang laughs down the phone. "So there are hearts all over me, are there? If I've got ten hearts stuck on me, which one is you?"

Lishui says nothing for a moment, then complains, "Why are you being nasty to me when there are ten of us in the sisterhood?"

Yi Guang starts to laugh again, then abruptly stops.

"Can you take another look at him?" Lishui asks.

"Sure," Yi Guang says, and cuts the call.

Lishui feels very tired. She has to steady herself against the wall on her way back to the ward. Zihua is still asleep, so she turns off the light and sits on the edge of the bed. The sisterhood once talked about how you can divide people into two. Xu Qi and Si Yinan split them into rich and poor, Yan Nianchu and Feng Ying into beautiful and ugly. Lishui figures that they thought like that because of their upbringing and circumstances. Personally, the only distinction she makes is between men and women. She thinks about Hu Sheng and Wang Beixing. If she compares the two men, she can see that they each have their strengths and their shortcomings. She wavers. Sometimes, everything is crystal clear, at other times, nothing is clear. She goes back to the stairs and calls Yi Guang again.

But his phone is off. Back in the sickroom, the duty nurse comes in to check on Zihua. Lishui is gazing at the wall and does not immediately react.

"Why don't you take a nap?" the nurse suggests.

"I am napping," says Lishui.

"With your eyes open?"

"Uh-huh."

"How's the patient been?" asks the nurse.

"She's fine," says Lishui. Then she asks, "What's the name of her doctor and the ward sister, and your name? Tomorrow I'll go and buy some books and get Yi Guang to sign them, as a thank you to all of you."

The nurse is impressed. "Yi Guang, he's a big name. Can you really get him to sign?"

"Yes, we're old friends," says Lishui.

"That's wonderful! We used to read his essays at high school. I heard his calligraphy is fabulous too!"

"I can't ask him for calligraphy, his pieces are expensive."

"They say he's seriously into money, right?"

"Everyone's into money. They're always trying to blag his calligraphy off him. If he refuses, they say nasty things about him."

The nurse is about to say something else when Lishui's phone buzzes. It is Yi Guang again. She goes back to the end of the corridor by the stairs.

"My mobile was on charge," he says. "We're taking a break and eating pot noodles, so we can talk now." He pauses, then, "If you want me to find out more about him, you have to be open too, so if he asks, I can answer. Has your divorce come through?"

"Yes, I'm completely free."

"So all the sisterhood are single!"

"And Yike, Xu Qi and Yinan never married."

"Why does a good woman's marriage always end in grief?"

"It doesn't always. She needs to find someone who's right for her."

"Wang Beixing might not be right for you."

"Better look for someone else then."

"Right, a woman must have a family, and there's sex too."

"We've all agreed that when we're old, we'll go and live in sheltered housing together and stay there till we die. As for sex, anyone can find a man for that!"

Yi Guang laughs. "True. In the past, sex was about carrying on the family line, but now it's an art."

"An art?"

"You see, art is the process of turning the practical into the useless. Take calligraphy, it's just writing, isn't it? Writing is for memorising things, so it's practical. But calligraphy is not concerned with content, it's an expression of emotion through the style, rhythm and overall structure of the brushstrokes. The same is true for sex. It's not for reproduction, it's about unleashing desire and physical pleasure."

"Well said! I'll pass that on to Hai-jie and the others."

"I already told Hai Ruo, Yike and Feng Ying."

"And you didn't tell me?"

"I've told you now, haven't I? Forgive me."

"No, I won't! But I still love you, and I still want you to check up on Wang Beixing for me."

"Sure, sure," Yi Guang says. Before he cuts the call, he sighs. "You know, looking for a partner is really looking for yourself."

6. YU BENWEN • THE HOTPOT RESTAURANT

YU BENWEN IS UP EARLY. Tousle-haired, she shuffles into the bathroom and sits on the loo. Then she calls her assistant and tells him to prepare the largest private room on the fourth floor and set up two dining tables, each with a hotpot partitioned down the middle for hot and mild soup. She wants new tableware and fresh covers on the chairs.

Hai Ruo was against holding the dinner in the hotpot restaurant at first, but Benwen insisted, "It's my treat and I run a hotpot restaurant. Are you saying that hotpot's not good enough? It's true, it's usually cheap and cheerful food, but it depends what you put in it. I can serve it with different seafoods. If you don't want to hang around there too long, then we can move once we've finished our meal. We can take the best wine, the Château Lafite, as well as the German dark beer, cold cuts, pastries, yogurt, cola and fruit and move to the teashop."

Hai Ruo finally agrees. "You make sure all the sisterhood come, and we should invite Mr Wu too, and Yi-laoshi, and we can ask Eva to join us at the teashop."

Benwen goes through the names, calling Lu Yike, Xiang Qiyu, Ying Lihou and Yan Nianchu. Feng Ying can't come because she is in the Philippines, and Xia Zihua is in the hospital. It is Xu Qi's turn to be with Zihua so she can't come either, but Si Yinan agrees to give

Zihua's mother a lift there and collect Xu Qi and bring her along later. Xi Lishui's phone is turned off so Benwen texts her. She calls Mr Wu's assistant, but the assistant says that her boss is on a retreat, just into his second day, and will not be able to come.

Yi Guang is delighted at the invitation. "What serendipity, I've not been eating a lot and I'm craving a hotpot! So it's your turn this time, is it? You're a rich dame, and you don't mind showing it!"

"It's taken seven months to get to my turn," says Benwen. "I have to put on a good show, but I'm not rolling in it and I'm not a rich dame."

"All right then, 'sister'."

"Did you write calligraphy on some of their fans a couple of weeks ago?"

"I wrote four characters on Yike's fan. It's her birthday, and she's having problems with her business. She's muttering that she might have to leave Xijing. Then Yinan, Qiyu, Lihou and Nianchu want me to write on their fans too, so I have to play fair and do all of them. Why don't you come over?"

"OK, when I have time," says Benwen.

"You're prepared to beard the lion in its den, are you?" says Yi Guang.

"Of course I am!"

"Excellent!"

Then Yi Guang asks, "Which men have you invited?"

"Mr Wu's on a retreat, so you're the only one."

"Oh, right, I'm the Party representative in the Red Detachment of Women! Although as it happens, I've just been told by the head of the Xijing Organisational Department that they have a VIP guest from Beijing who's read my books and likes them very much. I've been invited to their banquet this evening. I have to attend."

"Oh, if it's an official invite, we can't compete."

"I'm still part of their bureaucracy, there's nothing I can do about it," says Yi Guang with regret.

"Yes, it's a shame," says Benwen. "We two seem to be fated not to get to know each other! Come to our gathering in the teashop after you've had your dinner."

"Sure."

Having made the arrangements, Benwen cleans her teeth, washes her face and combs her hair. Then she dresses with great care in a white pencil skirt, and drives to the hotpot restaurant.

Yi Guang arrives at the teashop at nine o'clock sharp. Standing under the small window in the gable end on the east side of the building, he can hear the gentle hum of voices from the floor above and the ripples of laughter. As he walks around the corner of the building, he is forced to dodge a three-wheeler that screeches to a halt beside him.

A young man jumps down, and greets him, "Yi Guang-laoshi!" Before Yi Guang can react, the young man continues, "I saw you on the TV news. Now here you are in the flesh, alive!"

xiao-Tang comes out of the teashop and says sharply, "What on earth are you talking about?"

But Yi Guang laughs. "The year before last I was in hospital, and a reader came to visit me. He said that he had been thinking on his way to the hospital how regrettably short the lives of gifted people were. As soon as the words were out, he clapped his hand over his mouth, but what he said came from the heart. So who's this one?"

"This is Gao Wenlai," says xiao-Tang. "He writes poetry."

"Have you had any published?" asks Yi Guang.

Wenlai does not answer. Instead, he goes and fetches a stool from the shop for Yi Guang.

"Please come inside," says xiao-Tang. "There's no need to sit outside!"

Wenlai claps himself on the head and ushers Yi Guang inside. "I'm just learning, I haven't published anything yet. Mrs Hai said that if I came here, she would introduce me to you, but I still can't quite believe you're here."

"And I landed right in your net!" says Yi Guang.

"I'm incredibly honoured," says Wenlai. "Do you live around here?"

"The top floor of Unit Three, Building Two."

Wenlai is clearly thrilled but xiao-Tang warns him, "Yi-laoshi is very busy, we don't like to bother him. Don't go knocking on his door at all hours!"

"Understood."

xiao-Tang takes Yi Guang upstairs, and Wenlai unloads four cases of red wine from the three-wheeler, picks one up and clatters up behind them.

A large Eight Immortals table has been laid out with plates of cold cuts, pastries, yogurt, ice cream, beef jerky and fruit. Hai Ruo, Yike, Benwen and Eva sit on the couch. With Benwen hosting them this month, Yike after that, the bar is constantly being raised. Who knows which fancy restaurant they'll end up in next?

Yi Guang bursts into the room, and everyone stands up.

"See? I said he'd come!" says Hai Ruo. "And so smartly dressed too!"

"Dear Yi-laoshi!" Benwen greets him effusively.

Yike pouts. "No need to overdo it, Benwen. He didn't come to your hotpot restaurant, did he?"

Benwen puts her hands over her face and pretends to weep.

"Put some spit in your eyes!" says Yike.

"Benwen really pushed the boat out today," Hai Ruo tells Yi Guang. "We had salmon, huge lobsters, sea crabs, oysters, sea cucumbers and sea urchins."

"I really couldn't get away. Benwen knew I couldn't come, and she still gave you the best food!" Yi Guang protests.

"My seafood's straight from Australia. Come another day and you can have whatever you want!"

"I've missed you and your enthusiasm," Yi Guang tells Benwen. "I couldn't make the hotpot, but at least I'm here for the drinks. As it happens, after we finished our dinner, the departmental boss arranged for a performance by three famous Qinqiang Opera stars, but I said I had to get home, something urgent came up, and I rushed over here."

"If you hadn't come," says Hai Ruo, "Benwen's dinner would have been a failure."

Everyone laughs. Yi Guang pulls Hai Ruo aside and whispers, "Didn't you invite General Secretary Ning?"

"Benwen was issuing the invites. Mr Ning doesn't know the rest of the sisterhood. I didn't invite Mr Gong either."

Yi Guang raises his voice, "Benwen, where are the others?"

"On their way. I said you were definitely coming, so they all went home after the hotpot to get changed. Who is it you're looking for?"

Yi Guang looks embarrassed and rubs his face, a little like a cat.

"Yi-laoshi is so shy," remarks Yike. Everyone looks at Yi Guang and smiles, and Eva laughs out loud.

"It makes him more attractive, going all shy, doesn't it?" says Hai Ruo.

But Yi Guang's eye has suddenly been caught by Eva. "Hey, I see we have a foreign friend here!"

Hai Ruo brings Eva over and introduces her to Yi Guang. Wenlai has carried all the wine upstairs and stands to one side watching Yi Guang intently. Hai Ruo introduces Wenlai too, and Yi Guang says that they have met downstairs. Then he smiles at Eva.

"Oh dear!" says Yike and whispers something in Eva's ear.

"What did you say to Eva, Yike?" Yi Guang asks.

"I'm telling her the story of the snake and the rat. When the snake is about to eat the rat, it mesmerises it with its stare so the rat moves closer instead of running away."

"So who's the rat and who's the snake?" Yi Guang asks with an air of bemusement.

Yike and Eva burst out laughing.

"Yi-laoshi's used to getting a lot of respect," Hai Ruo says. "We're pretty casual here. Maybe too casual!"

At the head of the stairs, Wenlai is opening the wine while xiao-Tang brings up wine glasses.

"There's a rhyme doing the rounds on social media," says Wenlai. "He's so lovable, he makes flowers bloom and car tyres go boom."

"Don't talk nonsense," says Tang. "You say that about girls, not men."

"Everyone likes Yi-laoshi," says Wenlai.

"Yi-laoshi likes everyone even more," says xiao-Tang.

Hai Ruo asks Yi Guang for his opinion on the décor. Does he think it works? But Yi Guang is wholly in favour. All the furniture, and the couch too, is very well chosen. The furniture is Ming reproduction but it looks very comfortable. He can see that due consideration has been given to the feng shui, and the most basic requirement of feng shui is to be comfortable.

"Have you ever brought a child in here?" he asks Hai Ruo.

She shakes her head.

"A dog?"

"No."

"Try it. When kids come in without making a fuss, and dogs don't bark, that's because it's a liveable room. Is that table made of nanmu wood? The face of the Buddha statuette is exquisite, it must have been made by a true artist. It has an impressive, ancient feel. And you have so many books – literature, economics, picture albums, calligraphy copybooks, books on the tea ceremony, on porcelain, flower arrangement, jade and jewellery – the *guqin* is in a good position too."

"But the thing I'm most proud of is the thing you've not mentioned," says Hai Ruo. "What about the mural?"

"I'm leaving you to tell me how good it is!" says Yi Guang with a laugh. He glances at Eva, who is busy putting out the dishes. "Is it painted by Wang Ji?"

"It is."

"I've never seen such a large mural in Xijing. Only Wang Ji could paint one like that! But it reminds me of a tomb painting."

Hai Ruo is impressed. "It's a copy of a tomb painting from White City, the Xia capital," she says.

"Why did Wang Ji copy that one?"

"Because I asked him to."

"But why? The Xia is a minor dynasty. A fifth-century marvel, but ephemeral. A flash in the pan."

"Somehow, the first time I saw this mural in a book, I had a special feeling about it. Besides, my Living Buddha visitor is from Tibet and the painting looks appropriate for him, so I got Wang Ji to come here and paint me a reproduction."

"I see," says Yi Guang.

Yike puts in, "Yi-laoshi and Mr Wang are the two monarchs of Xijing's literary and art world. Kings don't like to meet as equals, right?"

"Are you saying that I'm deliberately belittling this mural? Wang Ji and I are adversaries but we're friends too. It takes a general to appreciate a general. We have no fear of each other!"

Yike applauds, and Hai Ruo joins in.

"When is the Living Buddha arriving?" Yi Guang asks.

"Mr Wu just says this month, there's no exact date yet," Hai Ruo tells him.

"I'd like to make a point," Yi Guang says. "When I got to know you and you opened the teashop, I wrote the shop sign for it. People often think I own this teashop, or have shares in it. But even though we know each other so well, you've never given me a studio to do my calligraphy in, or set up a literary salon for me. While the Living

Buddha's only coming for a few days, and you've completely redecorated this enormous room for him, in the height of good taste!"

"But I'm a lay disciple!" protests Hai Ruo. "I'm hosting the Living Buddha, and these four women want to meet him and convert." She laughs. "I think you're jealous! But we don't stand on ceremony with you. You're a friend. And when the Living Buddha's gone, I'll be able to relax in this room, and the sisterhood can use it to meet up. Of course, I hope you'll come to do your calligraphy and run a literary salon here!"

As she speaks, Qiyu arrives, wearing a red dress with spaghetti straps and wide dropped sleeves, a pleated skirt and a deep neckline. At her throat, she wears a jade pendant. She minces up the stairs in a pair of black high heels, then holds a pose at the top.

"You said you were going back to change, but whatever made you dress like that?" exclaims Benwen.

"Hai Ruo's turned the teashop into a cultural centre, and Yi-laoshi's here, so although I'm not educated, I have to look rich and classy!" says Qiyu.

"Rich, maybe, but classy?" says Hai Ruo.

"I'm still learning," Qiyu excuses herself.

Just then, Lihou arrives, also wearing a strappy dress, only grey. The straps are tied in bows on her shoulders, and she has a jade pendant too. She has brought two shopping bags in one hand and is carrying a mini-backpack in the other.

Qiyu greets her with, "Hey, you're wearing a strappy dress too! I like that little backpack."

"I was passing by the shopping centre just now, and planning to buy a pair of shoes. Then this new Korean bag caught my eye so I bought it. Do you like it?" she asks Yi Guang.

"It's great!"

"Really?"

"It suits you down to the ground."

Lihou's eyes tilt up at the edges as she smiles.

"Fox eyes!" Qiyu says. "Yi-laoshi likes a woman with fox eyes. No wonder Lihou has bought four brand-name bags since last year!"

Then they hear, "A woman dresses up for someone who truly appreciates her!" All heads turn in the direction of the voice and they see Xu Qi and Yinan coming up the stairs. The voice is Xu Qi's.

Xu Qi's long hair hangs loose, and she wears a jade pendant as well as a silver Miao necklace. She wears a black shirt and skirt, and long, black high-heeled boots. Yinan looks like she has just washed her short hair and sprayed it into spikes. She is in black too: black shirt and shorts, but topped with a denim jacket. Her shoes are brown and she has on a backpack, as well as a small bag that she carries in one hand. Xu Qi is out of breath by the time she gets to the top, and has to stop talking.

Yinan gives Xu Qi the bag, and Xu Qi whispers, "You're not wearing jade!"

Yinan pulls her collar down to show the cord for her pendant, and says, "It's underneath."

"Hah, we judge people by their clothes, and horses by their saddles," Yi Guang exclaims in delight. 'You're all dressed so beautifully today. Since you've made such an effort, let me give you a hug. I'll just hug your clothes!" He spreads his arms and goes towards them, but they scatter like magpies.

Nianchu comes a little later, wearing sunglasses, a white shirt and a leopard-print long-sleeved coat, which hides whatever she is wearing underneath. She has long, straight legs, and her left ankle is adorned with a small flower tattoo.

She is greeted by enthusiastic cries from the shop assistants, "Yanjie, you're such a trend-setter!"

When she goes upstairs, Yi Guang exclaims, "You're a sight for sore eyes!"

Nianchu pushes her sunglasses up to her forehead. "Thank you!" she says.

There is a moment of silence, then Hai Ruo claps her hands. "The only one who's missing is Lishui. She was late to the hotpot, and now she's late again. Let's not wait for her!" And they all gather around the table.

A round table is egalitarian, there is no seat of honour. Yike makes Eva sit on the west side with her. Qiyu sits on Yike's right. Nianchu is on the south side, Yinan and Xu Qi on the east side. Lihou is about to sit between Yinan and Xu Qi, but Yinan puts Xu Qi beside her, and Lihou sits between Xu Qi and Nianchu. Then Benwen takes a chair on Yinan's right.

Yi Guang sits next to Qiyu, but she pulls a face at him and says, "You go and sit with Nianchu!"

"I want to sit with you, you've got such a sexy pout," says Yi Guang.

Yike snorts with laughter. Finally, Hai Ruo finds an empty seat for herself.

xiao-Tang comes over and asks, "What kind of tea would you like me to get out, Hai-jie, Yunnan black tea or Moonlight Beauty?"

There are exclamations, "You've got tea called Moonlight Beauty?"

"It's just come in," xiao-Tang explains. "It's called Moonlight Beauty because it's picked by lovely women, and dried and stored in a dark room. Then at night, it's taken outdoors to absorb the essence of moonlight, for ten consecutive nights."

"Let's not all drink the same tea," says Hai Ruo. "Everyone here has different personalities and different tastes. So we won't use a teapot. Bring glasses, the Italian crystal ones, and brew whatever people want."

Qiyu agrees. "Right, only the same kind of people drink the same tea, and we're all individuals. I'll have jasmine tea."

"I don't know what the new variety tastes like. Eva and I will try the Yunnan black tea," says Yike.

"I'll stick to Anji white tea, please," says Benwen.

"Wuyi rock tea for me, Narcissus brand," Lihou says.

"Chinese cinnamon," says Yinan.

"Longjing, please," says Xu Qi.

"Horse meat or beef?" xiao-Tang asks Yinan.

"Horse meat or beef?"

"The cinnamon from Horse Head Mountain is called horse meat, and the cinnamon from Ox Clan Mountain is called beef."

"Horse meat then," says Yinan.

Xu Qi looks down and says, "Well, you're the expert. Forget my Longjing, I'll have the same as Yinan."

xiao-Tang turns to Nianchu, who wants a glass of plain water. Then she asks, "What would you like, Hai-jie?"

"Yi-laoshi should go first," says Hai Ruo. "What are you drinking, Yi-laoshi?"

"You're all a feast for the eyes," says Yi Guang. "I didn't share your hotpot just now, and now I'm drinking in your beauty. I won't have tea."

"But you must have some tea!" says Hai Ruo.

"Then I'll have Moonlight Beauty!"

Hai Ruo orders a glass of Iron Bodhisattva. xiao-Tang makes everyone's tea, places their glasses in front of them and goes to the top of the stairs where Wenlai is serving the wine.

Wenlai eyes xiao-Tang's chest as he fills the glasses. In response, xiao-Tang flicks a few drops of wine from the glass she is holding into Wenlai's eyes. "What are you looking at?"

"Your neck."

"Have I got flowers growing out of it?"

"I'm looking for your jade."

xiao-Tang is speechless for a moment. She wipes the wine from Wenlai's face with a tissue before saying, "And where would I get jade from?"

"They're all wearing jade pendants."

"Hai-jie gave pendants to all of them, as gifts."

"Oh, now I know why you didn't get one."

"Because I'm just an employee."

"Because you're too fierce!"

xiao-Tang stops wiping his face and drops the tissue.

After the wine is served, everyone scrapes their chairs back and gets to their feet, clinking their glasses and thanking Benwen for "splashing out on such a feast".

"Don't thank me," says Benwen. "We meet every month, how many times have you all invited me? The reason we came back to the teashop after dinner is that this is where we first met and formed the sisterhood, and got to know Yi-laoshi. This teashop has nurtured our new lives in the same way Yan'an nurtured China's revolution. Hai-jie has done up this upstairs room and brought us here to see it. When the Living Buddha comes, this will be the shrine, and when he's gone, it'll become our meeting place. Come on, let's drink to the teashop and Hai-jie. Propose a toast, Hai-jie!"

"You're the host, why do you want words from me?" Hai Ruo objects.

"Because this is where the sisterhood was formed," says Benwen. "We were like loose grains of sand, and you've packed us together into a tight ball."

Yi Guang looks down and whispers to Nianchu, "You can't ball sand. The tighter you squeeze, the more it runs through your fingers. You're all so prickly, like hedgehogs, you snuggle up and then you stab each other."

"Is that how you see us?" asks Nianchu.

"I'm taking Benwen's words to their logical conclusion."

Hai Ruo sees Yi Guang and Nianchu whispering to each other, but she cannot hear what they are saying.

"Yi-laoshi, you come and say a few words," she says.

"I'm a guest, my mouth's only duties are eating and drinking."

"What do you want me to say?" Hai Ruo asks Benwen. "That you've raised the bar by serving all these good things to eat and drink, and the next host will have a hard act to follow?"

Benwen waves dismissively. "Eating and drinking are just what we do. Tell us why you got this upstairs room, prepared it for the Living Buddha's visit, and are making it into a meeting place, what it means to you and how it will work."

"All right, a few words then," Hai Ruo begins. "No matter what we do in today's society and how, and what new technologies we use, the problems that Shakyamuni wanted all sentient beings to solve are still there. We can't always go and meditate or recite sutras in a temple, but we can practise meditation in our daily lives to rid ourselves of our worries. Of course, our sisterhood can't do that here yet. But by expanding the teashop upstairs and receiving the Living Buddha here, and using it as a sanctum, a meditation room, then we can begin to worship the Buddha. We're all sitting here today, but what force brought us together? Superficially, we're here to eat and drink. In fact, it's our past karma that's drawn us here, and the urge that each of us has to resolve the doubts in our lives."

The atmosphere suddenly becomes solemn. There is total silence.

Hai Ruo breaks the spell. "It's out of character for me to speak like this, and it's out of character for you not to eat or drink! Go for it!"

They relax again and someone says, "What a good speech, as good as a government leader! And now for the good food and wine!" And they set to, demolishing the food, gulping their wine and clinking glasses. They get so merry that Yike admonishes them, "Manners, ladies, manners!"

Lihou, who is sitting next to Nianchu, accidentally knocks her chopsticks off the table. When she bends down to retrieve them, she is confronted by a forest of bare thighs. As Yike is talking, she touches Nianchu's rump and whispers, "Are you not wearing trousers?"

"What's up? You think I've got nothing covering my bum?" says Nianchu, and she gets to her feet and hikes up her top.

"You're wearing hotpants!" Lihou exclaims.

And she holds up her wine glass and takes over from Yike. "Sisters, this name we've been calling ourselves, the ten maidens, it's not right. If it's a reference to the twelve ladies of *A Dream of Red Mansions*, then it's such a cliché, plus they all came to a bad end. We should call ourselves the ten beauties."

"That's so old hat, such a cliché!" declares Qiyu.

Yi Guang puts in, "Speaking of beauties, I've just remembered the lines from a poem, 'The scholar gets older, the beauty retains her looks'."

"Yi-laoshi, are you mocking us for being old?" says Xu Qi.

"Xu Qi's still young, of course," says Benwen. "But apart from her and Nianchu, the rest of us are all fading."

"A fading beauty can still look glamorous when she makes herself up," says Yi Guang. "But now I'm past fifty, my forehead is furrowed with wrinkles."

All this talk of the passing of the years makes everyone look at each other. They begin to touch up their make-up and tidy their hair. They have to admit with a laugh that time is a butcher's knife and their handsome friend is finally getting old.

Hai Ruo comforts him. "But you're still attractive. Guys can be old and attractive, right?" Then she says, "Let's raise a glass to Yi-laoshi. Thank you for attending our gatherings over so many years, bestowing your knowledge and wisdom on us, exerting your influence over us, raising us up and being so kind to us!"

They all clink glasses.

Yi Guang begins to speak, "I agree with Qiyu about not calling the sisterhood 'the beauties'. Can I suggest that since each of you is wearing a piece of jade, you call yourselves the Xijing Ten Pieces of Jade?"

After a moment's surprised silence in which they stare at each other, there are cries of approval, "Brilliant! We are the Xijing Ten Pieces of Jade! How did you think of such a clever image, Yi-laoshi?"

Yi Guang says, "There's a woman writer in Xijing called Feng. In one of her novels, the four women are called the Four Pieces of Jade." He fixes his eyes on Eva, who is watching and smiling silently. "Of course! Eva should be a piece of jade too!"

"I forgot to introduce Eva to the rest of you," says Hai Ruo. "Eva's from Russia. Yike, Benwen and Xu Qi already know her, the rest of you are meeting her for the first time today. Eva, this is Xiang Qiyu, who made tens of millions selling some land she owns, and has set up a therapy centre. This is Ying Lihou. She deals in property and has twenty-three shops she rents out. This is Yan Nianchu, who used to have a lift business, and now deals in medical equipment, which she does very well. This is Si Yinan, the owner of the largest mahogany furniture store in the city."

Eva greets them all by name, adding a respectful *jie* after each one. There are murmurs of approval. "What a nice, quiet girl! Hai-jie, why don't you give Eva a piece of jade? Ask her, Eva!"

"I saw you all wearing jade pendants, and I wondered why. Hai-jie, I'd like one too!" says Eva.

"I have one here," says Hai Ruo. "I just haven't had time to give it to you." She goes to the couch, rifles in a basket holding a collection of beads and cords, takes out a white jade pendant and hangs it around Eva's neck.

"Eva, that piece of jade is worth tens of thousands of yuan, and I won it for you!" says Yi Guang.

Eva bows to him, hands clasped. Everyone holds up their mobile phones to take pictures, and Yi Guang exclaims, "How beautiful Eva is!"

"So we're not beautiful?" the others protest.

"You're all beauties!" Yi Guang says. "Just senior beauties."

The wine glasses are refilled three times, and then Nianchu lights a cigarette, picks up the plate of pastries and goes to talk to Eva. Everyone else stands up and begins to circulate with their drinks too; here, a couple stand by the window, there, three sit on the couch, laughing and talking.

Hai Ruo takes Benwen downstairs with her. In the cubicle, Wenlai has lit the gas and turned it up high, and the water hisses as it comes to the boil.

"I know you're busy, but mind you don't let the water boil over and put the flame out," says Hai Ruo. "We don't want a gas leak."

"Don't worry," replies Wenlai. "I'm keeping an eye on it. I can tell by the sound anyway. Boiling water goes quiet."

Benwen suddenly says, "Oh, I forgot to buy cigarettes. Some of our guests smoke."

"Wenlai, go and buy cigarettes," Hai Ruo orders. "Here's five hundred yuan."

"Can you watch the stove then?" says Wenlai, before leaving.

"Why are you paying?" Benwen asks.

But Hai Ruo does not answer. Instead, she says, "Mr Wu didn't come, what did his assistant say?"

"He's on a retreat, and it's only the second day."

"Funny," says Hai Ruo. "I went to borrow *The Surangama Sutra* from him less than a week ago. He never mentioned a retreat. I wonder if it's one week or two. It looks like the Living Buddha won't be here till after that, right?"

"Probably not," says Benwen.

"Anyway, let's make a plan to receive him," says Hai Ruo. "We should take him to the Famen Temple and the Guangren Temple. You need to make sure we have a decent car."

"We've all got decent cars. Nianchu and Lihou have Mercs. But there'll be a lot of people going with us. I think we'll need a minibus. You know the general secretary. Can you get hold of one like the kind they send to pick up an important delegation, fitted with a desk?"

"We can't rely on a government bus," says Hai Ruo. "If a delegation needs to be picked up, it won't be available. We should hire one privately."

"Mr Gong's property business is doing well. He should have one," says Benwen.

"He has an RV and a van."

"An RV would be great," says Benwen. "A friend of mine has one, I'll get hold of it."

"That's settled then," says Hai Ruo.

She glances out of the window. Night has fallen and the street lights in the distance shine brightly. The streets are still crowded with pedestrians. Suddenly, they hear a loud noise.

Everyone in the teashop looks out in horror.

"Is that thunder?" xiao-Zhen asks.

"If only!" xiao-Su says. "If we got a bit of wind, there might be no smog tomorrow!"

Wenlai hurries in, a carton of cigarettes in his hand, his clothes spotted with rain. He wipes his face and says, "Hey, a builder's rubble lorry hit someone at the crossroads!"

"Is the person dead?" Mrs Zhang asks.

"She was lying at the side of the road," says Wenlai. "But when I got to her, she stood up. Must have just fainted. The driver got out, but when he saw she was all right, he drove his truck away. It's beginning to rain, by the way."

"Really?" xiao-Zhen says.

xiao-Su ignores her. "These rubble lorry drivers are crazy. I saw on the TV news that three people have been killed just in the last three months. I thought the local government inspects these lorries. How come they're still driving so fast? Even if they don't knock anyone down, the lorry doesn't have a tarpaulin cover so the dust flies off and adds to the air pollution, which is bad enough as it is!"

A customer who has come in to buy tea says, "These inspection campaigns never work unless they tackle the root cause."

"What's the root cause?" asks Wenlai.

"These rubble lorries are all privately contracted," the customer explains, "and the contractor pays the driver per trip. So obviously the drivers go as fast as possible so they get more money. Get it?"

"No," says Wenlai.

"Forget it," says the customer. "It's not gonna make any difference whether you understand or not."

Wenlai grunts, and he goes into the cubicle to give the cigarettes to Benwen.

It is raining harder now and the drops thud against the window panes. "If only this rain would go on all night," Hai Ruo says to Benwen. "I wonder why Lishui still isn't here. Why don't you call and chase her up?"

"Right," says Benwen and goes upstairs. The water in the kettle has boiled by now, and Hai Ruo turns the gas off and takes the kettle upstairs. Just then someone comes into the shop with a dog, both of them wet through. Before Hai Ruo can say that no dogs are allowed in the shop, Wenlai has stepped forward. "If you're sheltering from the rain, there's a pavilion on the left outside."

"I've come to buy tea! You do sell tea, right?"

"Yes, yes, we do, but leave the dog outside," says Wenlai.

"This is my dog," the customer protests.

"We don't have dog tea here," says Wenlai. Hai Ruo smirks as she goes up the stairs with the kettle.

There is a haze of smoke in the upstairs room. Almost everyone is smoking.

"Just look at how you ladies hold your cigarette between the index and middle fingers, take little puffs, then straighten your arm away and hold it aloft. So chic and graceful, so *'taiwei',*" says Yi Guang admiringly.

"What's *taiwei?*" asks Xu Qi.

"The essence of a woman. It's like the light emanating from the Buddha, the flame of the fire, the gleam of precious stones or jade," explains Yi Guang. "Xu Qi's like a rose. Sometimes, her face lights up in a smile. Other times, she looks like she's been blasted away in a storm." He reaches out, in spite of himself, and pinches her nose. "You have such a cute face."

The neon street lights outside shine through the window, colouring their smoke rings and bringing the murals to life. It is a dream-like scene, a fantasia.

Hai Ruo is beginning to find it hard to breathe, and hurriedly opens a window to let the smoke and alcohol fumes out. By now, the rain is pouring down, but they all ignore it. Yike, Yinan, Xu Qi and Yi Guang have gathered in the corner of the room by the long table and are chatting about the Living Buddha's visit.

"Hai-jie became a lay Buddhist follower a few years ago when Mr Wu introduced her to the Living Buddha," Yike is saying. "Now the Living Buddha's coming again, and Lishui and I want Hai-jie to introduce us so we can convert too."

"If you and Xi-jie are going to convert, then so will I... how about you, Yinan?" Xu Qi says.

"You and me both," says Yinan.

"You talk like converting is a fashion," says Yi Guang. "And why do you need to be converted by a Tibetan Living Buddha when there are so many local Buddhist temples and monks in Xijing? That's like going to a temple to burn incense. There's no need to burn incense to every Buddha – lighting incense to one Buddha covers all of them."

"That's not the same at all," says Xu Qi. "Don't they say, 'the Buddhas fight over every incense stick'?"

"Suppose you have three or four pockets. What's the difference between putting your money in one pocket and dividing it between all your pockets?" says Yi Guang.

"You're right," Xu Qi says.

"Next time think before you speak," says Yinan.

Xu Qi pulls a face, looks up to see Yi Guang looking at her, smiles quickly then lapses into silence.

"Lishui asked me to find her a man," Yi Guang goes on. "Is she going to convert too?"

"It's two different things, and there's no conflict between them," says Yike. "Living Buddhas have families too. I know there are temples and monks in Xijing, but recently, people have begun to think Chinese Buddhism is less pure than Tibetan Buddhism. Besides, we have an actual Living Buddha coming."

"Do you know what a Living Buddha is?" Yi Guang challenges her.

"It's a living reincarnation of the Buddha."

"Living Buddhas are the most important religious figures in Tibetan Buddhism. We call them Living Buddhas in Chinese. In fact, the proper name is *tulku*, or reincarnated sages."

"You're so knowledgeable," says Yike.

"I'm not a believer like Hai-jie, I'm a writer, and that means I need to get my facts right."

"What else do you know about Buddhism?" asks Yike.

"Well, Buddhism talks about predestination, it says that various phenomena occur due to the combination of relationships. The same is true for writing novels, you're writing about these relationships, about daily life. My current novel is about daily life. And Buddhism believes that the universe is formed by the activities of sentient beings. The lives of sentient beings are defined by the recurring cycles of suffering: birth, ageing, sickness and death, plus the pain of having to part from those whom one loves, of having to meet with those whom one hates, and of being unable to obtain what one desires. Over the course of time, our good and evil actions bring karmic retribution and we feel the consequences in our lives. Hence, the vicissitudes of life. The same goes for novels. The purpose of the novel is not to help us live better, or more meaningfully. A novel focuses on our pain, it doesn't teach us how to get rid of it."

"I don't understand how you write a novel," says Yike, "or what you mean by the vicissitudes of life and repeating cycles of suffering. Tell us more."

"Suffering comes from selfishness and vinicchaya, 'discrimination', and this makes one feel anxious, unhappy and incomplete. Evil actions triggered by human desire necessarily bring karmic retribution."

Xu Qi goes pale. "Aiya! Surely you're not talking about me?"

"I'm not talking about anyone in particular," Yi Guang says. "Everyone's like that."

"What about you, are you the same?" Yinan asks.

"Of course, what worries me is being unable to obtain what I want."

"But you have fame and fortune, a reputation and a family too. What else do you want that you can't get?"

Yi Guang laughs. "Are all those guaranteed? Can they satisfy me?"

"I feel like the sparrow that's unable to divine the lofty ambitions of the swan," says Xu Qi.

"Human desires are insatiable, and that causes an endless cycle of suffering, don't you think?" Yike suggests.

"Well, that's the reason I'm not going to convert to Buddhism," says Yi Guang.

"Judging by what you say, I shouldn't convert either, right?" says Xu Qi.

"You don't need to worry, you've got your Hai-jie," says Yi Guang.

Hai Ruo catches her name.

"Are you talking about me behind my back?" she says.

Yi Guang says with a quick smile, "I wouldn't dare. You should never bite the hand that feeds you, or rather, offers you delicious tea!"

The women on the couch call, "Yike, Xu Qi, Yinan, come over here, we want to hear what you think!"

"Think about what?" asks Yinan.

The women are flushed. Eva's youthful looks have made them painfully aware of the pitiless assault of time on their own bodies. How they wish that their own skin were as firm and tight, dewy and moist as hers. They are too late for botox injections now. Next year, they'll be at the hospital for face-lifts. Everyone begins to talk about cosmetic surgery in South Korea. Feng Ying is the oldest of the Ten Pieces of Jade, but after a complete face-lift, she looks younger than the others, they all agree.

"Qiyu, if you could go back twenty years, would you do it?" asks Lihou.

"Of course I would. You never appreciate your youth until it's gone."

"What about you?" Lihou asks Benwen.

"You mean go back twenty years economically as well?"

"Of course. You'd have to be as poor as you were before, but at least you'd have your youth and your looks."

"I've worked hard for two decades to get where I am today, so I wouldn't go back. I'd rather be old and ugly than have no money."

Qiyu says, "I'd go back, even if Benwen wouldn't, and even though I wasn't a pretty young thing. Who else is willing to go back to their youth... put your hand up!"

Yike and Yinan raise their hands.

"If I could turn the clock back twenty years, I'd know how to enjoy myself," says Yinan. Xu Qi begins to raise her hand, then puts it down again.

"You don't want to, Xu Qi?" asks Lihou.

"I can't make up my mind."

Nianchu doesn't put up her hand. She is smoking a cigarette, tilting her face up and blowing smoke rings into the air. "Are you sure you want to go back in time?" she says. "You're all living like the goddesses on this mural, flying through the sky. You really want to come tumbling down to earth?"

Qiyu whispers to Xu Qi, "She's really kept her looks, hasn't she?"

"Of all the women in the sisterhood, she's the one we all think hasn't aged a bit," replies Xu Qi.

"And that's why she doesn't care. She's beautiful, and if you're beautiful that changes everything."

"What are you two whispering about?" asks Yinan. Qiyu stops whispering, and clinks her wine glass with Yinan's.

As they laugh and chat, Hai Ruo and Yi Guang join them. Yi Guang is chuckling.

"What's so funny?" Nianchu asks.

"It's the idea of you all as flying apsaras."

"You mean you think we're not?" asks Nianchu.

Yi Guang goes on, "Well, we live in a society where women are supposed to have raised themselves up and thrown off oppression by men, and yet society is still male-dominated. Let me give one tiny example. Every single list of participants at meetings at all levels, from a city sub-district to the municipal government, the provincial government and even the central government, always adds (女) in brackets to indicate a woman. Do men get listed with (男) after their name to show that they're male? No!"

"This society treats women so unfairly," says Hai Ruo. "That's why we've got out of the public sector and out of the family."

"And is that why you're getting into business?" queries Yi Guang.

"We want to win economic independence. You can't be psychologically independent if you're economically dependent."

"Even so, you're all like broody hens," says Yi Guang. "The eggs you lay are different sizes, some are soft-shelled, others have shells covered in muck and blood, but you're all going, squawk, cluck, cluck, cluck!"

There is an outcry. Hai Ruo punches Yi Guang between the shoulder blades and cries, "Is that how you see us?"

Yi Guang mops his brow. "It's just metaphors, and all metaphors are lame. Of course, you eleven pieces of jade – no, let's leave Eva out of it – you ten have done really well, you're fine-looking, talented women. You all have a solid financial base. You can go wherever you want, and buy whatever you want. You don't need to go to official meetings, you're not under anyone's thumb, you have no ties, but do you feel really free, really psychologically independent? You've risen high but do you want to go higher? How big are your wings? Has the earth lost its gravitational pull for you? Wanting to rise is a desire in itself, and the more you desire, the heavier your body, the more claggy mud clings to your feet. That's why I say you're not flying goddesses, because you can't fly." He turns to Hai Ruo. "What do you think?"

Hai Ruo says, "Nianchu, give me a cigarette." Nianchu obeys and lights it for her. Hai Ruo takes a puff and exhales slowly. Wisps of smoke wreathe her cheeks and penetrate her hair, so it looks as if she is on fire. "That's why we need a visit from the Living Buddha."

Yi Guang is about to go on when they hear an indignant cry, "Are you saying I'm fat and have claggy shoes? Well, I don't, even when I'm soaking wet!"

"Xi-jie's arrived!" exclaims xiao-Tang.

And there she is. Swooping up the stairs, arms spread wide like a bird in flight. Lishui is wearing a pair of jeans, a white shirt and a backpack closed with a drawstring, all of which are dripping wet. "Sorry I'm late," she gasps. "Quick, pour me some wine, I'll drink three glasses as a penance!"

7. XIN QI • XI LISHUI'S HOME

EARLIER THAT EVENING, Xi Lishui went home from the hotpot restaurant to change. She opens the door to leave for the teashop again – to find Xin Qi standing outside, her long hair blowing about her face.

"You scared the hell out of me!" Lishui says. "What are you doing out here?"

"I want to talk to you," says Xin Qi. "I'd just got here when you opened the door."

"Good timing, let me take you to the teashop then. The sisterhood's meeting there tonight. You should come to meet them. If you get on with the group, you'll be able to see us often and share our good times."

At this, Xin Qi breaks down in tears.

Lishui hates seeing a woman in tears. "Crying again!" she exclaims. "Such a lot of tears! Are you still having a rough time with Tian Chengbin?"

"We've separated."

"But weren't you dying to get away from him?" asks Lishui. "The moment I split with Hu Sheng, I felt so relieved. I was so happy that I walked down the street, laughing out loud. But here you are, in floods of tears. Are you still pining for him?"

"No, it's not like that," says Xin Qi.

"Then come with me," Lishui urges her. "Have a few drinks. Let's celebrate your separation from him."

"No, thanks," says Xin Qi. "I'd just be a laughing stock. You and your friends have really made it. When I'm making a decent living too, we'll be able to talk as equals. You go, I'll wait for you outside."

This is awkward for Lishui. "What kind of a friend would I be if I left you waiting outside? You don't have to go to the gathering, but I do. How about this, you just stay here at my place? I'll be back in a couple of hours. You can boil some water if you're thirsty. There's tea in the fridge, and coffee in the thermos on the table. If you're hungry, there are noodles and eggs in the kitchen, and yogurt and cereal. And if you're tired, you can take a nap in my bed." Her words are so kind that Xin Qi starts crying again.

As Lishui is leaving, Xin Qi says, "You can lock the door from the outside."

"I'm not worried you'll go off with my belongings!" Lishui laughs.

As she reaches the ground floor, it occurs to Lishui that she should not have made that quip. Just a while ago, Xin Qi came with a video projector, a microwave and three blue-and-white porcelain vases she had taken from the home she shared with her husband and asked Lishui to look after them for her. Lishui almost kicks herself.

Lishui met Xin Qi when she first started her car dealership. Back then, Xin Qi was working at a kindergarten nearby and often dropped in to look at the cars. She spoke a rather awkward Mandarin, mixed with Hong Kong and Taiwan catchphrases she had picked up. "What's the model of this car? What's that one called?" she used to ask. Or she would strike poses by the cars and have her photo taken. It was Lishui who showed her how to edit the photos to make her look prettier.

There was a touch of the exotic and foreign about the younger woman's face, Lishui thought. She once asked, "Are you really Han Chinese?"

"Sure, I am," replied Xin Qi.

"We Hans all have faces flat as a wall. How come yours looks like an outside corner?" persisted Lishui.

"Maybe my great-great-great-granny was raped by a Hun," said Xin Qi with a giggle.

"Wash your mouth out," scolded Lishui. But she does like Xin Qi's exotic touch.

As they got to know each other, Lishui learned that Xin Qi is from the countryside in southern Shaanxi Province. She came to Xijing as a migrant worker at sixteen, and is constantly strapped for cash. Xin Qi has borrowed money from her on several occasions. Sometimes, she has paid some back, at other times, Lishui has told her to forget it. Then she finds out that Xin Qi is spending the borrowed money on clothes and shoes – ten times as much as she spends on food. Xin Qi often has stomach problems, and when she gets her period, she suffers terrible cramps.

Lishui tries to advise her, "Clothes are for others, food is for yourself."

"I'm a country bumpkin," replies Xin Qi. "I have to look cool."

Xin Qi's looks are fashionable: she has good features and a good figure. Now she has mastered Mandarin and is more citified than the local city folk. So she has married one of them, Tian Chengbin. He has a job and a flat, but he is only a low-grade public servant who earns a pittance, and he is stubborn. The couple bicker and fight, and threaten divorce constantly, though neither carries it through. The two women have found common ground in their bad marriages, and Lishui suggests that Xin Qi call it quits with hers. In three years' time, she'll be able to file a divorce application. Xin Qi moves out of the matrimonial home and rents her own place. When she leaves, however, she takes a lot of stuff with her.

So Lishui regrets her slip of the tongue. You should never hit someone when they're down, she thinks. She hopes she hasn't hurt Xin Qi's feelings. Perhaps she should go back and say she is sorry? But it begins to rain and she hurries to the teashop.

As she drives along Good Luck Street, it turns into a downpour. One of her car's windscreen wipers chooses that moment to break and Lishui parks outside a garage and asks the mechanic to change the wiper. Just then, she feels a tap on her shoulder, turns around and comes face to face with a man whom she recognises as Xu Shaolin.

Shaolin is a schoolmate from her middle school days. He used to like her and asked her out once, but she didn't fancy him. He was shorter than her and she couldn't help noticing that one of his socks had a hole in. Worse still, she could see his ankle through the hole, and it was filthy. Disgusted, she turned him down flat. Time passed and they both went to university. When they graduated, Shaolin was assigned a job in the city's Urban Management Bureau, while Lishui went to the Power Supply Bureau, but then quit and started her own business. They have not been in touch for ten years or more, though they hear news of each other every now and then. What were the odds of running into each other at a garage on a rainy night? Lishui could see the genuine joy glimmering in Shaolin's eyes, and cries out in equal astonishment, "Wow, it's you! What are you doing here?"

"My car's got a puncture," replies Shaolin. "It's the weather, heaven sent, heaven meant!"

"What do you mean?"

"We wouldn't have met if it hadn't been for this rain."

"Everything fine with you?" asks Lishui, smiling. "Oh my, isn't this a fine car!"

Shaolin chuckles. "It's my work car."

"Right, I heard you've made division chief. So it's true then!"

"Just a run-of-the-mill job."

"You've got yourself a wife, a son and a nice promotion. Why are you being so modest about it all?"

"It's not all win-win. I might have a better job, but it's a mess back home."

"What? Are you getting a divorce, too?"

"No, no, not a divorce. It's my son. He's a real headache."

"You mean he's too short? Or a poor student? Like father like son, Xu Shaolin!"

"For decades I was ashamed of my height," Shaolin smiles. "Until I finally found a tall wife. My son's taller than me now, and he's a handsome boy. His schoolwork is fine but he's fallen for a girl, and he keeps wanting to wine and dine her and splash out on expensive clothes. 'Why are you being so extravagant?' I ask him. 'Stop throwing my money around.' And you know what the little brat says? That I was spending his money! Me? Spending his money? His argument is, 'I'm your only son, so the family money is mine! And you're spending it.'"

This makes Lishui laugh. "What genius! I can see him making a big official someday."

"Huh, you're just teasing me."

"I have to get into your good books from now on. You're a division chief after all. Don't forget me if a good project comes up."

"I've never forgotten you in all these years! Oh, by the way, the municipality is installing huge LED screens at road junctions. I'm in charge. Are you interested?"

"You bet! That's a big deal, I'll do it!"

"You really want to?"

"Absolutely!"

"So, get one of the city officials to have a word with our bureau chief, and I'll make sure it goes your way."

"Are you making fun of me? Don't be daft. If I could pull strings with a city official, why would I need you?"

"Well, you could wait for the day I become bureau chief."

"By that time, I'd be starving!"

At the teashop, Lishui downs three glasses of wine as a penance for being late. "You've got to drink to every single one of us!" the others insist, but she cannot manage that, so Eva takes over and finishes the round for her. Lishui is more and more taken by the girl. "Teach me some Russian!" she begs. Eva tries to teach her how to roll her "r"s, but Lishui fails miserably, and only manages to wet the back of Si Yinan's neck with her spittle.

Lishui abandons her Russian and chats with Lu Yike about their businesses. She brings up the giant LED screens and asks if Yike is interested. Yike is onto it immediately. "You must nail this," she says, "you really must. I'll see what I can do to get hold of an official in the city government. I'd also like to meet your school friend, Xu Shaolin, as soon as possible."

"All right then," says Lishui, "bring a piece of calligraphy from Yi-laoshi when you meet Xu Shaolin."

"He charges a hundred thousand yuan a piece!" exclaims Yike. "I've never asked him for favours like that."

"You're trying to catch a big fish here. Go and ask him, he won't charge you."

"Why would he not?"

"He admires you. Every time he looks at you, I can see it in his eyes."

"Nonsense!" says Yike. She gets a bottle of Japanese eye drops from her pocket and hands it to Lishui.

"What's this for? My payment as go-between?"

"There's commission for you when it's done."

"Forget that. When you ask Yi-laoshi for some calligraphy, just get me a small piece, too."

Three hours later, Lishui arrives home to find Xin Qi curled up on the sofa fast asleep, her head propped on her crooked elbow, on the armrest. She has a mass of thick, soft hair, tied in a ponytail, which falls over her back and reaches to her bottom, making her look startlingly like a fox spirit. Lishui stands by the sofa for a while but Xin Qi does not stir. She feels sorry for the younger woman, and fetches a blanket to cover her. But before she can do so, Xin Qi wakes up.

"How did I fall asleep!" she exclaims, jumping to her feet. "When did you come back?"

"I'm terribly sorry for being late," says Lishui.

"It's me who should apologise, for bothering you so late in the evening," says Xin Qi.

"Then don't go," Lishui offers. "I won't go to bed, either. Let's have a nice, long chat."

She boils some water and makes tea for her guest and a cup of coffee for herself. She puts the cups on the low table, takes off her slippers and sits cross-legged on the sofa.

She thinks Xin Qi wants to talk about her divorce again, so she is astonished when Xin Qi confesses to having an affair with the head of a Hong Kong company. The company is very well-known in Xijing and although Lishui has never met the boss in person, she's seen him on TV. He is an old man – in his seventies.

"How extraordinary," she muses. "What a lot of things have happened today. And now you tell me you're in a relationship with a big shot!"

"We've been together for more than a year now," says Xin Qi.

"So is it meeting him that made you want to divorce Tian Chengbin?" asks Lishui. "You'll marry him after the divorce?"

"That's what I've come to talk to you about," admits Xin Qi.

Lishui can't help feeling a twinge of jealousy. "Well ... that's nice. You're always short of money, now you'll be rich."

"He is wealthy," agrees Xin Qi. "I've never met anyone with so much money. But he only ever gives me pocket money."

"With a second marriage, both the man and the woman are bound to be a bit cautious, at first. Things will be all right once you marry. His money will be yours, surely?"

Xin Qi's mouth opens in a wail, and the tears pour down her face.

"What on earth's the matter?" Lishui asks.

Finally, Xin Qi dries her eyes. Her face fills with rage and she spits furiously. "He's got one foot in the grave, and he's a lecher and a cheat!" And she tells Lishui the whole story of her affair with the Hong Kong tycoon.

"I'll be honest, I made a beeline for his money," she begins. "Otherwise, I'd never have ended up with a fossil like that. His false teeth threaten to fall out every time we kiss."

"I got a vaginoplasty done, so I could fake my virginity," she goes on. "And he takes pills so he can get it up and perform like a young man. But we never talk about stuff like that, of course. As soon as we're alone, we get hammered, then we turn the light off and hop into bed. I shout, 'I'm dying! I'm dying!' when I come – and it does feel like dying too. I can't wait to wake up the next morning. I always knew he had a wife and family in Hong Kong and wouldn't marry me. But it was after I met him that I started thinking about getting a divorce. Am I just going to end up with a hundred-square-metre flat plus some clothes, bags, watches and necklaces?"

"You must be disgusted with me, Xi-jie," she finishes.

Lishui feels her heart beat faster. "But you're just being a home-wrecker, aren't you?" she says. "Anyone can get a divorce, it's your right to divorce if you can't get along. I divorced, and most of the sisterhood have come out of their marriages and stayed single. But why do you want to be a mistress?"

Xin Qi's pretty face suddenly twists. "Unlike you and your friends," she hisses, "I'm not a businesswoman!"

Lishui is enraged. She glares at Xin Qi. The young woman's lips are slightly asymmetrical, something she used to find oddly attractive, but now it only annoys her. Why did I ever become friends with this woman? Lishui asks herself. Marriage is supposed to be the union of minds and hearts that think and feel alike. Is friendship the same? Do the differences in background, social standing, education and way of life inevitably come between you, even if you get on fine at first?

Lishui would have loved to act so coldly that Xin Qi would just go of her own accord. But it is not in her nature to be brusque. She falls silent for a while, then stands up to make another cup of coffee, noticing, as she does so, that she has her slippers on the wrong way round.

She finds herself contradicting her previous thoughts: I shouldn't be imposing my own standards on my family or my family's standards on my friends. Yi Guang once said that when you look for your other half, you're actually looking for yourself. By that token, when I make friends with other people, I'm linking up with someone like myself. Xin Qi's good points are the same as mine, of course, so her failings are my failings too. What would we be like if I didn't run my own business, if the sisterhood weren't all financially independent?

"Let me refill your cup, Xin Qi," she offers.

"I'm good," says Xin Qi.

Lishui goes to make the coffee, then comes back to the sofa – still with her slippers on the wrong way round.

"This is serious. If it's been dragging on so long, why didn't you tell me before?" asks Lishui.

"I wanted to make it work and spring it on you then," explains Xin Qi. "I never knew it'd be so hard."

"Now what? Mend your fences with Tian Chengbin?"

"If I could, I wouldn't have left home. I'm here to ask you a favour."

"Sure, I'll do whatever I can to help – except get you a piece of calligraphy!"

"Can you go with me to Hong Kong?" asks Xin Qi. "All expenses on me – plane tickets, hotel bookings, food, everything."

"Hong Kong?" asks Xi. "I just went to Hong Kong and Macau two months ago!"

"So you won't want to go there again, I suppose. Do you have any connections in a hospital there?"

"Are you sick? Why Hong Kong?"

"The old fossil has gone back home and probably won't come back to Xijing," explains Xin Qi. "He's always worn a condom before, and I realise now that he didn't want me to get pregnant. I want to go to Hong Kong and find a hotel near a hospital. Then I'll get him over, and make sure I preserve his semen. I'll take it straight to the hospital and have it frozen. That way, I can bring it back to Xijing and have a test tube baby. If it's successful, I'll go and tell him. If he refuses to acknowledge it, I'll have a paternity test. Even if he doesn't care about me, surely he'd care about his own flesh and blood!"

Lishui is so shocked that she starts to quiver. Her vision blurs, and she sees two Xin Qis in front of her, their lips flapping open and shut.

"Xi-jie, Xi-jie!" Xin Qi is calling her.

Lishui groans at the sound of her voice.

"So you won't help me?" Xin Qi is saying.

"I don't know any doctors in Hong Kong," Lishui manages. "I don't know anyone there. Do you think your plan will work?"

"Anything's possible if I put my mind to it."

"You've succeeded before, by being imaginative and brave, so now you're convinced you'll never fail, as long as you're bold enough. But Xin Qi, think about it, things can go badly wrong. Suppose you go to Hong Kong and ask him to your hotel. Will he really come? Even if he does, will you be able to preserve his semen? And get it frozen in time? Will it make a baby? Let's say that you manage to jump through all these hoops when you confront him with the baby in your arms, there'll be a huge stink and it'll involve not just him, but his wife and children as well. There'll be a lawsuit and it will take ages to resolve. By then, you might—"

"But it's the only thing I can do, Xi-jie!" protests Xin Qi.

"You've just got a bee in your bonnet," Lishui says. "There are so many other things you could do if you just dropped this."

Xin Qi drains her tea. She shakes the tea leaves into her mouth and chews them too. "I won't give up!" she insists.

"Are you hungry?" asks Lishui. "Let me do some noodles for you?"

"I'm fine, I should go," says Xin Qi.

"Didn't we agree you'd stay the night? It's getting so late."

"It's a long time till daybreak, I'm just a nuisance to you here, I'd better go." She puts on her shoes, gathers her shopping bags, and picks up one of the phones on the coffee table.

"I can't help you with this business, Xin Qi," says Lishui. "But how about if you go for the test tube baby in Xijing? I do know someone here. I'll take you there."

Xin Qi gets to her feet, realises she's taken Lishui's phone by mistake, puts it back and picks up the other one. She checks it, then puts it in her pocket.

Lishui fetches two umbrellas, gives one to Xin Qi and accompanies her downstairs. The rain is still pitter-pattering down. A taxi comes and Lishui drops a 100 yuan note through the driver's window. Xin Qi makes no comment, and the taxi drives off into the night.

8. LU YIKE • ENTERPRISE STREET

After three days of rain, the weather finally clears up. The smog evaporates, white clouds emerge, and the Qinling Mountains are visible in the distance from the teashop's upstairs window. Hai Ruo is inspecting newly-delivered tea packaging samples.

"Quick, come and look, xiao-Tang!" yells Gao Wenlai. "A cloud dragon's coming from Qinling!"

"That's not a dragon," says xiao-Tang. "Dragons fly, this one's running."

"Then it's a dinosaur!" says Wenlai.

The running dinosaur disperses in an instant, leaving just a tuft of cloud that rests on top of the shopping centre building like a spider.

"Where's the tea for our *shifu?*" demands Hai Ruo.

xiao-Tang makes tea and offers it to the man who brought the samples.

"I'm fine, I'm not thirsty," says the man. But he drinks it anyway.

A few days ago, the teashop acquired some fine Yixing teapots and wide, shallow Jianyang teacups. They have asked a fabric store on Second Prince's Street to make some cloth bags. The man has come with two samples, one in pale yellow and the other in maroon. Both are of velvet with an embroidered dragon and phoenix design, and are fastened with a triangular flap and a diagonal row of knot buttons. The characters for "Sojourn Teashop" are printed on the bags too.

"We'll take the yellow," Hai Ruo instructs. "In fact, let's use Buddha yellow. But dragons and phoenixes are on everything, they're such a cliché. Can we have a single apsara instead? 'Sojourn Teashop' should be smaller, and should be placed at the bottom left."

Just then, Lu Yike strolls in, carrying a plastic bag with a book in it. Hai Ruo asks her opinion on the cloth bags.

"The opening could use a better design," Yike says. "A drawstring, maybe?"

"That's it," says Hai Ruo. "The cord should be thick, make it as thick as a chopstick."

"And the colour for the cord? How would ochre brown look?"

"Make up your mind!" says Hai Ruo.

"Then ochre brown it is," says Yike.

The man leaves with his samples.

"What's happened to you? Your skin's sallow and you're looking thin," says Hai Ruo.

"You know my skin went sallow when I slimmed down," replies Yike.

"You should put some foundation on before you go out."

"I'm fair-skinned everywhere except from the neck upwards," protests Yike. "And what's wrong with not wearing make-up? Do I have to package myself to enter the teashop?" Yike eyes xiao-Zhen and xiao-Su.

Hai Ruo does not buy pre-packaged tea. Instead, every year, she sends someone to Fujian, Anhui and Yunnan, the main tea-producing provinces, to source loose tea direct from local farms. The teashop then packages the tea in boxes and bags and sells it under their own label. Currently, xiao-Zhen and xiao-Su are busy measuring tea leaves on a scale and pouring them into elegant cardboard canisters.

"No one's over-packaging the goods here, Lu-jie," says xiao-Zhen. "Our tea is of the highest quality!"

Yike pulls a cheeky face. "I was just winding up your boss!"

"Hah! You're welcome to try," says Hai Ruo.

"It's not surprising I'm thin and sallow," Yike goes on. "I can't sleep night after night. The business is in the doldrums. If we carry on like this, we'll have to lay off staff. That's if we don't go broke first."

"I can't stand people whining about being poor," says Hai Ruo. "If you keep this up, you'll go broke for real."

"I am broke," says Yike.

"But you just nabbed a deal on a billboard."

"Yes, but only one."

"I see. So you want a favour from me!"

"Exactly," Yike grins. "You've got to help me."

"I don't have any extra hands that I can spare for you, or any extra money!"

"It'll just take a few words," says Yike. She lowers her voice and confides in Hai Ruo about the LED screens. "Exciting, see?"

Hai Ruo is unmoved. "Lu Yike," she begins, "here's a tip for you: a low-level official will say, 'Of course, I'll do it if you get my boss to OK it.' And the boss will say, 'Sure, I'll approve it but only if you get my junior to put in a request.' They'll run rings around you."

"No approval's needed," Yike persists. "I just want the city's general secretary to put in a word for me. Who knows? It might work."

"What?' asks Hai Ruo. "You mean Xu Shaolin should ask for a direct instruction from the general secretary himself?"

"I just thought the general secretary would do."

"What makes you think he would listen to me?"

"I know he would!"

Hai Ruo falls silent for a while. "I've never talked to him about a project before. Even if I try, I can't guarantee he'll listen."

"Not a problem!" says Yike.

Some customers come in and xiao-Tang approaches them. "Would you like to buy some tea?"

Hai Ruo takes the plastic bag from Yike. "You were busy, huh? And you had time to go browsing in a bookstore?"

"I wasn't browsing," Yike protests. "It's business."

Hai Ruo takes out the book. It's by Yi Guang, published ten years ago. She turns to the title page. It carries a handwritten inscription: "For my good friend Lin Fucai. I welcome your comments!"

"I was at the Ghost Fair this morning," Yike says. "It was almost over, only one stall owner was still there, packing up second-hand books. I spotted this one. I imagine Lin Fucai must have been a friend of Yi-laoshi's, but he sold his signed copy. I bought the book to give it back to Yi-laoshi."

"Well done," Hai Ruo congratulates her. "And how do you think Yi-laoshi will react?"

"He'll go red in the face and have some colourful things to say about Lin Fucai!"

"You can't be sure of that. He might write, 'For my good friend Lin Fucai – again.' And then mail the book back to him."

They both laugh.

"That's odd," says Hai Ruo, giving Yike a straight look. "You always sleep in, so how come you got up early today and went to the Ghost Fair?"

"I wanted to get here early to ask you that favour."

"Is that so? Did you go anywhere else?"

Yike grins. "I couldn't come empty-handed, I did drop in on a friend first," she confesses.

"Don't keep stuff from me next time!"

"Did you know, UNESCO has listed the Xijing wind and percussion *guyue* as an Intangible Cultural Heritage of Humanity?"

"I heard from my *guqin* master. *Guyue* ensembles are a relic of ancient Chinese music. They should have been on that list long ago."

"Yes, but did you know there's a performance to celebrate the listing?"

"When?"

"Tonight, at the Ancient Capital Grand Theatre."

"Have you got tickets?"

"My friend said I could pick up tickets from his place, but there were only three left."

"I see," says Hai Ruo. "What a pity the Living Buddha hasn't arrived. There are three repertoires: Buddhist, Taoist and secular. It would have been so nice to have the Living Buddha join us. And only three tickets left? Who's getting them?"

"One for you, one for me. Xu Qi lives close by the theatre on Enterprise Street, so let's invite her. It won't matter for the others, they aren't interested in that sort of thing."

"How do you know? Even if they aren't, it'd be nice to introduce the music to them."

"You think the tickets were easy to come by? I had to badger my friend for these three."

"Fine. I owe you a dinner then!"

"No need for that. Let's get Xu Qi to take us out."

In the afternoon, they go to Enterprise Street. The western end of the street climbs up a low hill to the highest point in the city. Now it has been redeveloped, and the Grand Theatre stands on this vantage point. Looking east, the street has a linear park between the carriageways, planted with an exotic selection of lush flowering plants, shrubs and trees. Spectacular. Xu Qi lives in a housing estate towards the eastern end of the street. She has just come back from the market with a basket full of *yinchen*, a kind of capillary wormwood. She picks the herb over, blanches it, squeezes the water out and divides it up into portions that she puts in the freezer. The blanching water will not go to waste either: she pours it into zip-lock bags. She is delighted when Hai Ruo arrives with Yike and the tickets.

"Awesome!" she exclaims. "I'll go and buy some meat. Let's have *yinchen* dumplings tonight!"

"We want something pricier!" says Yike.

"Pricey stuff isn't necessarily better," says Xu Qi. "*Yinchen* has just come into season. It's fresh and tender, and it nourishes the liver and the lungs. It's diuretic and laxative too."

"Don't mind Yike," says Hai Ruo. "Let's have dumplings."

"You're our resident gourmet, Hai-jie!" says Xu Qi. She changes, brushes her hair, puts on some make-up and is ready to head out, neat, clean and tidy.

"Let me do the shopping," offers Yike. "You can tell Hai-jie all about keeping healthy." She opens the door and goes downstairs.

Xu Qi was in a folk opera troupe in Huaxian County to the east of the Qinling Mountains before coming to Xijing to start her own business. She has never been robust and is obsessed with staying healthy. Naturally, she is only too happy to share tips with her friends.

"In spring, as the yang qi rises, your liver's prone to flare up, so you should eat more bitter melon, celery and tubers," she lectures them. "In summer, the general view is that you should abstain from high-calorie food, but actually that's the perfect time to treat winter ailments. Mutton, for example, can drive out the body's dampness. In autumn, you must have an egg every morning. No seasoning, and no sugar, an egg poached in plain boiled water will enhance your vital energy. When the weather's cold, you must eat mooli. Stew a pot of it and eat some whenever you feel like it. I get through a hundred kilos of it every winter…"

She drives most of her friends mad with her long-winded sermons. Only Hai Ruo indulges her. "If you don't fasten the seat belt, your car will keep on beeping and annoying you," she tells them.

Now that she has the nod from Hai Ruo, Xu Qi became even more insistent. She hails from three generations of TCM doctors, she says. You have to take Rehmannia Six Formula in the morning and at night. This deep-sea fish oil from Australia is superb; those eye drops from Japan are excellent; and that cold cream from Thailand is a must-have. At their get-togethers, Yike steers clear of Xu Qi and Xiang Qiyu. Xu Qi never tires of offering health tips, and Qiyu drones on about the stock market.

With Yike out buying pork, Hai Ruo starts peeling spring onions, then pounds garlic with a pestle and mortar, while Xu Qi mixes the dough.

"You've got acne, Hai-jie!" cries Xu Qi suddenly.

"Me? Acne, at my age?" Hai Ruo is sceptical. "Maybe because I've had too much internal heat lately."

"Do you suffer from constipation?"

"I have for ages."

"Did you drink the Tibetan Plateau chrysanthemum tea I gave you?"

"I took it for a week, but I didn't see much effect."

"You really must have a lot of internal heat! Try some laxatives from Japan. One tiny pill, and it takes care of all your troubles."

"I've tried them before. They did work well, except that I got stomach cramps."

"Did you? Then don't take any more. How about some Betel Nut Sixiao pills? They're a powerful purgative, but they won't give you cramps, and you'll have a normal bowel movement the next morning. Yinan had pimples all over the back of her neck, but she took these for three days and it cleaned out her bowels, and now she's fine."

Hai Ruo only smiles at this.

"You don't believe me, either," says Xu Qi.

When the dough is mixed, Hai Ruo kneads it on a wooden board. Xu Qi takes out the *yinchen* from the fridge and chops it.

"*Yinchen* is precious," Xu Qi continues. "I'll give you a few bags to take with you. You can boil it, stir-fry it or eat it cold… Oh, and have you finished your Rehmannia Six Formula?"

"I took it for a week, but I kept forgetting, so I stopped."

"You should keep it up. My grandpa took it all his life. He was still going out on a bike when he was ninety-six. Yi-laoshi has been taking it for years now. Just look at him, he doesn't remotely look like a man in his fifties! It might not seem to work for a month or two, but give it six months and it's magic. Yinan has taken it for a year. I remind her every morning. I'll text you daily from now on."

"You could open a health and nutrition business, Xu Qi."

"I am considering it."

Yike brings back some pork and Hai Ruo instructs her to mince it while Xu Qi rolls out the dumpling wraps. Hai Ruo herself washes her hands and goes to sit on the balcony.

"Tired of having your ear bent?" Yike teases her. "Need a bit of peace and quiet?"

The trio eat their fill of the dumplings and walk to the Grand Theatre along the greenbelt. They admire the trees, agreeing that you can feel life pulsing through the trunks, branches and leaves, and yet the feeling is hard to put into words. Is it the same with humans? If you're living a good life and feel fulfilled, will people be able to see an aura shining from your head? Will you have a Buddha halo when you become really spiritual?

"What tree is this?" Hai Ruo asks Yike, pointing at one with broad, thick, almost waxy leaves.

"Loquat, maybe?" says Yike.

"How can it be loquat? It's a persimmon," Xu Qi corrects her. "Persimmons are very common in our county. When they ripen all over the hills in autumn, the trees look like they're draped in tiny red lanterns. Persimmons need grafting. If you don't, the fruits are small as jujubes. They're called 'soft jujube', you can't eat them. You pick the persimmons in late autumn, but you must leave a few on the top branches – those are for the *laogua*."

"What are *laogua*?" enquires Yike.

"Crows," says Xu Qi.

"A very rustic name!" says Yike. Just then, her phone rings and she takes the call. She falls behind, and does not catch them up for a long time.

"Hurry up," urges Xu Qi. "How important can a call be?"

Yike only waves her hand. Hai Ruo and Xu Qi walk on.

"Is that a pomegranate?" asks Hai Ruo.

"The leaves are similar, but pomegranates aren't so tall. It's a *huai*, a pagoda tree."

"So the *huai* flowers sold in the market come from this tree? They're delicious steamed with rice."

"Oh, those are the flowers of the foreign *huai*, the black locust. This is the native *huai*. You can't eat pagoda tree flowers."

Xu Qi goes on to point out a walnut, a chestnut and a nearby Chinese honey locust tree. Yike finally finishes her call and catches up with them.

"I know this one. It's got to be a cherry," she says, pointing.

"It's a mulberry," says Xu Qi.

"I raised silkworms when I was little," says Hai Ruo. "I remember my father used to take me to the city outskirts to pick mulberry leaves. But those trees weren't so tall."

"They must have been young," explains Xu Qi.

"What fruit will this tree bear in autumn?" asks Yike, indicating another tree.

"Chilli peppers," answers Xu Qi.

"Chilli peppers? Are you making that up?" says Yike.

Xu Qi smiles complacently. Yike asks more questions, and Xu Qi reels off the answers.

"Of course, you're a small-town girl, aren't you, Xu Qi?" remarks Yike. "No wonder you're a tree expert!"

Xu Qi suddenly goes quiet.

Yike runs ahead and calls back excitedly, "How about this tree? And this one?"

"Don't ask me," says Xu Qi. "I'm from Xijing, a city dweller like you. I know nothing about trees and plants!"

At the Grand Theatre, the crowds surge and bustle around the brightly-lit square. The three of them go to get a programme for the show, then buy popcorn and mineral water. They are just going in when Yike's phone goes off again.

"Bother!" she says. "You can't get away from it anywhere!"

She glances at the caller's name, then says to Hai Ruo and Xu Qi,

"You go on ahead!" She hurries to the edge of the square and takes the call.

It is Xi Lishui. She asks Yike where she is. Unwilling to admit that she has invited Hai Ruo and Xu Qi to a *guyue* performance, Yike says she is at home.

"Good," says Lishui. "We're at a restaurant near you, come on over, quick as you can."

"What's all the urgency?" Xu Qi asks. "Are we under siege or what?"

"Xu Shaolin and his friends are at the Impressions of Chengdu Restaurant and he invited me. This is a golden opportunity to talk business, Yike."

Yike is in a quandary now. One white lie, and she has to fabricate more to cover it up.

"Are we at that stage already?" asks Yike.

"If we're lucky, we could close the deal!" says Lishui.

"Well, someone just gave me a ticket for a show. Another time, perhaps?"

"What's so special about a show? Is it more important than business? You'll never have a better chance to get a hold of him. Hurry!"

"All right, then."

Yike contemplates going into the theatre to tell the others about her change of plan but is too embarrassed, as it is she who invited them. Why not go to the restaurant and have a quick meeting with Xu Shaolin? She hails a taxi.

Twenty minutes later, she calls Lishui from outside the Impressions of Chengdu.

"How many people are there?" asks Yike when Lishui comes out.

"There are six of them," says Lishui. "With the two of us, that's perfect for one table."

"Should we talk business over dinner?"

"I've told him about you. I said you are in advertising, and the project will be in good hands. If there are too many people there and you don't want to talk about it, just get to know him for starters, and then we'll play it by ear."

"I'll pick up the tab."

"Of course. We're talking about dozens of LED screens here!"

"Should I give him Yi-laoshi's calligraphy now?"

"You've got it? When?"

"Just this morning."

"Impressive! One word and he does it for you."

"I paid for it."

"You're a tease! And what about the small piece I asked you for?"

"I mentioned it to him. He says to ask him yourself."

"Hmm. If he'll write me one for free, why would he take your money?" Lishui pinches Yike on the cheek. Yike chuckles.

They go into the side-room where Shaolin and his friends are dining. The table is a jumble of dirty crockery and everyone is slumped in their seats, very drunk.

Lishui introduces her friend. "Isn't she stunning? My women friends are all beauties, but she's one in ten thousand."

"A woman is no judge of another woman," Shaolin slurs.

"Are you saying she's not as pretty as me?" asks Lishui.

"You're both gorgeous," says Shaolin. "Feminine beauty is either in the skin or the bones. Yours is your skin, and hers is in her bones. Beauty in the bones lasts a long time. The older the woman, the better she looks!"

"Spot on!" says Lishui. And she seats Yike beside him.

"Let me drink to you all first," says Yike.

She pours Shaolin three glasses of spirits and three for herself. They clink glasses and drink every last drop. She then does the same with the other guests, all of which she manages without getting even the slightest bit flushed.

Finally she sits down. "Are there enough dishes? Let's get some more!" she suggests.

Lishui calls the waiter in and orders three more dishes.

"What a generous friend you've got, Lishui!" says Shaolin.

"Yes, indeed," says Lishui. "This is your first meeting and Yike's brought you a present." And she turns to Yike. "Don't be shy, Yike, these are all Mr Xu's friends. Show them your gift."

Yike brings out a four-*chi* piece of calligraphy. It is huge, a full 138 centimetres long.

There are astonished cries when they see the artist's inscription. "Wow! It's by Yi Guang! That'd sell for a hundred grand!"

"You know the prices his work goes for?" says Lishui.

"We certainly do. The city government always takes his calligraphy to Beijing when they want to make sure of a deal."

Shaolin glances at it and carries on drinking. "I don't like this man's calligraphy," he says.

Everyone freezes. Both Lishui and Yike are startled.

"You don't like it?" asks Lishui.

"His brushwork looks like he's writing with a fountain pen," says Shaolin scornfully.

"I happen to know that he hasn't put in much time studying the ancient calligraphy masters," someone chips in. "He's not that good. His work is expensive because of who he is, not how good it is."

"I don't have a lot of respect for the man, either," declares Shaolin. "He has a very high opinion of himself, and the city officials seem to think a lot of him. But he's only a piece of gold leaf when they need him. Otherwise, he's just a bit of glass."

Yike almost leaps to her feet, but Lishui presses her back in her seat.

"He's also an adviser to the city government," says Lishui.

"That's just for show!" says Shaolin. "He's so arrogant. He acts as if he were a famous intellectual, and turns up in public wearing a traditional jacket and smoking a fancy pipe. Have you seen his business card? A CPPCC member, an adviser, a cultural consultant, this and that award for some work, a top-tier writer, the equivalent of a professor, and an expert who's paid a government allowance. The government's just using him, and he's doing well from it!"

His listeners look at each other, speechless. Yike's cheeks are blotched red and white with outrage.

"You've had too much to drink," says Lishui. "I'll take it if you don't like it!"

She rolls the calligraphy scroll up, but pushes it into the bag that hangs over the back of Shaolin's chair.

The meal is finally over, Yike pays the bill and she and Lishui walk Shaolin and his friends to the exit. Shaolin is unsteady on his feet. Lishui tugs at his sleeve. "I want a word, Shaolin."

"Shoot, no time like the present!"

"The LED screens," says Lishui. "I want Yike to deal with you directly."

"Fine, fine. Just as soon as I get word from a city official, there's absolutely no problem."

When they have all gone, Yike asks Lishui, "Did he really not want it, or was he just pretending because he was with the others?"

"It might have been just a show. I put the calligraphy in his bag anyway."

"Whatever he was doing, how could he badmouth Yi-laoshi like that? If you hadn't held me back, I would have argued back, or just upped and left. What a horrible man! And he wanted to go out with you? Thank heavens you turned him down!"

"Let's just stick to working on our deal. It doesn't matter what kind of man he is."

"But will he help us? I shouldn't have given him the calligraphy so soon."

"What's done is done. Besides, you didn't pay for it."

But Yike is still furious as she says goodbye to Lishui.

Meanwhile, Hai Ruo and Xu Qi have been waiting for Yike, wondering what is taking her so long. Xu Qi goes outside and looks around, but there is no sign of her. The show starts. Hai Ruo is quite familiar with Xijing *guyue* but it is the first time Xu Qi has seen it. Hai Ruo tells her the name of each piece as the show goes on.

First, the ensemble plays marching music, *Sixteen Bars*: a melodic song called *Circling the Immortals' Hall*, a giocoso tune named *Outgoing Drums*, a chant entitled *Looking East* and a copper drum piece called *Each Step Lovely*. Next comes an entire suite of indoor music in eight bars, featuring the double cloud gong. First *Tri-Strand Whip, Cloud Drum Prelude, End of Cloud Drum, Prelude to First Xia* and *First Xia*. This is followed by *Holding the Golden Goblet, Prelude of Second Xia* and *Second Xia*, then *Shaking the Door Bolt* and *Prelude of Third Xia*. The last part includes a giocoso tune, *Third Xia*, another giocoso tune featuring wind instruments only, and the final piece features drums and percussion instruments.

When the first half of the indoor music is over, there is still no sign of Yike. By the time the second half starts, Hai Ruo and Xu Qi are getting worried. They leave the theatre before the performance ends to look for her. And there she is, hunkered down at the edge of the square, her head buried in her arms, looking like she has been turned to stone.

9. SI YINAN • HARVEST LANE

Si Yinan spends a day and a night at the hospital looking after Xia Zihua. Then it is Yan Nianchu's turn, and Hai Ruo arrives with her. Zihua has not shown any sign of improvement after the platelet transfusion. Instead, she spikes a fever and develops a hacking cough. Her friends are distraught. They debate whether to try traditional Chinese remedies again, or even to transfer her to another hospital.

Hai Ruo has a long discussion with Zihua's doctor and relays the doctor's words to Yinan and Nianchu. "Apparently, the TCM treatment had no effect, and worse than that, it meant she missed the optimum window for chemo treatment. This is the best hospital in town, and a transfer would be disruptive. She could deteriorate, especially now that she has a fever."

"Illnesses are karma, that's what I heard," says Nianchu. "What you did in the past, you pay back in this life. It's like a prison sentence – three years, five years, whatever it is, you have to do your time. Then things will get better after that. But poor Zihua is having such a hard time." And she puts her palms together and intones, "Amitabha…"

"We could use the Buddha's blessing right now," agrees Hai Ruo.

"When is the Living Buddha arriving?" asks Yinan.

"About three weeks' time. Have you booked a hotel?"

"Let's book the Peach Blossom, I can get a discount. How many are coming with him? How many rooms should I book?"

"Five for now."

They go back into the sickroom. Zihua is asleep. One foot is exposed and they see the oedema; her skin is translucent, and the slightest pressure leaves a dent that takes a long time to disappear.

Hai Ruo tucks in the quilt and says quietly to Nianchu, "Tell the nurses to disinfect the room twice a day. If Zihua needs the toilet, don't take her there, give her a bedpan, so she won't get a chill. Her hands and feet are swollen from the IV, so cover them with raw potato slices. Try not to let visitors in. If anyone insists, get rid of them as quick as you can. Make a note of her condition every hour, and tell the doctors if you notice anything unusual. Call me straight away as well, but don't tell Mrs Qi." And, having issued her instructions, she leaves with Yinan.

Downstairs in the lobby, Yinan goes to the cashier's window to pay a further instalment. She is hurrying to the toilet when Hai Ruo stops her. "It's such a fine day, I'm thinking of taking Zihua's mother and son on an outing to the Qinling Mountains. Can you join us?"

"I don't mind going without sleep for three nights in a row," says Yinan. "But the furniture shop called last night. The new stock has arrived, and I need to go and check it. Also, I'd better book the rooms at the Peach Blossom as soon as I can."

Hai Ruo leaves and Yinan finally makes it to the Ladies.

On her way out, she bumps into a woman hurrying in. The woman glances at Yinan and hesitates. "Is this the Gents?"

"It's the Ladies," Yinan tells her.

The woman eyes Yinan again, then scrutinises the sign on the door before going in. Yinan knows she has been mistaken for a man. "Get yourself a pair of glasses!" she mutters, annoyed.

Yinan has good features – a prominent nose and double eyelids – but she is stocky and has a short neck. Her build, together with her short hair and androgynous style of dressing, means she is often taken for a man. In the sisterhood, Yinan is the most hard-working and generous with her time, so whenever there is a problem, Hai Ruo always calls on her first, confident that she will take care of it. Yinan once had a furniture factory and retail outlet, producing solid, bulky pieces, square Eight Immortals dining tables with marble inlay and heavy Qing-style chairs with high backs. She offered to give the teashop two tables for free, but Hai Ruo declined. It isn't her style, she said, and the tables wouldn't go with the teashop décor. Then three years back, Yinan acquired some hardwood known as "Brazilian *huanghuali*". It was a substantial plank, 1.3 metres wide, two metres long and twenty centimetres thick. It was too wide for the staff to get through the factory door, so they stood it on its edge, but even with six men, three on each side, they were still unable to lift it. Four more men came to help. Now they had five men on each side, but some were stronger than others, and when they lifted it, the plank tipped over, pinning the senior carpenter underneath. They could not lift the plank off him in time and the man died from crush injuries. It was Hai Ruo who stepped in to negotiate a settlement with the victim's family – Yinan agreed to pay substantial compensation. She vowed to shut both factory and shop, but Hai Ruo managed to calm her down and suggested that she should keep the shop, but focus on trading in furniture instead. Hai Ruo now buys all her teashop's furniture from manufacturers in Fujian Province. She passed them on to Yinan, who bought some elegant Ming-style furniture from them. Her new business thrives, and she has expanded the shop. Hotels are some of her best clients, and the connections get her substantial discounts whenever she or others in the sisterhood need to make bookings.

But after the hospital, Yinan does not go to her furniture shop, or to the Peach Blossom Hotel. She goes to a supermarket, buys some fish and heads for Prosper Street.

Prosper Street is the place for snacks. It is lined with stalls and eateries, selling mutton *paomo*, wonton, soup-filled *tangbao* buns, hand-pulled noodles – flat *chemian* and thick *latiaozi* – steamed dumplings and pot-stickers, whole *hulu* chickens, minced beef steamed with rice meal or wheat, sweet barley wine, rabbit heads, *maocai* hotpot, stinky tofu, mung bean cake, sweet rice wine, and hot and numbing *mala* soup. This Xijing street is one long dining table, where vendors of snacks and specialities from across China jostle for space. There are always throngs of customers and businesses flourish. Over time, changes have taken place: where once the eateries made their own steamed *liangpi* noodles and *shaobing* flatbread, nowadays these are made offsite and delivered on three-wheelers. The delivery man jingles his bell outside the shop, and the owner emerges with a basket, to check the delivery and offer a cigarette, which is usually stashed behind one ear as the man rides cheerfully away. Even speedier are the boys delivering takeaways, another new phenomenon on the street. Their electric bikes weave to and fro through the crowds and if, occasionally, one falls off, he gets up, ignoring any scrapes to his arms or knees, and instead checks the delivery box to see if any food has spilled. So long as everything is in order, he rights the bike, gets on, and off he goes again. There are cries of "Mind yourselves! Mind out!" as the egg man barges through the crowd with a basket of eggs on each end of a shoulder pole. He doesn't care if he hits someone, he just does not want them to hit his load.

There is the usual long queue outside the *laniurou* salt beef shop. The owner, a big fat man, thumbs through a wad of banknotes as he greets an old customer: "Hi there!"

"Hi!"

"You're looking well today!"

"Nah, it's my dicky heart that give me these red cheeks."

"You have to take care of yourself as you get older."

"Exactly! My old lady only ever makes me rice porridge, and I need meat!"

The owner weighs out some beef, but before he can wrap it up, his customer reaches over, grabs a lump and stuffs it in his mouth.

At the door of the *hulutou* shop is a pot of *bangbangrou* containing gourd-shaped chitterlings, heart and liver, and dried tofu, all smoked to a rich brown.

"Get me something lean," says a customer.

The owner takes a pair of bamboo tongs and stirs the contents around, finally picking out a piece of the chitterlings. With a few quick thwacks on the board, he chops it into pieces. Meanwhile, he has been keeping an eye on his neighbour's shop. The display stand outside is heaped high with walnuts, jujubes, peanuts, apricot kernels and almonds. A passer-by grabs a jujube and tosses it carelessly into her mouth as she walks on by.

"Laosan, Li Laosan!" calls the *hulutou* shop owner. "Are you letting your stand look after itself!"

The shop owner comes out and glances at the jujube thief, who is some distance away. "It's no big deal. Just one hair from nine ox hides, as they say."

"Is that so? Next time, I'll keep my mouth shut!"

Yinan buys some braised chicken wings and spicy duck necks. She still wants some *bangbangrou*. She transfers the assortment of shopping bags into her right hand, takes out her phone with the left, and calls Xu Qi.

"Are you home, sweetie?" she asks.

"My feet are killing me!" says Xu Qi.

"Why are you wearing high heels at home?"

"I'm in the shopping centre, looking for shoes for you."

"I've got plenty already! Why are you buying me more?"

"Because when you go out, you need to look good. We've got to have you looking presentable from top to toe!"

"Any more presentable, and I won't be myself! Do you see any Mercs or BMWs with ornaments? Only a forty-thousand-yuan wreck gets decorated with graffiti!"

"Then I'll buy you brand-name shoes, Adidas maybe!"

"No, no, I won't wear them. I'm heading over to you now. I've bought a fish, let's have it braised in soy sauce."

"You've left the hospital?"

"Nianchu took over from me. I'm just getting some *bangbangrou*."

"No, don't! Smoked offal gives you cancer."

"Fine. Dried persimmons, maybe?"

"I'd love some honey *zongzi*."

Yinan hurries to the *zongzi* shop, where she can buy the chunks of boiled sticky rice. The woman is about to dribble honey on the pieces, but Yinan stops her, and spends another ten *kuai* on a small jar of honey, so they can add it themselves at home.

She passes by a sex shop, a tiny one, its door almost hidden behind a concrete lamp post. Yinan looks around her. It is a beautiful day, everything smells fresh and new. A girl passes her, no older than eight, holding a candied hawthorn stick. She is not exactly eating it, just sticking out her tongue and taking little licks. She walks straight into the lamp post, but does not seem to have hurt herself, stumbles, then runs off. Yinan chuckles and slips into the shop. She buys a bottle of sensuous massage oil and some cleanser, wraps them swiftly in some tissues and tucks the package in her shoulder bag. She walks out, smiling, and catches sight of the display board outside the duck neck shop next door. The model on it is also smiling, albeit shyly.

Her mobile rings. It must be Xu Qi, Yinan thinks, but it is Ying Lihou.

"Where are you, Yinan?" Lihou sobs down the phone. "Can you come? Please come, now!"

Yinan is startled. "What's happened? What's up?" she asks, anxiously.

"I ran someone over! Please come!"

"I'm coming, don't panic. Where are you?"

But Lihou is vague. "I'm not sure," she says. "Do you know the Xijing South Hotel? I came out of the arts and crafts place, passed the Xijing South Hotel, and turned west. There's a cinema opposite, a bit further down. Wait, I know! It's Harvest Road, Harvest Road West."

Yinan goes back to her car and speeds off. Of all the women in the sisterhood, she is the fastest driver.

When Lihou took her first ride with Yinan, she asked, "What fuel do you use?"

"Ninety-five octane."

"How come the engine feels jerky? It's like the petrol's got dirt in it."

"Are you taking the piss out of my driving skills? I didn't learn at a driving school. Hai-jie bought a car, so I asked her how to turn the engine on, and where the accelerator and the brakes were, and she told me. I just drove the car straight onto the street. Maybe I put my foot down too hard."

"Slow down, for heaven's sake!" Lihou implored her but Yinan only accelerated, screeching to a halt about an inch from the car in front.

When Lihou bought a car, Yinan offered to teach her to drive, but Lihou said no. Instead, she spent the entire three months at a driving school and emerged a super cautious driver. Her way of driving is to sit behind the wheel, her back ramrod straight, eyes staring straight ahead. Yinan pities Lihou's timidity, and Lihou mutters to herself that Yinan is a wildcat driver. Over the years, however, Yinan has never had a single accident, while Lihou is always being scraped by another driver, or getting too close and running into the back of the car in front.

Yinan spots Lihou's car as soon as she gets to Harvest Road. Her friend is standing beside it. A man lying on the ground has her leg firmly in his grip and she is trying unsuccessfully to shake him off.

"I don't think there's much wrong with you, is there? Why don't you get up and take a few steps? Let me see where you're hurt," she is saying.

"You must be sorry you didn't finish me off! I can't get up, and I can't walk!"

"Well, stop clutching my leg like this!"

"If I don't, you'll make a run for it! I'm no match for four wheels!"

"Where are you hurt? Let's go to a hospital and get you treated first."

"I've no time to go to the hospital! Why can't we settle this between you and me?"

"Between you and me? You want compensation? Well, here's three hundred yuan."

"Three hundred! What are you thinking of? A thousand! Not a cent less!"

"I only have five hundred on me. I'll give you all of it."

"You're wearing expensive clothes and driving a Cayenne, and you expect me to believe you're penniless?"

By now, a gawking throng has gathered. Lihou pleads with the onlookers for support but no one comes forward, and the man starts howling in pain.

Tearfully, Lihou tells Yinan what happened. Yinan takes off her sunglasses and peers at the man. It is true there is a trail of blood oozing, worm-like, down his arm. She bends down and brushes the blood off his arm. She can see the cut.

"Let go of her!" she barks at him.

The man quivers. "No way, she hit me, she has to pay!"

"Are you going to let go or not?" Yinan raises her voice.

"No!" shouts the man.

Yinan shoves him suddenly and with such force that he skids three metres down the road. He scrambles to his feet, apparently with no difficulty at all and protests, "She hit me so hard that I'm bleeding, and now she won't pay me and you're beating me up!"

"That's right. Come on, hit me back! You can't? Well, I've got news for you: you're just a junkie faking a crash for a few quid. Except that your technique's not up to much!"

The man freezes, then says meekly, "OK, bruv, three hundred's enough."

"I'm not your bruv! Bugger off, you're not getting a cent!"

The man glares at Yinan, mumbling as if he has a walnut in his mouth.

"Get lost!" Yinan yells.

And he scuttles away, covered in dirt.

Lihou heaves a sigh of relief. "You reckon he's an opium addict?" she asks, fanning her face with both hands.

"Didn't you notice how sallow and gaunt he looks? His cheeks were as flat as an empty sack."

"Oh! I've heard about people faking accidents! But how did you know?"

"I rubbed away the blood and saw a cut, but it wasn't a graze or from hitting the ground. It was a clean cut, obviously made by a blade." Yinan takes a look around and sure enough, finds a razor blade beneath Lihou's car.

"How did you end up on Harvest Road?" asks Yinan.

But Lihou only says, "I've been feeling down the past few days, and bad things keep on happening to me."

"What on earth could be bothering you?"

Lihou sighs, is about to say something, swallows it back, then changes the subject. A few days ago, she says, she was out for a walk when she found a plain scholar fan at the arts and crafts place behind the Xijing South Hotel. She took it to Hai Ruo to get a pearl attached as its pendant. But Hai Ruo said for such a nice piece of work, she had something better. She'd just acquired some white agates with a single red dot, and was having them made into vajra pestles.

"Why don't you buy a few more fans?" Hai Ruo suggested. "We can use the vajra pestles as pendants, and give a fan to everyone."

But when Lihou went back to the workshop, only six colt tooth jade bamboo folding fans were left; the others were autumn fans with wider opening guards. Lihou insisted on having the colt tooth variety, and the dealer promised to source some from other shops, and asked her to come back in two hours. So she was just on her way to the shopping centre to while away the time when she ran into the fraudster.

"A fan is a fan, period. What's all the fuss about plain scholar and colt tooth?" says Yinan.

"The colt tooth is a type of plain scholar folding fan," Lihou explains. "The scholar fan is about seven centimetres shorter than an ordinary autumn fan, and it has an even number of sticks, one pair fewer than the larger fans. Its head is shaped like the tooth of a colt. It's an exquisite design, perfect for women."

"You're beginning to sound like a real arts buff, just like Hai-jie," says Yinan. "How much cool air can a tiny fan generate? You can buy plain scholar fans for the others, but please get me an autumn fan. I'll ask Yi Guang-laoshi to write a few words on it."

"Whoa! Why didn't we think of that? Now that we're having vajra pestle pendants made for each fan, we should ask Yi-laoshi for some calligraphy."

They chat for a while and Yinan takes her leave. Lihou looks at her watch. "There's still an hour before the fans are ready. Forget about the shopping centre, let's go to a cafe, I must thank you properly."

"Honestly, you don't need to. Besides, I have to go to the Peach Blossom to book rooms for the Living Buddha."

"After I've picked up the fans, I can join you."

Yinan hesitates, then says, "That's fine, but I've got another errand to run as well. How about this? You go to a cafe first, and I'll join you when I'm done."

Yinan drives like the wind to Xu Qi's place. As soon as she arrives, Xu Qi shows her the shoes she has bought and asks her to try them on. Yinan takes off her own shoes, hurriedly washes her feet and puts the new shoes on, parading back and forth in the sitting room.

"Do they fit?" Xu Qi asks.

"They're so nice, my feet are so lucky!" says Yinan, going over to kiss Xu Qi.

"Go and brush your teeth first!" Xu Qi commands.

Yinan obeys, but when she comes out, Xu Qi is in the shower, so she goes into the kitchen to slice the cold *zongzi*. She pours honey on the sticky rice triangles and takes the plate to the dining table, then guts and descales the fish. Xu Qi has still not emerged. Yinan picks up the massage oil and cleanser, and goes to put them by Xu Qi's bed, but when she opens the bedroom door, there is Xu Qi, freshly bathed, lying on the bed.

"We don't have time," says Yinan. "I have to book rooms for the Living Buddha at the Peach Blossom."

"You think I haven't got stuff on too?" says Xu Qi. "I need to go to the tax office in a bit."

Yinan smiles, and joins her on the bed.

Later, Xu Qi says, "Hai Ruo's had hyaluronic acid injections. Should I get my face done too?"

"Your face is nice and small, why bother?" says Yinan.

"But my nose is too flat."

"Eva has a big nose, but she's a foreigner. You're the traditional Chinese type. It'd be weird if you had a beaky nose."

"What is the traditional Chinese type?"

"A village girl, that's the ideal."

"A village girl! Is that what you're calling me?"

"Bad choice of words, I meant a pretty girl-next-door type."

"And the princess-type, like Yan Nianchu? You fancy her, do you?"

"No, she's not my type, and I'm not hers. Those airs she puts on… Did you notice her nose job's too big? It's always red at the tip."

Xu Qi gets up to look at herself in the long mirror when, all of a sudden, there is a crash. They spin round to see the frame fall off the wall opposite, hitting the wardrobe underneath. The glass cracks in several places, shredding the painting inside.

It is a small, traditional flower-and-bird picture by their friend Feng Ying. Xu Qi once asked Feng Ying to teach her painting. But Feng Ying was reluctant.

"Your strong point is your pretty face," she said. "Why bother dabbling with paints?" And she gave Xu Qi the painting as a present.

"The hook's still there, how did that happen?" says Xu Qi.

"The cord might have come undone," says Yinan. "Anyway, no big deal. Your looks are literally stunning, they brought the picture down off the wall."

"I'm here every day, why did it only come down just now?"

"Because I'm here and that makes you look even better."

Yinan reaches down to retrieve the picture. Oddly, the cord has not broken. As the glass and painting are both damaged, she does not rehang it. "Ask Feng Ying to do you a new one," she says.

"When is she due back?" asks Xu Qi, sitting on the edge of the bed, holding a pillow in her arms.

"Not for a week or two. Did you hear, there's a man called Liang Lei in the delegation. Feng Ying really likes him."

SI YINAN

Xu Qi is intrigued. "I wonder what he's like. She's very choosy about men."

"I've never met him," says Yinan. She gets up and puts on one shoe, but the other shoe is nowhere to be seen. Hopping on one leg, she searches under the bed.

They finish the honeyed *zongzi* and get ready to go out. Xu Qi puts on a pink skirt that barely skims her bottom, and poses in front of the mirror. "What do you think? It's not too bright or tacky, and it holds my belly in and makes me look thinner."

Yinan sits on a chair, admiring Xu Qi and her reflection in the mirror. "Why don't you wear the tracksuit bottoms?" she suggests.

"Why?"

"Your backside is an O-shape. It's rounded and firm, but a bit flat."

"I'm going to sign up for a yoga class next month," declares Xu Qi. She admires herself again, then takes off the skirt and puts on the trousers, which are straight-up-and-down, sort of H-shaped.

But Yinan does not put on her new shoes. "I look good enough already, don't I? I don't want to overdo it."

Xu Qi looks intently at Yinan. The whites of Yinan's eyes are so white they made her pupils look very dark, and especially luminous. She presses Yinan down on the sofa, puts her new shoes on for her, and throws her old shoes onto the balcony. "No one from an old Xijing family would wear such shabby shoes!" she declares.

10. YING LIHOU • PEACH BLOSSOM

SI YINAN ARRIVES at the cafe to find Ying Lihou sitting at a table nursing a steaming cup of coffee and looking despondent.

"Sorry I'm so late," Yinan apologises.

"No, it's not about you," says Lihou, "I was thinking about the accident."

"Forget it! It's not worth it."

"What I can't get over with is that there were so many gawkers, but none of them supported me. Worse still, they were all saying that I wasn't offering the man enough money."

"You're disadvantaged."

"Me, disadvantaged? How do you make that out? I'm not a migrant worker! I'm not a cripple!"

"There's a huge gap between the rich and the poor. You drive a high-end car, wear brand-name clothes, and on top of that, you're attractive. They're all jealous. Why should they help you?"

Lihou falls silent, her eyes on Yinan. "So, I should act arrogant?"

"Of course you should!"

This makes Lihou smile. "I've got the fans." She lays out fifteen folding fans, one autumn fan, the others plain scholar fans. Comparing the two designs, they decide that the scholar fans are finer.

Yinan changes her mind. "I want a plain scholar fan, too. When we ask Yi Guang-laoshi to write on them, we can give him the autumn fan as a gift."

"See? I was wondering why you didn't want a scholar fan."

They go to the Peach Blossom and ask for Mr Wei, the hotel boss. He is playing mahjong in an office on the top floor. Yinan tells him about booking the rooms; Wei says it's not a problem. He summons the front desk receptionist and dictates the number of rooms and dates, adding, "That's with a forty per cent discount."

The receptionist has barely stepped outside when Wei's assistant comes in with a business card. "A man came for you, Mr Wei. I've shown him into the lounge. Would you like to meet him? If not, I'll send him on his way."

Wei checks the card. "Ha! He's listed five positions! Just the day before yesterday someone said he was no longer the deputy chairman of the Xijing Art and Literature Society or the Chinese Culture Society." He picks up a pen and crosses out two titles on the card, but says, "I'd better see him."

His mahjong partners grow impatient. "We know you're so busy, Mr Wei, but you did promise us we could settle down for a quiet game!"

"Sorry," says Wei. "Stand in for me, will you, Yinan?"

"You think you're the premier of the State Council?" grumbles the man opposite as Wei walks out with a broad grin.

Yinan sits down. "Wonderful," says the player to her right. "It's always good to have the fairer sex along."

"I'm only a beginner," says Yinan.

"That's what we are counting on!" remarks the Grumbler. Everyone chortles.

Lihou sits behind Yinan and keeps an eye on the tiles for her. They play a hand and Yinan calls out, "Mahjong!" In the second hand, Yinan wins again.

"Back in our university, the cafeteria only offered the set menu," recalls Yinan. "The boys always sat at our table, thinking that we girls ate less and would give them the leftovers, but they soon found out that we could put away more than they did!"

The Grumbler is annoyed. "Mr Wei's not here, you should cut us some slack!"

"I want to, but the tiles won't let me," replies Yinan, picking up a tile from the stack. "*Ting!*" she declares triumphantly. She has a "ready hand", only one tile short of winning again.

"Let me play for a bit," Lihou chips in.

Yinan has tiles with a pair of two-dots and a pair of four-bamboos. A tile of either pattern will make it a "Mahjong". The player to Lihou's left discards a two-dot, but Lihou doesn't call a win. When it comes to her turn, she picks up a four-bamboo from the stack, but still she keeps quiet. Instead, she throws out one of her two-dots. It is Lihou's turn again and she picks up a one-dot, presses it face down against her forehead and tosses out the remaining two-dots. Then she watches the other players. As soon as the player before Lihou puts a one-dot on the table, Yinan announces, "Mahjong!"

"She pressed that tile against her forehead so hard it made a dent. Are you blind?" the Grumbler rebukes her.

Lihou looks at Yinan reproachfully, and stops playing.

All three men are puffing on cigarettes, filling the room with a haze of smoke.

"Go easy, smoking is bad for your health," says Lihou.

"The environment is so polluted, who cares about smoking?" retorts the Grumbler.

Lihou has a coughing fit and goes out to the corridor for a breath of air. The wall is lined with paintings, all in the traditional mountains-and-water style: precipitous rocky cliffs, dense forests, mist-shrouded streams, gigantic waterfalls. A bridge leads to a house, in front of which some women sit or stand. Lihou admires the paintings, wondering if she has ever seen scenery like this in the Qinling Mountains. Painters just exaggerate and distort these old-time scenes, she thinks. Those houses are skew-whiff, and the women all have long backs and short legs. In real life, painters all want to live in luxury mansions and marry beautiful, fair-skinned, wealthy women. How come they only paint tumbledown cottages and unattractive females? Does art have to be ugly?

Then she overhears Mr Wei talking to someone in the room directly in front of her. They seem to be discussing some city official.

"What a good thing you didn't get too close to him!" she hears his visitor say. "Nowadays you can't be standoffish, but being too closely associated is dangerous too. There's no telling who'll be the next to get caught. We can't see through the murk!"

The door has been left ajar and Lihou looks inside. The man talking to Wei is nearly bald, apart from a ridiculously thin ponytail at the back.

"But you and I should work together," continues the man. "I've got a cultural event in mind. You set up the venue, I'll round up the painters and calligraphers. Give them each a nice fat red envelope, and you get to keep all their works."

"How much?" asks Wei.

"Their food and drinks will all be covered, so five grand each should do it."

"Can you invite Mr Yi Guang too?"

The man sighed. "Sure I can, but you know, his calligraphy is so pricey, a red envelope wouldn't be enough. He'll have to be paid on his terms, I'm afraid."

"Fine. Can he do two pieces, maybe give us one more for free?"

"I don't think he'll go for that."

"Then I'll ask the teashop to invite him."

"The teashop at the foot of the building where Yi Guang has his studio? I know the owner, a woman called Hai Ruo. She has a friend named Lu Yike, doesn't she?"

"She has a bunch of close friends. They're all either leftover women or widows, and they're very easy on the eye, every last one!"

"I'm friends with all of them. We often get together for dinner or tea-drinking."

Lihou pulls a face and thinks, Nonsense, I've never met you in my life!

"Are you indeed?" says Wei. "Two of them are right here. Let me get them in."

Gotcha! Lihou says to herself.

"We still have a lot to finalise. Another day maybe," says the man.

She hears a shuffling of chairs in the room. It'll be awkward if they come out and bump into me, thinks Lihou, and she tiptoes back to the mahjong room.

It looks as if Yinan has not won any more. In fact, the thick wad of notes in front of her is half gone.

"What's keeping Mr Wei?" asks Yinan.

"Anyone who tries to beat Mr Wei ends up losing every hand," says the Grumbler. "But he's not here, so let's help ourselves." And he reaches over and grabs some money from Wei's pile. He passes each of his neighbours two notes, and sticks the remaining three in his own pocket.

"The... you..." stutters Yinan.

"Mr Wei has all the money he'll ever need," the man reassures her.

They hear footsteps in the corridor. Wei wears traditional cloth shoes, but the other man's leather shoes must have metal soles because they can hear his heavy tread.

"Go ahead and contact them. We can talk more later," says Wei.

"No need for that," says the man, "it's all settled!" He clomps away.

The door opens and Wei exclaims, "Good heavens, what a fug. Are you trying to smoke a raccoon dog out of its burrow?"

"Who was it that kept you so long?" asks the Grumbler.

"Something mega has happened," says Wei. "The chief has come a cropper!"

"What chief?" asks the Grumbler.

"Xijing only has one chief," says Wei.

The other two players both stop playing. "What's happened to him?"

"The Xijing Party Committee was having a meeting this morning," Wei goes on. "Inspectors from Beijing, from the Disciplinary Committee, turned up and marched him away."

The Grumbler drops the tile he is holding and it bounces on the floor. "Whew, there have been rumours for months," he exclaims as he bends down to retrieve it. "They really took him away?"

"I met him a few times," says the man to Wei's left. "He was a real 'brown-nose, look down your nose'. That's all very well as a strategy, but you have to have the courage of your convictions too."

"'Brown-nose, look down your nose'?" queries Yinan, puzzled.

"A provincial official is expected to look up to their superiors and down on their staff, but you've got to show integrity," explains the man. "Whenever Beijing officials turned up, that man bent over backwards to please them. A Pekingese puppy wouldn't have slobbered over them the way he did! But with his staff, he was a real tyrant, always barking insults and pounding on the desk."

"He didn't put much effort into his work, and he was a bully, but that wasn't the half of it," says Wei. "He was a political climber, always trying to curry favour. I know several tycoons were bankrolling him.

One of them, or so I heard, spent tens of millions on a fabulous painting by Qi Baishi, and gave it to a top Beijing official on his behalf. The official got into trouble and his home was turned upside down by investigators. They discovered the painting and it still had our man's CV taped to the back."

"And who bankrolled him?" asks the Grumbler.

"I couldn't possibly say, I'm not a gossip," says Wei.

"Sure, you're not a gossip, but you are a tycoon," insists the player. "How much did you slip him so you could build this grand hotel bang in the city centre?"

"You're a bad man!" laughs Wei. "I won this plot of land through fair bidding. And I'm not a tycoon. Tycoons fly to Macau to gamble, they don't sit around here playing mahjong with you!"

"All right, all right," says the player to Wei's right. "So the chief has been taken away, that's too bad for him. Now, let's get on with our game. Hey, my stomach's grumbling. Ask your chef to send something up."

"It is time for dinner," agrees Wei. "You two should stay, Yinan."

Yinan looks at Lihou, who says, "No, no, we'll be off, but thanks for the invitation, Mr Wei!"

"You won't find a finer roast duck in all Xijing," Yinan tells her.

Lihou is still shaking her head when the Grumbler says, "Who said anything about roast duck and Maotai? Much too expensive!"

Wei rises to the challenge. He points at the man and says, "Fine, roast duck and Maotai it is!" The players on either side of him applaud.

"Yinan always says how good your food is, and how generous Mr Wei is," says Lihou, "but we just had a late lunch. We have a job to do, over in the east side of the city. We'd love to join you another time."

"That's settled then, next time. I'll feed these guys today." Wei picks up the phone and orders the meal. "We can afford it, let's push the boat out!" he declares. "And here's something else: the chief was born and raised in our very own Xijing. He grew up on *hula* soup for breakfast. He's a top official now but he still loves his *hula* soup. Whenever he went to Beijing for a meeting, or led a delegation abroad, he always took along his own *hula* soup chef. This morning, as he was being taken away, he passed a *hula* soup stand. He knew he wouldn't be getting it again so he begged for one last bowl. They said yes, he got out of the car and went to the stall, and downed three bowls one after the other."

There is silence, broken only by a few sighs and sniffs. Yinan and Lihou take this opportunity to leave.

Down in the lobby, Lihou suddenly looks down and says quietly, "Do you see the guy ahead?"

Yinan puts her head on one side and takes a look. She titters. "He dresses so arty-farty, he can't be the real deal!"

"He was the man talking to Mr Wei, telling him about the chief being taken away. And guess what? He told him he was friends with everyone at the teashop. Do you know him?"

"Never seen him before," says Yinan.

They give him a good head start before they leave the hotel. Just outside the gate, an area has been roped off. A drain cover has been lifted and is lying upside down and some workers are clearing the sewage pipes. They have removed a large pile of rubbish: sludge, plastic bags, weeds and leaves, bits of rags and paper. They both hold their noses at the stench. Yinan has walked around the obstacle when one of Lihou's high heels gets caught in something, she lurches and almost slips over. She looks down and sees she has trodden on some condoms the workers have dredged out of the sewer. She hurries after Yinan then, suddenly feeling very sick, she bends double and retches, but nothing comes up.

"Hey, what's wrong?" asks Yinan.

Lihou chooses not to tell her about the condoms. "How did the sewer get blocked like that? How much can this city consume each day?"

"If all the city folk blow their noses once, we'd soon have a snot pond."

"Yuck!"

"The city's booming, and the more we consume, the more rubbish we produce," says Yinan, before she suddenly checks herself. "Why are you looking so sallow?"

"Am I? Well, you're looking a bit faded too."

"That's because I don't wear make-up."

They look up and see the sky is growing more yellow by the second, as if it is suffering from a severe case of jaundice. "Damned weather!" They laugh. "It was fine when we arrived, how come it's suddenly horrible?" Lihou goes behind a big newspaper display stand to fix her make-up, but Yinan simply says, "I can't help it if I'm looking faded, as you put it."

She then launches into a tirade, "The terracotta warriors started out colourful, but they faded after they'd been dug up. Nothing's like it used to be any more. There's no distinct summer or winter in Xijing, the seasons all blur together, there's no proper cold or heat. There's artificial lighting everywhere, so the day's never really bright and the night's never really dark. All our looks are fading, even the young are losing their youthful bloom. We've lost our sense of wonder at new things, we don't condemn evil any more, we've lost our passion for work, our respect for the old folks and our care for children, and even love, we've lost that too. What is it that has made us fade? Is it greed? Or envy? Or the pursuit of wealth and power?"

"Oh my, where's this big speech coming from?" says Lihou.

Yinan smiles. "I was very good at reading and writing back in middle school."

"Well, go and tell it to Hai-jie," says Lihou.

Yinan has to go to her furniture shop and Lihou insists on accompanying her. They drive to Second Lane in the old part of the city in their separate cars. The new batch of furniture has been delivered but is still piled up in its original packaging. Yinan tells the workers to open the wooden crates. There are three long, narrow side tables, four sets of display shelves for antiques, two wooden armchairs and two folding armchairs. On reaching the last three crates, however, they find that a wide-seat chair for meditation – a zen chair – has one leg broken.

Yinan calls the manufacturer. "Is that so?" says the furniture maker. "We packed it up really carefully. We've never had deliveries damaged before."

"You think I'm lying?" says Yinan furiously. "This zen chair is the most valuable item in this whole batch to me, and it's broken! I'll send you a video."

"Calm down, Yinan," says Lihou, and she calls one of the staff to come and take the video.

That in turn sends Yinan into a fury. "Is this how you shoot a video? I asked you to film the broken leg, and you just took one shot from the top!"

The worker goes scarlet, and he squats for another take. They forward the video over and the manufacturer agrees on a replacement. Yinan tells the staff to crate up the damaged chair and make sure it is dispatched before dark. She sits down, still fuming.

"Come on," says Lihou, "I'm famished. Let's go out and eat."

The lane has a dozen small eateries. The first one they go into sells buckwheat *hele* noodles. There are only seven or eight tables, where half a dozen migrant workers in filthy clothes, coated in dust and paint spots, are sitting. Cigarette butts dangle from their lips and they are playing drinking games, yelling at the tops of their voices and thrusting splayed fingers across the table over their drinks. Lihou drags Yinan outside.

"You don't like *hele*?" Yinan asks.

"It's not that. Look at me, dressed up like this, and you want me to sit in there?"

They try three more eateries before finally deciding on a Western meal – a steak with slices of bread on the side, and a cup of coffee each.

"Look at the cashier. Doesn't she look like Nianchu?" Lihou whispers to Yinan.

Yinan is amazed at the likeness. She takes out her phone and snaps a furtive picture which she attaches to a text to Nianchu with the message, "Did you ever lose a sister?" The joke gives them a good laugh.

"How much money do you think Nianchu has now?" Yinan asks all of a sudden.

"Why do you care?" asks Lihou.

"Just curious. Everyone thinks you're the richest, but Nianchu's living like a princess. She drives a Land Rover, lives in a villa, and a few days ago, she went golfing with a bunch of big shots. She asked me to join them, but I didn't go."

"So, driving a fancy car, living in a villa and playing golf makes you a princess! If anyone in our sisterhood's a princess, it must be Feng Ying."

"Feng Ying? Sure, she makes lots of money and she knows how to spend it."

"That's the pot calling the kettle! You're a spendthrift! Let's go through the list: you said you wanted to play Go, so you bought a top-grade *nanmu* chess board and *yunzi* stones, and you threw a banquet to begin your studies with a master. Six months later, you'd moved on to bowling, you drove around with five different kinds of balls in the boot. A month later, you fell in love with taekwondo. As for rock'n'roll, you've got a roomful of instruments and they're just gathering dust!"

"I just have a lot of interests. Hai-jie's the same!"

Just then, the door blows open in the draught, and grunts on its hinges.

"You compare yourself to Hai-jie? See? Not even the door believes you! You're both extravagant with money, but you just let it run through your fingers, whereas Hai-jie gives it out to other people."

"Hai-jie can't do anything wrong in your eyes!"

"She and Yike are both lookers, but Hai-jie doesn't tart herself up."

"Then she's just like me!" says Yinan. Their coffee arrives.

"Hai-jie used to wear only black or white, but I talked to her about it, and now she's transformed," Lihou goes on. "You'd look so much prettier with long hair and a skirt, Yinan."

"If I was pretty, I couldn't have browbeaten the man who faked your accident. In a temple, there are bodhisattvas and guardian warriors – I'm the guardian of the sisterhood."

"Thanks, you really helped me out today. And don't even think of paying. Here, your health! With coffee." Lihou turns to the waitress. "Where's the latte art? Your ad at the door boasts about your latte art, where is it?"

11. HAI RUO • A HOUSING ESTATE

HAI RUO CHANGES into a white shirt and a pair of jeans to visit Xia Zihua's mother. On the way, she stops by a bank to send money to her son Hai Tong. There she runs into Wu Xiaolin's mother, who is sending money to her daughter.

"Hey, I almost didn't recognise you!" exclaims Xiaolin's mother shrilly. "You're not wearing your Chinese gown." They grab each other's hands, beaming.

The woman beside her is introduced as her elder sister.

"Really, your sister?" says Hai Ruo, incredulously. She is struck by how much white there is in her friend's hair.

"We sucked at the same breast!" says Xiaolin's mother. "You think she looks younger than me? I don't dye my hair."

"If all your hair had gone white, you'd look nice without dyeing it," says her sister. "But salt-and-pepper hair makes you look really old."

"It's all the worries I've got," Xiaolin's mother laments. "At my age, I've got nobody to love me, so why would I bother dyeing my hair?"

"You're not the only one supporting an overseas student," her sister points out. "Look at Hai Tong's mother, she's so full of life. Just look at her face and her figure!"

"She's got her own company, and she has no pressure moneywise," says Xiaolin's mother.

"That's not true," says Hai Ruo. "I'm four or five years younger than you, but my hair's going white too. As I spot one, I pull it out but another one grows in its place."

Just then, the sister plucks a hair from Hai Ruo's head.

The trio leave the bank and carry on chatting cheerfully in the car park.

"What have you been up to lately?" Hai Ruo asks Xiaolin's mother.

"My sister's here to talk to me about starting a business. You're a business woman, do give us some advice. Should she open a fabric shop or a restaurant? My sister wants to sell made-to-measure curtains, but I think a restaurant selling crayfish or noodles is a better idea."

"Huh, you and your noodles!" says her sister. "You've been banging on about a noodle place for two years."

"I only agreed because you wanted to sell furnishings and you were so enthusiastic about it, but then you gave up on the idea."

"So you've been discussing this for a few years?" Hai Ruo chips in.

"That's right," says Xiaolin's mother. "We have to find a way to earn money. A noodle shop's more realistic, I think."

"It's back-breaking work, though," Hai Ruo demurs.

"And never mind the work, how much can you make on a bowl of noodles?" says the sister.

"But everyone eats noodles!" protests Xiaolin's mother. "However little you make on each bowl, we can easily make half a million in profit a year. If we split that fifty-fifty, that's enough for Xiaolin's studies."

"Would that be enough?" says Hai Ruo.

"Of course it would be," says Xiaolin's mother. "How much do you send Hai Tong each year?"

"Well, Hai Tong has a lot of expenses. I suppose, yes, that should be enough," Hair Ruo concedes.

"Now that he has a girlfriend, he has to spend money on her, too. Let me know when he's coming home and I'll get him to bring back a mobile for Xiaolin. Hers is broken."

"He just left after Spring Festival. He won't be back any time soon."

"But Xiaolin told me, he went to Shanghai."

"To Shanghai?"

"Xiaolin said his girlfriend went on a business trip to Shanghai, and they arranged to meet there. Your Hai Tong is so handsome and he's so good with people. And now he's got a girlfriend. My Xiaolin's so young for her age. They went abroad together... pity there was no spark between them."

Hai Ruo mumbles something indistinct.

All this while, the sister has been on the phone. "They've got news," she announces. "There's a place with three rooms and a big frontage going for a reduced rent. They want us to check it out."

"In that case, you'd better get going," says Hai Ruo.

As Xiaolin's mother turns away, she says, "Let's stay in touch. Do call me when you send money next time."

Hai Ruo watches the sisters leave and suddenly feels upset. She leaves the car in the car park and walks. It's a rare fine day, the sun has finally come out and is shining brilliantly. There's some public housing in the distance, of the sort called *tongzilou*, tube buildings, from the tube-like walkways on each level. On one of the roofs, a flock of pigeons coo hypnotically, then take off into the sky.

Every house has dark corners, every person has dark secrets. Hai Ruo is no exception. When she divorced, she got custody of her son. She was sure she could raise her little cockerel so that he grew into a fine crane, but the boy had become a rebel by the age of twelve. He made no effort to study, and was always doing stupid things, like taking cold showers in cold weather, eating hotpot at the height of summer, wearing trousers with the crotch down at his knees, insisting on trainers and doing high jumps so he could leave his footprints at the top of a white-painted wall. If anything annoyed him, he'd go to his room and slam the door behind him. Hai Ruo did not approve of the *gaokao* system for getting a university place, and she had hoped that a change might help Hai Tong settle down, so when some of his school friends talked about studying abroad, with some going to Europe or the US, she let him go to Australia with his classmate, Wu Xiaolin. To her dismay, once he was free of her clutches, he lost his way completely. He failed his IELTS three times, and instead, got himself a girlfriend.

"Don't you dare come home before you've got into a university!" Hai Ruo told him fiercely.

She then reduced her son's monthly allowance from 30,000 yuan to 18,300 yuan. "Not a cent more!" And now, her son is meeting up with his girlfriend behind her back! She wants to tell him that you have to do what is right for each stage of your life, and this isn't the time to get a girlfriend. She supposes it's normal, but at least he should not miss his classes. Everyone in my sisterhood wanted to run as soon as we learned to walk, she says to herself, and we all still dream of flying. How come my son has no get-up-and-go? He's rolling downhill like a stone – and enjoying the free fall!

Suppressing her rage, Hai Ruo dials her son's number three times, but the phone is turned off, even though Hai Tong normally has it on during the day. Maybe he has gone back to school. Then she looks at her watch and realises it's night-time in Australia. The thought calms her and she walks on, muttering to herself, How did I end up with a son like this?

The pavement is thronged with people: a middle-aged man leading a dog that looks exactly like its owner, a grandmother pushing a pushchair, the baby inside just a few months old, a skinny little thing with red cheeks, looking just like a monkey. Hai Ruo remembers the saying, you learn about the parents by looking at the children, and vice versa. She sighs long and hard. She wonders if she failed her son, or if Hai Tong's problems come from his father. Or maybe from both sides.

She walks on in silence. Occasionally she looks back. Her shadow trails behind her like her double.

She gets to the housing estate and pauses at the entrance to the building, rubs her face and stamps her feet a few times to shake off her gloom. She does not want to infect Zihua's mother with her low mood. This building must be more than forty years old. It seems odd that it is still standing when the city around it is changing so fast; whole neighbourhoods are being pulled down to make way for new high-rises. The exterior walls are stained with damp, and large patches of plaster are peeling off. The small windows have all been fitted with iron grilles that look like rusty cages, and the sills appear to be cluttered with stuff. Poles poke through the grilles, hung with quilts, trousers, socks and bras.

The building has a lift, but Hai Ruo chooses the stairs. She wants to break a sweat with the stiff climb, and feel gravity pulling her back as she goes up. But she is human and her arms are not wings. By the ninth floor, her legs are leaden and aching. The slightest touch of a finger behind her knees would make her legs buckle, and her underwear is soaked in sweat.

She knocks for a while on the door. Finally someone comes. It sounds like they are limping, each step followed by a long pause. The door opens and she sees Mrs Qi propping herself against it.

Hai Ruo smiles. "It's me, Auntie!"

"Good to see you!" The old woman's wrinkled face creases in an answering smile.

"The smog lasted so long, I can feel the weeds sprouting inside me. But it's bright and sunny outside, let me take you to Qinling for a stroll."

"Come in, please, do come in. It's so kind of you to visit me when you're so busy," says Mrs Qi, showing Hai Ruo to a chair. Then she goes on, "My legs are playing up again, they're stiff as sticks, and so painful I can hardly walk."

Hai Ruo looks at her friend's mother. She appears pale and drawn, and her back is stooped. She must have been weeping because her eyes are puffy and as red as overripe peaches. Hai Ruo feels a pang of sympathy. "I'll get someone from the teashop to catch some bees and bring them over for your legs."

"Don't bother, Hai Ruo. I had a nightmare last night. A swarm of bees was flying at me, and they all had human faces. It dawned on me that every time a bee stings me, it dies. The stings haven't done my legs any good, and I have so many lives on my conscience."

The thought of these sacrificed lives has never struck Hai Ruo before. After a long pause, she says, "You're overthinking it, Auntie. A bee's venom is dispelled when it makes honey as well as when it stings your arthritic knees."

"Then that venom ends up in me, doesn't it? You know what they say: as the parents get older, they hold their children back. If I'd died younger, Zihua would have recovered her health."

Hai Ruo pulls Mrs Qi into her arms. She is stick-thin. Hai Ruo sheds a tear, then says, "I know you're having a really hard time, Auntie, but no matter how bad it feels, we're here for you. Be strong and brave. We need you to live a long, healthy life, and Zihua *will* get better. But where's Xia Lei?"

"He's been racketing around the flat all morning, but he finally got tired and fell asleep."

Hai Ruo gives xiao-Su a call in the shop, then she goes to Xia Lei's bedroom to check up on him.

As she goes in, she catches sight of a pair of red shoes, one pointing at the corner, the other lying on its side in a pile of wooden building blocks. They remind her of her own son when he was little. Hai Tong had shoes like that. Every time she came home, she would see those tiny red leather shoes tucked in among the row of grownup shoes lined up at the door, and feel a surge of love and happiness. She picks up the shoes and sits down on the edge of the bed. Xia Lei is fast asleep, breathing as lightly as a puppy. One leg is sticking out from under the sheet and she takes it gently in her hand. It feels like a ball of cotton wool, shrinking as she holds it.

Then she hears the door open and someone comes into the sitting room. She comes out of the bedroom to find xiao-Su holding a small box covered in gauze to keep the bees in. Behind her is Xiang Qiyu, carrying a bag of rice.

"You arrived together?" She is surprised.

"A friend sent me some rice from the northeast, from Wuchang," says Qiyu. "It's delicious simply steamed and eaten on its own. So I brought Auntie a bag, and I ran into xiao-Su downstairs."

Mrs Qi nods and thanks them profusely.

As Hai Ruo and Qiyu watch, xiao-Su brings out the bees but cannot get them to sting in the right place. "Relax," Hai Ruo tells her, and takes Qiyu to the kitchen.

"Has Hai Tong been in touch with you by any chance these last few months?" asks Hai Ruo.

"Not really," says Qiyu. "I used to call him, and this year he called me twice and sent some photos. What a handsome young man!"

"Did he ever borrow money from you?"

"No. Borrow from me? Why? What's happened?"

"Nothing. I've cut down on his allowance this year and I'm worried he might ask you or the rest of the sisterhood for money. I don't want him getting into more bad habits."

"Why are you sending him less money? A child in a foreign country without any family needs money just to breathe! You're so mean!"

"You know what they say, a girl needs to be brought up rich, a boy should be brought up poor."

"Yes I know, but how much do you send him a month?"

"Eighteen thousand, three hundred yuan."

"That's much too little."

"No it's not. He's a student. He only needs to cover his rent, food, study materials and a few clothes. If he ever comes to you, remember, don't give him a cent."

Qiyu nods, but says nothing. She just looks at Hai Ruo.

"Why are you looking at me like that?"

"I'm looking at what your face is saying while you're talking to me. I can see you're worried that Hai Tong is having a hard time. You're telling me this because you want me to say, yes, you're right, then you'll feel better. You're an oyster, Hai-jie – the harder your shell is, the softer your body."

"But grit gets into an oyster's shell," Hai Ruo says with a laugh.

"Then you'll just make more pearls," says Qiyu.

"I've got to hold my ground this time, or he'll never mend his ways."

"Hai Tong's a good boy. He's your son, Hai-jie, he won't turn bad. Even if he does, how bad can that be?"

"Well, grains are better than grass seeds, as the saying goes, but only after they ripen. Before that, they're no good for anything."

"Granny!" comes the boy's shout from the bedroom. No one answers.

"Gran… nee!!!"

Hai Ruo and Qiyu are the first to arrive, and find the boy standing on the bed, stark naked. Hai Ruo tries to dress him, but he won't let her. His granny leaves the bees and comes to the rescue. "You'll catch a cold," she says, ruffling his hair and patting his back. The boy stands passively as she puts his clothes on. "Pullover, over the top… left foot," she commands and he raises his leg and she guides it through the trouser leg. "Right foot," and they repeat the same routine.

The boy is like a puppet. "Pee-pee!" he says, spreading his feet wide apart. Mrs Qi fetches an old enamel iron mug from under the bed, and holds it up for him.

Qiyu and Hai Ruo glance at each other. "He's three now, he should be using the toilet," Hai Ruo says.

"He's used to this," says Mrs Qi. Then she turns to the boy. "Lei Lei, are you hungry? What do you want to eat?"

"Let's go out and have some pork or fish on rice," suggests Qiyu. "The Anhui restaurant on Peace Road makes very good stinky Chinese perch."

"I want *geda*," says Xia Lei.

"You and your food!" says Mrs Qi. "I'll do some steamed egg custard, it's very good for you."

"No, no! I want *geda*!" demands the boy.

"Let's give him what he wants, I'm quite good at making it," says Hai Ruo.

"OK then," his grandmother agrees. "Don't go, Qiyu and xiao-Su, join us for the meal."

Hai Ruo kneads the dough until it is soft and elastic, then rolls it flat, slices it up and cuts the strips into small chunks. A firm roll under the thumb, and the chunk becomes a little shell called a "cat's ear". Meanwhile xiao-Su has the water boiling. As the cat's ears are being cooked, then drained, Qiyu chops up courgettes, Chinese celery, wood ear, dried long yellow daylily, tofu and turnip. Then Hai Ruo stir-fries the vegetables with the cat's ears to make the *geda*.

Two hours later, the serving bowl is placed on the table. Xia Lei reaches for it, but Mrs Qi stops him. She rests the chopsticks on the bowl, puts her palms together, casts her eyes downward and chants, "*Taotie, Taotie*, please help yourself." This she repeats four times before passing the bowl to her grandson.

"What was that, Auntie?" asks Qiyu.

"Lei Lei always eats too much and his tummy gets bloated, then he's sick. He won't listen when we tell him to eat less. Xu Qi was here the other day. She said Lei Lei must have a greedy *taotie* in his belly. She said if I invited the monster to help itself first before each meal, Lei Lei wouldn't eat so much because the *taotie* would be satisfied."

"Hah, Xu Qi's right," Hai Ruo says. "Let the *taotie* eat first."

As they all eat, Mrs Qi calls Zihua for a video chat so she can see the meal prepared by Hai Ruo, Qiyu and xiao-Su, and how Lei Lei is eating. Zihua lies in bed, saying nothing but smiling through her tears.

After the meal, Hai Ruo, Qiyu and xiao-Su leave together. "Hai Ruo," says Qiyu, "Xu Qi has really gone round the bend, what's all that nonsense about *'taotie'* before each meal? When did superstitions ever work? But you agreed Xu Qi was right!"

"Mrs Qi doesn't know whether she's coming or going. She just needs something to calm her nerves, whatever it is," explains Hai Ruo.

"The way I see it, the old lady's fine, it's Xu Qi who's behaving weirdly," says Qiyu. Hai Ruo glances at Qiyu, but holds her tongue.

12. GAO WENLAI • THE TEASHOP

FAN BOSHENG LEAVES the Peach Blossom Hotel and heads for Yi Guang's studio on Lotus Road. He knocks, and knocks again, but nothing moves inside. He takes his usual place sitting on the edge of the raised flower bed outside, and waits. But this time he miscalculates. Two hours later, not a single female has emerged from the building. He's really not in, thinks Fan, and he potters off to the teashop.

"Hello!" Gao Wenlai greets him at the door.

"Where's your boss?" asks Bosheng.

Wenlai feels a sudden itch on his head and scratches the spot. "She's not in."

"What a day, nobody's where they should be," says Bosheng. "I'll have a quick tea then." He heads inside.

With one hand still scratching his head, Wenlai steps in Bosheng's way. "We only sell tea leaves here. There's a teahouse just around the corner, you can drink tea and play mahjong there."

"Why can't I drink tea if you sell it?"

"We sell tea, but not water."

"But I want to drink tea!"

Wenlai raises both arms and plants his feet wide, blocking the entrance like the Chinese character for "big" – 大.

"What do you think you're doing?" demands Bosheng.

"I work here."

"What kind of an assistant do you think you are?" And Bosheng gives Wenlai a resounding smack across the face.

Nobody in the shop pays any attention when they hear Wenlai raise his voice. On any given day, there are plenty of people coming in looking for a cup of tea, being told that only tea leaves are sold here, and leaving. But they hear the loud slap. As Wenlai lunges forward to hit back, xiao-Tang rushes out and inserts herself between the two men in the nick of time.

"He's a customer, Wenlai," she tells the young assistant. "Let him in if he wants."

Blood is trickling from the corner of Wenlai's mouth and he spits. "He's a trouble-maker!"

Meanwhile, Bosheng has taken a seat at one of the long tables. He is seething. "I thought the Sojourn Teashop had a certain reputation! What kind of a shop assistant are you? A well-trained dog knows better than to block a customer's way!"

xiao-Tang tries to appease him. "Please don't be angry, sir. Wenlai has only just joined us. He didn't mean to offend you. Wenlai, go and make a cup of tea for our guest!"

"Oh, so it's OK to drink tea here after all!" says Bosheng.

Scowling, Wenlai fetches a cup, throws in a pinch of leaves and goes to the cubicle for hot water. The thermos is empty. He turns on the gas cylinder to boil water, which seems to take forever to heat up. He stands by the stove, still panting with rage. A fly buzzes in through the small window. He waves an arm furiously at it, but misses the target. He grabs a fly swatter from the cabinet and renews his attack, but fails to get any closer to the intruder. In the end, the insect lands nimbly on the swatter. By the time the water boils, the young man is spitting profanities. He pours water into the cup, then spits in it.

Outside, Bosheng sits with one leg crossed over the other, casually swinging it back and forth. "What's your name?" he asks xiao-Tang.

"Tang Yinyin, just call me xiao-Tang."

"Do you know who I am?"

"I'm afraid I don't, sir."

"Your boss is a friend of mine," says Bosheng, handing her a business card.

"Ah, Mr Fan. Please forgive us. Our boss has something to attend to today. She's not in this morning."

"For a business to thrive, its owner must be at the coalface," declares Bosheng. "Have you heard of Yi Guang?"

"Are you a friend of Yi-laoshi?"

"We go way back! I'll let you into a secret. I'm sure you're well aware how valuable his calligraphy is. Well, I've got so many of his pieces at home, I put them under the mattress."

"Wow, so you're literally rolling in it!"

"Hah! It's not about money, it's friendship!" His leg is now swinging so merrily that the shoe dangling from his toes drops to the floor.

"Well, Mr Fan, we really do only sell tea leaves here, we don't offer tea for drinking. But in your case, we're happy to make an exception." And she calls out, "How's the tea getting on, Wenlai?"

Wenlai waits until Bosheng goes into the toilet before coming out of the cubicle. He can't stand the cheek of the man. He plonks the mug down on the table, spilling a little of the tea.

"Could you get that porcelain jar down for me?" says xiao-Tang.

The young man steps on a stool and reaches up to the shelf for the jar.

"Oh, here comes the water delivery man. Bring the water in, would you, Wenlai?" says xiao-Tang.

Wenlai hurries out. Large bottles of distilled water are being unloaded from a three-wheeled cart. Wenlai grabs a bottle by the neck in each hand, carries them inside, then goes back for two more. Just then, four people arrive: three men each hefting a bundle of books on one shoulder, and a young girl holding a bunch of magenta-coloured flowers.

"We came to ask Yi-laoshi to sign these but he's gone out," explains one of the men. "He said we could leave the books here with our contact number. You can let us know when he's signed them."

"Put the books down here," says Wenlai, and he takes the girl's bouquet. "Are these for Yi-laoshi?" The girl nods. "Fragrance lingers on the hand that gives roses," says Wenlai.

"What fine words from a shop assistant!" exclaims the man. "I see that Yi-laoshi's learning has rubbed off on you! Rub against cinnabar and you go red, as they say."

"You must be hot, carrying all those books. Can I offer you some tea?" asks Wenlai.

"Don't worry about the tea. We'll just sit down and have a breather, if we may. These books are treasures, even a small bundle weighs a ton."

"Good paper comes from wood pulp, and that bundle of books represents a tree trunk," says Wenlai.

"We were just discussing on our way here, how many logs Yi-laoshi must have consumed!"

"Yi-laoshi has published so many books and each one has a print run of hundreds of thousands. And he's done so much calligraphy too. If you count all the different kinds of paper he's used over the years, that's several mountains' worth of trees felled, plus a whole reed bed, and a hundred or so straw stooks!"

"Are you accusing Yi-laoshi of destroying the environment?" says xiao-Tang, who is sitting at one of the round tables doing her bookkeeping. Wenlai and the visitors laugh.

"A friend put me in touch with Yi-laoshi," continues the man. "I've never met him in person. I thought he must live in a villa, with guards at the gate, but we went there just now and found out he lived in a high-rise just like everyone else, with no one guarding the door. Spring Festival is less than two months ago, and there were no couplets on the door."

"How could he put up couplets?" asks xiao-Tang. "If he did, someone would have them off in no time."

"Exactly!" agrees the man. "Does Yi-laoshi dress in smart suits and leather shoes? Is he a commanding figure who never deigns to talk to anyone?"

"Nah, he's just like you," xiao-Tang says with a giggle. "In fact, he's shorter than you. You're wearing a suit, but he just wears a regular jacket, year in, year out, and you'll often see him hunkered down by a fried *liangfen* stall, with a bowl of noodles in his hand."

"Really!" exclaims the man.

"Before I met Yi-laoshi," Wenlai chips in, "I thought he was a god. I couldn't imagine him ever having a crap or farting–"

"Wash your mouth out, Wenlai!" xiao-Tang scolds him.

"But I really did think that," insists Wenlai. He gives his face a little slap and goes to talk to the girl. "You've read Yi-laoshi's books?"

"I'm too young to read him," says the girl.

"Yi-laoshi is so busy, he has so many books to sign, he needs a bit of feeding up," muses Wenlai casually.

"Quite so," the man promptly agrees. "We were going to invite him to dinner."

"Well, since he's not here, why not buy him some tea? White tea is his favourite," says Wenlai.

Both xiao-Zhen and Mrs Zhang chuckle. "You're a natural salesman, Wenlai!"

"This is about paying homage to Yi-laoshi," replies Wenlai.

"Absolutely!" says the man, reaching for his wallet. "A canister of white tea, then."

"Which kind of white tea?" Wenlai asks. "There are two types, dry-fried and fermented. The first includes Anji, Ya'an, Yangxian, Thousand Islands Lake and Shangnan varieties. The fermented type comes in round, flat cakes, and the best-known is Fuding. It has a very long shelf life. In its first year, it's just tea, a year later, it's acquired medicinal properties, and by its third year, it's become a precious commodity. From the fourth year onwards, it's considered priceless."

"Then I'll have the priciest type," says the man.

Wenlai wraps the tea cake and puts it down on the book bundle. The man pays and Wenlai escorts them all to the door. Five middle-aged women stand outside, looking up at the shop front sign and trying to peer inside.

"Not a minute's peace," mutters Wenlai to himself, approaching the newcomers.

"Is this the teashop of that writer Yi Guang?" asks one of the women.

"Oh no, Mrs Hai is the owner," replies Wenlai.

"But Yi Guang's written the shop name!" insists the woman, pointing to the calligraphy over the shop.

"Yes, he did, but he doesn't own the place."

"His writing costs a fortune. If he did that, he must have shares in the business, surely?"

"Nope."

"We heard he runs this teashop and he's often seen here. So we've decided to come and look at him, so we can see what such a clever man looks like!"

"He's often here, just not today."

Bosheng returns from the toilet and raises the cup to his lips. Just in time, he spots something suspicious floating on the surface of the liquid. He scrutinises it, and exclaims, "What tea comes with spittle!"

xiao-Tang hurries over and sees something that should not be in the tea, but says, "Spittle? Not possible! Wenlai must have used the old tea by mistake. You know the aged leaves tend to froth. But I'll get you a fresh cup of this year's tea." She empties the cup outside and shoots Wenlai a murderous look.

But Bosheng won't let it go. "I'll be damned if that wasn't spittle! Son of a bitch, you spat in my tea, didn't you?" He grabs hold of a tea tray on the table and hurls it at Wenlai.

The young man dodges as the tray hurtles by and crashes into a small cabinet behind him. One of the three shallow teacups displayed on top tumbles onto the floor. There are shrieks from xiao-Tang, xiao-Zhen and Mrs Zhang. They rush over, but the teacup lies broken in three pieces.

"Oh, my God!" xiao-Tang cries. "These three were made by a ceramic artist, in the most beautiful glaze too. They cost three thousand yuan each! And now one's broken!"

Bosheng hears the women, but does not turn around. He throws himself at Wenlai, who is shouting, "You've got to pay for it!" Bosheng kicks out, but misses and, in the meantime, Wenlai seizes his chance and scores two punches. He is so quick that no one sees the attack. He straightens up and sneers at his opponent. "Come on, you can do better than that!"

But Bosheng has a stitch and bends over to ease it. Then he shouts, "Motherfucker! Take this!" He snatches a bamboo *ruyi* talisman from the table and swings wildly at Wenlai. The young man swiftly catches Bosheng's wrist, forces it backwards, and knocks Bosheng on the head with it. Bosheng drops the *ruyi*, gripping a lock of Wenlai's hair with his free hand.

xiao-Tang wedges herself between the pair. "Are you trying to trash the shop? We'll call the police!" She reprimands Wenlai, "Why are you shouting? Has a dog been teaching you to bark?"

Amid the row, footsteps are heard coming down the stairs. It is Eva.

All this time, Eva has been upstairs with Yan Nianchu. Nianchu was looking after Xia Zihua at the hospital when she got a call at lunch from Wang, the director of the Lotus Road Dental Hospital, telling her to be at his office at 3 pm. Nianchu gives 100 yuan to the ward's cleaner and asks her to keep an eye on Zihua, promising to return before dusk. She can't go and see Wang empty-handed, Nianchu thinks. She has already bought him a shirt and a jumper, as well as expensive health foods like sea cucumbers and swallow's nests. Tea makes a good gift too, so she calls xiao-Tang to ask if Hai Ruo is in. When the answer is no, she hurries over to buy some premium Longjing tea and a silver teapot. The bill comes to 10,000 yuan.

"This is a serious gift, who's it for?" xiao-Tang asks.

"Please, don't ever breathe a word to Hai-jie that I came by, or she would never let me pay," Nianchu says.

xiao-Tang wraps up the tea and teapot, then ushers Nianchu upstairs to while away the time over tea. Eva, meanwhile, is back from a bookstore where she found the books Hai Ruo wanted. On her way back, she has been to a flower market and bought armfuls of blooms too. Nianchu sips on her tea, chatting with Eva, who is trimming the flower stems with a pair of scissors and arranging them in vases.

"How tall are you, Eva?" Nianchu asks.

"One metre seventy-four in my bare feet," says Eva.

"I'm the same, but you look a lot taller!"

"I might be slimmer."

"How do you keep your figure? You're slim, but you've got all the curves you should have. If I go on a diet, I might lose a few kilos, but my breasts and buttocks shrink too. Are you taking something special to lose weight?"

"I'm not on a diet."

"No way! You're gorgeous!"

"You're the gorgeous one."

"Chinese medical equipment isn't on a par with foreign products, and the same with Chinese people and foreigners. Hey, are Russians Slavic?" Nianchu starts asking about Slavic history, geography, products, climate and cuisine. Eva tells her everything she knows.

"You were born in such a wonderful land, but you chose to come to China!" exclaims Nianchu.

"I came to learn Chinese. China's wonderful too, and I've made such good friends with all of you!"

Nianchu smiles, then her eyes light on Eva's ankle boots. "What's the brand? Where did you get these?"

"I bought them in St Petersburg. I can call a friend there if you really like them. They'll buy a pair for you and ship them over in no time. What's your size?"

"Thirty-eight."

"Me too. Here, try them." She starts taking off a boot.

They hear the uproar downstairs just as Mrs Zhang is coming to clear up the cut-off leaves and stems.

"What's that all about?" Eva asks.

"A guy came in and said he knew our boss, but none of us has seen him before. We didn't take him very seriously, we thought he was just spouting off. And then he got into an argument with Wenlai."

"He says he knows Hai-jie and yet he picks a fight in her shop?" says Nianchu. "Who is this guy?" She goes to the top of the stairs and peers over, then comes back.

"Who is he?" asks Eva, holding one boot in her hand.

"Don't know."

"If you don't, then Hai-jie won't either," says Eva. "Is he drunk? Why's he making such a scene?" She hobbles to the stairs. Then she exclaims, "Good heavens! That's Mr Fan?"

Bosheng has raised one arm high in the air, then slams his hand down on the table. He has seen Eva and, at first, pays her no heed. Then, just as he is raising his arm again, he checks himself. "Oh, it's you, we've met. You're that *laowai*–"

"My name is Eva. Hai-jie, Lu-jie and I had dinner with you the other day," Eva reminds him.

"Did you hear that?" Bosheng asks xiao-Tang. "Am I a friend of your boss or not? And I had to put up with this mutt?"

"How can you call him a dog?" asks Eva. "Are you drunk? Why are you acting so crazy?"

"I haven't touched a drop," says Bosheng. "He is a mongrel, a brainless mongrel!"

"Even if he is, you ask the owner before hitting the dog! You're being a bastard!"

"Why?"

"Because you're getting abusive in public!"

"Huh!" Bosheng grunts in annoyance.

"Huh! Huh, indeed!" Eva retorts.

"Please, don't be angry, let me get you a fresh cup of tea," xiao-Tang says, trying once more to placate Bosheng.

"As if anyone cares about tea! I'm fed up with you lot!" Bosheng slams out.

When Bosheng is at a safe distance, Wenlai spits at his retreating back. "What's the hurry if you were in the right?" he mutters.

"Stop spitting," xiao-Tang reprimands him. "He was in the wrong, but you shouldn't have spat in his tea. Now you're the bad guy even though you were right. If it weren't for Eva, he would have made an even bigger scene."

"Thank you, Eva," says Wenlai.

"But I didn't do anything for you," says Eva.

"I'm sorry for what you went through, Wenlai," says xiao-Tang. "If I were a man, he would never have smacked you across the face."

"He was out to make trouble *because* you're all women. I was just trying to protect you," says Wenlai.

"Who needs protection? Before you came, no one ever raised their voice in here," says xiao-Tang.

"And we never broke anything either," adds xiao-Zhen. "Look at this teacup? It's three thousand yuan! Who's going to pay for it?"

"I'll tell Hai-jie about it," says xiao-Tang.

"Oh, no, please, don't tell her," says Wenlai. "If you do, that'll put paid to my salary for this month. Please, Tang-jie, let me write you a poem."

"Who wants your doggerel?" xiao-Tang rebukes him. Eva giggles.

Nianchu comes downstairs, handing the boot to Eva. "It's getting late, I must get back to the hospital."

Wenlai grabs her shopping bag with the tea and the teapot, and trots cheerfully behind her to the car park.

13. YING LIHOU • THE PAOMO RESTAURANT

M<small>R</small> W<small>ANG CASUALLY STASHES</small> the packet of tea in the fridge, then examines the teapot. "I may not be an expert, but is this silver?"

"You know your silver and gold all right, but you're no expert on tea," Yan Nianchu tells him. "That packet of Longjing costs over ten thousand yuan. Make sure you keep it to yourself!"

Wang laughs. "I'm not fussy about tea. Isn't there a saying, it's not what you eat that matters, it's who you eat with? When it comes to tea, it's the teapot that counts. I was at the Department of Health offices last month, and I saw the director, Liu, had a silver teapot. I was wondering when I'd ever get one like that, and here it is!"

"A wish come true! I bought the teapot in Japan, and I've treasured it ever since."

"Then why would you let it go?"

Nianchu pushes her sunglasses up into her forehead. "As Confucius put it, 'Don't do unto others as you wouldn't have them do unto you.'"

Wang snorts with laughter at the mangled quote. He sits down in his chair, leans back and lights a cigarette. Nianchu takes the stool by the desk. The stool is only half the height of the desk, so she's looking right up at his Adam's apple. It resembles a pyramid threatening to pierce his skin at any moment.

"So, is the contract drafted?" asks Wang.

"I've printed three copies," says Nianchu. She crosses her long legs, and her skirt rides up, so she takes the scarf off her neck to cover her thigh.

"Good, that's good. Oh, you're a smoker too, I almost forgot." Wang tosses over a cigarette and Nianchu catches it. "Take that scarf off," says Wang. "It covers your skirt. If someone comes in right now, they'd think you've got no knickers on underneath!"

"So what if I haven't? Surely they wouldn't think you're that kind of guy!" Nianchu giggles, then asks, still smiling, "Well, have you thought about acquiring the equipment?"

"Close the door."

Nianchu gets up to shut the door. As she comes back, she catches sight of a magnificent asparagus fern in a pot in the corner. Its delicate stems and finely-cut leaves rise in spirals around a supporting stick, for nearly two metres. "Someone here has green fingers!" she comments.

"The head of the hospital Party Committee, the deputy director and me, we all have an asparagus fern in our offices. I smoke day and night and never pay it any attention, but it thrives on neglect. It's much healthier than theirs." He takes several drags then exhales and the smoke completely shrouds him. "The Party Committee had a meeting this morning just for this, and decided on open bidding."

"Oh," says Nianchu. She straightens her back and moves the stool closer to the desk, resting both hands on the edge. All her nails are polished and painted, and one is adorned with a tiny diamond.

"Is that the real deal?" Wang asks, looking at it.

"You like it?"

"Sure."

"When I get rich, I'll get real diamonds on my nails to show you! You said it would pass at the meeting without any problem, so why do you still want open bidding?"

"Have you heard what happened to the Xijing Party chief? Things are really tense just now. Any new projects have to be seen to go through the bidding process, step by step, and it all has to be recorded. That's good for everyone."

"So the chief was really arrested?"

"Not just him, his wife too. They went through their residence with a fine-tooth comb. They found three hundred kilos of gold alone, I heard. By the way, how many brand name bags have you got?"

"About a dozen."

"Their daughter had more than three hundred."

"That many! Gifts that just fell into her lap, I suppose, while we have to sweat for each cent. But Mr Wang, there are so many medical equipment suppliers, am I really going to win the bid? I finally talked Ying Lihou into meeting you. You've got to help me out on this!"

"All these years I've always helped you out, I've never left you in the lurch. Sometimes I wonder if I'm atoning for some past sin against you."

"You do owe me," says Nianchu, pouting a little.

Wang leans over the desk, stares at Nianchu and lowers his voice to a whisper, "I'll give you the base price. Put in a lower bid and you'll get it for sure."

"What's the base price then?"

Wang reaches over the desk. Instead of taking her hand, he catches her fingertips between his. Nianchu lets him do it, and says with a smile, "You know villagers are supposed to bargain by pinching the other person's fingers to indicate what figure they're offering. Do you do this too?"

"My father was a peasant," says Wang,

"Aiya, that's a quarter of a million gone up in smoke!" exclaims Nianchu, once she has figured out the base price from the pressure on her finger joints. "And I was going to buy you a car too." She draws her hand back and straightens up.

Wang is puffing again. "I don't need your car, I've got a work car. I wouldn't drive it even if you gave me one. I can't drive and I've nowhere to park a car. I'd be eternally grateful if this whole business with Ying Lihou would just go away! Has she read the contract?"

"We're in this together. You choose a time. Should we go to her place, or ask her over here?"

"Call her and ask if she can join us for dinner. It's easier to talk over a meal."

Nianchu picks up the phone and calls Lihou.

Lihou is still feeling depressed. So she leaves her car at home and walks to the Golden Flower Shopping Centre where she scans the merchandise. First, she buys a pair of leather shoes with an Italian logo, then a Hermès scarf and a pretty little incense burner. In the cosmetics department, she chooses a Givenchy lip balm, as well as Lancôme face cream and serum.

She takes Nianchu's call. "Darling, we're having dinner with Mr Wang, the hospital director. I've booked the Riverview Mansion by the west section of the moat. We'll have mutton *paomo* tonight."

Just hearing Wang's name rekindles Lihou's rage, but she takes a couple of deep breaths and softens her tone. "I haven't got the car with me today, and the Riverview Mansion is so far away. I'll skip it if you don't mind."

"Please come, we need to discuss things properly with him," Nianchu urges her.

Lihou gives in and hails a taxi. The driver is very chatty and calls her "Gorgeous!" Lihou answers him in monosyllables, then ignores him. He's hitting on me like I'm just a kid, she thinks in annoyance. When they reach the western moat outside the old city wall, the fare is eighteen yuan. Lihou takes out a twenty-yuan note. "Keep the change," she tells him as he rummages for coins. She opens the door and gets out, head held high. When she reaches the Riverview Mansion, she realises that she does not have the big plastic bag with all her purchases in it. She whirls around and searches the street but the taxi is long gone. She is furious with herself.

In the restaurant, Nianchu and Wang greet Lihou with smiles. They chat about the weather, the stock market and the Party chief being hauled in by the Disciplinary Committee. Wang rubs his chin and pulls whiskers out, while Nianchu says how much she likes Lihou's suit.

"Navy blue is a great choice, elegant but not flashy. What material is it? Did you buy it off-the-peg or was it tailored? Nice clean lines, and powerful shoulders too!"

To Lihou, the other two are just trying to ignore the elephant in the room. She replies briefly, then remarks, "It's so hot." She pushes open the window and gazes down at the scenery outside.

In the gathering dusk, the water in the moat is like glass. A breeze ruffles the surface, shattering the glass into a myriad fragments and projecting onto the city wall strange, wonderful images that mutate from silver grey to smoky blue. A few cyclists are riding on top of the wall, three of them on a tandem. It takes around four hours to complete the entire circuit, but these people are not there for exercise. They are just enjoying themselves, stopping to take photos, sometimes poking their heads through the gaps in the battlements, shouting in excitement. They try unsuccessfully to catch the attention of passers-by below. They are reflected in the water of the moat, however, and to the fishermen they look like a string of heads suspended from the parapet. There are children swarming over parts of the wall. The rows of bricks have been laid sloping slightly inwards as they rise, with the edges of the bricks protruding by just about three fingers' width. This offers hand and foot holds, but it is still a risky game. Time after time, a kid gets one or two metres up, only to tumble down – then get up and try again. The winner is now more than four metres from the ground. An old man potters along the tree-shaded path to the foot of the restaurant. He has no facial hair and his wrinkled lips look like a baby's bum-hole. They move as he mumbles something inaudible. The short grass along the path is studded with small blue flowers that gleam like stars fallen from the night sky. The old man has passed the Riverview Mansion and disappeared among some trees. There people sit quietly gazing at the ripples on the water, oblivious to the din of the traffic and the people on the opposite bank.

Singing drifts from an octagonal pavilion in the distance, where a group of amateurs are amusing themselves singing Qinqiang folk opera. They are mostly retired actors and opera lovers who have been practising for decades, and gather every day in their spare time. They need to sing – it keeps them happy and healthy – but it is not a hobby to do at home, it annoys the family and the neighbours. So they come here to scratch the itch. The singing quickly draws devotees who sit on the ground to listen, and reward the exceptional singers with *guacai*. The word used to mean "war commendations", but nowadays it just involves a ten yuan note. A bandy-legged old man does the rounds collecting the money and passing on the accolades to the singer, who comes to the centre, bows and launches into another aria. Cicadas, which have appeared earlier this year than usual, chirr in the trees. They take a break when humans sing, but pick up again whenever silence falls, singing at an ever-higher pitch, and as one cicada stops, another takes up the chirring. The wind gets up, the audience disperses, but the singers keep on. Every now and then, a gust catches a singer in the throat, playing havoc with the aria's rhythm. There is one listener still sitting there, his head drooping on the chest. By now it is completely dark, and the old man collecting donations can no longer see his own bowed legs. "Hey!" he addresses the lone listener. "How can you doze off in this wind?"

Lihou has a strange expression on her face. She is not smiling as she speaks, the way she usually does, nor is she glowering, but her eyes are screwed up, as if they are uncomfortably sensitive to the light. When a plateful of *tuotuomo* is brought to the table, she rests the bowl on her lap and pulls the small flatbreads apart with her fingers, turning to look outside the window from time to time.

"I've got a question for you, gorgeous," Wang begins.

"I'm not gorgeous," replies Lihou coldly.

"Of course you are. People admire slender women with big eyes, arching eyebrows and cherry lips, or they go for big breasts and wide hips, because they think they're good for child-bearing – that's the peasants' mindset. But you're different! You have perfectly symmetrical features, such a sophisticated look. You're the same height as Yan Nianchu, but I've never seen you in high heels. With your broad shoulders, long neck and slender legs, you're the ultimate clothes-horse."

"I'm nothing but a clothes-horse, I haven't got a brain," says Lihou.

Wang chokes on his food. He turns to Nianchu, laughing loudly to cover his embarrassment.

"Lihou always speaks her mind," says Nianchu, trying to smooth things over.

"I like a plain speaker," says Wang. Then he turns to Lihou. "Did you know, gorgeous, why our Dukedom of Qin was able to defeat all six other states in the Warring States period?"

"No idea," Lihou says curtly.

"We had the best stallions, for one, and the food was awesome. On any expedition, our soldiers marched on mutton and *tuotuomo*. Out in the wilderness, they boiled up the mutton, and soaked the pieces of flatbread in the soup. The hot meal was tasty and sustaining, and quick to prepare. When they charged into the enemy's camp, their opponents had barely finished washing and steaming the rice, cleaning and cooking the dishes. Before they took a single bite, everyone was turning tail and running for their lives."

Lihou is unimpressed.

"You're not breaking the flatbread small enough, Ying-jie," Nianchu tells her. "Here, let me. First, break it in half, then do it again. Now, pinch off pieces the size of a mung bean, and make sure each piece has a bit of the crispy outside."

"So much effort to put into a bowl of soup!" says Lihou. "Leave my chunks as they are. I've had dinner, I'll just try a bit to keep you company."

"No matter how little you eat, you've got to do it properly," Wang says. "The old folk around here always order two portions of *tuotuomo* when they come to a restaurant for the first time. The first simmers with the mutton soup while they prepare the second portion of flatbread, which they wrap in muslin and take home with them. The next day, they bring it back to the restaurant and it's ready for the chef to cook for them. While they're waiting, they start breaking up another flatbread into pieces. So at every meal, they're preparing the next day's flatbreads."

Lihou picks up some of her larger pieces and pinches them into smaller bits. They're finally done preparing the flatbreads and a waitress takes the pieces into the kitchen to be cooked in the soup. Lihou takes out a cigarette.

"You smoke too?" asks Wang.

"Yes, when I'm feeling down," answers Lihou.

"Well, I'm on a real downer," says Wang. "For weeks, I've had night sweats and haven't managed a wink of sleep. There's no getting away from it. It's a catastrophe!"

"No need to moan," says Lihou. "I've already agreed with Nianchu, I'm prepared to forget about the unpaid interest. What we need to talk about over dinner is how you plan on paying me back the principal."

Wang stands up, then sits down again, shifting his chair. "Right, Ying Lihou, first of all, let me say how grateful I am to you! Mr Hu may have done a runner but I've been keeping an eye out for him. The moment he shows up, I'll make sure he pays your principal back, not one cent less. If there's no sign of him in six months, a year, eight years, or even if he's dead, rest assured, I'll pay you the principal. I'm the guarantor, I won't walk away from this! But the thing is, I'm pretty stretched, there's no way I can produce ten million yuan now. I'm really hoping you can cut me some slack. I've told Yan Nianchu, and she probably told you, that I can pay you in instalments: one million in the first year, two in the second year, three in the third year and four in the final year."

"That'll make it four years," says Lihou. "I can't wait that long! You might as well give me a teaspoon to eat an ox."

"It will take a long time, Ying-jie, but is there any other way around it?" asks Nianchu. "You did receive a million and a half of interest. If you consider that as interest on your ten million over four years, it's still much higher than any bank could offer. In fact, why not look on it as a bank deposit?"

"Well, what can I say? So be it," says Lihou.

"Did you bring the old contract with you?" asks Wang.

"I've been carrying it around for days," says Lihou.

"Yan Nianchu and I have both brought our copies. Let's tear up the old contract right here, and sign the new one."

They put the documents together. Wang drops the papers on the floor, lights them with his lighter and, when the flames have consumed them, he stamps on the ashes. Nianchu shows Lihou three copies of the new contract.

Lihou checks them and confirms, "What Mr Wang just said is all here."

"Exactly," agrees Nianchu. "Exactly the same as what I told you, all in writing. If you don't have more questions, let's sign it now, and we can each keep a copy."

Lihou goes through the text again and signs her name. Then Nianchu signs, hands Wang the pen, and he signs too.

"I'm just nipping to the toilet," Wang says. Once there, he undoes his flies and starts to pee, exhaling slowly. It sounds as if he is emptying the Yangtze and the Yellow River combined. On his way back, he tosses the pen out of the window.

The room now feels much warmer. Wang slumps into his chair, smoking a cigarette, and offering Lihou and Nianchu one each.

Nianchu declines. "I don't like the thick ones." And she takes out her own packet of slim smokes.

"Too skinny. No kick to them. I go for the thick ones, they are good," says Wang.

"Slim ones are much better," insists Nianchu. They argue the merits of their favourite brands, laughing loudly, neither prepared to back down.

What do we really want? Lihou thinks to herself. Traders want profits, officials want power, a dog wants a bone. Her head feels heavy and achy, and she doesn't join in the bantering. She sits there, takes a few drags, then flips the cigarette on the ashtray. She carries on flipping the butt until no ash is left – if only bad luck could be flipped away so easily.

Three bowls of *paomo* are brought in. Wang takes a bowl from the waitress and places it solicitously in front of Lihou. "Bring us sweet pickled garlic, hot pepper sauce and coriander, quick as you can!" he tells the waitress. "And tissues, a packet of tissues!"

Lihou picks out a morsel with her chopsticks and places it in her mouth. It is scalding. She tongues it frantically but has to spit it out.

"Blow, blow gently on it," says Wang.

Lihou is embarrassed. She bends down and wipes the spit off the floor with a tissue. Then she stirs her soup with her chopsticks to disperse the steam.

"Don't mix it up, you'll make the soup sludgy. Eat the pieces from the outside in," says Wang.

Lihou sits with her mouth open, letting the burning sensation gradually subside.

14. HAI RUO • THE TEASHOP

THEY PART COMPANY at the Riverview Mansion, and Lihou goes home and straight to bed. She sleeps until noon the next day. She feels no desire to get up, and lies there turning things over in her mind. When she was younger, her first thought in the morning was of a man. She was in love back then. But now, her head is churning with the thing she least wants to remember – that contract. Aware that this train of thought is going to make her depressed, she tries to force her thoughts into different channels. What's the weather like today? Has the smog gone? Has it thinned out or thickened? What shall I eat after I get up? Rice porridge with mung beans and coix seed? Or scrambled eggs and a nice cup of milk? That white T-shirt, will it go with the dark blue skirt? Wait, that skirt is patterned, I'll look like a country hick in it. How about that pair of high-waisted harem trousers, or my mint green skirt? Those cute white trainers will go well with that. That reminds me, I bought those trainers at the Capital Trade Plaza with Nianchu after we signed the old contract! That damned contract again. Put it out of your head! But how can I? I mustn't let myself dwell on it, otherwise it'll blow out of all proportion. It's like a sneaky little draught… once it finds its way through the door, it blows into a gale. Just thinking of those trainers is getting me in a state again!

Lihou breaks out in a cold sweat and a surge of rage threatens to overwhelm her. She thinks, I could have raked in a lot of interest by lending out this money. I could have bought another street-front property. Instead I've lost out on the rest of the interest, and I can't get the principal back for four years. What a shambles! And I have no one to blame but myself!

She can no longer lie still, so she decides to take a shower. Then a more sinister thought creeps into her mind: if Wang's friend has done a runner, will Wang really pay me back in four years? Can he? When the original contract was signed, both Wang and his friend swore a solemn oath that they would honour it, and now look what's happened! Is there any guarantee at all that the new contract won't go the way of the old one?

Her heart begins to pound. For years now, whenever Lihou is in a mess, she prays to the Buddha. Burning incense and kowtowing to Shakyamuni, murmuring prayers, has always given her solace. But the Famen Temple is too far away, and so is the Longxing Temple, in the eastern part of the city. Hai Ruo's teashop comes to mind. Why not go and burn incense to the Buddha there?

She calls Hai Ruo and asks where she is.

"At the teashop," says Hai Ruo.

"So you're not out?" asks Lihou.

"Do you want me to be at the teashop or not?" Hai Ruo is confused.

Lihou does not answer immediately. Deep down, she would rather not see Hai Ruo – she might blurt out the contract business and embarrass herself. But she cannot say that she's not going to the teashop either.

"Wait for me," she says. "I've got the plain scholar fans, I'll bring them over." And she drives to the teashop.

Meanwhile, it has been a morning of excitement at the teashop. Shortly after they open for business, Xi Lishui arrives with a man at her side. In front of xiao-Tang, xiao-Zhen and xiao-Su, she tells Hai Ruo that this is Wang Beixing, the boyfriend Yi-laoshi introduced to her.

Before Hai Ruo gets a chance to speak, the others exclaim in delight and applaud. "Our Xi-jie never fails to bring us happy surprises!"

"Lishui always says how wonderful the Sojourn Teashop is, the boss, the sisterhood, and the staff too, so I've come to meet you all!" says Beixing.

"It's not you coming here to check them out, it's for everyone to check you out," Lishui says. "Everyone, any comments, however nitpicking, will be most welcome!"

Beixing is not much of a looker. He has a nice square 国-shaped face, but he is on the porky side. "I work at the Xijing Sports Bureau," he says, smiling politely. "We've got facilities for tennis, badminton, swimming and table tennis, do come anytime you want some exercise."

"Any discounts for us? Or is it free?" chips in Gao Wenlai.

"We do charge a fee," says Beixing.

"Hah! You're a division chief, and you're still going to charge my friends?" Lishui chaffs him.

"Wow! You're a division chief!" exclaim xiao-Tang, xiao-Zhen and xiao-Su in chorus.

Lishui splays her fingers. "He's only the pinkie!"

"I can't bend the rules," says Beixing. "What I can do is to buy you tickets out of my own pocket, and throw in a hot drink for everyone."

There are more cries of enthusiasm. "Haha! Lishui has fallen right into your lap!" someone jokes.

"Lishui is wonderful," replies Beixing.

Hai Ruo takes him to a chair and asks xiao-Tang to make tea. She tries to hush the rest of them. "Mr Wang's in the government. They don't joke around the way we do, don't scare him."

Lishui pays no attention. "Come on, get up!" she orders him. "To the door! Now back to the tea cabinet!" Beixing obeys. "OK, you've shown us your paces and we've seen you from all angles. Off to work with you, I'm staying here. I've got some catching-up to do."

Before he can leave, Hai Ruo instructs xiao-Tang to fetch him two boxes of Maojian tea from southern Shaanxi. Beixing offers to pay, but Lishui stops him. "Don't be so formal. Hai-jie's offering it, so take it."

"But I'm much older than your boss," protests Beixing, smiling back.

"Whatever your age, Lishui treats me like a big sister, so you should too!" Hai Ruo pats Beixing on the shoulder and walks him to the door.

Once he has gone, Lishui asks them, "Well? Does he pass muster?"

This triggers more banter. "He doesn't carry himself like a division head," someone comments. "Officials boss other people around, how come you had him on a lead like a puppy?"

"When a man goes out, everyone notices his head and feet first," adds another. "He'd score with that brilliantined hair and shiny leather shoes! But he's a bit swarthy, don't you think? That's karma for you, Lishui, when you've always been proud of having the fairest skin in the sisterhood!"

"He looks healthy though," someone else says.

"You lot are just jealous," says Lishui. "All I want is a boyfriend, and you all take the piss out of me. The moment I drop him, you'll be all over him, fighting tooth and nail to get him!" She throws her arms around xiao-Tang, laughs, and the others join in.

In the end, Hai Ruo calls Lishui upstairs. "Getting married is serious, don't turn it into a farce," she says sternly.

"I've never been more serious in my life," protests Lishui. "I brought him here so everyone can have a proper look. It's the same as the government publicly appointing and sacking officials."

"But all this leg-pulling and teasing, he might not like it and then what would he think of you?"

"If he judges a book by its cover, I'll be well rid of him – there's no shortage of good men around."

"You're the most unsettled of all of us. You're always finding fault with this and that man, like you're plaiting *mahua* dough! If you like each other, you should take him seriously. Was it Yi-laoshi who introduced you?"

"Uh-huh."

"You see? Yi-laoshi does care about you! Have you bought him the matchmaker's shoes?"

"I brought Beixing for you to check over and if you OK him, then you're our matchmaker too. I'll get you a pair when I buy the shoes for Yi-laoshi!"

After Lishui leaves, Hai Ruo is sorting out the miniature agate vajra pestles when Lihou calls to say she's bringing over the plain scholar jade bamboo fans. Well-timed, Hai Ruo thinks.

"You usually work all day and come for tea in the evening. How come you're free this morning?" she asks when Lihou arrives.

"I miss you!"

"Where did you suddenly acquire the gift of the gab? You didn't use to be such a flatterer!"

"I've come to bring the fans," says Lihou, with a laugh. She takes the fans out of her shoulder bag.

"Anything else?"

"That's all."

Hai Ruo leads her upstairs. The décor seems to have changed slightly. On the long, narrow table on the north side of the room, the statue of the Buddha is now flanked by a small crystal stupa on the left and a pile of thread-bound sutras on the right. In front of the statue is a lower table with an incense burner, a bowl of clean water, a lamp and a vase of fresh flowers on each side.

Lihou scurries over to light a stick of incense and plant it in the incense burner's ashes. She falls to her knees on the square prayer mat facing the lower table. With her palms together, she looks up and mutters.

"What's this all about?" asks Hai Ruo as she pours tea into a cup. "You're in a hurry to say your prayers!"

"I'm asking for Lord Buddha's protection," replies Lihou. She finally stops murmuring, gets up and sits down beside Hai Ruo.

"One burns incense to honour the Buddha, but lights a cigarette to honour oneself. Here, have one." Hai Ruo hands Lihou a cigarette. Lihou lights it. "When you beg the Buddha to get you out of a mess, the Buddha won't grant you your wishes," Hai Ruo continues. "To ask the Buddha for a blessing, you have to ask yourself first."

"But I can't extricate myself," says Lihou. She takes long, deep drags on the cigarette so that its end burns fiery red. Soon, half of it is gone.

"Good heavens, why are you smoking like this! What's happened?"

"Nothing. I just feel empty inside."

Hai Ruo doesn't say anything. She spreads the fans on the arhat couch, then browses the sutras, noting down four-character phrases for Yi Guang to write on the fans:

境界现前 *faced with one's own perceptions*
染净不二 *purity and impurity are one and the same*
阿鞞跋致 *Avinivartanīya*
清风在握 *grasping the wind*
旷野无尘 *a wilderness free of dust*

逸翩独翔 *a lone bird swoops and soars*
高尚其事 *taking pride in what one does*
鸣鹤在阴 *a pair of cranes whoop in the shade*
被褐怀玉 *wearing hessian and holding a jade*
澹然无极 *supreme serenity*
格物致知 *pursue knowledge in depth*
解衣般礴 *stretch out on the ground bare-chested*
得大自在 *attain great freedom*
有孚盈缶 *as brimful of sincerity as a wine jar*
幽闲贞静 *reclusive, leisurely, chaste and serene*

They hear chirps coming from a corner.

"A cricket already?" remarks Lihou.

"We have year-round vegetables, why shouldn't there be insects year-round?" retorts Hai Ruo.

"In this room?"

"Outside the window, maybe."

"We're too high off the ground, a cricket couldn't get this high."

They fall silent again. Hai Ruo goes back to her books, and the pages rustle as she turns them. Lihou finishes her cigarette. "Are you going to listen to me?"

"But you don't want to tell me."

Lihou chuckles, then stops abruptly. "Put your books down, pin your ears back."

Lihou tells her story: Yan Nianchu is an old friend of Mr Wang, the director of the Lotus Dental Hospital. Mr Hu, a friend of Wang's, has been running some big projects – he's into new-builds and he has a vocational school.

"Wang is a good man, so is Hu," Nianchu assured Lihou at the time. "They're both excellent people and have plenty of funds to back them. They've known each other for ten years or more, and given me a lot of help."

Nianchu then explained that Hu was temporarily cash-strapped because he had not managed to sell his latest premises but wanted to expand the school. "Could you loan him ten million yuan? The interest is half a million per month."

And, through Nianchu and Wang, that was just what Lihou did. For the first three months, she did get the full interest, but nothing came in the following month. Then she heard that Hu had disappeared. Apparently, he had borrowed so much from so many people that he was up to his eyes in debt and eventually went to ground to escape his debtors.

Hai Ruo thumbs through a book as Lihou tells her story but puts it on one side as Lihou breaks down in tears. "Oh dear, this is terrible, why didn't you ask any of us for advice? There are so many scams like this but I never thought you'd fall for one!"

"The interest payments were so high that I got greedy," Lihou admits. "Besides, it was Nianchu who involved me."

"So what have you done about it?"

"Nianchu told me there's no hope of getting any more interest now, but she agreed I must recover the principal. She said Wang's willing to pay me back on behalf of his friend, but he doesn't have much money right now, he'll pay me back over four years."

Hai Ruo is tight-lipped. She lets out a long breath. Then she lights herself a cigarette. "So now you're worried whether the principal can be recovered at all?"

"Just thinking like that makes me burn up inside! You've got to help me out, Hai Ruo!"

"Did you think of me when you were raking in the money?"

"Don't you see? That's why I hate myself!" Lihou pounds her own head with both fists.

"Stop doing that. Fists can't make an idiot any wiser. Do you have a contract?"

"I signed one with Nianchu, Wang and Hu. But we've just torn up the original and signed a new one."

"Did you bring it?"

Lihou takes out the document and hands it to Hai Ruo.

Hai Ruo scrutinises the contract word for word, muttering, "The interest is sky-high, didn't you ever smell a rat? If something seems too good to be true, then it is!" She pauses, then goes on, "When you first made the loan, was Wang the direct guarantor?"

"Yes, he and Nianchu were both direct guarantors."

"Hmm, Wang is the direct guarantor all right, but here it says Nianchu is the indirect guarantor."

"What? Nianchu? Indirect guarantor?" Lihou bends over to read the contract. Sure enough, in front of Nianchu's name are the words "Indirect Guarantor". Instantly Lihou's face turns ashen.

"Who drafted it?"

"Nianchu. It was Yan Nianchu who drafted it."

"But why did you sign it without checking?"

"I did check it. But I've been so freaked out since Hu did a runner. All I've thought about is how to get my money back. So the only words I saw on the new contract was how much I'll be repaid each year."

Lihou suddenly erupts in rage. "How can Yan Nianchu do this to me? If it weren't for her, I would never have met Wang, or Hu. I only agreed on the loan because I trusted her, and now she wants to wriggle out of it? How can she do this, Hai Ruo? When everything went to pot, I said I'd just recover the principal, and over four years, because I value our friendship. And she's done the dirty on me! Hai-jie, Hai-jie…" Her outburst ends in floods of tears.

Instead of trying to comfort her friend, Hai Ruo chain-smokes three cigarettes. Lihou curses, then cries some more. Half an hour passes. She grabs a phone on the table all of a sudden and stands up.

"What are you doing?" asks Hai Ruo.

"I'm going to find Yan Nianchu. I need to confront her!"

"You've picked the wrong phone." Lihou stares at the phone in her hand then realises she is holding Hai Ruo's. "What do you plan on doing when you find her?" Hai Ruo asks. "Yell at her? Beat her up? Kill her? You won't get your money back if she's dead!"

Lihou bursts into more tears and slaps her own cheeks. "What a fool I've been, Hai-jie! Nianchu sold me down the river and all I did was help her count her profits! Please help me, Hai-jie. That money is all the savings I've got. They've got me trapped. If they say they can't afford to pay me back, I've got no money to live on! I've never treated anyone in the sisterhood so badly. If Yan Nianchu asked me for a jacket, I'd give her the trousers as well. She lured me to a cliff, watched me fall into the ravine, and it wasn't enough for her to turn her back on me, she got some branches to sweep away all her footprints!"

"Nianchu's not the kind of person to set you up intentionally," Hai Ruo says. "It's a knee-jerk reaction to protect herself. I'll talk to her. At this point, she's going to have to fight your corner for you, whatever the costs. She must get Wang to pay you back."

"What if he doesn't?"

"Trust our friendship."

"You want me to trust our friendship?"

"I'll be asking Nianchu to do the same."

Lihou sobs and sobs, until she eventually calms down.

An hour later, Hai Ruo sees Lihou off. "You have to talk to Nianchu, Hai-jie, I'm out of my mind with worry," are Lihou's parting words.

"I'm more anxious than you are!" says Hai Ruo. "This is about much more than the ten million yuan. Our sisterhood can't afford to lose anyone." Lihou puts her arms around Hai Ruo. "There, there," Hai Ruo says soothingly. "Once you get back home, hang a mirror on the wall facing the front door."

"Is that to drive away bad luck?"

"No, it's for you to take a good look at yourself."

15. EVA • THE CLOUD-GATHERING HALL

SOON AFTER SHE ARRIVES at the teashop, Hai Ruo gets a phone call. A multitude of expressions chase each other across her face. She speaks softly, chuckling from time to time. Gao Wenlai, xiao-Tang, xiao-Zhen and xiao-Su creep around, afraid to make a sound, their eyes on her. Finally, they hear Hai Ruo say, "Thank you... Please give my regards to…" but they can't make out the name.

"Who's calling her?" whispers Wenlai.

"Don't be so nosy!" says xiao-Tang.

"There's an aura over her head, it must be something good."

"I'm sure it is."

When she gets off the phone, Hai Ruo tells them that the Xijing authorities are holding another convention to attract investment funds, and need two hundred canisters of Houkui tea.

"Whoa! That's a big deal!" exclaims Wenlai.

"Come on, let's get the tea ready," says xiao-Tang.

The shop hums with activity. One after another, bags of top-grade Houkui are packed into elegantly-designed cardboard canisters. xiao-Zhen puts an "Exclusive Domain Tea" sticker on each, and Eva stamps the label with the Sojourn Teashop's seal. They stack the canisters into four large boxes and load them into Hai Ruo's car. She hands xiao-

Tang the key. "Take them to the Haiqing Hotel, that's the convention venue."

"Did Mr Qi get us this deal?" xiao-Tang asks in a low voice.

"No," replies Hai Ruo.

"I thought the Party chief just came a cropper! Why are they holding a convention at this juncture?"

"Where did you hear that?"

"From some of our clients. I wanted to check with you."

"Hmm..." Hai Ruo is non-committal.

"I hope it's not going to involve Mr Qi," says xiao-Tang, sounding anxious.

"I called him, but he's not picking up. No, it shouldn't affect him. This is a city government convention, not a Party Committee event." Hai Ruo hands xiao-Tang a gift card.

"For General Secretary Ning again?"

"Yes, he's been looking after us."

"The same amount in the card? But they've only ordered two hundred canisters. Should we charge them a bit more per canister?"

"No!" says Hai Ruo, poking xiao-Tang in the forehead with her finger. "You're so tight-fisted!" She calls Wenlai and says, "You go with xiao-Tang. And take a few more canisters of tea. You can drop some off with Mr Wu on your way back. Ask if he's finished his retreat, and when the Living Buddha's arriving."

xiao-Tang and Wenlai spend the better half of the day driving around the city. They come back with ten jars of chilli bean paste and a bagful of steamed buns. Hai Ruo has been out too, and is flipping through the photos on her phone for the others to see. She has captured the shadows of old pines cast by sunlight on a roadside wall.

"Why shadows?" asks Wenlai, peering over others' shoulders.

"Can't you see how the shadows of the crisscrossing branches stand out, and throw the light and shade into sharp relief?" says Hai Ruo.

"Oh," Wenlai grunts.

"Mr Wu is still on retreat," xiao-Tang reports. "They don't have a specific date for the Living Buddha's arrival. But his staff gave us the chilli bean paste and the steamed buns as a present. It's all Qinling Mountain farm produce."

"The sourdough makes tiny holes in the buns so they're light and elastic. They're heavenly with chilli bean paste," says Wenlai.

Hai Ruo gives everyone a bun. They split them, spread the spicy paste inside, and take a large bite. They really are a delicacy. As they munch the snack, Wenlai asks Hai Ruo, "But where did you get the idea of taking pictures of tree shadows?"

"I've been learning how to draw, but I've never managed to do a passable sketch, even when I'm sitting right in front of a tree," says Hai Ruo, with a smile. "I decided it was easier to draw them from their shadows."

"If Hai Ruo's in a toilet which has marble floor tiles, she sees images of people in the patterns," says xiao-Tang.

"She's right! Art and literature are both built on observation and imagination," says Wenlai.

"That's a good way of putting it!" says Hai Ruo. "Let me ask you a question now: have you been to the thicket of *huai* trees by the eastern moat?"

"I was there once. You couldn't move for courting couples. I never went there again."

"Did you see patches where the grass has been worn down to the roots, but a couple of sunflower seedlings are growing nearby? And what do you make of that?"

"I never saw anything like that. Even if I did, I'd probably think that some goats had eaten the grass down, and someone sowed the sunflower seeds."

"Hah! I can tell you've never had a girlfriend."

"I did once, but she wanted a house and a car, which I couldn't afford, so it all went pear-shaped."

Eva, xiao-Tang and the others burst out laughing.

"Just imagine, once upon a time, a couple might have sat on that very spot on their first date," Hai Ruo continues. "The boy says something, and the girl is so shy she turns away and starts pulling out grass stems without being aware of what she's doing. That makes a bald patch in the grass. Meanwhile, the couple are eating sunflower seeds, until the wind gets up and there's a sudden shower. The couple beat a hasty retreat. The rain flushes the sunflower seeds into the soil, including some that never got roasted and still have a live kernel. And soon enough, they germinate."

"You must have done creative writing, Hai-jie!" exclaims Wenlai.

"Actually, I haven't, but I do like reading."

"You've got a way with words!" Wenlai exclaims in admiration.

"Leave some of the buns and paste, don't scoff them all," says Hai Ruo. "Eva, take two buns and a jar to Yi-laoshi, please."

"OK," says Eva. She knows that Yi Guang's studio is in the housing estate behind the teashop, but is not sure which building.

"It's 1501, Unit Three, Building Two," recites Wenlai.

"How do you know?" asks Hai Ruo.

"Those people who came with the books for Yi-laoshi to sign, they said so."

"Good thinking. Then you can take Eva there, but don't hang around, come back straight away and don't keep him from his writing," Hai Ruo instructs them.

After Wenlai's fight with Fan Bosheng, Hai Ruo gave him a severe telling-off, but she did not dock his wages or make him pay for the broken teacup, even though it was hand-painted by a master craftsman. Instead, she kept him away from the customers and gave him all the chores to do –mopping the floor, carrying water and boxes, cleaning the toilet, taking out the rubbish and directing customers in cars to the parking spaces. So today Wenlai is elated that Hai Ruo has sent him to Yi Guang's along with Eva. From his shoulder bag, he takes out some newly-composed poems and slips them inside his jacket. He takes Eva there, and they get into the lift all the way to the top floor.

When the doorbell rings, Yi Guang is sitting on the toilet, grunting and straining because he suffers from severe constipation. "All right, don't come out then," he mutters to himself, getting up to answer the door.

He opens up, to see Eva. "What a surprise! Welcome!" he exclaims in delight, giving her a big hug and patting her on the back with both hands. Then he spots Wenlai standing to one side, holding a plastic bag.

"Good morning, Yi-laoshi!" the young man greets him.

"I see you've brought a bodyguard?" remarks Yi Guang.

Eva explains, "Someone gave Hai-jie some chilli bean paste and steamed buns and she asked me to bring you some. Wenlai came to show me the way."

"Ah, goodies! Wonderful!" he says, showing them into the flat. The sitting room is cramped. It is gloomy too, since all the curtains are tightly drawn. He switches on the light.

"This is a pilgrimage for me," beams Wenlai. "Thank you for letting me visit your home."

"It's not my home, it's my studio," Yi Guang corrects him. "I usually come here in the morning, and go home in the evening. Don't thank me, thank Eva. Are you working at the teashop now, Eva?"

"Yes. It means I get to spend more time with Hai-jie, and I'm picking up more knowledge about tea," says Eva.

"And with all this knowledge, are you going to open a teashop in St Petersburg?"

"Oh, I don't know if I could do that," Eva says, modestly.

"Why don't you open a Western restaurant here?" says Yi Guang. "The Chinese love Western cuisine nowadays. I can find a place for you with a good shopfront, and I can bring groups to spend their money there every day."

"Really? And do you like Western food?"

"I do, and wine and coffee too."

Wenlai can't get a word in edgeways, so he admires the décor as they talk. "Amazing!" he mutters. "I can imagine Yi-laoshi writing his great works in a place like this!"

"I write in that room just in there, go and have a look," Yi Guang says.

Wenlai goes into the study. Then they hear a cry, "Wow, oh my god, can I take some photos, Yi-laoshi?"

In the sitting room, Eva is admiring a cabinet that sits against the east wall of the room. Inside the locked glass doors are shelves with stacks of books, in front of which are antiques, strange-looking rocks and figurines. Then she turns around, props herself against the cabinet and looks at another one against the opposite wall.

"Fine, take whatever photos you like." Yi Guang calls to Wenlai. He goes to stand beside Eva and drapes one arm over the cabinet.

Eva is fascinated by the curios in front of her. "It seems strange that you're so into your national culture and love Western food too," she says.

"There's no contradiction in that," he replies. Then he adds, "You're beautiful!"

"Thank you," says Eva, turning to look at Yi Guang. His answering gaze is soft. "But I'm not really beautiful. I've got freckles, can you see them?"

"Your freckles are pretty too. Beautiful women in ancient China used to paint moles on their faces."

He makes as if to touch the freckles on the bridge of her nose, then suddenly pushes Eva back against the cabinet door and presses his lips against hers.

Eva is taken completely by surprise. She catches her breath, her eyes widen, and her cheeks turn crimson. A long minute passes before he lets her go. Eva is panting.

"What? Why?" she exclaims. "You're my mentor, my laoshi!"

"So what? Hasn't anyone kissed you before?"

"But you should have asked me! You pounced on me... you never gave me a chance to say if I wanted it!"

"But I mean it, Eva, I admire you, the way I admire a lovely flower."

"But this flower doesn't belong to you, laoshi!"

"I see its beauty and I smell its fragrance!"

"Are all scholars lecherous?"

Yi Guang laughs heartily, then calls, "Wenlai, come and take a picture of us!"

Wenlai comes out of the study. "Yi-laoshi, I always imagined your desk must be huge, but it's tiny."

"Your mouth is tiny, considering the amount of food you put through it in a lifetime," Yi Guang retorts. "Eva, let's take a photo."

Eva is still red in the face. "Excuse me, I'm rather hot, I need to use the toilet."

"The blush becomes you," murmurs Yi Guang.

Eva goes anyway. Her heart thumps fast and loud. "You so-and-so!" she mutters to herself. Her lipstick is smudged, making her lips look fat. She hurriedly rubs them clean, then washes her face and reapplies her make-up before coming out for the photo with Yi Guang.

Wenlai talks on and on as he focuses and clicks. "Yi-laoshi, what I can't figure out is, your books have so many characters and such convoluted plots, but they're all carefully laid out and crystal clear, full of vivid details. How do you do it?"

"Easy. I just close my eyes, things come to me, and I jot down the scenes as they take shape. Make sure you pay attention to the composition in the photos."

Wenlai takes a step forward, then back, crouches down, then raises himself on his toes, and clicks one photo after another. "Hah, what you just said will infuriate a lot of writers!"

"Are we done?" Eva interrupts. "We shouldn't take up any more of Yi-laoshi's time. Let's go."

"You haven't seen my study. Come and pay it a visit," says Yi Guang. He guides her in and explains in detail the history, provenance and artistic value of each objet d'art, and how he acquired it. Then he steers her towards the attic.

"There's more upstairs?" Wenlai says, trotting after them. Through the attic's glass roof, they can see the sky and a lone cloud drifting by. Wenlai exclaims in admiration.

"You seem to have a poet's sensibility, Wenlai," remarks Yi Guang.

"Actually, I do write poems." Wenlai produces some papers from his inside pocket. "Your generous guidance would mean so much to me, Yi-laoshi. Could you see if I have what it takes to be a writer?"

"You'll know that better than me," says Yi Guang.

"But how?"

"When you go to dinner with someone you don't know and they serve you a bowl of rice, you know if you can finish it. If you know you can't but you take it and start eating, you're going to leave them half a bowl of wasted rice."

"You're right," agrees Wenlai, but he hands Yi Guang the poems anyway.

"Did you show them to Eva?" Yi Guang asks.

"Yes, and I felt like I was trudging through a swamp! It was exhausting," says Eva.

"What do you mean?" cries Wenlai.

But Eva has found something far more interesting, the large desk Yi Guang uses for calligraphy and painting. She picks up the brushes, paperweight, bamboo knife, seals and pigment boxes one by one for a closer look. Then she bends over to examine a porcelain bowl full of clean water.

"That's called a *bixi*," explains Yi Guang. He sticks the poems on a shelf.

"*Bixi?*" asks Eva.

"It's where you rinse the brushes."

Eva picks up a porcelain frog with a long protruding tongue crouched by the inkstone.

"You fill its belly with water, which trickles out of its mouth. You can use it to dilute the ink and lighten the tone. It's called *dishui*, a water-trickler."

"What a long tongue, yuck!"

"Eva, let me write you something on a fan to commemorate your first visit," says Yi Guang, bringing out a round fan from beneath the desk.

"No, thank you," says Eva.

"You don't want it!" Wenlai is incredulous. "Yi-laoshi's calligraphy is priceless! A large four-*chi* piece goes for over a hundred thousand, a fan costs between twenty and thirty thousand!"

"Forty thousand," Yi Guang corrects him.

"Really? So expensive? All the more reason why I shouldn't accept it," says Eva.

Yi Guang chuckles. "But I insist," he says. He fetches a slender brush, dips it in ink, and writes a line of tiny characters from top to bottom on the fan:

Amid a fragrance of peach blossom, a fair maiden arrives.

"What does it mean?" asks Eva.

"Have you heard of Liu Rushi?"

"Is that a person?"

"I know who she was, a Ming dynasty poet and courtesan!" says Wenlai eagerly.

Yi Guang glares at him and turns back to Eva. "It describes a lovely woman walking through a peach orchard in full bloom in spring. You could say the flowers burst into blossom the moment she sets foot in it."

"Is that about me?" asks Eva.

"Exactly," confirms Yi Guang.

Eva accepts the fan, and asks Wenlai to take a photo of her.

The three of them head down the stairs single file, with Wenlai in front. Eva looks up from the fan and turns to Yi Guang behind her. "Thank you for this."

Yi Guang leans forward in the hope of snatching another kiss, but too late – Eva is already on the step below.

As his guests prepare to leave, Yi Guang finds some newspaper to wrap the fan, then puts the package in a paper bag. "Don't let anyone at the teashop see this fan, Eva."

"Why not? They can share my appreciation of it," says Eva.

"They'll just be annoyed that I never wrote them anything quite like this."

"Not even for Hai-jie?"

"Well, I did, soon after we met."

"When you first met her? Like what happened to me today?"

"What an idea!"

But Wenlai is asking, "What did you write? Was it 'The phoenix dwells close to the sun, the crane dreams of living in the clouds'? Or 'Sunlight brings the springtime to the earth, a rain shower settles the flying dust'?"

"Someone's done his classical homework," Yi Guang acknowledges with a nod. "I wrote, 'The scholar gets older, the beauty retains her looks'."

"Wonderful!" Wenlai claps his hands warmly. "Who wrote that?"

"I did," says Yi Guang.

"And what does it mean?" asks Eva.

Yi Guang smiles, but says nothing.

Before they leave, Yi Guang says, "There is something I want to ask you for, Eva."

Eva is confused. "But I didn't bring anything."

"You have it with you. A hair, may I ask for a hair of yours?"

"Hair?"

"As a keepsake."

Eva gathers her hair to the front, picks one and pulls it off. Yi Guang raises the hair above his head for a better look, then twirls it around a finger, knots it and places it in a little pottery bottle. He opens one of the cabinets and puts the bottle inside.

When they are downstairs, Wenlai remarks, "Yi-laoshi is so romantic!" Eva remains quiet. "What a gentle, warm man!" Wenlai exclaims again. Still Eva does not reply.

16. HAI RUO • THE TEASHOP

IN THE EVENING, Hai Ruo goes for moxibustion treatment at the TCM clinic opposite the housing estate where she lives. Back home, she turns off her phone before going to bed. She is looking forward to sleeping in as the teashop is closed on Sundays. However, she wakes up at 4.30 am, and cannot get back to sleep. She stares at the window. Outside, under the lintel, there is no sign of movement in the swallows' nest.

It was the year before last when she first noticed the birds. They were just building their nest. To have swallows in a big city, and to have them nesting in the worsening smog, is a lasting delight to Hai Ruo. "A household can have no better auspice than a swallow building its nest or flowers blossoming on a beam," Hai Ruo has read somewhere in the classics. That first year, she checked every inch of the ceiling where wood was exposed, but found no mysterious blossoms, and worried that the swallows might give up, and go and check out better sites. For two weeks, she didn't dare touch that window. However, luckily, ever since the nest was finished, the swallows have been returning every year. This spring, they arrived twelve days early. Every time she contemplates her feathered neighbours, a saying from Laozi comes to mind: "Swallows are above and beyond". Swallows come close to humans, but they don't mingle with us like cats or dogs do. They perch on the door lintel, roof beam or window frame, keeping a respectful distance.

Eventually, Hai Ruo gets up. She pours hot water into some milk powder, adds rolled oats and has her breakfast. "A swallow lives better than I do," she mutters. Then she heads out to the teashop.

Even at such an early hour, the streets are bustling with people and an endless stream of cars passes by. One cannot say a new day begins to unfold, she thinks, because the earthly world never ceases its spinning. It suddenly occurs to Hai Ruo to wonder where all the millions of people live in this city. Why hasn't she heard of anyone mistaking someone else's home as their own? She takes in the forest of high-rises, their myriad windows already lit up. These concrete behemoths seem to her full of emptiness, sunyata.

The sky has still not brightened when she reaches the teashop. Instead of going inside, she heads for the dawn market behind it. Mr Wu has a *qing* chiming stone in his Buddhist sanctum. It came from the dawn market, he told her. She rarely comes so early, so it'd be nice to find a *qing* for her room upstairs the teashop. The dawn market happens so early that you can barely make out the sellers and buyers. There is only a rippling sea of bodies and a low murmur of voices. Hai Ruo wanders around the market. No chime stones, but she spots a brass gong. It dates all the way back to the Ming dynasty, the seller claims, and he bought it from the family of a night watchman who centuries ago beat it as he patrolled the streets and announced the hours. Hai Ruo doesn't care if the story is true or not, she is delighted with the gong – its former master was always up early, reassuring citizens that all was in order. She carries the gong back to the teashop.

To her surprise, she finds the door open and xiao-Tang and Gao Wenlai rolling up the bamboo blinds and wiping down the windows. xiao-Tang tells her she got a call at five in the morning from the Neighbourhood Office.

"Are you the owner of the Sojourn Teashop?" they asked.

"No I'm not, our boss is Hai Ruo. I'm Tang Yingying, a shop assistant," she told them.

"The teashop gave us two mobile numbers, one's turned off, so I'm trying the other," complained the woman. Then she goes on, "It doesn't matter whether you're the boss or not, we have an urgent instruction. The mayor's coming on an inspection this morning. All the work units and private businesses in our area have to start a clean-up outside their premises at six o'clock. Your teashop is responsible for the road and square outside your frontage. Clear up all the rubbish, dust the benches and make sure there's no waste paper, plastic bags or dead twigs and leaves in the holly bushes."

"Good heavens!" exclaimed xiao-Tang. "Why not order the smog to disperse while you're about it?"

"What was that?" the woman said. "Hello?"

xiao-Tang hurriedly put the phone down. She got out of bed and called Hai Ruo, but her phone really was turned off, so she called Wenlai.

"The mayor can go ahead and inspect anytime he wants," xiao-Tang tells Hai Ruo. "But it's ridiculous for the Neighbourhood Office to make such a fuss about everyone cleaning up in advance."

"Just finish what you're doing, then go home and grab some sleep," says Hai Ruo and she goes upstairs.

She hangs the gong at the head of the stairs. The room is dim in the early morning light and all the furniture and ornaments seem fast asleep. She strikes the gong three times and smiles, imagining to herself that the loud, ringing tones arouse everything, making them vibrate until they become sentient, awakening their functions and investing them with an aura of energy. From now on, I'll strike the gong three times as soon as I arrive, Hai Ruo tells herself.

At this, xiao-Tang pounds up the stairs. "A van's just stopped, and it's full of houseplants, money trees, devil's ivy, orchids and calla lilies. Should we buy some?"

"Yes, our money tree's looking a bit poorly, get a new one. How many calla lilies do they have?" Hai Ruo asks.

"Two big bunches."

"Get them all! I have time, I'll trim them and fill a few vases."

xiao-Tang goes out and asks the man if he will swap the old money tree for a new one. If so, she'll buy all the calla lilies he's got. They haggle, then lug the pot with the new money tree into the shop, carry the old one out and take the bunches of lilies upstairs. Hai Ruo pays the seller and xiao-Tang sees him to the door.

"It wasn't a wasted trip, we've got ourselves a new tree!" says xiao-Tang happily.

"You're the only rake with any teeth in our shop!" jokes Hai Ruo.

"This rake has teeth, but our cash box has no bottom!" xiao-Tang retorts.

"Are you trying to say I'm extravagant?"

"You're dead right. Our teashop makes good money, but you spend it like there's no tomorrow."

"That's why I can't do without you!" laughs Hai Ruo.

xiao-Tang chuckles. "I'll boil some water for tea."

"Don't bother, I don't want tea."

"Maybe you don't, but the God of Tea does."

xiao-Tang boils the water downstairs in the cubicle. She prepares a cup of tea and places it in front of the statuette of the tea master Lu Yu, then places her palms together and bows three times. She makes another cup and carries it upstairs. Hai Ruo is trimming the calla lilies. xiao-Tang puts the cup down and goes back to wiping the tables and mopping the floor.

Wenlai gets a broom and sweeps the steps outside the shop, then begins to sweep the little square. The sky brightens as if it has just opened its eyes, and the first burst of sunlight gilds the rooftops behind the teashop. There is hardly any smog, but the PM2.5 reading on his phone's air quality app is alarmingly high. "There's no such thing as a fine day any more," Wenlai mutters to himself. Then he sees some people emerging from the alley down the side of the shop. He can tell a government official from a customer straight away. This group are striding along, legs wide apart, arms swinging and faces sombre. If they aren't here to collect taxes, Wenlai figures, they must be here about public security or street hygiene. He pretends not to know who they are, but watches them going into the shop as he waves a customer into a parking space.

"Back, more... more!" he directs the driver.

There is a crunch as the car's rear bumper hits the steps. "Why weren't you looking!" the driver says angrily.

But Wenlai keeps his mouth shut. He is much more worried about their visitors and, putting the broom down, he goes in after them.

Inside, Hai Ruo is asking, "Has the mayor arrived?"

"He's been and gone," says a man with a leather briefcase tucked under his arm.

"I've been outside the whole time, but I didn't see the mayor!" remarks Wenlai.

"You know the mayor?" asks the man.

"No, but when he shows up, he brings a whole retinue with him," says Wenlai.

The man stops paying him any attention and turns to Hai Ruo. "The mayor likes unannounced inspections. He gets himself driven around, stopping for a quick look here and there. He didn't get out in our area, or even stop, so that means he was satisfied."

"So this unannounced inspection, how did you know in advance?" Hai Ruo presses him.

"I get wind of these things."

"Then perhaps you could let us know a bit earlier next time. If we'd cleaned things up last night, it wouldn't have caught us off guard this morning," says Hai Ruo.

"We told you early enough!" says the man. "We only got the tip-off an hour after midnight. This mayor is a workaholic, he's known for making decisions around midnight and summoning his men right then and there."

"Does he ever sleep?" Wenlai interjects.

But the man is telling Hai Ruo, "Unless you're super-fit, you won't reach the top rung of the official ladder!"

"Yeah, but power keeps you healthy too," says Hai Ruo.

They fill a canister of tea for each of the visitors before they leave.

"Huh! They keep us at it all morning, and the inspection's over without the mayor even showing up!" grumbles Wenlai when the group is gone.

"Do you want to do some more cleaning?" xiao-Tang rebukes him.

"Go home and catch up on your sleep," Hai Ruo urges them, and she takes out 200 yuan and gives them each a hundred. Tang refuses it, and Wenlai follows her example. Hai Ruo insists. "The others didn't come, only you two. You've worked overtime, just take it!" She shoves them out of the door, locks it from inside and goes back upstairs.

By now, the streets are drenched in sunlight. In the square by a clump of trees, a dozen middle-aged women are doing their dance exercises. They have red sashes tied around the waist and hold large gaudy fans as they perform the simple, repetitive moves. Perhaps these exercises are addictive, the way opium is. But then so many things are addictive. Eating, drinking alcohol and tea… And as for gossip, just look at those country girls gathering under the cherry blossom trees with their dogs. They're in Xijing to earn money and they're still single, but they're keen to find a suitable mate for the dog – of the same breed, of course, so that the progeny are pure-bred. As the dogs sniff around each other, the girls stand holding their leashes, chatting about getting better jobs, the fluctuations of the stock market and the ever-rising rents.

"Everything is so expensive in the city, and now you need to pay for bottled water and air purifiers, too!" one laments.

Then they move on to discussing whether, if they quit their jobs, they would be better off starting an e-commerce channel, or becoming influencers. They cannot decide, and instead begin to exchange whispered comments about the gnarled old man sitting on the bench in the square.

"He's a scientist," says one under her breath. "Apparently, he never retired. He still works at some nuclear research institute."

"You mean, atom bombs?"

There are squawks of astonishment and they look at the old man with new respect, until one remarks, "What a pity, nothing brilliant in this world is ever put to actual use."

Upstairs in the teashop, Hai Ruo has finished trimming the flowers, leaving a pile of leaves, stems and roots. She stands up and flexes her muscles to ease them, then picks up the phone to call Yan Nianchu. The teashop is shut and all is quiet. It would be a good moment for a serious talk. But Nianchu's phone is switched off. By the time she has cleared away the mess and arranged the vases, half an hour has passed. She tries Nianchu's number again, still without success. For the last seven or eight years, Hai Ruo has on occasion turned off her phone before bedtime, whereas Nianchu always claims she will answer any call 24/7. Why is her mobile off in the middle of the day? What a ton of trouble you've caused, and now you won't even answer the phone, she thinks, suddenly uneasy.

She brings out the *guqin* and decides to play *A Fisherman Singing at Dusk* to calm her nerves. She has learned the exquisite Tang dynasty melody by heart, but today the rhythm remains elusive. The images should be of a small boat gliding nearer under the bright moon, rowed by an old fisherman. But the plying of the oars under her fingers is jarring and the boat is not drifting across placid water, it is being jolted against the rocks. She leaves the instrument on its table and goes to the writing desk to leaf through the classic *Painting Manual of the Mustard Seed Garden*. But after a few pages, she is bored again and sits on the couch where she runs her hands over the beads and scholar fans.

She grunts, and smiles at herself. Lately, she has been feeling increasingly jittery. She is assailed by worries. She is not far off the menopause. Is it going to warp her personality? Yi Guang once pontificated that "a good woman should be tranquil as well as pure". But Hai Ruo rarely finds tranquillity these days. There are a ton of things to attend to, how can she? She has so many spiritual and emotional needs, but they are irreconcilable with the baggage of everyday life. It's as if someone is obsessed with losing weight but has kidney trouble – to treat the kidneys, you need hormones, which in turn make you put on weight. Hai Ruo cannot see her way forward. Should she focus on the big things and let the little things take care of themselves, or vice versa? It is her anguish that led her to convert to Buddhism. Since her initiation, Hai Ruo has often joined other lay followers at Mr Wu's shrine, and she has offered to host the Living Buddha. But recently, things have not gone smoothly: she has not been told if or when the Living Buddha is arriving, her son has let her down again, Xia Zihua has taken a turn for the worse, and now Ying Lihou is distraught that Nianchu has altered their contract. On top of all this, she feels a growing unease that the Xijing Party chief's downfall might implicate Mr Qi as well. She knows full well that she is neither powerful nor particularly capable. She feels like a well down which people have chucked so much stuff that she is nearly filled to the brim.

Hai Ruo scoops up beads in both hands. She picks through them and finally settles on ten, which she begins to thread. But somehow she cannot get the cord through the hole. She reaches for the magnifying glass and knocks the bowl of beads with her elbow. It falls to the floor with a crash and the beads scatter, leaping and rolling in all directions. Just then, a couple of bees squeeze in through the gap in the window frame and buzz insistently around the room. Hai Ruo sits down. She does not pick up the beads or swat the bees. She takes out a cigarette and lights up.

Half-way through the cigarette, she calls Xiang Qiyu, who is looking after Zihua at the hospital.

"Hey, you're early today!" says Qiyu.

"How's everything?" Hai Ruo asks.

"I assume you're asking about Zihua. I can see you don't care if I got any sleep last night, or if I had any breakfast," Qiyu complains.

"It sounds like Zihua must be doing OK."

"She's not," says Qiyu, lowering her voice. "She seems to be worse than a few days ago. She won't sit up even when I try to help her. She's just lying there."

"Is she still half-asleep a lot of the time?"

"Yes. She woke up towards evening yesterday, saw Xia Lei wasn't here and started weeping again."

"Mrs Qi didn't bring him to see her?"

"They came by in the afternoon, but Zihua wouldn't wake up. Mrs Qi sat there crying, I had to send them away. Then Zihua woke up and asked for instant noodles."

"She shouldn't eat those."

"I didn't think she should either, but she insisted. She said she was desperate for noodles. So I made her a bowl, but she only took a mouthful."

"Did you tell the doctors? What did they say?"

"They said they've been doing their best, and they are giving her the best medication available in the country. All we can do is to keep her under observation and hope for a miracle."

Hai Ruo falls silent and cuts the call. It occurs to her that she could really do with a drink. She runs over to the cabinet and grabs a bottle of expensive, high-proof *baijiu*, China Red Xifeng. Back upstairs, she begins to swig it straight from the bottle. There are no titbits in the teashop to go with it, except for the dried fruit and nuts they offer with the tea and it's too much of a hassle to go back down again for them. In no time at all, the bottle is half empty. Her head is heavy, her eyes are glued together and the muscles in her face feel wooden. She slips sideways and falls flat. The bottle slips out of her grasp and rolls away, not onto the floor, but towards the back of the couch. It comes to rest against the backboard and the liquor glugs out. Hai Ruo looks at the bottle, eyes glazed. The bottle must be drunk, too, and it's leaking transparent blood.

In her drunken state, Hai Ruo has a sudden desire to make contact with her friends and family. She grips her phone hard, as if it is the only thing saving her from drowning.

First, she calls her cousin, who works for Mr Qi. A fortnight ago, he went to Fujian Province to check out a building project and offered to source some tea for her.

"I'm still in Fujian," says her cousin. "This year the yield is low for the Four Great Tea Cultivars, but the quality is even better than previously. I got fifteen kilos each of White Cockscomb and Golden Turtle, twenty-five kilos of Iron Arhat, and twice the amount of Big Red Robe. They're all packed up and with the courier. You should have them in a couple of days."

"What about your boss?" asks Hai Ruo. "Where is he? I haven't been able to reach him for days, his phone is always off."

"The day before I came to Fujian, he went to Macau. Mr Qi doesn't use his usual mobile when he goes away."

Hai Ruo knows that Mr Qi has been to Macau to gamble several times, and always loses. Why can't he learn his lesson? "Are you sure he's still in Macau?" she pursues.

"I was on the phone with the company office yesterday, he is in Macau."

"Can you get a message to him? He's got to come back!"

"Is something up?"

Hai Ruo takes another swig from her bottle, and chokes. She tries to say an emphatic "Yes!", but it comes out as a feeble croak.

After the call to her cousin, Hai Ruo sits up and suddenly sees that the beam of sunlight coming through the window is teeming with dancing bugs. She leaps up to swat them, and feels like she is flying. Amazing! She wants to share this extraordinary sensation with the sisterhood. In her contact list, she hits some numbers randomly but her finger will not obey her and either misses the numbers totally, or hits two at a time. The phone beeps in protest and she rages at Xi Lishui, Lu Yike, Yu Benwen, Xiang Qiyu, Ying Lihou, Feng Ying, Yan Nianchu, Si Yinan and Xu Qi, yes, and Eva too. "Pick up! Come on, pick up!" Then she pulls herself together and, holding the phone right up to her face, she stares intently at it and presses each number with great care, grumbling, "You go ahead and ignore me. I'll call Yi Guang. Yi Guang will talk to me."

Hai Ruo often turns to Yi Guang when she is upset, and especially when she's had too much to drink. Yi Guang humours her and lets her talk for two or three hours at a stretch. A few times, she has even passed out on his couch. With him, she is all woman, at ease in her body, just like she is in her own bed, or in the bathroom, or in front of the mirror or her dressing table. She listens to him talk and laugh and poke fun at people, and it makes her go soft and lethargic. Her eyes close kitten-like, and she melts into molasses running stickily through his fingers. Yi Guang, however, has always behaved like the perfect gentleman. He has never embraced or kissed her or even shaken her hand since the day they first met. Does Yi Guang not have feelings for me? Hai Ruo wonders. He has so many young women friends, after all, and she's friendly with some of them too. They are all stunning, but she has observed him closely, and she trusts her powers of observation and her intuition: Yi Guang does love me. He has made his views plain more than once. "As soon as a man and a woman have sex," he said, "they either grow closer, or stop seeing each other and become complete strangers." She supposes that Yi Guang has feelings for her and the rest of the sisterhood, but does not want sex to get in the way.

Hai Ruo calls Yi Guang. It rings but he does not answer. What's wrong with them today? Everyone she calls has either turned their phone off or is not picking up. Why won't Yi Guang answer? He should have arrived at his studio by now. He might be at a meeting or some event or other, but even so, he could answer a call. Maybe he's entertaining one of those young women at his studio? She winces at the thought and, in a fit of temper, presses his number again, and then again. *I don't care if he gets annoyed,* she tells herself, rooting around under the couch for her shoes and pushing her feet into them. She's going up to his studio without waiting another minute. Her phone suddenly rings loudly. The vibrations make it spin on the table and she can see the caller's name: Yi Guang. Hai Ruo snatches it up, lets it slip through her fingers, then grabs it again.

He speaks quietly, "Sorry, my phone was on mute, I didn't hear your call."

"Rubbish, you're going cold on me," Hai Ruo accuses him. "You used to call me before I called you, then you wouldn't call me if I didn't call you, and now, you won't even answer my calls. I feel pathetic! What were you doing anyway, putting the phone on silent?"

It sounds like he is laughing. "I was playing mahjong. I've been playing all night and I'm still playing," he whispers.

"Mahjong? I thought you valued your time. Someone like you, playing mahjong all night? Who are you playing with?"

"Three men, including General Secretary Ning," Yi Guang explains patiently.

"Really? Put him on the phone."

"He lost, and then stormed off to work in a huff. One of the other two's in the toilet, the other's gone to wash his face. I lost, too, and I'm just reviewing the game in my head."

He's telling the truth, Hai Ruo can tell. Mr Ning is intelligent and capable, and he's been most helpful to her. But he has an explosive temper, not like Yi Guang, who loses at mahjong and then spends time reviewing his moves. Yi Guang's equable nature is his strong point. "Can I come over?" she asks. "Did you tell Mr Ning about Yike?"

But Yi Guang puts her off. "Now's not a good time. The three of us are going to play some more, and it won't help anyone if you turn up. I've told Mr Ning about it, but he's in difficulties himself. With the chief gone, they're all running scared. No one's going to risk putting in a good word for her."

Hai Ruo is feeling less drunk and wants to say more, but before she can speak, Yi Guang says, "I'm doing my review, I'd better go now." And he cuts the call.

Hai Ruo sighs. What a pity they did not talk for longer, she has so much to tell him. She really wants to hear his reassuring tones as he explains things.

Her phone jingles once more. She picks it up without looking at the caller ID. "You said you were reviewing your game, what's up now?"

"Who's got your back up today?" exclaims the voice at the other end.

Hai Ruo sobers up instantly. It's Lishui.

"Hai-jie, Hai-jie, I'm in so much trouble, please let me come and talk to you!" Lishui implores her.

"Why are you always dumping your troubles on me?"

"But who else can I turn to? No one else in this whole huge city seems to have ears. Who else can I talk to? Do you want me to die bottling it up?"

Hai Ruo sits upright and harrumphs, "You could try drowning your sorrows in drink at home. Or go out for some fresh air."

"I am out. I'm outside the teashop. Are you closed today?"

"I'm upstairs."

"Aiya, you're a true sister to me. You're always there whenever I need you most."

"Worse luck for me. How did I end up with you lot?"

"Come on, there aren't that many of us in the sisterhood. The emperor had to look after the population of an entire empire!"

Hai Ruo makes her way unsteadily down the stairs, the steps feeling like cotton wool under her feet. She opens the door, and sure enough, there is Lishui's car parked outside.

"Lock up and hop in!" Lishui calls.

Hai Ruo obeys, but she is not happy. "Are you sick?" she grumbles.

"If I am, you're my medicine!" Lishui says as she starts the engine. "Have you been drinking? And all on your own? You should have called me!"

"No way. Drinking reduces you to a snivelling wreck. I'd never call you."

"Fine, you can keep your bottle to yourself. But now I've got you in my car, you're meat to my chopping board and I can mince you up how I like!"

Lishui drives around aimlessly, up and down one street after another.

"Where are we going?" Hai Ruo asks.

"Wherever the wheels take us!"

Lishui does not talk about her marriage problems. Instead, she relays what Xin Qi told her.

"You certainly hang out with a clever bunch of people!" says Hai Ruo.

"She is clever," admits Lishui.

"Cowardice is clever, and so is cruelty."

"Do you think I should go to Hong Kong?"

"It seems like it wouldn't take much to persuade you!"

Lishui is distracted for a moment and the front wheel mounts the curb. She spins the steering wheel and the car bumps down onto the road again, making Hai Ruo bounce in her seat. "This isn't bumper-cars!" She exclaims. "It's me here, not a sack of potatoes!"

Lishui laughs. "Then be nice to us! Even the car's finding you a bit brutal... Nah, I can't imagine myself going to Hong Kong, it's a definite no."

"Tell her, she mustn't go either!"

"Xin Qi's had a tough life, but I never thought she'd be so ruthless. I'm beginning to regret getting close to her. I've thought about backing off, but she's so needy. She cries all over me and then I feel sorry for her. The thing is, Hai-jie, she's the kind of person whose love life is always a disaster zone, and I'm stuck with her. I don't know what to do with her."

"Well, you've made her your friend, and she clings to you because you let her."

"Just like I cling to you?"

"Are you telling me your troubles or taking the piss? Get serious!"

"I'll be serious. Go on, please."

"Here's an example," says Hai Ruo. "I used to know this young guy, he couldn't find work after college, so he got a holiday job as a tour guide at the Quhu Lake Scenic Area. Somehow he found out that I was friends with the head of Quhu New District. This guy kept coming to see me, pleading with me to recommend him to the director. I did, and he got a short-term contract. A year later, he got to know a deputy mayor, and tagged along behind him until he got a transfer to the Tourism Bureau. From then on, he was convinced that if he kept on at his superiors, he could get whatever he wanted. He was promoted to section chief, then deputy division chief, but that wasn't enough. He really wanted to be the office director. So he bribed the director of the Tourism Bureau, and at the same time, he wrote anonymous letters slandering his rivals. But then the bureau director was arrested for corruption, there was an investigation and this man was rumbled. He lost his job. Now, your friend here, she might think she needs to do this to survive, tricking the old man in Hong Kong for her own protection, but if she goes on being this ruthless, it's going to end very badly. If we keep putting ourselves first, we actually weaken our position, and we'll never make it to a better place."

"You're right, that's exactly what I've been thinking, but I can't put it in words like you do. Can I bring her to see you and the others some day, and you could perhaps talk to her face to face?"

"All right. Have you met the old man from Hong Kong?"

"Not yet."

"And her husband?"

"Once. A good-looking guy, not very bright though, and a nasty temper. She says he's beaten her up."

"Domestic violence?"

"I've seen her black and blue a few times."

"Poor woman. Same as Feng Ying."

"I'm all for her leaving him. She's moved but she wants to get some of her furniture out and she's asked me for help. If she carries that through, could you find a van and a couple of strong men for her, and rent a small place in your housing estate so she can store her stuff?"

"No need for that, she can just put it in Yinan's furniture warehouse. I can get men and a van to her when the time comes." Hai Ruo pauses, then asks, "Do you happen to know any debt collectors?"

"No I don't. Who's not paid their debts?"

"It's nothing, forget it."

They drive around until almost noon, then stop for ramen noodles. Lishui takes Hai Ruo to the hospital. A fire must have broken out somewhere, the fire brigade sirens are wailing.

17. XIANG QIYU • THE ENERGY TANK STUDIO

XIANG QIYU LEAVES the hospital and goes home. She is free in the afternoon, so she takes Xia Zihua's mother and son for a trip to Quhu Lake. It is huge, covering nearly 700 hectares, and the lake shore is bright with peach and plum trees in flower. It is the height of the cherry blossom season, too. Mrs Qi's legs will not carry her far, and she takes a seat in a lakeside pavilion. Qiyu and Xia Lei chase butterflies on the grass. A dragonfly settles on a nearby rock.

Qiyu amuses the boy by addressing it, "You have a nice rest, Mr Dragonfly, I'm after Miss Butterfly, not you."

The dragonfly keeps quite still and Qiyu grabs it and hands it to the boy. She turns to admire the lake. The wind is whipping up ripples, making the lake surface boil. Troubled thoughts flit across her mind and she frowns.

Qiyu has very fair skin compared with the rest of the sisterhood, and a neat, delicate nose too. But her lips are unattractively thin and she frowns a lot. She has had lip filler injections, and brightens her face with carmine lipstick, but she cannot break the frowning habit. As soon as she furrows her brows, it looks like a caterpillar has crawled between them. "You're such a worrier, you'll make yourself ill!" Hai Ruo once told her.

Qiyu rubs her eyes, stops looking at the lake water and does a few stretching exercises. She glances over her shoulder and sees Xia Lei pulling off one of the dragonfly's wings and throwing it up in the air, but it can no longer fly and falls to the ground. He is just about to pull off the other wing when Qiyu flies into a rage and gives him a terrible telling-off. All her fond feelings for him have evaporated.

Her phone rings. It is Shen, an old friend who works at the Industry and Commerce Bureau. "Are you at your studio?"

"No, I'm out."

"Here I am, bringing you new clients and you're not here. It's too bad," he complains.

"Ask the manager to look after you. I'll be right back," says Qiyu. She drops Mrs Qi and her grandson back at their housing estate. The boy ignores her and she avoids looking at him too. She talks to Mrs Qi instead.

Qiyu used to run a plastics factory with some other people, until it was shut down by the government for polluting the environment. Since then, no matter what she turns her hand to, she has been dogged by bad luck. With great difficulty she managed to wangle a licence to open a pharmacy, but it is not in a good location, and is too small, so it has still not achieved the projected turnover. Then last winter, she took out a loan and opened the Terahertz Energy Tank Studio. So far, it has not attracted many customers but she knows that it takes a year or two for any new business to build up its clientele. In the meantime, she is hard put to keep up with the interest on the loan. Shen has been supportive, coming several times and bringing new customers. When Qiyu reaches the studio, the guests have settled into the tanks for their therapy, while Shen is sipping tea in the lounge.

"Aiya!" exclaims Qiyu. "Don't you want a session?"

"No, not me. All I'm interested in is bringing you more business," says Shen.

"That's why I respect you, you haven't a selfish thought in your head."

"I just wanted to see you."

"Huh, I'd believe you if you said that ten years ago."

"There is only one constant in this ever-changing world – feelings between people. I admired you a decade ago, and my feelings haven't changed. I'm telling you the truth."

"Then the truth is what I'm hearing! Did you bring any women today?"

"When did I ever bring a woman here? No, these are three men. One is a government official and the other two are treating him."

"That's good. Bring more officials, they've got clout. Once they've experienced it for themselves, they can encourage more people to come." She tells the manager to bring Shen a new pot of tea.

The manager brings some premium Longjing, with a lidded bowl on a tray. "My deepest apologies, Mr Shen," she says. "This is my boss's own tea, I'm not authorised to serve it when she's not here."

"Shen is our friend!" Qiyu instructs her. "Any time he brings clients, serve all of them quality tea. And if he's here on his own, everything's on the house."

Shen sips his tea. Then he recites:

The first bowl of tea moistens lips and throat;
The second disperses my melancholy;
The third inspires me to write five thousand scrolls;
The fourth releases sweat through my pores, taking my grievances
  with it;
The fifth cleanses muscles and bones;
The sixth connects me to the immortals;
I cannot drink a seventh, I already feel a cool breeze lifting me...

"Amazing! I never knew you had such literary talents!" says Qiyu.

"I've read a smattering of the classics. This is from the tea writings of Lu Tong," Shen explains.

"I'll copy it down for the boss of the Sojourn Teashop. She could have it written out and displayed in her shop, what a perfect advert!"

"You know her too?"

"We're practically sisters."

"I hear they sell the best tea in Xijing."

"Absolutely," Qiyu confirms, getting up to pour more hot water for his cup, and then pulling open the curtains.

Qiyu's studio is in the southeastern corner of a large compound. Nearly 2,000 square metres are filled with trees of various sizes – pine, willow, cherry blossom, Chinese crab apple, lilac, dwarf elm, pagoda tree and peach. At the foot of the trees, roses, peonies and canna grow. China rose bushes have scrambled up the compound wall and made a dense thicket on top.

"Such a nice spot for your studio," says Shen.

"How so?" asks Qiyu.

"There are so many trees here, and they really understand the environment in which they live."

"Is that so?"

"Once a tree is planted, it never moves, but every tree dreams of flying. See how their leaves are cut like feathers?"

"Are you talking about me or you?" asks Qiyu. "I didn't know you were so knowledgeable."

"I know a few bits and pieces about plants, that's all," Shen chuckles. "I normally don't talk about it, but you get me going. I hope you don't think I'm showing off?"

"I like it when you show off."

And so he does, and Qiyu indulges him. "Slow down, I'm trying to take notes, so I can show off to other people," she says, scribbling on a piece of paper.

Shen begins, "Cherry blossom is the most unconventional. It flowers brazenly before any leaves appear, as if it were pregnant before marriage. Willow is full of affection. In the past, when a scholar set out on a long journey, he'd receive willow branches as a parting gift. When the new leaves bud, the whole willow turns a misty green. The pagoda tree is a liar – many of its flowers are sterile. The toon tree's leaves can be eaten raw or cooked. The pomegranate is sexy! A ripe fruit splits open and reveals the seeds, just like a glamorous woman showing off her cleavage. The walnut cycles between years of good and poor harvests – to get a good harvest every year, you need to ring the bark with a knife. You need to graft the persimmon, too. Otherwise they only have fruit the size of a jujube, called 'soft jujubes'. Do you see that tangle of dodder vine, climbing up that pine? It's parasitic, and yet it seems to cling with real emotion. See that pile of white rocks? Eventually, it'll be covered in moss. You've heard of Ningxia goji berries? It is a prolific plant, one goji bush can bear tens of thousands of berries each year. And its roots extend for scores of metres, nobody has ever dug them out completely. Then there's *suoyang*, which has yang energy and is medicinal. Its roots grow underground all through the winter and produce heat – for thirty centimetres around it above ground, it's always frost-free. Oh, and peonies grow wild in southern Shaanxi. When water boils, it looks like a peony bursting into flower, so the locals call boiling water 'peony water'."

Shen is in high spirits and only stops his botanical musings when the three men emerge from their therapy tanks, and shower and get dressed. He introduces them to Qiyu. The man with whiskers up the side of his face as far as his ears is the official, she learns. Of the two thin men, one is the man's subordinate, the other his friend. The official gets out a cigarette.

"I'm so sorry," says Qiyu hastily. "I don't smoke, and I always forget to offer cigarettes to our guests." She sends the manager to buy some, and goes to make tea for the guests. The thermos is empty and she turns on the kettle to boil some more. She carries the tea tray into the lounge in time to overhear Shen saying something about the official's healthy complexion.

"I had the tank very hot, that might be why," says the official. "The truth is, I'm not in good health. I've had too much to do for years, and I'm exhausted. I'm under so much pressure, and it's sent my cholesterol, blood sugar and blood pressure sky-rocketing."

"It is a difficult job you've got," Shen says.

"You're not kidding!" the official's subordinate exclaims. "We've just had an inspection team from Beijing, and that means meetings, interviews, reports, dossiers... and taking them to inspect a dozen *danwei* units. We've been working non-stop day and night for nearly two weeks. I'm shattered."

His boss has been sipping his tea and smiling. Now he puts the cup down and says, "We're among friends so I'll be frank. It's the hardest thing to behave well *and* be an official. You get a stiff neck, what with looking up to your superiors looming above you, and down on your juniors. And things change in the twinkling of an eye. People blow hot and blow cold, yin changes to yang... it's hell."

"Yeah, but a lot of people would die to have some of that hell!" remarks Shen, and all four men laugh.

There is a brief pause. Qiyu takes a moment to add water to everyone's cup, while Shen reaches over and touches a piece of jade hung on the other thin guy's belt. "Ms Xiang here has a jade pendant, and you have a piece of jade on your belt. It's a very nice one."

"It's a Hetian jade pebble, I had it carved into a *pixiu*."

"Just right for a businessman! The winged lion that protects wealth as it keeps on eating but never shits!"

The amulet's owner grunts agreement. He turns to his friend and asks, "Why don't you show him yours?"

The other man lifts the hem of his jacket – there is a piece of jade hung on his belt too.

"Oh wow, is that a copy of a Han dynasty *gangmao*!" exclaims Shen.

"*Gangmao*? What's that?" asks the official.

"It's an amulet inscribed with incantations," explains Shen. "In the Han dynasty, high-ranking officials wore them for protection and to show their desire for power and authority."

These last words make the skinny man turn bright red. He sneaks a glance at his superior. "This *gangmao* is just right for an official." And he starts to untie the knot on his belt.

"No, no, I couldn't take it. It's not my place to wear something like that," his boss says. "The Han dynasty was two thousand years ago, we're living in completely different times."

"But you can just keep it in your pocket," Shen reassures him. Then he turns to the *gangmao's* owner and says, "Yours is Qinghai jade. Why don't I get hold of a really good one for you to give your boss? I know a Professor Kan, and he's just given me a white jade pebble which I'm having carved."

"Professor Kan?" asks the official. "A professor who collects jade?"

"He teaches physics in the university," says Shen. "But he's obsessed with jade. Over the decades, he has collected enough jade to fill a two-room flat. The name over his study door reads Jade Mansion."

"I didn't know we had eccentrics like that in Xijing!" says one of the thin men.

"He's quite an oddball," says Shen. "First of all, he only collects uncut jade, stones that come from Hetian in Xinjiang. And he never sells any of them. They're worth well over a hundred million yuan, but he lives hand-to-mouth."

"Then he's a custodian," says the official.

"Another oddity is that he was single for so long. Everybody thought he'd die a bachelor. And guess what? At fifty-five, he married a much younger woman who's very glamorous."

"She got herself a sugar daddy, eh?" says one of the skinny men.

"She must have her eyes on the stones. I bet they've had a good few fights since then."

"Maybe so," agrees Shen. "But they had a daughter, and that is the third oddity."

"Every family has a skeleton in the closet," says the leader. "I once read a classic that says, 'We go through hell and high water to get a wife and a son, and they cause us all sorts of trouble. A family is like a thicket of brambles – you wade through it and the thorns cling to your clothes at every step.'"

"And the fourth oddity is that they got a divorce when their daughter was barely a year and a half," Shen continues.

"See?" one of the skinny men interrupts. "They did split up. So the woman took half of the jade collection?"

"That I'm not sure of," says Shen, "but Professor Kan got custody of their daughter. I ran into them a few times on the street. He was carrying the toddler, and a bottle of milk and nappies too. I felt sorry for him, but he seemed fine about it. He said to me, 'Isn't my little girl lovely? We're looking after each other.' The girl was indeed lovely, but she didn't look like him at all."

"Let's see," says Skinny Two. "The professor married at fifty-five, and the kid was a year and a half old... by the time she turns twenty, the father will be... seventy-seven at least. How many years have they got to enjoy each other?"

"There you go, I said he's a custodian," the official sums up.

"But that's not the end of the story," Shen continues. "So many people remarked the girl didn't look like him, he got suspicious and did a paternity test. And you know what? It turns out he really isn't the child's father! So just a few days ago, he sent her back to her mother."

"That's terrible!" Skinny One exclaims. And they all agree the woman's a slut.

"A wife who's so much younger and prettier is no good," says the other skinny man.

"Let's not make sweeping generalisations," says Shen. "Good looks can have merit too. Think of a house, if it's well-proportioned and well-built, there'll be ample sunlight and good ventilation, and the house will last a long time. If the house is thrown together any old how, on the other hand, it'll be gloomy, damp and stuffy, and might even fall down."

All this while, Qiyu has been a quiet observer of their lively exchanges. Now she asks, "What's the woman's name?"

"Her surname is Yan, and she's called Nianchu," replies Shen.

"Yan Nianchu?" exclaims Qiyu, startled. "What does she look like?"

"Taller than you, and slender," says Shen. "Quite exotic to look at. She walks with head in the air, always has a pair of sunglasses on, and she's standoffish."

"Hmm," says Qiyu.

"You know her?" asks Shen.

"No!" says Qiyu emphatically.

After her clients leave, Qiyu cannot settle to anything. She is on edge, but she is not sure what she feels... anger, sympathy or schadenfreude? All she knows is that she is sitting on a volcano that could erupt at any moment. She grabs her phone, hurries out of the studio and heads for her office. On the way, she calls Lu Yike. It rings but then the call drops. She calls again but the same thing happens. Is something wrong with Yike's phone? Qiyu wonders. Or is Yike rejecting my call? If her phone's working, why wouldn't she answer? Has something bad happened? But what? What could be worse than this? Qiyu jumps into her car and drives to Yike's office. I have to tell her about it, she thinks crossly. When a hen's ready to lay, you can't keep the egg from coming out!

Yike is at her office. She is feeling thoroughly despondent. She has shut the door and laid out playing cards to try to tell her fortune. When Hai Ruo told her the general secretary will not put in a good word for her with Xu Shaolin's boss – it would not be good for anyone if he did – she knew the LED screens deal has gone up in smoke. For what seems like forever, her business has been in the doldrums. After Yike landed the billboard by the airport expressway, Xi Lishui told her about the LED screens, and she invited Lishui to dinner. At the time, Yike told herself that when someone's bad luck ends and their fortunes turn a corner, there are often three good omens. First, someone will offer help (Lishui). Lishui did not seem to have the means to help... but now she's met up with her old school friend, Xu Shaolin. Another omen is someone smoothing the way for her. (Hai Ruo. She's asked Yi Guang to put in a good word.) And finally, Yike is surprised to find her stomach has settled down. She used to get cramps if she ate anything that did not agree with her, but now she can swig an iced beer without any problems. However, the response from the general secretary has left her crestfallen.

This morning, one of her father's younger brothers called. Her uncle has started a design company in Chengdu, the capital of the neighbouring Sichuan Province. His business is thriving and expanding, so he is offering Yike the job of deputy general manager. She is tempted, but it is a hard call to make, hence the playing cards. Everyone in the sisterhood knows how to tell fortunes. There was a time when they used to forecast each other's love lives. Today, however, she is making a serious attempt to decide whether to stay or to go. She lays the cards on the table and arranges them over and over. The first round tells her to go. Will I really go? she asks herself. She plays again. Stay. So she shuffles the cards for another round. If I get the same answer three times in a row, it's obviously meant to be, she thinks.

She is still busy with the cards when the phone rings. "Damn!" she says, cutting the caller off without even glancing at their ID. The phone rings several times, and she silences it each time. By now she has played half a dozen rounds without getting a clear answer. Dad, tell me what to do, she implores. Make yourself known through someone... anyone! Then I'll know not to go. Dad, Dad... And she sits there, lost in thought.

Qiyu arrives to find Yike gazing at a table covered in playing cards. "Hey, I'm desperate to see you, and you've been telling your fortune! Are you still looking for Mr Right? It's all rubbish, you know. I've washed my hands of it. I don't believe in love or marriage any more!"

"What's brought you here?" asks Yike.

"You didn't answer any of my calls, I was worried something had happened to you."

"What could happen to me?"

"You could have landed a huge deal and been busy counting the money. Or you could have been kidnapped by a handsome young man!"

"Huh! No such luck. Come on, tell me, what's up?"

"Have you seen Nianchu these past few days?"

"Her phone's been off. I know Hai Ruo hasn't been able to reach her."

"Is that so? Then maybe it's true."

"What may be true?"

"I don't know if I should tell you."

"Try stopping that mouth of yours!"

So Qiyu repeats what Shen said. "How can she do this?" she goes on. "We don't mind who she marries, we'll support her. And if it doesn't work out and she wants a divorce, we'll support her in that too. But if the baby really isn't her husband's, she's crossed a basic moral line!"

"Wait, don't jump to conclusions before we've seen Nianchu."

"But don't you think this news is worrying? Nianchu is one of us!"

But Yike repeats, "We don't know the whole picture, what are you making such a fuss about?"

"I've known Shen a long time. I'm sure he doesn't know how close I am to Nianchu. But he's definitely not the kind of man to spread baseless rumours."

"Even if it is true, kill it now," says Yike. "Not a single word to anyone else!"

"Who would I tell? It's humiliating!" Qiyu exclaims.

18. YAN NIANCHU • THE TIANPEIZI RESTAURANT

IT'S ANOTHER GLOOMY DAY. Does smog gather on a gloomy day, or is it gloomy because of the smog? Hai Ruo arrives at the hospital to find Xu Qi sitting at Xia Zihua's bedside. She has been there since yesterday. Why hasn't anyone relieved her? Hai Ruo asks her.

"It was Benwen's turn," explains Xu Qi. "She called to say that Nianchu offered to take her shift, but Nianchu didn't show up this morning. When I called, Benwen said she'd gone out of town to buy chilli and Sichuan pepper. I couldn't reach Nianchu, either, her phone's turned off. So I stayed."

"If Nianchu offered to come, how can she not show up *and* keep her phone off?" says Hai Ruo.

"Just what I was wondering," says Xu Qi.

"Have you seen her in the last few days?"

"The day before yesterday, she dropped by early in the morning, and asked if I'd find her a *baomu*. She thought I could ask around in my family's hometown."

"But Nianchu's hardly ever home during the day, why would she need a housekeeper?"

"Anyway, I told her I've been away too long, I don't know anyone. So she left. Maybe it's for her mother? She's nearly eighty now, and she lives by herself."

"Possibly, but why turn her phone off?"

Zihua is still drowsy. Hai Ruo bends close to her ear and calls her name several times. Zihua's eyes open but do not move or show any signs of recognition. Then they close again. Hai Ruo's brows draw together in a deep frown. She and Xu Qi look at each other wordlessly. Then the door opens and Xiang Qiyu bursts in.

"I was on my way to the Tax Bureau, but I'm in good time, so I thought I'd check on Zihua," Qiyu explains. She's brought a bagful of food: bread, dragon fruit, raisins, Coke, yogurt. "A cousin of mine from Qinghai arrived last night and brought a box of yak milk yogurt. It's really good for you."

"What a lot of food! Didn't anyone tell you she's asleep most of the time?" says Hai Ruo.

"I figured that if it was that serious, she'd be in ICU by now. And she's not, so maybe she's just a bit woozy. Once she wakes up properly, she'll ask for food or drink and we need to be prepared."

"She did wake up last night and ask for stir-fried *liangfen*," Xu Qi puts in. "I ran down to the night market and bought some takeaway but she only took a mouthful, and spat it out. She definitely won't touch all this."

"If she can't eat, I'm sure you two can," says Qiyu. She takes the bread and yogurt out of the bag, then goes to ask the nurses for a knife to cut the dragon fruit.

"You eat if you want to," says Xu Qi. "Wow, whatever are you wearing?"

Qiyu has on a pair of beige harem trousers and a tight-fitting white spaghetti strap top which reveals her cleavage. "What do you mean? Why are you staring at me like that?"

"I'm not staring at you, I've just got big eyes," says Xu Qi.

"And I've got big breasts," retorts Qiyu.

Xu Qi pretends not to hear her. She takes the thermos and goes down the ward to get hot water from the boiler.

"Why's she taking the piss out of me?" Qiyu asks Hai Ruo. "Did you know she's got a thing going with Yinan?"

Hai Ruo gets out a carton of yogurt and inserts a straw. She looks at Qiyu as she sips.

"So you haven't noticed anything?" Qiyu pursues.

"Noticed what?" asks Hai Ruo between sips.

"Don't you think there's something odd going on? Every time we get together, they show up and leave together. The way they look at each other, it's weird, it gives me goosebumps!"

"You think too much. I don't want to hear stuff like that."

"You don't? Well, here's something you'll definitely want to hear. Yike said you've been trying to contact Nianchu. Has she gone missing?"

"Yike said that to you? We shouldn't be telling you anything."

Qiyu leans over, regardless. She pouts her plump, scarlet lips and whispers mysteriously, "She's turned off her phone because she has to!" She recounts Shen's story about Professor Kan. Hai Ruo has finished her yogurt and the carton is empty but she carries on sucking noisily.

Xu Qi has filled the thermos. She hangs around outside until she reckons Qiyu has gone, but when she opens the door, Qiyu is still there. Qiyu shoots a glance at Hai Ruo, who looks dazed.

"Are you angry?" Qiyu is saying. "It's quite understandable if you are. If she's gone missing, then forget her. She must be too ashamed to look us in the eyes. Let's pretend we don't even know her."

"You'd better be off to the Tax Bureau," Hai Ruo says.

Qiyu glances at her watch and utters a cry of alarm. She gathers her tote bag and gets up. At the door, she turns back and says, "Don't be so upset, Hai-jie. She's not worth it."

Hai Ruo gets to her feet and calls Nianchu one more time. To her surprise, Nianchu answers. As they talk, Hai Ruo acts as if nothing has happened: she's neither happy to hear Nianchu's voice, nor upset at her keeping her phone off for days on end. When Nianchu says she's at the Zhongda International Shopping Centre, Hai Ruo says she needs a new handbag, and asks her to wait on the second floor by the escalator.

"That must have been Nianchu," says Xu Qi when Hai Ruo cuts the call. "She's the only one of us who can afford to go shopping there! If you need a new handbag, she should give you one as a present. You do know she has an entire room full of luxury goods, don't you? Three big shelves of high heels, and more than a hundred brand-name handbags."

"Are you jealous?"

"No, not me. Everyone should live the way they want. She spends all her money on clothes, I spend mine on food. What you wear is for others, what you eat is for yourself."

"And that's how you get so skinny?"

Xu Qi giggles. "I don't eat just for the sake of eating. I'm thin where I should be, and curvy where it matters." She is still speaking as Hai Ruo walks out of the room.

Hai Ruo drives to Zhongda International and spots Nianchu's Land Rover parked alongside another car. Nearby, there is a man hunkered down, taking long drags on a cigarette. Something about him looks familiar. Then it dawns on her that this is Nianchu's cousin, Zhang Huai. She remembers him from the time they met in the street and he delivered Feng Ying's message. Hai Ruo keeps out of sight and goes across the square to call Yi Guang.

"Where are you?" Yi Guang mumbles, sounding as if he has just woken up.

"At the hospital."

"How's Zihua? Shall I come to the hospital?"

"Don't bother, she's slipping in and out of consciousness. Better wait until she's improved."

Yi Guang heaves a sigh, then says, "Let me know if I can be of any help."

Hai Ruo thanks him, then says, "I just want to ask you one thing, do you happen to owe Feng Ying any money?"

"I do, a hundred and fifty thousand yuan. But how did you know? Did Feng Ying tell you about it?"

"So it's true! If you're not strapped for cash, you should pay the whole lot to Zihua, because Feng Ying borrowed two hundred thousand from her. Right now, Zihua needs money for her treatment."

"She should have told me herself. And isn't she in the Philippines?"

"I got the message from someone else. She wanted me to pass it on to you."

Yi Guang is startled. "She told someone else about it? Why couldn't she talk to me directly? This isn't right, it makes me look bad, as if I'm not going to pay her back."

"I don't know why she did it like that."

"All right, I'll get the money together in a few days and give it to you, so you can pass it on to Zihua. I want a receipt from you," says Yi Guang brusquely.

So Yi Guang does owe Feng Ying 150,000, and Nianchu's cousin was telling the truth, Hai Ruo thinks, but something still feels off. She doesn't want to go over and say hello to the man. She dislikes everything about him: his looks, his clothes and his expression. She goes into the shopping centre and spots Nianchu waiting by the escalator upstairs. She is wearing a baseball cap, a pair of sunglasses and a brown windcheater. She is carrying an assortment of shopping bags, and there is an old woman beside her.

"What a smart jacket," Hai Ruo compliments her. "It's so eye-catching, I spotted you right away."

"I just bought it," says Nianchu. She brings out a long, belted skirt in ice blue, and a pair of mid-grey cropped trousers.

"So is this the minimalist look?"

"You know about the minimalist look?"

"You think I'm old just because you're young!"

As the two laugh and chat, the old woman gazes at Hai Ruo.

"Who's this?" Hai Ruo asks.

"My *laogu*, my father's youngest sister," Nianchu explains. "She's turning eighty this year so we're celebrating with a big birthday bash on the twenty-third. My cousin wanted to give his mother some jewellery and asked my advice. I brought her here and we got a pair of gold bracelets, gold earrings and a gold ring."

"So much gold!" Hai Ruo says.

"My *laogu*'s spent most of her life in the countryside. She only moved to Xijing a decade ago, to live with her son. She does love a bit of gold. She says when she was young, she saw the landlord's wife wearing gold and silver jewellery, and now she's old, she wants to live like them, even if it's not for long." Nianchu chuckles, then goes on, "The year before last, when I visited her over the Spring Festival, I asked what she needed and said I'd buy it for her. 'Buy me a gold bar,' she told me. So I bought her a gold bar for three thousand yuan, and she's been keeping it under her pillow! She's fixated on the idea that only gold is valuable!"

"Don't talk like this, she'll hear you," says Hai Ruo.

"She won't, she's deaf as a door post," says Nianchu. She leans close to her aunt's ear and shouts, "This is my friend, Hai Ruo!"

"What a nice-looking girl," the old woman shouts back. "Lovely fair, round face, very lucky. Not like you, you never eat properly, and you're skinny as a grasshopper!"

Hai Ruo and Nianchu burst out laughing. Nianchu gives Hai Ruo three carrier bags and asks her to wait there while she sees her aunt off. Through the window, Hai Ruo watches as the old lady gets into the car parked next to the Land Rover, and Nianchu's cousin, Zhang Huai, drives his mother away. As Nianchu comes back up the escalator, the man in front of her turns round and leers at her. Nianchu holds her head high and ignores him. When the man reaches the end of the escalator, he is not looking, catches his foot and falls flat on his back.

"Which one do you like?" asks Nianchu.

"Huh?" asks Hai Ruo.

"Didn't you look inside? I bought two handbags, one's French, the other's Italian. Choose one, a gift from me."

Hai Ruo takes out the handbags, both top brands. "I like both, but I don't want you to give me one. I'll pay you the exact price, no service charge! Choose one and the other's mine."

"Fine, when I go to your teashop, I'll pay for every cup of tea I drink," says Nianchu. She scribbles the letters "F" and "I" on two bits of wrapping paper, crumbles them into balls, hides them behind her back, then brings her hands out in front. "It's in the lap of the gods," she says.

Hai Ruo points at her right hand, and Nianchu opens it and flattens the scrap of paper: "F". Hai Ruo retrieves the receipt from the French bag, and counts out the cash, down to the last yuan and cent. Nianchu tries to refuse the small change but Hai Ruo insists. Then she recounts a story that Yi Guang once told her.

A university professor, seventy-six years old, took a taxi to a conference, and when it was over, got a ride home from someone. Then he realised that he had forgotten to claim back the fifteen-yuan taxi fare. So he hailed a taxi and returned to the conference.

"Why did you do that?" asked someone. "You're spending thirty yuan on a round trip to claim back half that amount."

"But I have to claim it back," insisted the professor. "I like to do things properly, and if it costs me, then so be it."

"Is that a joke?" asks Nianchu.

"No," says Hai Ruo as she hands Nianchu the change. "Now, let's go and find somewhere to put something nice in our stomachs."

"I know a Muslim restaurant down the lane ahead of us. How about *yangza* soup?"

"There's always a long queue for the sheep offal soup. And you're really going to stand out in that outfit."

"That's a no, then. There's also a *tianpeizi* restaurant, that's a quiet spot."

Tianpeizi is made of fermented highland barley. Served cold, it is a refreshing dessert, sweet and winey. Nianchu orders two bowls of *tianpeizi* and two dishes of chicken feet and wings, then goes next door for two bowls of *yangza* soup, which she carries back to Hai Ruo.

"Not very classy are we?" says Hai Ruo. "More the earthy types. We just go for the offal."

"We're certainly no empresses," agrees Nianchu. "But hens have feet to kneel on, '*gui*', and wings to fly with, '*fei*'. And Guifei was the famous imperial consort, so that adds a touch of class to our chicken feet and wings!"

Hai Ruo watches Nianchu slurping down the peppered mutton soup, her forehead beaded in sweat. She makes up her mind. "Are you looking for a *baomu*?"

Nianchu is taken aback. "Did Xu Qi tell you this?"

Hai Ruo does not answer directly. "Xu Qi's been away from home for years, she has no contacts there. Even if she managed to find one, the woman would need training. I used to have this great *baomu*, you know. She stopped coming six years ago, but she's still in town, and we've been in touch. You could have asked me, I can call her. Ideally, she could work for you. Otherwise, she could recommend someone reliable."

"Well, I don't want to put you to any trouble."

"You've done that before without worrying! Why are you suddenly so considerate? Is this for your mother?"

But Nianchu gives a non-committal grunt. She looks out of the window. On the street, someone is holding a balloon that keeps bobbing up into the air, but is anchored by a bit of string. Then the balloon and its owner pass the window and are gone.

"Niu Niu is back," Nianchu says, out of the blue.

"Really? Niu Niu's back? Your little girl?"

"I took Niu Niu back from her dad. He's getting old, and it's hard for a man to bring up a toddler on his own."

"I thought you should have insisted on getting custody. I was worried that if you didn't, you'd grow apart and you'd never have that close mother-daughter relationship. It's good you've got her back."

"I still don't have time to look after her, so I've left her with my mum. They really need a *baomu*, but I haven't been able to find anyone suitable. It's put me in a foul mood, but I don't want to be grouchy to my friends, so I switched my phone off."

"It's been off quite a few days. And just burying your head in the sand won't make the trouble go away!"

Nianchu takes off her sunglasses, opens her mouth to speak, but says nothing.

"When a potter makes a basin or a jar, they know that if they leave a single crack, it'll leak for sure," says Hai Ruo.

Nianchu sighs. "My marriage has been a total debacle."

"Well, it's not as if the rest of us have lived happily ever after, is it? You can't tell how spicy and smelly a peeled clove of garlic is just by looking at it. You have to suck it and see. We all know that, but we panic when we're faced with the unpalatable truth. Let me help you find a *baomu*, don't worry about it. What I really want to talk to you about is that business between you and Lihou. She's told me her side of the story, but I'd like to hear your side so I can get the full picture."

Nianchu grunts. Then she looks up at her friend. "You are not here to buy a handbag, Hai-jie, you are here to lance a boil."

"An abscess won't heal if you leave the pus inside."

Nianchu begins, "I feel like a fugitive on the run… so nervous that I'm actually relieved when the cops finally catch me." She spreads her hands apart and says, "I'm the injured party here. I wanted to tell you about it, but I was afraid you'd be angry with me. I had no idea she'd already come to you! I was trying to help her make some money, and she did earn a lot of interest in the first three months. She invited me to dinner and gave me a box of South Korean cosmetics, as a thank-you. But you never know what's around the corner in this life, and suddenly things went pear-shaped."

"She didn't come to me about this," Hai Ruo says. "It was me who noticed that she'd lost a lot of weight, and she wasn't bothering to colour her hair any more. She only confided in me when I pressed her.

She's grateful that you were helpful, and that's why she agreed to drop the interest and only ask for the principal back. What made her angry is the new contract – you're now the 'indirect guarantor', instead of the 'direct guarantor'. No wonder she believes you've thrown her under the bus to safeguard your own interests. The sisterhood have been together for so many years, what we feel for each other is precious. Of course, Lihou wanted to make some quick money out of this deal, and any speculator should be wary of the risks. But Lihou is such an open book, there's no malice in her, and when she discovered the change of wording from 'direct guarantor' to 'indirect guarantor' in the new contract, it's not surprising she was distressed."

"I've been thinking about it, Hai-jie. Maybe I was selfish, and got a bit scared, and I shouldn't have tried to be too clever. I phoned her, but she was in a rage. She called me names and hung up, and refused to see me after that."

"Direct or indirect, you are still the guarantor. If you can't guarantee the repayment, we'll all try to think of a way out. It's a lot of money, we can't let it just disappear."

"The loss of Lihou's money has upset me too! And I've lost a friend over it, and that's even more upsetting."

"Good, this is what I came to you for."

"I've been asking Mr Wang to repay the money, come what may, and he has given his word."

"Did he lend the money to his friend?"

"Yes, Lihou lent the money to Mr Wang, who lent it to his friend."

"So he gave it to his friend, and this friend did a runner. Hardly surprising that Lihou's worried that Mr Wang won't repay her."

"He has to, he took a cut from the interest."

"So – Mr Wang was making money from Lihou's loan!" exclaims Hai Ruo.

Nianchu can think of nothing to say to this. Hai Ruo persists, "You've got to be honest with me, did you get a cut from it, too?"

"No, I didn't! Not a single cent. Cross my heart and hope to die!"

"But you introduced Lihou to Mr Wang, just so you'd get into his good books and sell him medical equipment! Let me ask you something else."

"I've fallen in your estimation, haven't I, Hai-jie? You're practically interrogating me!"

"If I thought any less of you, I would never have come to see you. This is not an interrogation, I just want to get my head around this whole thing. Mr Wang is the head of a state-owned hospital, so he only earns a basic salary. How on earth is he going to pay Lihou back?"

"He must have savings. Besides, he has a shop selling construction materials, his wife runs it."

"Huh. If it were me caught in this mess, I'd sell the store so I could pay back the full amount up front. Why let someone else run away with my hard-earned money?"

"There's two reasons why he's not selling the business – because one, he has to live, and two, he needs to earn money to pay Lihou back."

"What if he goes back on his word? Or if his business goes down the tubes and he can't pay her back?"

Again, Nianchu has no answer.

"You all tore up the old contract, and I wouldn't put much faith in the new one, either. It's urgent to get the loan back," insists Hai Ruo.

"I'll keep pushing him."

"I'm sure you will, but I can see why you changed your guarantor status from direct into indirect. It's because you've got doubts about him. Isn't that so?"

Nianchu has gone bright red in the face, and there are beads of sweat visible on her nose. "Waiter!" she calls. When the waiter comes over, she asks, "Do you have any Lafite?"

"I'm afraid we don't."

"How can you not have Lafite if you're running a restaurant? What wine do you have?"

"Great Wall, and Ansenman."

"Ansenman? Where's it from?"

"From here, from Shaanxi."

"Two glasses, then."

Glass in hand, Nianchu carries on, "What should I do, Hai-jie?"

"Pile the pressure on. The larger the debt, the less the motivation to clear it. It's up to you and Lihou to make him pay. Do you know anyone in the debt-collecting business?"

"Lihou would have to approach them."

"Of course."

"My cousin Zhang Huai's running a debt-collecting company with a partner. I can give Lihou his phone number," says Nianchu.

But Hai Ruo says, "Give it to me, I'll contact him."

"But Hai-jie, you'll be implicated in this mess."

"We stick together through thick and thin, our sisterhood," says Hai Ruo. So Nianchu gives her the phone number.

At the end of the meal, Hai Ruo brings out her money but Nianchu is having none of it. The two of them fight over the bill.

"Everyone's going to laugh at us if we keep squabbling. How much is it anyway? I'll let you treat me when we have a grand feast," says Hai Ruo.

"When did the two of us ever have a feast?" retorts Nianchu.

But Hai Ruo has thrust her cash into the waiter's hands. Nianchu reaches over to pick up the carrier with Hai Ruo's handbag and knocks over a cup, splashing half a cup of tea onto her new windcheater.

19. XIN QI • THE TEASHOP

THE NEXT MORNING, Hai Ruo arrives at the teashop and phones Zhang Huai, Yan Nianchu's cousin. The young man hurries in, and xiao-Tang ushers him upstairs and serves him tea.

Hai Ruo then phones Ying Lihou. "I've found a debt collector, you need to get here right now," she begins, but before she can go on, the phone slips through her fingers and clatters to the floor. She picks it up and sees a crack at the bottom right corner of the screen. "You think I'm pushing you too hard, eh?" she says, stroking it, and goes upstairs.

Zhang Huai and Eva chat as she adds water to his tea cup. He had some garlicky sheep's blood pudding at a roadside stall on his way here and his breath stinks so badly that Eva backs away, but he just leans in closer to her. As Hai Ruo comes up, he says, "You've gone all international, missus! How much do you pay this foreign chick?"

"Eva's not an employee, she's my friend from Russia. She's just in Xijing for a few days," Hai Ruo tells him.

"A friend? Then you must be from the northeast."

"Why? Do I speak with an accent?"

"No, your Chinese is very standard, but this *niwa*, this girlie… is that even her real name?"

"It's not *niwa*! It's 'Eva', ee-vah…"

"She speaks such fluent Chinese! Is she from the border area then? There are a lot of hookers up there who try to pass themselves off as Russians."

"Eva is from St Petersburg! You must have heard of it!"

"Hah! A real pure-bred Russian! Here, take a photo of me with her." And he hands his phone to Hai Ruo. She points the phone and he grabs Eva around the shoulder and poses.

"Be serious!" Hai Ruo reprimands him. "Get your hand off her, stand straight, look at me!" She takes a few shots.

Zhang Huai takes his phone back and swipes through the photos. Hai Ruo shoots a glance at Eva, who leaves them and goes downstairs. "Let me pour you more tea," Hai Ruo says. "And mind you don't go sharing those on WeChat!"

"Would I do a thing like that? She's stunning though, isn't she?"

"She is, and the streets in St Petersburg are full of them. When I go there again, you can come with me."

"It's a deal!"

"It is, but not until you've sorted this business for me."

They hear a commotion below, then Lihou runs up the stairs, sweating profusely. "You've caused a lot of excitement!" says Hai Ruo. "That's what happens when you don't come around for days."

"It has nothing to do with me," says Lihou. "A new batch of tea's just arrived and everyone's busy unloading and unpacking."

xiao-Zhen comes upstairs. "Mrs Qi and Xia Lei are here. We were going to send her some bees, but the kid wanted an outing so Tang-jie got Wenlai to go and pick them up."

"Fine, you all look after them," says Hai Ruo. "I'm in the middle of something. And make sure we're not disturbed."

Hai Ruo introduces Zhang Huai and Lihou, then cuts to the chase. She wants the debt collector to get Lihou's money back. Lihou tells him the whole story from beginning to end, then brings out a photo – a head shot of Mr Wang – and a scrap of paper with his mobile number, and the name and address of his building materials company. Next, they negotiate Zhang Huai's commission. After a good deal of wrangling, they eventually reach an agreement: if he's successful, his commission will be ten per cent of the amount recovered.

Zhang Huai sounds confident. "No problem, dear ladies, I'll have good news for you in no time at all. And don't talk about 'the amount recovered', I'm going to get every cent for you in a single payment!"

Lihou is elated. "Fantastic! If it's a single payment, you can have an extra two hundred thousand on top of the ten per cent."

"What methods do you use?" Hai Ruo asks.

"I've got a few tricks up my sleeve, don't you worry," replies Zhang Huai.

"Then let me be quite clear," says Hai Ruo. "No one loses their life, or even gets beaten up. And absolutely no kidnapping or maiming."

"Quite right," Lihou agrees. "We only want the money back. You must give us your word."

But Zhang Huai is brutal. "These mother-fuckers, you gotta screw them over! It's the only language they understand!"

"What did you say?" exclaims Hai Ruo, alarmed.

"Is my language too rough for you? I'm just telling it like it is."

"I repeat, we only want the debt repaid, nothing else," says Hai Ruo sternly. "You came to us through Yan Nianchu, and she's given me her word that you're straight."

"All right, all right," says Zhang Huai.

Lihou takes wads of banknotes out of her bag and gives them to Zhang Huai. "Here's fifty thousand as a down payment," she explains. "Plus an extra five thousand that I was going to use to take you to dinner, but we aren't going out tonight, so just take it and treat yourself."

Zhang Huai pockets the money. He stands up to go, then turns back and empties his tea cup, before heading downstairs. Hai Ruo and Lihou see him to the door.

After he has gone, Lihou says, "So, this Zhang Huai is Yan Nianchu's cousin?"

"Yes, she was really upset when you wouldn't talk to her," says Hai Ruo. "It was she who suggested her cousin's debt-collecting company. You should cut her some slack."

"Did you know her ex-husband has sent her kid back to her? He did a paternity test and found out the girl wasn't his!"

"Who told you that?"

"Qiyu."

"What a blabbermouth!"

"Yan Nianchu deserves to be exposed."

"And you think it's OK to gloat? No one's squeaky clean in this life! Nianchu did wrong, but it's in the past. Why re-open old wounds? Qiyu's not using her head. She hasn't thought about the consequences of her gossip. If this business comes out, it will drive Nianchu away from the sisterhood and then what will happen to her?"

"You have my word that I won't tell anyone else about this," Lihou reassures her. "But my concern is, if that's the kind of person she is, can we trust her cousin?"

"He's running a debt-collecting business, he's not a blackmailer," says Hai Ruo. "But why did you give him the fifty thousand in such a hurry?"

"I figured he'd be more eager to do it if I gave him some incentive."

Back in the shop, Hai Ruo finds Mrs Qi in the cubicle, making the bees sting her knee joints. She chats to her and plays with Xia Lei, then tells Wenlai to take the boy to the shopping centre and buy him some toys. Taking Lihou back upstairs, she asks Eva to make two fresh cups of tea.

"The potato's gone, has it?" says Eva, putting down the tea cups.

"What potato?"

"The man who was here, a short-arse with a puffed-up face and a round head. He looked just like a big potato!" says Eva. Hai Ruo laughs out loud. "He asked for my phone number, I said I didn't have a phone. His breath really stank!"

Lihou also laughs at Eva's thumb-nail sketch. "Nowadays people are either extremely kind or extremely evil. Be careful he doesn't latch onto you."

"No worries," says Eva. "He won't dare offend Hai-jie, so he won't offend me, either." She pulls a face and goes downstairs.

Lihou stretches luxuriously and gets up to leave. "I haven't slept for nights," she yawns. "But now he's set my mind at rest. I'm going home to sleep for two whole days and nights."

"Not before you get that hair of yours washed," says Hai Ruo.

"Are you saying I'm a mess?"

"Too right. Tidy yourself up before you come here again." Hai Ruo calls xiao-Tang upstairs, and asks her to take Lihou to the hair salon to the right of the teashop, and put the cost on her tab there.

In the salon, xiao-Tang and Lihou spot a familiar face. Xi Lishui is sitting in the lounge, admiring fingernails she has just painted a hazy blue.

"Hello, Xi-jie, how come you're here and not in the teashop?" xiao-Tang greets her.

"I'm here with a friend. I was taking her to the teashop, but she insists on getting her hair done first," says Lishui, and jerks her chin towards the back of the salon.

A woman is sitting at a dressing table, touching up her make-up. She's wearing a long, khaki-coloured dress and matching high heels, and her wavy hair cascades down over her shoulders. She must surely be able to see Lishui talking to Lihou and xiao-Tang, reflected in the mirror in front of her, but she seems oblivious to them, completely engrossed in painting and prettifying the other self that faces her.

"What a beauty!" Lihou exclaims.

"Everyone I bring to the teashop is a beauty. Is Hai-jie in?" asks Lishui.

"She is," Lihou replies.

"Xin Qi, Xin Qi!" Lishui calls. The woman comes over and Lishui makes the introductions, "This is Ying Lihou-jie and xiao-Tang-jie."

"Forget about the 'jie', I'm only the shop assistant," says xiao-Tang.

"But if Hai-jie is the captain, you're her first mate," Lishui says.

"How lovely to meet you both," Xin Qi says warmly. xiao-Tang arranges for Lihou's wash and hair colouring to be put on Hai Ruo's tab, and Lishui and Xin Qi head for the teashop, their dresses swaying gracefully as they walk.

When Xin Qi meets Hai Ruo, she sits primly on her stool, legs tilted sideways, knees together, hands placed on top of them, her small lips opening and shutting.

"You're a sweet girl, Xin Qi!" Hai Ruo exclaims. "You remind me of the names Yi Guang gave his *huanghuali* tree trunk and the Hetian jade pebble – Soft Jade and Gentle Snow. The names suit you perfectly! Wait, let me get you a present to mark our first meeting. I'm sure you'll love it!" She gets up and goes downstairs.

Xin Qi heaves a sigh of relief. "I was so nervous, my palms are sweating."

"See? There's no need to be shy, Hai-jie is big-hearted and open-minded," Lishui reassures her.

"And Ying Lihou, the one we met just now at the hair salon, is she in the sisterhood?"

"Right."

"And the one making tea for us?"

"That's xiao-Su."

"Not in the sisterhood?"

"She and xiao-Tang, they're the assistants."

"And downstairs there's a girl who looks like a foreigner."

"She *is* a foreigner, she's Hai-jie's friend from Russia."

"How glamorous you all are! Who's the best-looking of your sisterhood?"

"I couldn't possibly say but the ugliest is definitely me."

Xin Qi laughs. She brings out a small pocket mirror and refreshes her make-up again. "Who's this Yi Guang that Hai-jie was talking about just now?" she asks.

"You haven't heard of Yi Guang?"

"No, what does he do?"

Hai Ruo is coming up the stairs and overhears Xin Qi's question. She laughs out loud. "Finally, here's someone who doesn't know who Yi Guang is! He ought to be here to hear this."

"Yi Guang is a famous writer, a celebrity in town," explains Lishui. "He lives in the building behind the teashop. He's friends with all of us."

Xin Qi goes red with embarrassment. How can she not have heard of him?

"A lovely girl like you, you'd better steer clear of him," remarks Hai Ruo. From behind her back, she brings out a small circular fan. The silk fabric is mounted snugly on the fan's "eyebrows" – the thin bamboo frame – and is hand-painted: a cicada rests on a weeping willow, its wings translucent and silvery, its head tucked in, its tail erect, so vivid you can almost hear it sing. "This was a gift Feng Ying gave my son before he went abroad," says Hai Ruo. "It's just right for you, with your build, your looks and your manners."

Xin Qi receives the gift with both hands. "I love it. Thank you, Mrs Hai!"

"Less of the 'Mrs'!" Hai Ruo says.

"It was Feng Ying's present for your son, and now you're giving it away to Xin Qi," Lishui laughs. "What a pity Xin Qi is a dozen years older than Hai Tong, otherwise people might think you've earmarked her as your daughter-in-law and it's an engagement token!"

Xin Qi blinks in embarrassment.

Hai Ruo is disapproving. "Lishui tells terrible jokes!" Then she turns to Xin Qi. "Please do call me Hai-jie. And if you like it here, drop in whenever."

"I'd love to," says Xin Qi. "Lishui has told me so much about you and the sisterhood, but I didn't want to push myself forward. I wouldn't want to lower the tone of your gatherings."

"Now Hai-jie's invited you, you should come," Lishui urges her. "We are all very close in the sisterhood. There's no rivalry, we're mirrors reflecting each other, and we're really free and easy! Aren't I right, Hai-jie?"

"We're just a bunch of like-minded women," says Hai Ruo. "But our lives are not free and easy. If only they were, but we're actually all entangled in our own problems, like insects stuck in a cobweb. As I often say, we get along well because we don't want to change anyone else. We're like different rivers, flowing where we want to, and cleansing and nourishing the land as we go. Still, without us being aware of it, things that need changing do change."

"Did you hear that, Xin Qi? This is what makes Hai-jie into the woman that she is!" exclaims Lishui.

"I'm listening," says Xin Qi.

"The sisterhood follow Hai Ruo's lead, and we learn from her," says Lishui. "I can't say I've changed greatly, but at least I've learned who I am, and that if I want to do well for myself, feel comfortable with myself and live decently, then everything I do matters. I try to see the big picture even when I'm busy with the here and now. I try to treat people with honesty and kindness, and always give a helping hand, even if it's just with a smile or a few nice words."

"This reminds me of my elder brother," says Xin Qi. "When we were little, there was a time when we only had this one small flatbread. We agreed to go halves. My brother started first. He put his finger in the middle to mark the half-way point. But as he munched away, his finger kept creeping downwards. He'd already had more than half when he took another bite, such a big one that he bit his own fingertip."

"A good example of how poverty makes a person greedy and cruel," says Lishui.

Xin Qi falls silent. She picks up her cup and takes a gulp of tea. It burns her mouth and she spits it out, shooting an embarrassed glance at Hai Ruo.

Hai Ruo glares at Lishui before turning to Xin Qi. "Where are you from? I'm guessing not from Xijing..."

"I'm ashamed to admit that I grew up in eastern Shaanxi, in a small country town," replies Xin Qi.

"Nothing to be ashamed of!" says Hai Ruo. "It's good to be from the countryside. Yan Nianchu comes from the suburbs, and both Si Yinan and Xu Qi are from small towns. You can hardly tell the seasons in the city, but Xu Qi knows all about it. She's always reminding us what to wear and eat for each of the twenty-four solar terms."

"I've forgotten all that, I've been here more than ten years," says Xin Qi.

"And you're about twenty-two... or twenty-three?" Hai Ruo guesses.

"No, I'm nearly thirty. I'm old."

"If you're old at not-yet thirty, Lishui and I must be fossils!"

"I've achieved nothing while all of you are big names in business."

"We're not! We just run small shops, and we help each other out. Yi Guang-laoshi likens us to a nest of snakes – so restless that we're always slithering around looking for something to eat."

"Does he think of us as beautiful lady snakes?" Lishui wonders aloud.

The three of them laugh. Hai Ruo calls down to Eva, who comes upstairs with Xia Lei, the boy clutching a brown teddy bear in his arms.

"Oh, what a lovely teddy!" exclaims Hai Ruo.

Xia Lei thrusts the teddy towards Hai Ruo, saying, "Bite! Bite!"

Hai Ruo pretends to dodge the attack. "Ouch, it hurts!" She turns to Eva and says, "We need some more fruit." She gets out two hundred yuan, but Eva doesn't take her money and hurries down the stairs again, with Xia Lei thudding close behind her.

Eva gets a basket of strawberries in the market. When she returns to the teashop, she finds Hai Ruo and Lishui trying to comfort a whimpering Xin Qi. Hai Ruo washes the strawberries and picks one for her guest. "No one should have to put up with domestic violence in this day and age! We're going to help you out of this mess," she says. "Let's stick to the plan. Whenever you are ready to move your stuff out, give me a heads up, and I'll send you the men and a van."

Xin Qi stops crying, accepts the strawberry and nibbles on it. Hai Ruo and Lishui go downstairs, leaving Xin Qi with Eva.

Xin Qi immediately takes to Eva, and tells her how pretty she is and how well she speaks Chinese.

"It's just because I'm not a Chinese that I want to be like one," says Eva.

"Same here. I come from the countryside. I'll never be a real city dweller, however hard I try," says Xin Qi with a giggle.

"You are laughing, that's good."

Xin Qi edges closer to Eva and puts her arm around her shoulder. "I don't know why, but I sensed a vibe between us as soon as I saw you. Maybe you were a Chinese in a previous life, maybe even from my neck of the woods."

"Same here. Maybe you were a Russian in a former life!"

When Hai Ruo and Lishui come back, the pair are getting on like a house on fire. "Well, well!" says Hai Ruo. "Lishui, don't you think they even look like each other?"

"Good-lookers all look alike. Ugly ducklings like Si Yinan and me are each homely in our own way," says Lishui.

"You're not ugly," Hai Ruo protests. "Every woman is a flower, each with her own brilliance!"

20. XIAO-TANG • QUHU LAKE

小唐

THESE DAYS, the first thing Xijingers do when they get out of bed in the morning is pull the curtains back and check the weather outside. Today, the sky is a depressingly dirty-grey, and the air is gritty with smog. Hai Ruo doesn't feel like putting on a new outfit this morning, or taking her new Dior handbag. When she drives up to the teashop, her employees are busy cleaning up. Gao Wenlai is standing on a stool, wiping the door and windows, coughing nonstop. Each cough ends in a lengthy harrumphing.

"OK, so you've got a cough, but what's the harrumphing all about?" asks xiao-Su.

"I'm telling the heavens off!" says Wenlai.

"Then I'll tell you off!" says xiao-Tang. "How do you expect to stop coughing if you don't wear a mask?"

"But I can't breathe with a mask," says Wenlai.

"I hear the primary and high schools are being given a day off," puts in xiao-Zhen.

"What's that supposed to mean? Are you annoyed we're not having the day off, too?" says xiao-Tang.

"You're trying to make me look bad now Hai-jie's here," complains xiao-Zhen.

"What good is a day off anyway? You still have to breathe at home!" laughs xiao-Tang.

Hai Ruo notices that the flowers in the vases are shedding their petals. She takes a quick look outside but can see no flower sellers with their three-wheelers. She goes upstairs. Today's a day for staying in. She picks up a book and sits down on her arhat couch. The book is by some foreign writer named Rumi. A few pages in, and Hai Ruo is enjoying it. Why didn't I start it as soon as Yi Guang sent it to me? she thinks. She circles the heading "The seven stages on the path to truth" with a red pencil:

Every soul, or "nafs" in Arabic, has to go through these in order to attain Oneness.

1. The Depraved Nafs. Most human beings have their souls trapped in worldly pursuits, struggling and suffering in the service of their ego, and always holding others responsible for their continuing unhappiness.
2. The Accusing Nafs. When people become aware of the ego's abased situation, they stop blaming other people but turn their criticism on themselves, sometimes to the point of self-effacement.
3. The Inspired Nafs. Upon experiencing the true meaning of the word "surrender", one will possess and display patience, perseverance, wisdom and humility. The world, now full of inspiration, will be beautiful and happy.
4. The Serene Nafs. With a high level of consciousness, one can feel generosity, gratitude and an unwavering sense of contentment regardless of the hardships in life.
5. The Pleased Nafs. They are pleased with whatever situation they find themselves in, as mundane questions no longer matter.
6. The Pleasing Nafs. They become a lantern, radiating energy to everyone who asks for it, and wherever they go, they bring about a big difference in other people's lives.
7. The Purified Nafs. Insan-i Kâmil, the perfect human being, is a state attainable for very few, and those who do attain it, never speak of it.

Well put, Hai Ruo thinks to herself, then wonders, Am I still in the first or the second stage? Just as she starts to copy the passage, the room suddenly dims. It grows darker by the second, as if night is falling. She rubs her eyes. No improvement. She can hardly read. She fumbles her way downstairs and asks, "What's happening?"

"We're being smothered in smog!" says xiao-Tang.

The sky above is churning and the city streets have a nightmarish feel. The buses are still running, but apparently without wheels, and passing pedestrians look like they are headless. The old caretaker of the housing estate is rummaging for plastic bottles in the rubbish bin. Then he goes to talk with the woman at the kiosk, gesticulating animatedly. His face is visible, but his hands and feet keep appearing and disappearing in the murk.

"Turn on the lights," says Hai Ruo. "Turn them all on."

Just then, the telephone rings, the sound sharp as a whiplash. xiao-Tang picks it up, then holds it out to Hai Ruo.

"For me? Who is it?" asks Hai Ruo.

"Mr Ma."

"Popped up again?" exclaims Hai Ruo.

Ma used to be in the coal business. He's also an old client of the teashop. Hai Ruo takes the call and Ma asks her to buy him three calligraphy pieces from Yi Guang.

"But you know Yi Guang yourself, why do you need me?" asks Hai Ruo.

"There are different ways of knowing. If you ask him, you'll get a discount!" says Mr Ma.

"Each piece is a hundred thousand yuan. I'll only be able to save you ten thousand or so. That's peanuts for a tycoon like you!"

"Ten thousand is ten thousand! Get them delivered to the New Epoch Hotel. I've invited some big shots, and I want to give them as presents over lunch. I'm transferring the money onto your card now."

And 270,000 yuan promptly appears in Hai Ruo's account. But she doesn't go to Yi Guang's studio. She asks xiao-Tang to go upstairs with her. From a cabinet she brings out the calligraphy pieces Yi Guang presented her with.

Seven years ago, Xijing was going through a growth spurt. Old villages were demolished to make way for highways, high-rises were flung up, plazas were laid out. Construction sites were everywhere.

This economic boom made everyone money-mad. Officials used their power to rake it in, business folk speculated, those with resources traded them in, those with skills put their hands to use. Back then, the parking space in front of the teashop was full of fancy cars. The talk inside was all about which restaurant served the best shark fins and swallow's nests, and which hotels had the poshest presidential suites. Or who had secured a prime plot of land, or been awarded a coveted seat in the provincial CPPCC. Mr Ma was one of them. When he turned up at the teashop, he was usually greeted by his fellow businessmen with raucous shouts of, "Here comes Blackie! His piss is as black as his coal!"

He never let it bother him. He'd just say something like, "How come there's no parking spaces left today?"

When everyone looked outside the window, there was an enormous Hummer with its two front wheels planted on the doorstep. "You've got yourself a new car!" they exclaimed.

"You switch wives, I switch cars. Buying it was easy, but getting the right number plate was a bit of a challenge," said Ma. His was "88888". This was an especially sought-after combination, known as the "Old Leopard" among collectors, because "8" sounded like "hit the big time".

One day, Mr Ma had stumbled into the teashop very drunk. "Go and buy me some calligraphy from Yi Guang, the more characters on it, the better," he ordered his assistant.

"And the blacker the ink, the better!" Hai Ruo teased him.

Mr Ma chuckled. "What's your most expensive tea? Give me two boxes, gift-wrapped."

xiao-Tang hurriedly packed the tea for him, and asked him to transfer the money. "You might regret it when you've sobered up!"

"Regret it? Me? How much can a bit of tea cost?" Then he turned to Hai Ruo. "Hey there, what's the most difficult number to break through?"

"What do you mean?"

Ma raised two fingers, then three. "From two to three, there's a bottleneck. But you're looking at a man who's finally made it to three after all these years."

Hai Ruo knew he was a multimillionaire, so she asked, "You've made three hundred million?"

"Nah, add another zero! I've broken through to the billions!" said Ma.

After the boom came the bust, however. Coal prices plummeted so steeply that mining companies lost thousands of yuan on each ton of coal they sold. A gas explosion at a coal mine killed and wounded twenty miners, and Ma had to pay out astronomical sums in compensation. The last straw was a national crackdown on polluting businesses: the government shut down all of Mr Ma's small coal mines. The coal tycoon no longer showed up at the teashop.

Now, Hai Ruo gets five pieces of calligraphy out of the cabinet, then settles on three.

"He's a wealthy man, why are we giving him such a discount?" xiao-Tang objects.

"He's a different man now," replies Hai Ruo.

"He shouldn't have flaunted his wealth back in the day!"

Hai Ruo gives xiao-Tang a reproachful look. "On your way to the New Epoch Hotel, buy him a nice shirt. He was one of our best customers for years. He might be in trouble now, but a half-starved camel is still bigger than a horse. We'll need his business in the future."

"He's not as kind to us as Mr Qi. Why buy him a shirt? Isn't a canister of tea good enough?"

Hai Ruo gives in with a smile.

xiao-Tang arrives at the hotel and finds Mr Ma drinking alone in his room. The man's hair has turned white and he looks gaunt.

"Ooh, you do look different," xiao-Tang says.

"Maybe because my pot belly's gone? I've been on a diet," replies Mr Ma. He takes the calligraphy scrolls from her, but his knowledge of art is quite limited, and he asks her, "Which one should I give to a top official, to wish him progress up the promotion ladder? And which one for a retired official, to wish him a happy retirement?" xiao-Tang makes the choices for him, and Ma makes a little mark on the bags the scrolls are packed in. xiao-Tang gives him the gift of tea and makes friendly enquiries about his business. He smiles. "So-so."

"Hai-jie was saying she wants to invite you to a meal some time," xiao-Tang says.

"It should be me treating you," says Mr Ma. "I was going to invite you all when I fetched the calligraphy. But I've not been well. Too much internal dampness. So I booked the hotel's masseur for a moxibustion session. Thank you for bringing the calligraphy pieces."

"Don't mention it, Mr Ma. But you know that moxibustion only helps with a localised infection. If your body has too much dampness, I'd recommend Xiang Qiyu's Terahertz Energy Tank Studio. She's just opened it. An hour in the tank and you'll feel reinvigorated."

"Who's Xiang Qiyu?"

"You don't know her? She's in Hai-jie's sisterhood."

"I must have seen her, but the name doesn't bring up a face. Good, I can go there for an hour's treatment and still make it for lunch."

"Aiya, I came out in such a hurry, I forgot to bring any cash," exclaims xiao-Tang.

"Good heavens, I didn't mean that you should pay for me!"

When they arrive at Qiyu's studio, xiao-Tang has a few whispered words with Qiyu, then Mr Ma is taken to one tank suite, and xiao-Tang goes into another. While the tank is switched on and heats up, she strips off, downs a fifty-millilitre glass of herbal medicine and climbs in. At first, as the tank's lid shuts on her, she feels like she's been shut in a coffin, but then the heat takes over. It is almost unbearable. Her body feels like a sieve, leaking sweat from every pore. Soon the sheet beneath her is drenched, and she can wring water out of the towel. An hour later, she emerges from the tank and takes a cold shower. Her eyes, ears, nostrils and mouth feel cleansed, her skin glows, her eyesight is sharper and she feels relaxed from head to toe.

A few minutes later, Mr Ma comes out of his suite. "How was it?" inquires Qiyu.

"Awesome!" exclaims Ma. "It's done more than steam my flesh, it's steamed right down to my bones. All my fatigue and my worries have evaporated!"

"Then you should come more often!" Qiyu urges him.

"I certainly will, and I'll bring my business associates with me," promises Mr Ma. They exchange phone numbers.

xiao-Tang heads back to the teashop but the car has a puncture on the way. She stops at a shack offering car repairs. While she is waiting for them to fix it, she takes a seat and looks across the street. Above her head, a spider dangles from the awning, attached to a strand of silk so fine it is almost invisible, so that the spider appears to be floating in mid-air. Workers are installing an advertising billboard across the street. Not the old-fashioned kind with a poster behind a glass, this is a hi-tech installation with light, sound and colour and constantly changing images. A woman seductively extols the virtues of a sour plum soup that will quench the thirst and do wonders for one's health.

Ahead of her, the street forks. Just where the street branches off to the right, a restaurant is being revamped. xiao-Tang passes by this street on her way between home and work, so she notes that it's the fourth time the place has changed hands in two years. For a few months, tiny "pearl *jiaozi*" dumplings were sold there, then it was Jiangyuan fish stew. Soon, the name above the eatery changed again: Thirteen Steamed Bowls. The repair shack workers are saying that the left branch of the fork points directly at the restaurant's door. "That's bad feng shui, no wonder they keep going bust," says a mechanic. Strangely enough, as soon as one business packs up, another arrives, then another. xiao-Tang feels the building's pain, as its walls and floors are constantly pulled apart and put back together.

Now someone appears at the restaurant door, a very young woman with a baby in her arms. She's arguing with a man. "You never took me to the hospital or gave me any money. Do you think I made this baby all by myself? You fucked a kid but you don't want to raise a kid!"

"Stupid cunt! If I had the money, of course I'd give it to you! I don't have a cent!"

"You think I've got money? You've never given me anything! Our baby's got a raging temperature!" says the woman. The man brings out three yuan. "You think that's enough for a doctor!" she protests. The man turns and stomps away. The woman is so distraught she sinks down until she's squatting on the ground. Finally, she struggles to her feet and carries the baby to a tiny clinic down the street, wailing all the while.

In the distance, xiao-Tang can hear a rumble of drum beats. It must be the local wind and percussion band, she thinks. Ever since the city's Tang dynasty court-style ensembles became famous, the residents of this street have been busy jumping on the bandwagon. Whenever they've got time, the group gathers to play the drums and other instruments. No one understands what they are thumping about, but the musicians seem to enjoy themselves hugely.

Just then, xiao-Tang notices an odd-looking man with very short limbs. He has appeared out of nowhere, and is carrying a wooden stick in one hand, and a turtle in the other. The turtle is huge, several times larger than the man's head. When he reaches the shack, the man stops all of a sudden and peers inside, a sinister smile on his face. xiao-Tang suddenly remembers seeing a chameleon snatching a praying mantis on *Animal World* on TV last night – this man has exactly the same reptilian expression. Meanwhile, the man has planted the stick in the ground and hung the turtle by its tail atop the stick. The turtle's head dangles out of its shell by quite some distance, at least the span of someone's outstretched thumb and middle finger.

"Hey, you, the turtle will die if you hang it like that," says xiao-Tang.

"No, it won't," says the man. "Two thousand yuan, and it's yours."

"Turtles are spiritual beings, why are you tormenting it?"

"Right, and if you eat it, that'll make you more spiritual."

"Huh!" xiao-Tang is disgusted. "OK, I'll give you a thousand yuan for it."

"Fifteen hundred."

"A thousand."

"You've got yourself a bargain. Half a kilo of pork costs fifty yuan these days. This turtle's fifteen kilos."

"Take the turtle down," xiao-Tang says, and she hands him the cash.

When xiao-Tang arrives at the teashop with the turtle, Hai Ruo jumps up and fetches a basin, fills it with water and gently lays the turtle inside. It barely fits. She brings out a large porcelain jar and empties its contents, asking, "Where's it from? I've never seen a turtle this big."

xiao-Tang tells her what happened. "He had this outlandish accent, maybe from the south," she adds.

"Where I come from, turtles are the size of rice bowls," says Wenlai excitedly. "This one's bigger than a winnowing fan. Imagine the broth it'll make!"

"I'll make broth out of you!" says xiao-Tang in annoyance.

"We've got to set it free," says Hai Ruo, handing 1,000 yuan to xiao-Tang. xiao-Tang refuses. "Come on, take it!" says Hai Ruo, sticking the cash into xiao-Tang's pocket. Together they carry the basin upstairs.

Hai Ruo asks xiao-Tang to message the sisterhood's WeChat group to say that they're releasing the creature into Quhu Lake in a *fangsheng* ceremony tonight. Anyone interested should be at the teashop at eight o'clock."

xiao-Tang clicks Send and says, "If this turtle were human, it'd be laughing at its good luck."

"There'll be laughing... and there'll be crying too," says Hai Ruo cryptically.

"Who'll be crying? Has Lishui brought Xin Qi over? I thought Xu Qi was a cry-baby, but Xin Qi beats her hands down!"

"The world doesn't just consist of our teashop!"

"When I become the Xijing Party chief, or the mayor, then I'll start worrying about the rest of the city."

"It is the Party chief I'm talking about."

"I thought he was up before the Disciplinary Committee?"

"And it's not only him. Mr Wu's PA dropped by this morning. She said the Disciplinary Committee hauled in two business leaders two days ago, then another yesterday. You can't dig up a mooli without mud sticking to it. I've been thinking about it and decided it's better to talk to you now, so we're both mentally prepared."

"Mentally prepared? What's it got to do with us? OK, so we've all seen the Party chief on TV, but would he know who we are?"

"Mr Qi is connected to him, and we're connected to Mr Qi."

"So they took Mr Qi, too?"

"He's in Macau right now but they're sure to get him the moment he comes back. If it's only petty sleaze, they'll soon be let out... in ten days, two weeks, six months or even a year, it's hard to tell. But once Mr Qi is in there, he might confess and drag us down with him."

xiao-Tang looks visibly anxious. "But we don't have anything to do with Mr Qi, apart from him buying expensive tea from us," she objects.

"I don't know if you're aware, but when I got you to buy two hundred kilos of gold with Mr Qi's money, it was actually on the instructions of the Party chief."

"That was the Party chief's money?" cries xiao-Tang, distraught. "I thought I was running an errand for Mr Qi!"

"Hush! Keep your voice down! No one's going to blame you, you were just running an errand. I'm going to remind Mr Qi of that, so he keeps his lips buttoned. I've called his office and asked his assistants to tell him to come back without delay."

"But if he comes back now, won't he walk straight into the arms of the investigators?"

"If something's really wrong, he has nowhere to run. Nor do we. If we do get dragged in, let's tell them absolutely everything. We just ran an errand, what's the worst that could happen?"

Crestfallen, xiao-Tang looks at the floor. She is silent.

"If I didn't tell you, you'd be even more upset and blame me," Hai Ruo goes on. "So don't look so gloomy now I've shared the information. Go home and get a good nap. I'll let you know if anything happens."

"I'll take a nap here. Don't let anyone come upstairs when you go out," says xiao-Tang, slumping onto the couch.

Hai Ruo spends the rest of the afternoon sorting and packing the newly-delivered tea leaves, taking phone calls meanwhile from Yu Benwen, Xiang Qiyu, Yan Nianchu, Si Yinan and Xu Qi. They all pepper her with questions: "What put it into your head to do *fangsheng* tonight? The air quality's terrible!" "Are we going to Quhu Lake again?" "Is it a fish, a snake or a *bie* turtle?" "A *wugui* turtle? Where did you get it? Is it the only one or are there several?" "Do these giants really still exist?"

"If we're meeting at the teashop at eight tonight, should we eat first, or are you inviting us to a banquet?" Lu Yike wants to know.

"Fat chance! Come after your dinner!" says Hai Ruo.

Ying Lihou is the last to call. "Is Yan Nianchu coming tonight?"

"She is."

"In that case, I'm not coming."

"Haven't you two made it up yet? Why won't you see her? You can't avoid her forever."

"I'm still really annoyed. I'm not ready to see her yet, I need more time. My face is an open book for anyone to read my thoughts. It'd embarrass everyone if I came. Best for me to stay away. It's Yinan's turn at the hospital, I'll do it for her tonight."

"All right then, but let's make it very clear, this matter stays between you, me and Nianchu. Don't breathe a word to another soul."

Eva is bubbling with excitement. "I'll be there, I've never seen a Buddhist ceremony like that before!" Then, just before the day's work is done, she gets a text. It's from Yi Guang, "Can you come to the Cloud-Gathering Hall tonight? I'll draw your portrait."

At first, Eva is thrilled at Yi Guang's invitation and his offer to paint her, but then the doubts creep in: Yi Guang backed me up against the cabinet and kissed me last time. What's he up to now? Then she tries to look at it in another way: writers and artists are romantics, what does a kiss mean anyway? Even if he's pushy, I still don't believe he'd hold a knife to my throat. So she texts back, "OK."

Another text arrives. "Great! I'll see you then. About the portrait, not a word to Hai Ruo and the others. They're always asking for my calligraphy and paintings, but I never give them any."

Fine, thinks Eva, and she says to Hai Ruo, "My landlady just called, she's had a nasty dizzy spell. I can't come with you to the lake, I have to go back and see if she needs anything."

After dinner, the other women gather at the teashop. They're all dressed up as if they're going to a party. The teashop has closed early. Wenlai puts the turtle in a hessian sack and they drive to the lake in five cars.

While the day has been dreary, this evening the illuminations light up the lake brilliantly. Now that the smog is invisible, the throngs of people ambling along apparently believe it's gone away, and none are wearing masks. Most are tourists drawn by the fame of this beauty spot. Everyone marvels at the great expanse of water that reflects the brightly-lit pavilions and other buildings dotted along the shore. Roosting birds, disturbed by human voices, take off and scatter into the night sky. Off to the side of the paths, nature has been allowed to run wild. Dewdrops twinkle like stars on the flowers and grasses. There are plenty of locals too, promenading along, or running past, the men bare-chested, while the outdoor gyms and children's play areas are full of women and kids chattering, screaming and laughing.

Hai Ruo and her friends try several spots, but none are satisfactory. Finally, they cross a low bridge that leads to an islet in the lake. A small pavilion is perched on the islet, looking out over rocks that appear and disappear as the water approaches and retreats.

"This is it," says Hai Ruo. She lights an incense stick, clasps it in her palms and bows several times towards the lake, then she plants the stick in the ground.

Lishui and Yike have tipped the turtle out of the sack. Two more pairs of hands join theirs to carry it towards the water. "One, two, three, in you go!" They launch the creature and it hits the water with an almighty splash. The turtle was quite still while they were carrying it, but as soon as it lands – upside down – its four feet thrust out and it paddles frantically until it rights itself. In an instant, it has dived to the bottom.

Qiyu is at the back and by the time she has pushed to the front, the lake surface is still as a mirror again. "What's the hurry? Did anyone take a video?"

"Doesn't it rain when you release a creature? So where's the rain?" asks Yike.

No sooner are the words out of her mouth than she feels a drop of rain on her face. Hai Ruo, Xu Qi and Qiyu also feel wetness. Suddenly, it is as if the surface of the lake is covered in dancing nails. Miraculous! They are about to raise a cheer when they see something even more extraordinary.

Just ten metres away, the turtle has reemerged. It raises its head high out of the water, and then dips it in a nod, once, twice, three times. They are speechless with astonishment. In a few moments, the turtle has disappeared into the water once more and the raindrops have ceased. Lishui finds her voice, "Oh my, was it thanking us!" They give it some rousing cheers.

Their *fangsheng* this evening has been such an amazing experience that they decide then and there that if they come across a turtle for sale in the street, they'll buy it whatever it costs. And they will come here again to set it free. They hang around at the pavilion for a long time, laughing and chatting. No one is in a hurry to leave.

Finally Yike says, "The turtle got its water, but we're still parched."

"I'll get some water at the store by the park entrance," offers Yinan. She sets out with Xu Qi on her heels.

"Hey, they're inseparable, aren't they?" says Qiyu, looking around at the others, but they ignore her comment.

"I wonder where the turtle's gone," says Hai Ruo.

They look at the lake, its surface studded with the shimmering, jewel-like reflections of distant lights.

"Gone to get something to eat, for sure," says Benwen.

"Food, that's all a restaurateur cares about," says Lishui.

Benwen laughs. "By the way, just so you know, we've had a delivery of naked carp from Qinghai Lake. Tomorrow I'm inviting you all for a very special fish hotpot. Raise your hand if you're in!"

"We're here to release a turtle, and you talk about fish hotpot!" objects Yike. "I'm vegetarian now, I won't touch anything that moves!" All the same, half-a-dozen other hands go up.

"Qiyu, you keep talking about taking the Buddhist initiation ceremony. Are you really going too?" asks Lishui.

"I'll have this one meal before the Living Buddha arrives," replies Qiyu. "Once he's here and I become a Buddhist, I'll abide by all the rules."

"I don't think Qiyu should become a Buddhist, do you, Hai-jie?" Lishui says.

Hai Ruo does not answer directly. She says, "There are three precepts in the initiation – to refrain from killing, stealing and lying. As long as you don't take a life, you can eat whatever you want."

"Is that so?" says Benwen.

"What exactly does 'lying' mean here?" Qiyu persists.

"Lying, or musàvàdà, covers anything from untruths to slander, abuse and sycophancy," Hai Ruo explains.

"Well, I'll refrain from all these after I'm initiated," says Qiyu.

"Is that even possible?" Nianchu cuts in. "How can you do business without spinning tales? Hai-jie, does spinning tales count as lying?"

"That depends on what's being said," replies Hai Ruo.

"Take adverts for example," says Nianchu, "they're all exaggerations. If that's lying, then Yike's advertising company will have to shut up shop."

"Right!" says Yike.

"I was just giving an example, Lu-jie," says Nianchu. "Please don't take it the wrong way."

But Yike doesn't reply. She gets up and heads for the water. Hai Ruo grabs the hem of her jacket as she passes and whispers, "What's wrong? Are you all right?"

"My company is going under!" says Yike.

"You only lost the LED screens, is that such a big deal?" asks Hai Ruo.

Yinan and Xu Qi hurry back. Besides a Coke and an ice cream for everyone, they have also bought bananas, pistachios, malted millet *qiongguo* candy, sunflower and melon seeds, plus two packets of cigarettes. Hai Ruo opens a packet, gives a cigarette to Nianchu and lights one for herself.

"How generous of you, Xu Qi," exclaims Qiyu.

"Actually, Yinan bought everything," Xu Qi says.

"Still, we have you to thank!" insists Qiyu. "If you weren't there, Yinan would have just got everyone a bottle of mineral water."

"No gratitude from you then," says Yinan.

"I'm just telling it like it is," says Qiyu. "You know the trick question, if we all fell into the lake, who would you save first. Well, who would you save first?"

Xu Qi has peeled a banana to give to Qiyu to stop her talking, but changes her mind and takes a bite out of it herself. She changes the subject. "What a pity Yi Guang-laoshi isn't here tonight, or we could have had some fine words to commemorate the evening. Wenlai! Wenlai!"

"I'm here," answers Wenlai, busy folding the sack.

"You ought to compose a poem," Xu Qi urges him.

"OK," he promises. He hands out paper napkins to everyone. "Remember to wrap up the fruit peel and melon seed husks."

"When we went to buy the food and drink," Yinan tells them, "a park warden who'd heard about the turtle asked us how big it was, so I said it was bigger than a winnowing fan. And guess what? The man told us off! He said we mustn't do that without their approval. He said we should only buy fish and *bie* turtle from them. I did see a huge water container in their office, it was teeming with fish and turtles. The fishes cost ten yuan each, turtles fifteen."

Yike says, "Why do I have this sudden feeling that they're catching the fish and turtles at night, and selling them to devout visitors to release the next day, and repeating the process every day?"

No one knows what to say to this. They hear splashing coming from the lake. Near another islet some distance away, they can just make out the outline of a boat and someone in it. Can it really be that the park wardens are netting and hooking fish and turtle?

"When I first came to Xijing, it was such a wonderful place," laments Yike. "Nowadays, we're smothered in smog, and the people are evil."

No one speaks. The lake is peaceful once more, but everyone feels a twinge of unease.

伊
娃

21. EVA • THE CLOUD-GATHERING HALL

EVA ARRIVES, and Yi Guang shows her straight up to the attic. A sheet of *xuan* rice paper is spread over the drawing desk, and porcelain dishes containing the pigments are arranged neatly down the sides. On a small square table in front of the desk, a large red candle is lit. Around it is an arrangement of fruit, snacks, wine and a very small cake. Eva is nonplussed. She is on the verge of shrugging, holding her hands up and pulling a face when Yi Guang claps his hands. "Happy birthday!"

"Is it the twenty-first today?"

"It is!"

Eva has not exactly forgotten her birthday but she has lost track of the days, and besides, she's in China. She is touched that Yi Guang has put in so much effort to celebrate it. On her way up in the lift, she envisioned all sorts of scenarios, and came up with a plan or two to deal with them. But suddenly all that has vanished, as completely as a white puff of breath exhaled in frosty winter air. She gazes at the candle's dancing flame and the soft, smooth trickles of candle wax, and finds that her eyes are moist with tears. "But how did you know it's my birthday?" she asks.

"The other day when we all met at the teashop, I asked you which

Russian city you were from, and you showed me your passport. Your birthday was in it."

Eva comes forward and pecks him on the cheek. Yi Guang smiles. He doesn't try to seize her in an embrace, or kiss her back, but neither does he wipe the lipstick from his cheek.

"Amazing, you remembered my birthday from one glance at the passport!"

"If I like a woman, nothing about her escapes me."

"So you really like me?"

"I do."

"But why? I'm a *laowai*, and I'm only in Xijing on a short visit."

By way of an answer, Yi Guang recites, "'People in this world treasure illusory things such as the Wine Spring, whose waters are as sweet as wine. Everyone drinks wine, but it's a sip of the Wine Spring waters that they yearn for.'"

"You've lost me. Are you quoting the classics?"

"Forget it. It just means that I like you. Come on, let's celebrate your birthday. May I wish you all happiness and joy while you're in China!"

Eva thanks him profusely. She has been to birthday parties in China, so she does what she has seen them do and inserts three small candles in the cake and lights them. As Yi Guang croons *Happy Birthday to You*, she puts her palms together and makes a silent wish, before blowing out the candles all in one go. Yi Guang busies himself with cutting the cake, finding glasses and pouring wine. They start drinking.

Eva is not impressed by the label. In fact she thinks the wine tastes a bit strange, but she clinks glasses with Yi Guang and they drink. When one bottle is finished, they open another. Before she realises it, her cheeks and ears have gone a flaming crimson and she can't see straight. She focuses on the big candle on the table, but the flame keeps moving – from the top of the candle one moment, to hovering beside it, bulging and shrinking by turns. She pats herself on the forehead and mutters, "My head's spinning..." Then she collapses onto her side on the sofa behind the table.

"Wonderful, stay there, don't move, you're ravishing!" Yi Guang exclaims. He's at the drawing desk, where he picks up a brush, dips it in ink and begins to sketch her. Obediently, Eva lies motionless and rigid, staring blankly at him.

Six or seven minutes go by, and Eva complains, "I'm exhausted!"

"I've got the outline done. You can take a break, get yourself a drink or a smoke," Yi Guang says.

"Can we go on chatting?"

"Sure. Hey, look in front of you, into that corner. That's right. Your eyes are delicious!"

"Chinese is a fascinating language! You say the eyes speak, or they're delicious."

"Right, for us Chinese, we can't decide if something is good or not until we take a bite of it."

"Hah, is that why you say to each other, 'You're my dish'?"

"That's right."

"So, am I your dish?"

"You tell me."

"You've got so many dishes already, I don't want to be another one!"

Yi Guang laughs. He passes a hand over his face.

"Hey, I've discovered a secret of yours."

"Oh?"

"You are enormously gifted. Even at your age, you're still witty and charming. But you're kind of shy. When you're talking to Hai-jie and the others in the sisterhood, you come over all awkward and rub your face, the way a cat does. You do know how attractive shyness is in a man?"

"Is that so? It's not intentional."

"But it's just that body language that you're not aware of that's made you into their dish."

"Hah! But there are so many of them in the sisterhood, a single dish is nowhere near enough!"

"You remind me of a St Petersburg poet, a famous romantic with a string of lovers. He was careful to keep his women apart, and met them in different places. Come Sunday, he knew they'd all try to arrange an assignation with him so, in order not to snub any of them, or let on who he was seeing, he used to hit the bottle as soon as he got up and drink himself into a stupor."

Yi Guang laughs out loud. "Clever man!" He shows her his sketch and is just saying, "Is it a good likeness?" when his mobile rings. He pulls it out of his pocket, looks to see who it is and puts his finger to his lips. Then he puts the picture down and goes to the window to take the call.

Eva says nothing. She inspects the drawing but she is listening to the call as well. She hears Yi Guang say, "Good evening, sir. You're working late! Yes, yes, I'm fine... Of course, of course... I'm still writing articles, and doing calligraphy and painting... No, I haven't sold any recently. Ah, I see. Go ahead, I'm on my own here. As far as I'm concerned, he deserves everything that's coming to him. What? Is it that serious? Oh, Oh."

The sketch shows Eva lying on the sofa. It is a very fine likeness. In particular, he has captured the contour of her temples and her cheek bones, the nape of her neck, her lower back, and the way her arms fall. *I really look good*, Eva tells herself.

The conversation goes on, "...Uh-huh, yes, I'm listening. I know him well, but only because I had to report to him at work. He made a big thing about being concerned for me. Of course, I'm drawing a line under all that now, I'll be having nothing more to do with him. What? The meeting is tomorrow? Do you think I should be there? Aiya, I have to go to the doctor tomorrow, I've just remembered. Can I skip the meeting? Uh-huh, OK. As you wish. I'll be there. What? I have to state my position? But what should I say? Fine, fine."

Yi Guang seems to have changed into a different person, Eva observes. He sounds flustered, and his mixed feelings are written all over his face. Is he putting on an act? She wants to ask him, but he is looking so serious that she doesn't dare.

The call ends and Yi Guang returns, looking despondent. He sits down on the sofa, sighing heavily.

"Who was that? What was that about?"

"It was our general secretary. He was telling me more about the Xijing Party chief being *shuanggui*."

"*Shuanggui?*"

"It means being investigated by a Party disciplinary panel."

"Huh?"

"There's a meeting tomorrow. I shouldn't be there, but I've been told to attend anyway."

"Why? Are you involved too?"

"If he's corrupt, it's his business. Why would I be involved?"

"But will you go to the meeting tomorrow?"

"I don't want to talk about it any more. Did you look at the sketch? Is it a good likeness?"

"Yes, it certainly is! I'm amazed that you're so good with the brush when you're really a writer."

"Writing, calligraphy and painting share the same *jingjie*. It's just that they each have their own language for expressing it."

"But what exactly is *jingjie*? How does one get it?" Eva asks. Yi Guang says nothing. "Am I asking foolish questions?"

"No, not at all. I just don't know how to answer them. The fact is that writers, painters and calligraphers today are nothing special. All we're doing is regurgitating the *dao* paths and the *li* theories that were explored by the sages of old, just in different ways. What am I to do? I just have to try to 'avoid being snared in a trap, or die in a net'. I accept things as they are, I write my articles, or do a bit of calligraphy and painting. But this is 'nourishing the bird with my own food, not with what the bird needs for its sustenance'. And sometimes even that doesn't work." Yi Guang looks despondent again.

Eva has no idea where the quotes have come from, though she's guessing it's some ancient Taoist sage. But she feels a wave of sympathy for his predicament. "But you're so very talented," she says. "Can you teach me? Can you nurture my talent, even just a little bit?"

Yi Guang turns to look at Eva. He leans forward and runs the back of his forefinger down her nose. "A woman doesn't need to be a genius," he chides her. "Your beauty is your talent."

"But I'm not beautiful," Eva says. "Look at my feet, they're huge. When I was little, I only got to wear my sister's castoffs. I grew fast and the trousers were never long enough. I had to wear her old shoes too, and they pinched my feet. Look, I've still got a bunion on my right big toe."

"I noticed. That's why I asked you to tuck your leg under you when I was drawing, but your right foot still shows."

Eva looks at the sketch again. She pulls a towel over her feet, then lies on her side on the sofa again. "Draw me again, please!" Yi Guang obeys and goes back to the drawing desk.

"To get a really good portrait, you have to draw the subject nude," he remarks.

"You want me nude? This is not an artist's studio, and I'm not your life class model."

"It would only be taking your clothes off, nothing more."

"Just you saying 'nothing more' means that something else did cross your mind."

"Last time you came, I kissed you," says Yi Guang, smiling, "but I haven't put my arms around you today."

Eva looks at him. "Huh, you're leading up to something, I can tell." She gets up and pours herself another glass, tips her head back and swallows it in gulps, then sits down on the sofa, readying herself into another pose.

"A work of art," comments Yi Guang.

"What was that?" asks Eva.

"You're a work of art." He comes over and moves her head to one side, then the other. Then he puts his arm around her waist, pulls her so she is sitting upright and instructs, "Tuck in your belly, move your hips forward a bit." Every time he touches her, Eva gives a twitch. "Relax!" he soothes her.

"When a cup becomes art, you can't use it any more, you have to display it on a shelf," says Eva.

"That's for sure."

Eva gives a sudden laugh. "Look at me, are you trying to make me look like those flying apsaras in the teashop?"

"Yes."

"But they're soaring upwards, and I'm falling down, aren't I?"

"Falling is another kind of flying."

"You're seducing me."

"I'm quoting a philosopher."

"Eh?" says Eva. But Yi Guang says nothing more.

He goes back to the painting desk, spreads out a fresh sheet of paper and begins to draw. But his heart doesn't seem to be in it and he is working very slowly. He observes her for a long time before he makes a single stroke then, dissatisfied, he tears up the paper and starts on a fresh sheet. After he has made three botched attempts, Eva asks him, "Still thinking about the call just now? Aren't I enough to take your mind off it?"

"It's not that, Eva. You know, drawing you is a torment, especially now."

"A torment?"

"Let me take a few deep breaths." And he begins to inhale and exhale.

"I'm relaxed, why are you so anxious? Surely it's not the first time you've done a woman's portrait?"

"In a way you're right. I've never seen a woman with a figure like yours in China."

"I'm a different race, that's why."

"They say Russian women are beautiful when they're young but put on weight as they get older."

"Not necessarily. My big sister's had three kids, but her body's just like mine, and I think I'll keep my figure too."

"Uh-huh, if that's right then there is something in this world that lasts forever." His phone beeps. Yi Guang checks it but it's only a spam message. He begins to draw her arm again, but cannot get her fingers right. "Move your hand forward," he says. There is no response. Yi Guang looks up, to find her head pillowed on the arm rest. She is asleep.

"Eva, wake up!" he calls a couple of times, but she does not stir. He goes to the sofa and observes her up close. The night is quiet. Suddenly, there is a creaking, maybe from one of the wall cabinets. The wood often emits creaks and groans as it expands or contracts with the change in room temperature. He wants to be sure, so he stands perfectly still, ears cocked. A few minutes pass, and silence falls again. All he can hear is a car or lorry whooshing past every now and then. In the lamplight, Eva's face and neck gleam opalescent, while her body seems to give off a faint warm smell. He checks his watch, and sees that the hour hand is pointing to one. "Eva, why have you gone to sleep?" he exclaims.

Eva is not asleep. She's just too tired to open her eyes. Let Yi Guang think that she is asleep. She is aware of him sitting beside her, gazing at her. His eyes travel across her hair, forehead, nose, lips, breasts, then down to her feet. She feels like an open book as she lets him examine her, and is quietly aware of her body's reactions. His head has not moved, nor have his hands. She wonders why he is doing this. Doesn't he want me? That can't be true. I saw him when he said I had a beautiful body. I saw his eyes and lips, the muscles of his face and hands. He really wanted me. Maybe he's still upset by that phone call. Or am I just a portrait to him? Just another task he has to complete, like sweeping the floor, cleaning the table or shutting a window that the wind has blown open. And he's waiting for me to wake up. Or maybe he thinks it would be ungentlemanly to make a move when I'm dead drunk.

Yi Guang gets up and pours himself another glass of wine. He gulps it down with such urgency that he almost chokes on it. The room is very quiet. There is a tap on the window pane. Is it the wind? Or a mouse having a nibble at something? Can mice even make it as far up as this floor? Eva peeks through her eyelids. The big red candle has burned down. In the puddle of wax, the last bit of wick still has a winking flame, as if it is determined to burn to the very end. The teapot, cups and saucers arranged around it are all dry. Eva hurriedly shuts her eyes again. She hears Yi Guang finish his drink and put the glass down on the table. "Are you asleep?" he asks again. But she is still feigning sleep. Finally he moves an arm and rests it on the back of the sofa. He moves his head closer, she feels his breath brushing her face – and she suddenly grabs hold of his neck with both hands, so that she is lifted off the sofa.

"You're awake!"

"You led me on, then you abandoned me!"

He tries to speak, but she covers his mouth with hers. Their limbs intertwine and they pant and cry out. They are struggling with each other's clothes. Buttons pop off and ping against the table. Then the wine bottles and the teapot jiggle and clatter and there is a crash as the table is overturned. The sofa slides a foot towards the window, like a boat through water, then jerks around.

His mobile goes off again. It is on the sofa. He hesitates, then reaches for it. "Damn the phone!" says Eva and kicks it onto the floor. It spins on the spot, flashing wildly. Yi Guang grabs it, swears and throws it into the corner. The phone stops moving and goes quiet. Meanwhile, they are making love. Or rather, they are not. Sweat and passion notwithstanding, Yi Guang is getting nowhere. "This has never happened before, never!" he mutters. They try again, but it is no good. He starts to kiss her from head to toe, and all the way back again. Finally, he lies on top of her, licking her like a dog and does not try again. Eva holds his head between her hands and sees that his face is glistening. She does not know if it is their sweat, her fluid or his tears.

22. YING LIHOU • A CAFE

Lu Yike takes Xia Zihua's mother and son to the Lotus Road Shopping Centre to buy some clothes. They choose new outfits and wear them out of the shop. Following lunch at the plaza, Yike drives them to the teashop. xiao-Tang is busy with some customers who have bought tea and want a teapot to brew it in. She is talking them through the pros and cons of aluminium, porcelain, glass and cast-iron pots, but comes forward to greet Mrs Qi, get her a chair and offer her some pastries. She turns to xiao-Su and says, "Pack this tea in canisters and paper bags for our customers, will you? And xiao-Zhen, we've got three silver teapots hand-made in Japan. Could you fetch them from that cabinet?"

Zihua's mother looks embarrassed. "You are so busy, don't mind me. I'll just take the weight off my legs for a moment."

Hai Ruo hears her and comes out of the cubicle. "Aiya, how smart you look today!" she exclaims.

Mrs Qi gets laboriously to her feet and turns around to show Hai Ruo. "Yike took me and Lei Lei to buy some new clothes. She's got really good taste and spotted this for me. It's perfect!"

"We should wear brighter colours as we get older," says Hai Ruo. "Now you're here, why not treat your knees? Wenlai, Wenlai!"

Gao Wenlai has been changing gas bottles in the cubicle. He comes out. "All done."

"Get the step-ladder and catch some bees," Hai Ruo orders him.

But Mrs Qi stops her. "I just had bee stings the day before yesterday. That's fine for now. Let me get my breath back and we'll be off. Lei Lei is tired, he's been running around the whole morning. It's time for his nap."

Yike and Xia Lei have come inside, and the boy protests, "I'm not tired."

"No, of course you're not," Hai Ruo tells him with a smile. "Wenlai, take Lei Lei to the kiosk and get him some comics." She makes a cup of tea and ushers Mrs Qi into the cubicle to drink it.

Wenlai takes Xia Lei by the hand. "Carry! Carry!" the boy cries as they're about to go down the steps, and Wenlai hoists him up and pins him under one arm. Xia Lei shrieks with delight.

"Do you like the clothes I chose for him?" Yike asks Hai Ruo.

"Are you trying to dress him like a girl?"

"Where I come from, we dress boys in girly clothes to keep the evil eye away from them."

"Fine. It'll be nice when he grows up and is around for his granny."

Yike changes the subject. "Every time I see Zihua's mother and son, I can hardly keep from crying," she sighs. "There's a window in her flat that doesn't shut, and the toilet doesn't flush properly either. I've arranged for someone to fix them tomorrow morning. I'll take them home shortly, then I'll drop by the supermarket and pick up some shopping for them."

"Benwen's had a delivery of rare-breed hens' eggs," says Hai Ruo. "She gave me a box this morning, it's upstairs. Take it with you when you go."

"Who's at the hospital today?"

"It's Lihou's turn."

Hai Ruo's answer reminds Yike of something and she beckons Hai Ruo to the stairs.

On the floor above, the desk is covered with plain scholar fans, some tied with an agate vajra pestle pendant, others waiting their turn. "You're giving little gifts to everyone again," Yike remarks. Then, without waiting for Hai Ruo's reply, she continues, "So Lihou's been swindled out of a fortune, has she?"

Hai Ruo is caught off guard and says nothing. "Have you and Lihou hired a debt collector?" Yike pursues.

Hai Ruo goes pale. "Does no one keep their mouths shut? Why don't we just shout it from the rooftops!"

"I heard it from Fan Bosheng."

Hai Ruo's lips quiver and it looks like she is going to swear. Instead, she tells Yike the whole story. "And how did Mr Fan catch wind of it?" she wants to know.

"He came to my office early today. He was looking for financial support. I told him no. 'I'm like a farmer whose pigs are half-starved,' I said. 'Where would I get extra grain to sell?' He tried to tell me how helpful he'd been to you and Lihou."

"What a blabbermouth. What did he help us with anyway?"

"He said he bought shares in a landscaping business. What with this Greening the City project, the company's been raking it in. They've been digging up trees galore – mature pines, locust trees, ginkgos and osmanthus – in the south and north of the province and transplanting them to the city."

"He's been investing in landscaping? I really hate the way these businesses transplant old trees to 'beautify' the city. It devastates the countryside, and a third of the transplanted trees don't survive."

"Well, anyway, the business is not just into trees, it also does debt collection, and that's how Mr Fan heard you and Lihou have found someone to collect her debt."

Hai Ruo is silent for a moment, then asks, "Did he say how it went?"

"He said they hired dozens of migrant workers. They've been promised three hundred yuan a day to stand in front of the debtor's shop, and shout and wave protest banners."

"That'll be the talk of the town!"

"That's the least of our concerns. What bothers me is that these peasants are dirt poor, and if the debt isn't recovered with the protests, they may take matters into their own hands. Aren't you a friend of Mr Qi? He knows so many city officials, why don't you ask him to pull a few strings. A hospital chief is just a small potato."

"It's next to impossible to get the general secretary to make a simple phone call. I don't think any other official's going to stick their head out right now."

"Well then, you'll have to take it to court."

"But Lihou desperately needs to get her money back. A lawsuit could drag on for as much as a year, not to mention that she really doesn't want people finding out."

After Yike has taken her charges home, Hai Ruo sits upstairs fastening pendants to the fans, but she is distracted and the plaiting of the threads is not going well. A line from a Siegfried Sassoon poem comes to her, "In me the tiger sniffs the rose". She wishes she had both feminine and masculine strengths. She wonders if Lihou has heard from Zhang Huai. Has he made any progress? But she brushes the thought aside and calls xiao-Zhen upstairs.

"Go to the TCM clinic across the street, xiao-Zhen, and see if it's busy. If not, I'll go over for a massage."

"Fine," says xiao-Zhen. Then she adds, "A lorry's outside, they say you're expecting them."

"Great," says Hai Ruo, hurrying downstairs.

There are two young men and the driver. "Si Yinan sent us," explains the driver.

Hai Ruo brings the three men in for a cup of tea. Turning to Wenlai, she says, "Xi Lishui and Xin Qi will be here soon. Can you help them with the furniture?" When everything's arranged, she changes her mind and, instead of having a massage at the clinic, she drives to the hospital.

Zihua has been moved to the ICU. Once a patient is in intensive care, the family can't stay with them, but they have to be instantly available in case there are procedures to authorise, so no one dares wander out of earshot. That is why there are always families milling around in the corridor outside the ICU. There is a shortage of chairs so they hunker down on the floor, or stand. They are wan-faced, and mutter in low tones to each other, but no one is really paying attention. Their eyes – full of sleepy dust and worry – are immediately drawn to the slightest sign of movement from inside.

Hai Ruo spots Ying Lihou in the crowd. She is sitting on a handkerchief on the floor, just to the right of the ICU door, a bottle of mineral water in her hands. She is slumped over, her head drooping, mussed-up hair falling over her face, probably dozing. Hai Ruo makes her way over, and stands silently beside Lihou without waking her.

A man is pacing back and forth, back and forth, like a zombie, getting on everyone's nerves. A woman goes up to the ICU entrance for the umpteenth time, glues one eye to the crack between the double doors and tries to see inside. When one eye is tired, she switches to the other. Her eyebrows look like she has rubbed them thin, but she has not managed to see a thing. Finally, she breaks down in sobs, and then everyone is weeping audibly, apart from the few who have silent tears running down their cheeks. A man hurtles through the waiting crowd and makes for the window at the end of the corridor. The window is half open, and the man takes gulps of fresh air, like a stranded fish.

All of a sudden the ICU's doors open a crack and a nurse puts one foot in the doorway. "Zhang Minsheng's family! Zhang Minsheng!"

Heads jerk up and everyone scrambles to their feet. Someone pushes through, saying, "Here! I'm here!"

"You've got more fees to pay!" the nurse says.

Half a dozen people are calling out names, asking the nurse for news, and if they can go in and take a look at them. But the nurse says nothing and shuts the door on them.

Lihou wakes up with a start, to see Hai Ruo standing beside her. "When did you come? Why are you here?" she whispers. "I thought Qiyu was taking over tonight."

"I just wanted to see her. Have you seen her?"

"They won't let us in. Why don't we move her somewhere else? She's really sick, she has no family or friends with her, it's so sad."

"Better follow the doctors' orders," says Hai Ruo.

"I dozed off just now and had a dream, a bad one," says Lihou.

One of the bystanders is looking at them, her face dripping with fat tears, and Hai Ruo takes Lihou by the arm and leads her to the corner of the stairs.

"Dreams are the opposite of reality," Hai Ruo tells her when they are out of earshot.

"Yes, that's what I was telling myself in my dream," says Lihou.

"However bad a dream may be, once you know it's not true, everything will be fine. Come on, don't take it to heart. I bet you haven't eaten. Let me go and buy you something."

"Don't bother, I'll wait till Qiyu takes over. How's Mrs Qi doing?"

"Not too bad. I haven't gone into any unnecessary details, I just said she shouldn't bring the boy on a visit for the moment. Yike took them to a shopping centre this afternoon and bought them clothes."

"Oh, that was nice of Yike."

"Everyone's being nice."

"People are always nice when things are normal. It's when something major happens that you really see what they're like inside. Yan Nianchu is not nice."

"Why do you still hate her so much?"

"I don't. I don't have any feelings about her one way or the other."

"Have you heard from Zhang Huai in the last few days?"

"I was going to call and tell you. I got a call from Mr Wang just two hours ago. He said, 'Are you getting people to threaten me?' I said, 'That money's my life, if I don't get it back, how will I live?' Apparently the debt collectors have organised protests in front of his shop and it's been going on for days. They're not doing any business and his wife has left Xijing in a hurry. The debt-collecting company has even sent him threatening messages, saying if he doesn't pay, they'll ramp it up a notch: they'll protest outside his hospital and kidnap his kid. They told him his kid's name, age and school, everything. When he told me what was going on, I was scared!"

"This afternoon, Yike told me Fan Bosheng knows. We stressed to Zhang Huai that he had to keep it confidential and now Mr Fan's got wind of it. Debt collectors don't follow the rules, and I've a horrible feeling that something really bad is going to happen. It's all my fault, I shouldn't have given them the job."

"Don't say that, Hai-jie. You were just trying to help me. But do you think they were bluffing about kidnapping Wang's kid?"

"That would be drastic, but it could well happen."

"The more I think about it, the more scared I am. To hell with Yan Nianchu!"

"Cursing her doesn't help. Yike says we should take it to court. The thing is, we were too quick off the mark, we were only thinking about getting all the money back quickly."

"Then should we stop the debt collectors?"

"That's what I've been thinking too. I came to talk to you about it. If you agree, I'll have a word with Nianchu and then we can decide."

Hai Ruo's phone has been ringing non-stop. First, Si Yinan reports that Xin Qi's furniture has been moved. Then Yike says that on her way back from taking Zihua's mother and son home, she stopped by the building materials place run by Mr Wang's wife. "The shop was shut, but the protesters hired by the debt collectors were brawling in the restaurant next door. They've been eating there every day, taking up four tables, but only ever ordering rice – no meat, fish or even vegetable dishes. The restaurant staff have been trying to get rid of them, and now they've all come to blows."

"I see," says Hai Ruo.

"What a lot of calls!" Lihou comments.

Hai Ruo gets a text, hushes Lihou, and reads it. It's from her son, Hai Tong. No message, just a bill.

- Monthly rent, 3,000
- Food, 2,000
- Study materials, 1,000
- Gas, 1,200
- Shoes, 500
- Laptop repair, 500
- Property management, 1,500
- Wallet lost with 2,000 in cash
- Glasses broke, replacement pair, 2,000
- Treatment for a sprained ankle, 800
- Cat food, 400
- Mobile bill, 1,000
- Toothpaste, shower gel, toilet paper, tissue paper, 300
- Electricity bill, 500
- Water bill, 600
- New coffee machine, the old one broke, 500

Something explodes in Hai Ruo's head. She types a reply, "What's this? Are you begging or protesting!"

Hai Tong replies instantly, "I'm going to get a job washing dishes in Chinese restaurants!"

"Then do it," Hai Ruo types. "You should have found part-time work long ago to see how hard it is to earn money!"

"Mum, you're so hard-hearted. Why don't you just abandon me if you don't want me any more? Give me to Li Ka-shing in Hong Kong, or Jack Ma."

"Listen here, Hai Tong, don't mess with me! And don't mess with my money!"

"I'm spending my money."

"Your money?"

"Aren't I your only child? So everything you own will come to me in the end? You are actually spending *my* money, Mummy!"

Hai Ruo is enraged but also amused. "What cheek!"

"Who are the texts from?" asks Lihou. "Yan Nianchu?"

"No."

"I must have been blind to make friends with her!"

"Then you should be telling me off. It was me who introduced her to you."

Lihou starts to weep again and puts her arms around Hai Ruo. "You're the only one who's kind to me."

When Qiyu arrives to take over from her, she sees Lihou's swollen eyes and thinks she has been crying for Zihua. She dries her own eyes and urges Lihou to go home and get some rest. Hai Ruo and Lihou head for the alley in front of the hospital, and look for somewhere to eat.

The lane is lined with small eateries offering noodles, *baozi* buns, wontons and *jiaozi* dumplings, and there are also shops selling flowers and fruit, funeral wreaths and burial clothing.

"Wreaths and burial clothing shouldn't be sold right in front of a hospital," complains Lihou. "Patients are here to get better. How's this going to make them feel?"

"Most people die in a hospital."

"When people die, do they know they've died? It's just like going to sleep. You know you've climbed into bed, but you don't know the exact moment you go to sleep."

"Maybe."

They try a wonton place but it's too cramped and they go to a restaurant selling *baozi* and rice porridge instead. Two of the three tables are occupied. At one of them, a woman is weeping softly while a man at her side tries to cheer her up. He keeps coughing and spitting into a rubbish bin beneath the table. At the other table, two men are slurping porridge noisily. One of them has a plaster on the back of his hand, which shows he has just had an IV infusion.

Hai Ruo pulls Lihou by the arm and they walk away. "Those are patients, who knows what they've got."

"So where shall we eat?"

Up ahead, in front of a flower stall across the street, a couple of people are pointing and haggling over baskets of flowers, before leaving without buying anything, muttering that they are not visiting their boss, it would be better to get something the patient can use. They choose a small box of milk cartons in the shop next door.

Outside the burial clothing shop, a board displays the prices for sets of men's and women's funeral outfits, "longevity wear", as it is called, ranging from one piece to three pieces. As with the hospital, there is no haggling here. An old man has just examined a three-piece set for a woman, and now he asks to see the men's outfits.

"Do you want something for a man or a woman?" asks the owner.

"Both. The doctors say my missus is going fast, I have to be ready. And I might as well buy a set for myself at the same time."

"Eh? What? You're buying for yourself?"

"Everybody dies, sooner or later," says the old man. He pays for the three-piece sets for himself and his wife and stands there looking at Hai Ruo and Lihou, apparently talking to himself, "Why are these things called 'longevity clothing' anyway? By the time you need them, you're dead."

Lihou glances at the eateries nearby. "Perhaps we'd better not eat here. I'll just boil myself a bowl of plain noodles back home."

"All right," Hai Ruo agrees. As they part ways, Hai Ruo says, "And make sure you drive safely. Don't get distracted."

But how can Lihou not be distracted? She has been defrauded of a fortune, and to make matters worse, everyone now knows about it. Nothing could be more humiliating. If this business ends in injuries or even deaths, she will be implicated, that is inevitable. If so, she'd lose not just the money, but her reputation, and possibly even more. The deeper she delves into the consequences, the more apprehensive she grows. Several times she almost drives into the back of the car in front. When she finally makes it home, she cannot find the key to her building. It's not in her pocket, and when she turns her bag inside out, it is not there either. Did she leave it in the hospital? She decides to call Qiyu, but where is her phone? She breaks out into a cold sweat. She runs back to the entrance and asks the security guard if she can borrow his phone to make the call.

"But your phone's in your hand, miss," he points out.

And there it is, in her left hand. She bangs the phone against her head in exasperation, and something scratches her – it is her key dangling from her wrist, though she cannot recall putting it there.

She hurries back to the entrance to her building, opens the door and tries to calm down. Then she dials Zhang Huai's number. "I'm putting a stop on the debt collecting, bruv," she says, enunciating her words slowly and calmly.

"What! You want me to stop!" Zhang Huai yells. "I got in a load of extra men and we've all worked our arses off, and now you want to pull the plug!"

"I know you've put a lot into it. We're putting a stop on the operation but of course, I'll make sure you don't lose out," she placates him.

"Of course I'll lose out! I've spent tons of money, and our company's reputation is on the line. What do you think you're doing here? Playing house? You swallowed it, you can't spit it out now! It'll give you an upset stomach if you try! We can't stop, we signed a contract!"

Lihou doesn't know what to say. It is further proof, if any were needed, that Zhang Huai is a thug and she made the right decision in cancelling the contract. She takes a few deep breaths and says, "Now listen to me, bruv, why don't we do it this way? I'll give you three hundred thousand, and we'll call it quits. No more debt collecting."

"Three hundred thousand? But we agreed on ten per cent!"

"That was when the debt was recovered in full. You haven't got a cent back yet, have you?" There's no reply. Lihou tries again, "Zhang Huai?"

"I've never met anyone like you! Fine!" Zhang Huai says.

"Are you free now?" Lihou says quickly. "Come to the coffee bar on the corner of Kangning Road and Xinghua Lane, and I'll give you the cash. And we'll rip the contracts up while we're there." Zhang Huai agrees.

The cafe Lihou suggests is two streets away from where she lives. She doesn't want the debt collector to come to her home, or to find out where she lives. She goes home, collects the cash and stashes it in a paper bag. As she goes out of the door, it occurs to her that she has paid Zhang Huai 50,000 yuan as an advance. So she removes 50,000 and leaves it behind. But what if Zhang Huai insists on the full amount? she asks herself. She puts the bank notes into her pocket. It's a bit late to be clever now, she berates herself. You should have been smarter when you lent the money.

She arrives at the cafe in good time and orders a coffee. She has drunk half by the time Zhang Huai arrives. She orders another cup for him.

"Just one more bundle of firewood and your beef would be cooked. Why are you taking the wood out from under?" he says.

"Look, Mr Wang and I are friends, I don't want to turn him into an enemy," says Lihou.

"He *is* your enemy if he doesn't pay you back!"

"He'll pay, it'll just take time. I'll wait."

"You must have loads of money then!" Zhang Huai is sounding friendly as he counts the banknotes. Then he says, "Why's it fifty thousand short?"

"I paid you fifty thousand in advance."

"Come on now! You gave me the fifty thousand as expenses while I was drawing up a plan. Your words!"

"My words?"

The young man snatches the paper bag containing the 250,000 yuan, and glares at her, revealing an alarming amount of white in his eyes. "Your words!" he insists, keeping his copy of the contract firmly in his pocket.

"All right, I'll give you the fifty thousand – I've already lost the ox, I might as well throw in the rope as well." Lihou takes the wads of bank notes out of her pocket and hands them to Zhang Huai, who brings out his contract. They put the two contracts together and rip them to pieces. Lihou asks him to write a receipt for the 300,000 yuan, specifying that she no longer wants him to collect the debt.

Zhang Huai scribbles on the paper. "How do you write the character for 'debt' again?" he asks. He attempts to write the ten-stroke character several times, pressing so hard that his pen makes three holes in the paper.

"How many years did you spend at school?"

"My uncle brought me to Xijing before I finished primary school. You won't laugh at me?" he pleads.

"Why would I do that? You've got your own business now."

Zhang Huai thanks her and leaves with the bag of cash. Lihou drinks her coffee, musing that she shouldn't have given him the

50,000. It was only his word against mine, she thinks. If I'd said I recorded our first meeting, that might have scared him into backing down... I'm not a very quick thinker, am I? When her second cup of coffee comes, she sits over it gloomily. Maybe he wasn't as bad as I thought. Maybe I should have let him carry on and finish the job.

23. XIN QI • THE WORKERS' HOUSING BLOCK

FOR THE REMAINDER OF THE NIGHT, Eva sleeps on the sofa in the Cloud-Gathering Hall. She wakes to find herself alone. She goes in search of Yi Guang but he is not downstairs in the sitting room, or in his study either. Back in the attic, she sits down, then spots a note on the small table: "I've got a meeting. Make sure the door's shut when you leave." Eva lies down on the sofa again.

She feels like staying there and sleeping through until dusk, but she can't get comfortable. She tosses and turns until her arms and legs are finally settled, but her mind is still buzzing. Fragments of the previous night surface in her mind, some vivid and clear, others less so, but all with a dream-like quality. She turns and looks up. Outside the skylight, two pigeons perch, glittering in the light. The sun's rays shoot through the glass like arrows to pierce the floor below. The floor is littered with balled-up tissues. She does not touch herself down there, but she doesn't feel any pain or discomfort either. She compares Yi Guang with her ex-boyfriend. Yi Guang looks much older; he has a paunch and his neck is saggy, but he makes up for it with his wit and his charm. He's a local celebrity. I don't feel I've got anything to complain about, Eva concludes. But how did it happen? Before I came, I had it all worked out how I was going to fend him off, but it took just one push and all my fences came tumbling down. One by one, the faces of Hai Ruo and her sisterhood pass before Eva's eyes. Does he sleep with them, too? It's possible, based on how he treats her, but then again, if you look at the way they act with each other, maybe not. In any case, Yi Guang made a move on me, an outsider he's only just met. She has mixed feelings about that: misgivings, trepidation, but a smidgin of self-satisfaction too.

Eva gets up to take a shower. Some of her hair has blocked the drainage hole and she picks it up and dumps it in the toilet, then sits on the toilet for well over an hour. With her body cleansed and her mind refreshed, she stops fussing about what happened last night. She stays where she is all morning. First, she texts Hai Ruo to say that her landlady is still sick and needs her. She's going to make her *jiaozi* and might be a bit late to work. Then she starts to clean the attic, sweeping it clean of cake crumbs, melon seed husks, fruit peel and used tissues, and clearing away empty bottles, and cups and glasses. Finally she applies her make-up meticulously, singing to herself as she does so.

Yi Guang still hasn't returned. Eva finds some noodles, eggs, a bunch of pak choi and garlic leaves in the kitchen, so she boils some water and makes herself a bowl of egg noodles. By the time she comes downstairs, it is almost dusk.

The wind is blowing the smog away. Wind has been forecast for many days now, and it has finally arrived, all the way from the deserts of Xinjiang. While it sweeps away the smog, it has brought with it sand and dust, so that the air is as murky as before. In no time at all, Eva's clothes, hair and face are coated in grains of sand.

Walking side-on to the wind and tucking her head into her jacket collar, she makes her way to the teashop. In front of the door a car and a lorry are parked. The lorry's engine is running. Perhaps it's on its way, or has only just arrived. It is shuddering as if it's throwing a tantrum, sputtering a stream of profanities. Xi Lishui, Xin Qi, xiao-Tang and Gao Wenlai are coming out of the door. Wenlai turns back for a pair of gloves.

Xin Qi spots Eva and calls to her, 'They said you weren't coming to work, how come you're here?'

Eva opens her mouth to reply and gets a mouthful of grit from a sudden gust of wind. She spits it out and says, "I'm just a bit late because my landlady needed me." She is unable to look them in the eyes. Instead, she looks at the lorry. "Are you off somewhere?"

"We're helping Xin Qi move some stuff. Wanna come?" asks Lishui.

"Eva's big and strong, she must come!" says Wenlai.

"The more the merrier! Hop in!" calls xiao-Tang.

So Eva gets in the car with Lishui and Xin Qi, wondering what she has got herself into, while xiao-Tang and Wenlai get in the lorry, and they set out in convoy.

Lishui is behind the wheel, and Xin Qi and Eva sit in the back. Lishui exclaims in admiration at Eva's complexion, "So much collagen! Your face gleams like porcelain!"

"You're right!" Xin Qi agrees, patting Eva on the cheeks. "Such perfect eyebrows!"

"It's eyebrow liner," says Eva. "My brows are naturally thin."

"That's normal," says Lishui. "An unmarried girl has eyebrows that grow together. They thin out when she's married."

Eva's heart beats hard. She bends down to tie the shoelaces.

"But Eva's not married!" Xin Qi corrects Li Shui.

"No?" asks Lishui, turning around to look at them.

"Xi-jie! Watch the road, Xi-jie!" Xin Qi cries.

Lishui is embarrassed. "Of course, the eyebrows rule doesn't apply to *laowai*. Eva, what are your people called again, S... v...?"

"Slavic," Eva fills her in.

"Anyway, she can still have a man before she gets married," retorts Xin Qi. "How many young women with growing-together eyebrows do you know these days?" She puts an arm around Eva and says, "You're so delicate, with such soft skin, I shouldn't have let you come."

Eva seizes her chance to change the subject. "Are you moving house?"

"Just some furniture," says Xin Qi. The car suddenly jolts, as the front wheel hits the curb, then jolts back down. Xin Qi jerks forward and hits her head on the front seat. "Xi-jie! Xi-jie!" she cries.

"Well, you two are ignoring me!" Lishui complains. "Light me a cigarette." Xin Qi hurriedly gets out a packet, lights a cigarette for Lishui, then another for herself.

"You smoke, too?" asks Eva.

"I just started," says Xin Qi.

"Smoking's bad for you."

"So be it, I hate myself anyway!"

They go up and down one road after another, and by the time they finally drive into a courtyard, the street lights have come on. "Here we are," announces Xin Qi. Eva looks out to see a single six-floor building. A large poplar tree is growing next to it, with twin trunks: one already taller than the building, the other arching over the courtyard. The leaves flutter vigorously, showing white and then green, and rustle like ghosts clapping their hands. Ivy has smothered the façade of the building, and undulates in the wind as if there's an earthquake. Even the small windows and the lights within are hard to make out.

"What's this? Is it a residential estate?" asks Eva.

"A residential estate? No, it's just a workers' housing block," replies Xin Qi.

"Housing block?" repeats Eva, confused.

But Xin Qi doesn't answer. She gets out carrying a rubbish bag and goes to the lorry.

"Back in the 1980s, the state-run work units, the *danwei*, built these blocks for the workers and their families," explains Lishui. "They're very basic, brick-built, with long corridors down the middle and flats leading off on both sides. There's only one toilet and washroom for all the residents on each floor." In a low voice, Lishui tells Eva about Xin Qi's marriage and why they are here to move the furniture. Eva cannot think of anything to say.

Everyone in the lorry has climbed down, carrying sacking and ropes. Xin Qi takes out pairs of shoe covers from the rubbish bag and says, "Put these on, try not to make any noise." Then she runs back to the car. "Watch the vehicles for us, Eva." And the group enter the building.

It is very dark by now. The residents are eating dinner or watching TV soaps, brushing their teeth, and soaking their feet in basins of hot water. The air is so full of sand that the lights atop the courtyard wall are scarcely visible. A dozen weeping willows along the wall look like nothing so much as quarrelling women, their hair lashed savagely by the gale, turning their backs in disgust. A cat quietly emerges, its body stretched like a hungry tiger. Eva is startled at first, then whistles at it. The feline ignores her and slinks over to the rubbish bin by the wall. Here, as in all the other city blocks where humans live, the dogs are petted and fed indoors, while the cats are left to fend for themselves.

Why do the Chinese prefer dogs to cats? Eva wonders. Is it because a dog is loyal and faithful while a cat acknowledges no master or mistress? But dogs are only loyal because it's in their interests to be. They obey their owners' commands, wag their tails and grovel. Cats would never do that, so they're on their own. Eva's philosophising leads her on to the thought that the existence of dogs and cats is no different from that of humans. What about me? And what about my friends in St Petersburg and Xijing? Who's done best for themselves in society? Who's been reduced to subservience by invisible forces? And what about the ones who turn their hearts to ice, and then, when the ice shatters, they turn the shards against their enemies and stab them?

Eva stands in the wind-swept courtyard, lost in thought. Soon the furniture starts to arrive. First to be carried downstairs are two cabinets, followed by chairs, chests, tables, a washing machine, a fridge, a TV, two sofas, a bed – frame and mattress – as well as bedside tables. Xin Qi accompanies each batch downstairs. The three men all agree that one of the bedside tables should be thrown out because its drawer sticks, but Xin Qi insists, so it is loaded onto the lorry. The six of them go back upstairs again to pack all the odds and ends into cardboard boxes. Eva waits by the car.

Just then, an old woman emerges out of nowhere like a ghost. Eva almost cries out in fright. The woman is carrying what appears to be half a bowl of food and heads towards the rubbish bins. She is as thin as a piece of origami and the wind almost blows her over. Three stray cats run up to her. Eva gives a cough, and the old woman looks up. She looks at the lorry piled with furniture and says, "Moving house, are you?"

"Just some furniture," Eva replies.

"Aren't you tall? Did you dye your hair, or is it the light? It's so yellow."

"It's naturally blonde."

The old woman comes nearer for a better look. A cat jumps up and claws the bowl from her hand, and left-over food spills everywhere. "Damn you, why are you in such a hurry?" the old lady says. Eva picks up the plastic bowl. "Are you a foreigner?" asks the old lady.

"That's right."

"You scared the hell out of me! A foreigner who speaks Chinese!"

Eva is amused, but before she can say anything, xiao-Tang comes out of the building entrance. Eva turns back and catches a glimpse of the old woman disappearing into the building through another door.

xiao-Tang is dragging a large sack and grunting with the effort. Eva hurries over to help her but the bag is too unwieldy for them to lift, so xiao-Tang takes the items out: an aluminium pot, a ladle for stir-frying, a kettle, a *mazha* folding stool, a bamboo basket, as well as a shovel, a pair of pliers, a hammer, an extension cable, a charger and a rolled-up plastic mat.

"What a collection!" exclaims Eva.

xiao-Tang pulls a face. "I told her to leave this rubbish behind, but she wouldn't."

"What will that man live on now she's taken everything?"

"I used to think that Xin Qi was a nice person, but after this, I've no respect for her."

"Is that because she's poor?"

"It's not about being rich or poor. But if she *is* poor, there must be a reason for it." And xiao-Tang does not make another trip upstairs.

Finally, the three men haul three giant cardboard boxes downstairs. Lishui comes behind, carrying a bag of rice, Wenlai has a gas cylinder balanced on one shoulder, while Xin Qi has a basin full of crockery in one hand and a wooden bucket in the other.

Eva goes up to Xin Qi. "Is the bucket for steaming rice?" she asks. She has seen some restaurants using buckets for this purpose.

"It's a foot bath," says Xin Qi.

Eva dares not ask more questions. With everything loaded, the lorry sets off. Eva gets in Lishui's car with Xin Qi, and they too speed away.

"Lishui, how about I take you and Eva to dinner?" Xin Qi offers.

"Do you want to go, Eva?" asks Lishui. "If you do, I'll take you and Xin Qi to Meridian Road. The Zhang's Roujiamo Restaurant is famous for its meat-stuffed flatbread. I can recommend *liangpi*, wonton, sticky rice *tangyuan* dumplings and meatball soup with vermicelli as well. I'm trying to lose weight, so I'll skip dinner."

"Don't go to any trouble for me," says Eva. "Stop by that mini-market ahead, and I'll buy some bread."

"If Lishui isn't having dinner, then let's do lunch another time. Eva, why are you just buying bread?" says Xin Qi.

"'Stop pussy-footing around!" Lishui exclaims. "Are you going back to the teashop or where you live, Eva?"

"It's late, I'd better go home."

"All right then, I'll drop Xin Qi off first, then you."

They drive east for twenty minutes before stopping by an alley that disappears into a rundown shanty town, originally a village but now swallowed up by the encroaching city. Xin Qi gets out, then Lishui turns the car back towards the old city.

"Xin Qi's moved here?" asks Eva incredulously.

"Yup," confirms Lishui.

"Did the lorry get here before us? And how's it going to get through a lane this narrow?"

"Her stuff isn't coming here."

Eva spots a corner shop ahead, and gets out to buy two buns and three sausages.

24. XIANG QIYU • ANQIAN

Lu Yike has been in touch with a property development company that wants her to create their adverts, but the slogans they have sent over do not exactly trip off the tongue. They are far too flowery. "Live like billionaires!"... "Created by the ultimate craftsmen!"... "Luxuriate in villa-style living!"... "Our reputation is dazzling" and so on. So Yike has suggested that the wording should be revised, and the client has asked her to his office to discuss it. For such an important meeting, Yike knows she cannot show up empty-handed, so she heads to the teashop to buy him a present. At Guangwei Road, the intersection is sealed off to allow a marathon to pass by. Yike asks a traffic police officer when the cordons will be lifted: in about two hours. Some cars are making a U-turn to find alternative routes but Yike turns left into a housing estate. She parks, walks to Unit Four, Building Nine, and takes the lift to the twenty-fifth floor, where Xiang Qiyu lives.

Qiyu's *baomu*, Ah Fang, opens the door, and recognises Yike. "She's still asleep," she says.

"At this hour?" Yike exclaims.

"The moment she gets home, she goes to bed. It's like putting your phone on charge."

This makes Yike laugh. "Get her up."

Qiyu came back from the hospital and fell asleep the moment her head touched the pillow. Ah Fang goes into the bedroom and shakes her awake. "What time is it?" Qiyu murmurs.

"A quarter to one."

"It's too early!" Qiyu says, and turns over to go back to sleep.

"Ms Lu's here," Ah Fang tells her.

This gets Qiyu out of bed. She opens a drawer, takes out three capsules of caterpillar fungus powder and swallows them. Then she goes into the sitting room. "Aiya! What are you doing here?" she exclaims. "Taking a moment to put your feet up? Or hoping for a cup of tea or lunch?"

"If I wanted to put my feet up, I wouldn't come all the way up here, would I? I do want lunch, though, but it doesn't look like you're going to give me any!"

"I'd cut off a slice of my flesh if you wanted it! Ah Fang, Ms Lu has honoured us with her presence for lunch. And she has high standards. Go and buy a grouper, and some shiitake and porcini mushrooms, then we'll need lily buds, Chinese yam and bitter melon."

"No, honestly, please don't put yourselves out! I didn't really come for lunch, I'm on my way somewhere and I stopped off. I just wanted to see you."

"Rubbish. You must stay for lunch, or you'll be ratting on me to the sisterhood that you turned up at lunchtime and I didn't give you anything to eat." And Qiyu tells Ah Fang to go and do the shopping.

As they chat, Qiyu notices a freckle on Yike's cheek. "When did you get that?" she asks, getting out her concealer, and dabbing it on for Yike. "Here, you keep this tube."

But Yike says, "No, you keep it. I'm always getting spots and freckles, especially if I haven't been sleeping well."

"Women's problems often arise from hormone imbalances," Qiyu lectures her. "Have you been finding it hard to concentrate? Are you feeling weak and listless? Have you lost interest in things?"

"Yes. I thought I was getting a bout of depression."

"Nonsense, you're not depressed! I came across something really nice recently. I'll get you some, it'll give you a real boost."

"It sounds like a miracle cure!"

"It's tiger bone tonic."

"Really? But you can't get genuine tiger bones these days, it's probably dog bones."

"A classmate of mine has a top job at Xijing Zoo. Last winter, one of their tigers died of old age and she gave me forty grammes of bone, which I made into a tonic. You must try it!" Qiyu gets up to fetch a jar from a cabinet. The list of ingredients reads:

Baijiu liquor 10 jin; bones 40g; papaya 30g; Szechwan lovage root (*chuanxiong / Ligusticum striatum*) 15g; niuteng (stauntonia) 30g; female ginseng (*dong quai*) 10g; Tall Gastrodia Tuber (*tianma*) 15g; saffron 20g; eggplant root 10g; acanthopanax root bark (*wujiapi*) 15g; *yuzhu* (*Polygonatum odoratum (Mill.) Druce*) 12g; *fangfeng* (*Saposhnikovia divaricata*) 15g; mulberry twig 30g.

Yike is impressed. "So many TCM ingredients!" She pours herself a small shot glass and gulps it down.

"How does that feel?" asks Qiyu.

Yike bares her teeth and claws the air. "I feel so powerful and energetic! Keep out of my way, I'm going to attack!"

Qiyu applauds. "Bravo! We can use that as an advertising slogan!"

But Yike's high spirits don't last. Soon she slumps on the sofa, looking dejected.

Qiyu pours two more shots and puts the jar back. She carries the glasses over and sits by Yike's side. "You've always been such a strong, sensible woman. What's got into you? Something happened with your business?"

Yike pulls herself together and smiles. "It's fine. I'm actually on my way to discuss a commission today."

"That's good! If your business does well, don't forget me. Send your clients my way and I'll make it worth your while. I'll give you a thirty per cent cut."

"Didn't I bring Mr Fan to you? He's on very good terms with a number of top officials and entrepreneurs."

"You mean the man with a pigtail? Why does a hunk of a man like him wear his hair like a woman? He doesn't even make a very convincing woman. No man would look at him in a million years!"

"Hey, don't be so mean. Neither of us has married again."

"We don't want to. We're going to age gracefully and in style! He did drop by my office, but he wasn't bringing any clients, he wanted me to sponsor him. If I give him two hundred thousand yuan for an event, he'll include my name in the leaflet, plus he'll give me two pieces of calligraphy by Zeng Shicun. Have you heard of this Zeng Shicun?"

"Never. He's probably a nobody."

"Exactly! Do I need his writing as wallpaper? So I told Mr Fan, 'Give me two of Yi Guang's pieces, then I'll consider your offer.' And he left fuming."

Yike doesn't know what to reply, so she changes the subject. "Ai, I haven't seen Yi-laoshi for so long. The year before last, it was the Year of the Monkey, and he wrote the character 'monkey' for each one of us. Last year was the Year of the Rooster, so he wrote 'rooster' for us. We've just entered the Year of the Dog, but Hai Ruo didn't want him to write 'dog', she asked him to write something on our fans. I haven't seen mine. Has he done yours?"

"If you don't have yours, he certainly won't have done mine. He's always been nicest to you and Hai Ruo."

"He's nice to Hai Ruo because they've known each other for ages. And she likes him too. Her staff at the teashop do all his housekeeping for him."

"I know. Anyway, apparently Yi-laoshi introduced Lishui to a young man."

"Yes, it's true."

"I heard he's a division chief in the government, his wife died last year. One's only just got divorced, the other's just been widowed. Why are they in such a hurry?"

"It'd still be nice to see them become a couple. We're beginning to look like the Yang Family widow-warriors."

"What do you mean?"

"The ones in the Song dynasty. They all ended up alone."

"But do you think they will get together?" Qiyu persists.

"Lishui said she loves him and he loves her."

"Bah! What's all that talk about love, they're just famished."

"You're so nasty!"

"What I mean is, she's several years older than him."

"But she looks younger."

"Because she scrubs up well," says Qiyu, dragging Yike by the hand to her bedroom. She opens the wardrobe and chooses a long-sleeved dress in velvet with embossed motifs, a short skirt in dusty pink, an off-the-shoulder black dress slit up the side, then a pair of jeans, a white T-shirt with a matching pleated skirt, and finally, a camel trench coat. "I bought these recently," she says. "Oh, and I got a white two-piece. Let me put it on so you can have a good look."

"Are you flashing your money at me, Xiang Qiyu? Are you fishing for compliments? I thought I was only here for a meal!"

"I was just like you before, I never gave my clothes a second thought. But look at me now. All the collagen's disappeared from my face. It's gone saggy and wrinkled, I've got panda rings around my eyes and my complexion's darkened. I always look as if I'm exhausted. We should follow Lishui's example and make sure we stay looking young."

"Fine, wear what you want, and let's see if it makes you look eighteen again!"

But Qiyu puts the clothes back into the wardrobe, and they return to the sitting room sofa and snack on fruit.

Ah Fang comes back with the shopping and begins to prepare lunch in the kitchen.

"Ah Fang, come and clean up the table!" calls Qiyu. Her *baomu* does as she is told then, as she goes back into the kitchen, Qiyu calls again, "Ah Fang, boil some water! We've been so busy talking, we haven't had our tea!" And soon they hear the hissing of water in the kettle.

"You're showing off again!" says Yike.

"You mean I'm ordering my *baomu* around?"

"Well, if I weren't here, would you be keeping her this busy?"

"She's a hard worker."

"Where's she from?"

"The south part of Shaanxi. Clever, nimble-fingered and hard-working too. Not like folk from the Guanzhong Plain. They're standoffish and snappy. I've had two from Guanzhong, neither lasted a month."

"Could Ah Fang recommend someone from her area?"

"You don't have a *baomu*?"

"No, I don't, and even if I did, I'd be hopeless at managing her. But this is for Zihua."

"But we're taking turns to look after her at the hospital. She's in ICU for the moment. It'd be a waste of money."

"No, not for her, it's for her mother, Mrs Qi. She's so frail now, she really can't get around any more. And Xia Lei is becoming quite a handful. Haven't you noticed how tired she looks nowadays?"

"Ah Fang? Ah Fang!" Qiyu calls again.

Ah Fang comes with two cups of tea. "I'm sorry you've had to wait for your tea. I should have done it before I went shopping," she apologises, setting down the cups.

"Ms Lu is looking for a *baomu*, do you know someone from your area?"

"What's the family like?" Ah Fang wants to know. "Is there an old person or someone who's sick? What about children? A baby, or a toddler, or an older one who's running around?"

"Both an old person and a child," replies Yike. "The kid is three, his granny's been taking care of him. We just need someone to help her."

"Let me think about it, it's got to be the right person," says Ah Fang.

Qiyu snaps her fingers. "Right! That's what we'll do then. Now go and make our lunch." Ah Fang goes back to the kitchen, and Qiyu turns to Yike. "There's something odd about Zihua's illness. Why's she got cancer?"

"What's odd about it? You know they say anything you eat can make you susceptible to any kind of illness," says Yike.

"Some illnesses are beyond the power of TCM or Western medicine to cure. Maybe more unorthodox methods might work... *qigong*, for example, or prayers to the Buddha, or getting an exorcist to expel the demons."

"We did try *qigong*, and not a day goes by without Hai-jie begging the Buddha for help. And I doubt there are any Taoist exorcists left these days. Where would we find one?"

"There are some in the Qinling Mountains, I heard."

"Do you ever stop to think before you speak? You heard – who from? Looking for an exorcist in the Qinling range would be like looking for a needle in a haystack!" says Yike in exasperation. She gets up to go to the toilet.

Yike comes back and looks out at the balcony. The wind has dropped, but the air is still full of sand and grit. "Such a dirty sky, it's high time it rained," she mutters.

Qiyu also comes over, stretching lazily. "If you think exorcism might help, I can find one. The year before last, a client was doing a physiotherapy session at my place. We had a chat and she mentioned that lots of people nowadays aren't really human."

"You mean they're supernatural?"

"She said, if you see someone running like a wolf, then they really are a wolf, and if someone wails like a ghost, then they are one."

"It's a figure of speech, Qiyu," Yike says. "Yi-laoshi often writes stuff like that."

"This client said that when people die, their souls usually return to the Samsara to be reborn into one of the Six Realms. But some souls don't want to leave the human realm, and others are stuck here for various reasons. It's like taking the plane from Xijing to Beijing. Some people are booked on the flight but decide not to go, others make it to the airport but don't catch their flight. These are stranded souls. They wander around in the world, trying to attach themselves to someone. If the possessed person has a lot of energy, the ghost inhabits the body with its host. They take it in turns to manifest, so sometimes the real person speaks and acts normally. Other times, it's the ghost who dominates and the person appears to have nonhuman thoughts and behaviours. If the possessed has low energy, he or she will lose control completely. We often see people who act weird, or seem to have clairvoyant skills that can't be explained. They might even speak in the voice of the departed, or grow to look like them."

Yike is startled by Qiyu's words. It reminds her of the day she saw the cobbler who was the spitting image of her dead father. "Grow to look like a dead person?"

"Yes, she maintains that everyone like that is possessed."

Yike's head fills with memories of her father. The sight of that man with her father's face prompted her to stay in this city, and put all her energies into her business. Her uncle has invited her to join him in Chengdu but she hasn't made up her mind whether to accept. She has told herself she'll stay if she sees her father's lookalike in the street once again within a month. For her, everything happens because her father is watching over her in heaven, protecting her. How can all this be the doings of some evil spirit? Red in the face, she exclaims, "Nonsense, what a load of superstition!"

"The client also said that what we call superstition can be regarded as dark matter in scientific terms."

"It sounds like you're possessed too!" exclaims Yike.

As they talk, a flock of crows wheel around in front of the building. There are a lot more of them perched along the rooftop of the high-rise right opposite them. Their droppings have daubed the wall white, like a coat of lime wash.

"Huh, I wish I were possessed," says Qiyu. "Then everyone in the sisterhood would be possessed too, including you."

Yike has had enough of this talk. "Why are there so many crows here?"

"This place was called Anqian, 'Fore-*An*', because there used to be a small *an* nunnery right behind, full of Taoist nuns. There was a ring of poplars around it. Every day at dusk, the branches filled with crows, apparently from every corner of the city. Then the nunnery was demolished and high-rises were built, but the crows still congregate here. It's almost as if they remember places the way humans do. Our memory's in our bellies. What we ate as children always makes us nostalgic. Crows remember with their nostrils, the scent brings them back to the same spot every time."

"You know this isn't a good place for you to live," says Yike. "You shouldn't live near a hospital or any kind of a temple. You should move."

"And you'll lend me the money, will you?"

"Do you need any?"

"I'm not going anywhere even if I could afford a new flat. This is where I live. It's right for me. When the Living Buddha comes, I'll become a lay Buddhist, and this will be my nunnery."

"But you're going to be a Buddhist, and the nunnery down there was for Taoists!"

Qiyu laughs. "Well, they say that Buddhists and Taoists belong to the same family."

After lunch, Qiyu gives Yike a small bottle of the tiger bone tonic, and Yike goes to the teashop. She pushes open the door, and xiao-Zhen greets her with a nod. "Come in, Lu-jie." xiao-Zhen is busy moving a large cabinet from the east wall to the north wall, with xiao-Su and xiao-Fang's help. Then they carry a table over to the window.

"Are you rearranging the whole room?" Yike asks.

"Uh-huh," xiao-Zhen says.

"It's better the way you've got it now. That cabinet didn't feel right on the east side."

"Do you know feng shui, Lu-jie?"

"Only in general. The fundamental rule is, to see if a room has good feng shui, ask yourself, do you feel comfortable when you step inside."

Both xiao-Zhen and xiao-Su look intently at Yike, but say nothing. xiao-Su places a sandalwood statuette of Guan Yu, the traders' God of Wealth, on top of the cabinet they have just moved. Then she lights incense sticks, places her palms together in front of her chest and bows three times before it, so deeply that her torso is parallel to the ground.

"When did you invite Guan Yu here, xiao-Su?" Yike asks.

"A while ago," says xiao-Su. "It's been stored in a cabinet. We just took it out so we could pay our respects."

"You're doing it with such reverence."

"I don't know if I'm doing it correctly. Please don't laugh, Lu-jie."

"You did it right. You've been honouring Lu Yu, Protector of Tea. Now you have Guan Yu too, business should boom!"

"Thank you for your good wishes."

"Well, here's another contribution from me to the teashop. Can you give me a kilo of the best Longjing please? How much is it?"

"It's free to you," says xiao-Zhen.

"No way! We may all be friends, but we need to do business too. If none of us paid, the teashop would go broke in no time!"

For some reason, xiao-Zhen looks at her feet and sniffs. Gao Wenlai comes down the stairs, gives a silent nod to Yike, then grabs a mop to clean the floor by the east wall.

Yike asks where Hai Ruo is. "The boss", she calls her, not the usual "Hai-jie".

"She's upstairs, I'll take you up," offers Wenlai.

But Yike pulls out a chair and sits down. "I'll wait here. She's obviously having a bad day."

"How do you know, Lu-jie?" asks Wenlai.

"Isn't it obvious? Your boss is all heart. When she's happy, you are too. When she's in a bad mood, you're all down in the dumps. And I can tell that because nobody's offered me a drink of water yet."

"So sorry, let me make you some tea, it's white tea, right?" xiao-Su exclaims.

"Yes please. Your boss might be sulking, but her tea's delicious!" Yike laughs.

As xiao-Su brings her a cup of tea, she whispers, "xiao-Tang's been taken away."

Yike misunderstands. "Called away? Where to?"

Fat drops of tears roll down xiao-Su's cheeks. "No, she's been taken before the Disciplinary Committee."

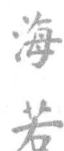

25. HAI RUO • THE MAHJONG ROOM

HAI RUO TELLS Lu Yike about the morning's dramatic events.

xiao-Tang was the first to arrive at the teashop and opened up. Then Gao Wenlai came along with xiao-Su and xiao-Zhen, followed by xiao-Fang and Mrs Zhang. Mrs Zhang bought five wholegrain *jianbing* pancakes at a stall and shared them with the other women.

"You didn't even ask if I wanted one or not," complained Wenlai.

"I didn't know you'd be in so early," replied Mrs Zhang. "Here, take mine."

"Thanks, you're too kind," said Wenlai. "But you go ahead and eat, and I'll put some water on for tea." He lit the gas stove, put the kettle on and went to sort out the rubbish bins as the water heated up.

Just then, a van screeched to a halt outside the entrance, barely inches away from the steps. Three men jumped out and barged through the door, demanding, "Is this the Sojourn Teashop?"

Wenlai was going out with the rubbish bags. "Hey, do you have to block the entrance? The square's big enough!" he protested.

"Stand right where you are! Don't move!" barked one of the men.

"What's this? A heist? We've got CCTV here!" said Wenlai.

The man reached into a pocket and flashed some sort of an ID in Wenlai's face. "We're looking for a woman called Tang Yinyin."

xiao-Tang came forward, her mouth full of *jianbing*, and mumbled something.
"Spit it out and answer me!" ordered the man.
xiao-Tang forced herself to swallow and then answered, "That's me."
"Come with us," snapped the man.
"Why? Who are you?"
"The Disciplinary Committee!"
xiao-Tang shot a quick glance at Wenlai, and repeated, "The Disciplinary Committee? What do you want with me?"
"It's about Qi Jiayuan."
"Qi Jiayuan? The disgraced Party chief?" interjected Wenlai.
"She knows what this is about," said the man.
"But... but I don't know the Party chief," said xiao-Tang, turning pale.
"He's plain Qi Jiayuan now!" the man corrected her.
"Right, Qi Jiayuan... But I don't know Qi Jiayuan, and he doesn't know me." The man clutched xiao-Tang's arm, and she pleaded, "Please, not while I'm wearing the teashop uniform."
The man hesitated, then let her go and change into her own clothes. xiao-Tang went into the cubicle, where the water was boiling merrily. As she dressed, the tears started falling. She came out and told the rest of them, "Tell Hai-jie to please get me out... and the water's ready."
With one in front and two behind her, the men escorted xiao-Tang away. Steam was seeping under the cubicle door by this time and xiao-Zhen went to turn off the gas. She found xiao-Tang's scarf on the hanger and ran out with it. The men had pushed xiao-Tang into their van, and were pulling a cloth bag over her head. xiao-Zhen patted the van door, but it roared away in a splutter of exhaust smoke.
Hai Ruo carries on with her story: when xiao-Su called her, she rushed to the shop and found its door locked and the window blinds down. The other shop assistants sat inside, visibly shaken.
On hearing what had happened, Hai Ruo started to tremble so violently she felt as if every muscle in her body was twitching. When she first heard of the Party chief's fall from grace, she had sensed that a storm might be in the offing – when you cast a stone into a lake, you get ripples. But it had never crossed her mind that xiao-Tang would be

taken away even before Mr Qi was back from Macau. She had no idea what to do.

However, she was the boss here, and everyone's eyes were on her. She sat down on a chair – her legs would not hold her up any longer – and tried to steady their nerves. "Don't cry, dry your tears and take a few deep breaths," she told them. "When you feel ready, open the door and pull up the blinds. It's business as usual. Not a word about this. You need to greet our clients with a smile."

She took her phone upstairs to call Yi Guang. She was a strong woman, but she still needed a bit of support at a time like this. Even if he couldn't support her, it would still mean so much to have him listen and say a few comforting words.

And so she broke the news to Yi Guang. Her words were punctuated by sobs and she sounded distraught. Yi Guang was appalled. After a long silence, he promised to find out as much as he could. All morning, she waited for him to call back, but there was no news.

It was the most anxious four hours of her life. She lit incense to the Buddha, kneeling before the statue and murmuring prayers. She thumbed through her books, searching for anything that might offer solace. She knew that bright, sunny days were always followed by rain, snow or hailstorms, but this did not prevent her from being thrown into a helpless panic. Now she understood why four ferocious Heavenly Kings always flanked the front gate of any Buddhist temple. Would Yi Guang be her protector? Surely he would, he must be able to, she repeated over and over, as she rummaged through the cabinets for the sandalwood statuette of Guan Yu and set it on the table to pray to. On a whim, she told the girls downstairs to rearrange the shop cabinets, shelves and tables.

Somehow, both upstairs and downstairs now felt as if the spirits had gathered to strengthen her resolve and give her energy. And sure enough, just about twenty minutes before Yike arrived, Yi Guang called.

He had not made inquiries with any city officials. Their leader's fall from power had sealed their lips. They were much too afraid to talk. But he had called Fan Bosheng and asked him to put out feelers and see what he could find out. Bosheng got everywhere, like a speck of dust. He had told Yi Guang that the Disciplinary

Committee were based in a guest house on a university campus and were conducting their investigations in rooms where the windows were nailed down, the walls hung with blankets and any sharp corners were wrapped in fabric, to prevent those placed under investigation from harming or killing themselves. Bosheng had even found that one of the guards was the father of a colleague of Feng Ying. The old man was taking it in turns with another guard to keep watch outside the room day and night. They were not allowed to go in or talk to those being interrogated. If anything happened, the guards had to report to the investigators in other rooms. Bosheng was unable to shed any light on how the investigations were being conducted and what leads were being followed. But one thing was for sure: any businessmen who confessed details of petty bribes they had offered the city chief – amount, time, place and method – would be allowed to go.

xiao-Tang was taken in because Mr Qi the businessman bribed the Party chief Qi Jiayuan, Yi Guang had explained to Hai Ruo. "But she shouldn't be in too much trouble. Once she explains what she did, she'll come back. She's not even a small potato. Don't worry, she should be fine."

"But what's it got to do with xiao-Tang? Why *her*?" Yike asks, now that Hai Ruo has concluded her story.

"Mr Qi is an old customer," says Hai Ruo. "Each time he buys tea, he spends hundreds of thousands of yuan. So he knows me pretty well, and the shop assistants too. He used to give top officials expensive watches, jewellery, pieces of jade, clothes and the like, but he didn't know what to buy so he used to ask me to get them for him, and I always asked xiao-Tang to deliver them. I think she might even have exchanged some gold for him once."

"Exchanged some gold?"

"Mr Qi came in one day and told me that the Party chief's wife wanted to buy gold. It was xiao-Tang who did the actual work."

"So she was just running errands?"

"That's right."

"Could there be anything else?"

"No, not that I can think of. xiao-Tang has always been so loyal and reliable and clever that I could ask her to do almost anything. And now look what a mess I've got her into!"

"It's no big deal," Yike reassures her. "xiao-Tang will be back as soon as she's explained."

"But how long will they keep her?"

"A couple of days maybe? Or she might be back tomorrow even. Calm down."

"Ai! I'm always the one doing the reassuring, and now the boot's on the other foot."

"So you aren't a saint after all," smiles Yike.

"But I'm still your senior!" insists Hai Ruo.

The two make a plan of action: first and foremost, they have to go and see Yi Guang tomorrow and get him to find out what's happened with xiao-Tang's investigation. Then they'll call xiao-Tang's family and tell them she's been sent to Fujian Province to purchase tea. They won't be able to get in touch with her for a bit, but if they need her for anything, they should call the teashop, and they'll do their best to help.

Having settled that, Yike tells Hai Ruo, "Now try to relax. It's going to be fine."

Hai Ruo breathes out a long slow breath, then asks xiao-Su to make two fresh cups of white tea. "Yike, as I sat here alone this morning, I thought of something else. When I opened this teashop, you were the first person I got to know, it was just you and me. How have we ended up with so many sisters?"

"What do you mean? Are you patting yourself on the back for heading up such a big group?"

"No. I'm not a *lingxiu*, not that kind of a leader. The cuffs and the collar, the *ling* and the *xiu*, are always dragging in the muck, but I'm not like that."

"You're a magnet then, drawing the wires, broken saw pieces, screws and nails out of the dust. Birds of a feather flock together, as they say."

"Well, that's true. But none of us is after political power, or wealth, or a perfect marriage. We want a good life and the freedom to please ourselves. Is that so much to ask? It seems to be. When I was young, my mother was always telling me off for having ideas above my station. And I still feel like a crane with the wings of a hen."

"Well, where does the fault lie? In us, or in the society we live in?"

"You tell me. Don't ask me questions," says Hai Ruo.

"It reminds me of when I was young too. There was one baking hot summer. I was covered in so much sweat that I stood in the sun to dry off, but I just got sweatier and ended up with sunstroke!" Hai Ruo lights a cigarette and doesn't reply. So Yike goes on, "Forget it, let's play mahjong. The game will take our minds off all this, with the first click of the tiles."

"Fine."

"You don't have mahjong here. Let me call Lihou, she has a mahjong room. Let's go to her place."

Ying Lihou is delighted when Yike calls. "Do come! This'll be the first time I've used the mahjong room. Bring plenty of money with you!"

It takes Hai Ruo and Yike no more than a quarter of an hour to drive to Lihou's place. To their surprise, Xi Lishui, Xin Qi and Eva are also there. Eva is embarrassed when she sees Hai Ruo. "I do apologise, Hai-jie," she says. "The bamboo curtain in the cubicle is broken, so yesterday afternoon xiao-Tang asked me to drop by Fuyou Street this morning and buy a new one. I ran into Xi-jie and Xin Qi on my way, and came here with them."

"You're not in any trouble," says Yike. "Hai-jie isn't properly employing you."

But Hai Ruo looks serious. "I'll have to dock your pay," she says.

"Aiya! This is my fault, I dragged Eva here. If you dock her pay, let me make it up to her," says Xin Qi anxiously.

"Fine, you owe her ten thousand yuan then," says Hai Ruo.

"Oh my god, where can I find that much money?" exclaims Xin Qi.

"If you don't have the money, then you must swear that you'll be extra-specially nice to Eva!" says Hai Ruo.

Xin Qi puts her arm around Eva's shoulders. "We're already besties!" She bumps Eva's forehead with her own and everyone laughs.

"What an incredible place your teashop is, Hai-jie," says Lishui. "The ten of us met at the teashop and became sisters. Then Xin Qi and Eva met there, and now they're best friends, closer than Xin Qi is to me!"

"No, it's not like that," protests Xin Qi. "You're still like my big sister."

"Take that as a compliment," Lihou tells Lishui. "So many customers have come to the teashop wanting Hai-jie's help over the last decade, and as soon as they get to know each other, they ignore

Hai-jie. They come dirt poor, but thanks to the connections they make there, they turn into tycoons, while Hai-jie is still running a small teashop."

"Things that burn seldom benefit from their own warmth," Yike says.

"Hey, are you praising me or mocking me?" says Hai Ruo.

"What I really resent is the way those country hicks-turned-tycoons swagger into your teashop," says Lihou.

"You're just jealous," says Hai Ruo.

Lihou moved into this new flat early this year. Yike has come here once before but it's Hai Ruo's first visit. Every flat in this housing estate comes fully furnished – and has the highest price tag in the whole of Xijing. Hai Ruo checks out the sitting room, kitchen, bathrooms and toilets, the master and guest bedrooms, and the walk-in closets. "You've done the sisterhood proud, Lihou. Think how much face your luxury address gives us!"

"This is the only thing I've got left," says Lihou.

Hai Ruo ignores her remark. "Where's the mahjong room? What a luxury to have a special room for it!"

Lihou shows her to another room, occupied by a mahjong table, an electric one made in Hong Kong that shuffles the tiles automatically. "This is not about luxury, it's about being lonely," explains Lihou. "I have no one to go to the cinema, drink coffee or enjoy the double bathtub with, all I can do is to get together a mahjong group."

"You've got a double bathtub?" chips in Xin Qi.

"Yes."

"Have you tried it, Xi-jie?"

"No," says Lishui. "I don't know if it's supposed to be for a married couple or lovers or friends. Anyway, the rich are rich because of the way they think, and we're poor because of the way we think."

"Xi Lishui, stop feeling sorry for yourself!" says Lihou.

"You're so vulgar, you two!" exclaims Hai Ruo. Then she asks Eva, "Did you and Xin Qi agree in advance or are you telepathic? You're wearing the same tracksuits!"

"Not just that, we've both got moles on the back of our necks in the same place," says Eva.

Lishui takes a look and says, "There are stories about moles like yours. Like, before the dead leave the netherworld to be reborn into a new life, Old Lady Meng offers them a sip of Broth of Oblivion so they have no more memory of their previous life. But some people refuse to drink it, and they have to go through hell and high water to get reborn. They're also marked out by being born with a mole at the nape of the neck."

"So, is it good to have this mole or not?" asks Eva.

"It's not about good or bad, it means you'll have many emotional entanglements in this life," says Lishui.

"She's right," says Xin Qi.

Lishui goes on, "Strange that Eva and Xin Qi have the same kind of mole – size, colour and position. Do you think Eva was Chinese in a previous life?"

"Or I could have been a Russian?" Xin Qi puts in.

"*Laowai* don't care about stuff like that!" says Lihou. "You know we Han Chinese all have a split down our little toe nails, so it looks like we've got a double nail. If you haven't got them, you're not Chinese." Xin Qi takes off her shoes for a good look, and so does Eva.

"Put your smelly feet away!" Yike says. "Come on, it's mahjong time!" And everyone pulls a chair up to the table.

There are six of them and four players, with Yike and Hai Ruo facing each other.

"Xi-jie and Ying-jie, you two go ahead," says Xin Qi. "Eva and I will sit behind you and keep our eyes peeled."

"I don't know how to play anyway," says Eva. "Let me serve the tea. Just don't forget to tip me at the end."

"Sure, a double tip from me, if I win, that is," promises Yike.

"How about this, everyone here should take turns to play a pot," says Lihou. "Let's make each pot worth five hundred yuan and lay out the money on the table. When one of us has lost everything, she drops out and someone else takes her place."

"You've sat down, so you should play first," says Xin Qi.

"Xin Qi, go to the kitchen and see if there's anything to eat," says Yike. "Hai-jie and I haven't had lunch."

"You've not eaten? Why didn't you say so?" says Lihou, standing up. "Take my place, Xin Qi. I'll fix you something to eat." So Xin Qi sits in Lihou's chair.

"What do you have?" asks Yike. "Are there any *mo* flatbreads? I'll just have one with some pickled chillies. What do you want, Hai-jie?"

"I'm not hungry, don't worry about me," says Hai Ruo.

"One wants nothing, the other just wants a *mo*, are you trying to insult me?" says Lihou. "I may not have a fridge full of delicacies but I do have *laniurou* beef, *pidan* eggs and cucumbers. I'll make them into three cold dishes and you can have a bowl each of dragon beard noodles with spinach and chopped spring onion."

Without further ado, Lihou goes to the kitchen and starts cooking. Eva makes tea for everyone, then opens a packet of cigarettes and distributes them. She joins Lihou in the kitchen to help her peel spring onions and crush garlic in a mortar and pestle. In no time at all, the lunch arrives at the mahjong table. Yike grabs a chunk of *laniurou*, then slurps down the noodles, all the while dealing out tiles. Her glasses are covered in steam, and she takes them off. Then she sees that Hai Ruo hasn't touched her food and is lost in thought.

"Hey, it's your turn!" Lishui urges Hai Ruo, who finally lays down a tile.

"Here, take a bite, it's delicious," Yike tells Hai Ruo.

"Will she get lunch, I wonder?" Hai Ruo mutters to herself.

Lihou mis-hears. "I made this just for you, don't say I'm not getting you lunch," she says.

Yike kicks Hai Ruo on the shin beneath the table. Hai Ruo looks at Yike, who frowns at her. Hai Ruo eats a piece of beef, but asks Eva to finish the noodles for her.

Eva takes the bowl to the sofa. The noodle strands are as thin as a dragon's beard. Lihou sits down beside her. Between mouthfuls, Eva asks about the décor and furniture. "Where did you get these sofas? How much were they? Is the curtain material French? And how about the door knobs, and the cooker hood and the bathroom and kitchen taps? And the shoe horn on top of the shoe cabinet? Are all the pieces Swedish? They're loads more expensive than Chinese-made products, right?" She burbles on, asking about the chandelier in the sitting room, the bedside lamps, as well as the toilets and wall lights in the bathrooms, but Lihou's answers are monosyllabic. In the end, she says, "Are you a Disciplinary Committee inspector, Eva?"

Hai Ruo's eyes glaze over at her words. When it gets to her turn at mahjong, the others have to wait a long time before she makes a move.

"Do stop babbling, Eva," says Yike. "You're distracting me, I've discarded a wrong tile. Go and chat in the bedroom if you want." Eva smiles and goes to the kitchen to do the washing up.

They have played three rounds and Hai Ruo only calls "Mahjong!" once. She's down to her last hundred yuan. "Lihou, take my place," she calls.

"You know I've had rotten luck lately, I'll lose for sure," says Lihou.

"Eva, sit behind Hai-jie and back her up."

"But I know nothing about mahjong," Eva protests.

"Hai-jie can teach you, you'll get the hang of it in no time," says Lihou.

So Eva sits behind Hai Ruo and learns how to pick up the tiles, arrange them and deal hands. "You do know something," says Hai Ruo.

But Hai Ruo loses this round again. She stands up and tells Lihou to take her seat. Lihou insists Eva should go. Eva tries to back out but Lihou takes 500 yuan out of her pocket and smacks the notes onto the table. "Go ahead, it's yours if you win, it's on me if you lose. I need a word with Hai-jie."

"We came to play mahjong because we were tired of talking. What's there to talk about?" says Yike.

"You don't know what's going on," says Lihou, taking Hai Ruo's arm and leading her into the bedroom.

Lihou shuts the door behind them, goes to the bedside table and gets out a bottle of *baijiu*. "You want a swig?" she offers, but Hai Ruo says no. Lihou raises the bottle and takes a big gulp. "I've stashed bottles by the sofa, in the kitchen and in the bathroom, so I can reach one whenever I'm cooking, cleaning or watching TV. I don't drink much, just a swig or two each time."

"You swig it on an empty stomach?" asks Hai Ruo.

"That's how my father drank it. He drank a lot after my grandmother died. I guess he was drowning his sorrows."

"You go ahead..." Hai Ruo pauses, then says, "You know so many things have happened in the past few days, I haven't had time to see Nianchu."

"It's sorted, Hai-jie. I've called off the debt collector."

"Called him off? But how?" asks Hai Ruo, looking anxious. Lihou tells her the arrangement she came to with Zhang Huai, but Hai Ruo is indignant. "I found the debt collector, why didn't you let me know before cancelling the deal?"

"I was so scared. If something bad happened and I dragged you into it, that'd be the end of me."

"You're such a simpleton, so impulsive! It really makes me wonder how you earned so much money!"

Lihou is hurt at Hai Ruo's comments and tears roll down her cheeks. Hai Ruo relents. "Fine, what's done is done. But how do you plan on getting the debt repaid now?" Lihou looks gloomier than ever, and she bursts into tears.

"Stop crying, they'll hear you!" Hai Ruo continues. "Do you want everyone to laugh or feel sorry for you?"

"But what should I do, Hai-jie?"

Hai Ruo thinks for a long while. "We'll invite Nianchu and Mr Wang to a restaurant tomorrow. I want to hear what Mr Wang has to say. If he shows any remorse and promises to pay you back, then Nianchu and I will pressure him to do so. If he gets on his high horse and is clearly trying to shirk his responsibilities, I'll pull a few strings and get onto his bosses. If all else fails, let's sue him."

But Lihou objects. "I've made it clear I'm having nothing more to do with them. How are we going to sit around the same table?"

"He's the one who owes you money, he did you wrong, you shouldn't be so apologetic! You have to sit with them even if you don't want to."

"I need a drink," says Lihou, grabbing the bottle for another swig.

Outside in the sitting room, Lishui is calling, "Hai-jie, I'm done, come and take my place!"

"I'll go out and play for a bit," says Hai Ruo. "Clean up your face, your make-up's all smudged."

Lihou sits at the dressing table and opens a drawer. "I've got some cash here if you want it," she says. But Hai Ruo has left the room.

The mahjong game lasts all through the night until seven the next morning. Everyone is pale and wan by the end of it. Their fingers look like chicken claws – where has the flesh gone? Out of the six, five have lost, and Lihou is the sole winner. "There's nothing more snobbish than money," remarks Lishui. "It only goes to those who are rolling in it."

Xin Qi is counting the pile of change in front of her. Three hundred in total. She counts again, and makes two hundred and eighty. "Aiya! I've lost a dress!" And she starts to count all over again.

"Don't make such a fuss. This is peanuts!" says Lihou, with a wry smile. She takes out 300 yuan and pushes it into Xin Qi's reluctant hands. Lihou hurries downstairs to get some steamed *mo*, pickles and fermented tofu at a corner shop. Back again, she heats the buns, fries twelve eggs sunny side up, then spoons milk powder into six cups, pours on boiling water and stirs. "Just something simple this morning," she says. "I'll invite you to a banquet on another day."

"Aiya! I can't eat *mo* in the morning," says Xin Qi. "Do you have any millet porridge? Just warmed-up will do. Milk upsets my stomach."

"Then I'll make some millet porridge," says Lihou.

"Just for me? No, no, forget it," says Xin Qi.

"You're so skinny, breakfast is the last thing you want to skip. Besides, it's easy to make porridge, the rice cooker will get it done in no time at all."

When breakfast is over, everyone gets up to leave. Hai Ruo tells Lihou, "Don't spend too long tidying up. Get some sleep. I'm going home to sleep too. I'll let you know once I've contacted them this afternoon."

Lihou looks at the dark rings around Hai Ruo's eyes, opens the fridge and gets out a small bottle. "Let a few tablets dissolve on your tongue, it really works," she whispers, putting it into Hai Ruo's pocket.

Hai Ruo takes out the bottle for a closer look. It's American ginseng. She pours three tablets into her palm and puts them in her mouth. "Open your mouth," she instructs the others, and drops three pills in each.

Yike drives Hai Ruo to the teashop before heading home. Lishui takes Xin Qi and Eva with her. They pass by a shopping centre and Eva wants to get off.

"You're going shopping now? Aren't you sleepy?" asks Lishui.

"No," says Eva.

"I was just like you ten years ago. I once played mahjong nonstop for two days," says Lishui.

When she pulls over, Xin Qi tells Eva, "I'll join you."

"You're no stronger than Xu Qi, don't you need some rest?" asks Lishui. But Xin Qi has hopped out.

At the shopping centre, Eva and Xin Qi head for the jewellery section on the ground floor. They ask the prices of necklaces, rings and earrings, then sit down to try some on. They admire each other and themselves in the mirror, and take selfies, but in the end, they buy nothing, and go upstairs to the fashion shops.

"It's the first time I've been here, everything's very glitzy," says Eva.

"I've been here twice," says Xin Qi. "Nothing good comes with a cheap price tag."

"We asked the price of so many things, but we didn't buy a thing."

"But we did wear them! I mean, we tried stuff on," replies Xin Qi. And they laugh.

The two floors above are occupied by top-of-the-range fashion from around the world. The two wander from one boutique to another. Eva is looking for jeans. She tries a pair at a shop on the first floor and they're a perfect fit. But Xin Qi stops her before she can buy them. "We need to do comparisons with other shops," she says. "Keep going, something better might be waiting for you."

They go upstairs where Eva tries on more jeans, before she spots a place specialising in leather trousers. She takes a pair and tries them on. "What do you think?" she asks.

"A bit tight?" says Xin Qi.

"They are a bit. You try them on, so I can see how they look," says Eva. Xin Qi comes out in the leather trousers. "They really fit you well!" says Eva.

"Comfortable too," says Xin Qi, getting ready to take them off.

"Keep them on, let me pay for them. They're a present," says Eva.

"No, no, I couldn't possibly!" protests Xin Qi.

But Eva is heading for the cash desk to pay and get the invoice. Xin Qi stuffs her old trousers into her bag and follows Eva.

26. XIA ZIHUA • THE HOSPITAL

THE WEATHER FORECAST PREDICTS RAIN, but only a few drops fall, splattering heavily on the ground, as if hurling themselves to their deaths, and leaving coin-sized marks. The sun refuses to show its face. Only the smog grows brighter, turning the air an orange colour.

The streets are jammed, as usual. The use of vehicle horns has been banned in Xijing, but someone toots their horn anyway, and immediately, dozens of cars follow suit. It's catching, like yawning.

The cacophony comes from a road leading up to a flyover, where so many vehicles are queued that there are now five columns of vehicles jostling for space in a three-lane road. A red car hesitates for a moment and another car nips in front, followed by another, then another car, so the red car is completely stuck and there are enraged hoots from those behind. When the driver immediately behind the red car finally squeezes into the moving traffic, he looks over his shoulder and sees that the red car driver is a young woman. Some local bigwig must have just given it to her, he thinks and spits in contempt.

Another car crawls by, its back window lowered. A Shar Pei sticks its nose out. They are generally known for being bad-tempered dogs, but this one seems to be immune from road rage. It is gazing placidly at the fly-posted lamp posts at the bridgehead. The spitting driver sees the advertisements too: Xijing is hosting its annual trade fair – the media is always trumpeting the multi-billion-yuan contracts signed at each fair. Huh! the driver thinks to himself, if that were true, Xijing would be paved with banknotes by now. But public services are still terrible and the traffic is getting worse by the day!

Hai Ruo goes to the bank to send her son Hai Tong a few thousand yuan, then meets Ying Lihou, Yan Nianchu and Mr Wang in a Japanese restaurant.

They eat and talk. Then just as they conclude their business, Hai Ruo gets a call from Si Yinan, who tells her, "Zihua's in a bad way!"

Hai Ruo, Lihou and Nianchu abandon their dinner, jump into their cars and race to the hospital. At first they drive in convoy, but soon lose sight of one another trying to navigate the traffic. When Lihou and Nianchu get stuck in a particularly congested spot, Hai Ruo turns off just in time and takes a shortcut down an alley. However, before she comes out at the other end, her car stalls. She keeps trying but it won't start. "You lousy bit of junk! Why are you dying on me now!" she swears at it.

She has had this Audi for over a decade and should have changed it before now. She has even talked to Xi Lishui several times about getting a new one. But although it has had a few glitches, it has never needed major repairs. And now, at the worst possible moment, it's given up the ghost. Hai Ruo is so stressed that sparks are coming out of her eyes.

She breathes out long and slow, telling herself to calm down. It's no good swearing at the car, I need to encourage it, she thinks, and pats the steering wheel. "Come on, you've worked so hard for me all these years, I know you're getting on, but I'll fix you, I won't abandon you. Please, just one more effort, we need to get to the hospital, Zihua is waiting for us."

She turns the key in the ignition, and the engine sputters into life. As she drives on, Hai Ruo mutters, "Good little car, I promise I'll get you serviced after this trip. I'll even take you to Lishui's shop for a facelift." She reaches the hospital, but there is no sight of Lihou or Nianchu.

Inside, she sees Yinan with her arms around Mrs Qi. The old woman bursts into tears as Hai Ruo approaches.

"I was coming to take over from Xu Qi," Yinan tells Hai Ruo. "Something made me stop and pick up the two of them on the way, I don't know what it was. It was so strange, Xia Lei wouldn't stop crying, no matter how we tried to calm him down. Eventually Xu Qi offered to take him to the cinema. The moment they left, a doctor came and told us Zihua is brain-dead. She's only breathing because she's on life support. The doctor needs the family to decide when they should switch the machine off. Mrs Qi fainted and it took me ages pressing on her philtrum to revive her."

Hai Ruo nods, then goes looking for the doctor herself. A long time passes before she emerges from the Doctors and Nurses Office, looking very pale. "We need to make a decision," she whispers to Yinan, and she starts calling everyone else in the sisterhood.

Finally, Lihou and Nianchu arrive at the hospital and Hai Ruo tells them what has happened. Lihou starts wailing and Mrs Qi makes a gurgling sound and slumps to the floor. Yinan tries to hold her up but fails. "Nurse, nurse!" she yells, and asks them to find an empty room they can take her to and lie her down. Meanwhile Nianchu knocks on the door of the ICU. It opens a crack but when the nurse sees it's a family member, she slams it shut again. Nianchu rejoins them, and soon Lu Yike, Xi Lishui, Xiang Qiyu and Yu Benwen arrive too, their faces wet with tears.

"They still won't let us see her, don't they have a shred of humanity in them!" Nianchu exclaims.

"But she's still their patient until she's taken off life support," says Hai Ruo, to stop Nianchu from making a fuss. "Has everyone arrived?"

"Where's Xu Qi?" asks Yike.

"I came to relieve her, she's taken Xia Lei out," says Yinan.

"Should we call Yi-laoshi?" Yike suggests. "And we could use some help from xiao-Zhen, xiao-Su, xiao-Fang and Wenlai too."

"All right, you call them," says Hai Ruo.

Hai Ruo delegates the tasks: Lishui and Nianchu are to purchase the funeral clothing, and the padded mat, quilt and pillow. Yike and Benwen will take Zihua's mother home and set up the mourning room there. Qiyu and Yinan will go to the mortuary to arrange the cremation. Hai Ruo and Lihou will stay at the hospital.

Xu Qi calls. "Should I come back and take Mrs Qi home?" she asks. "Or bring Xia Lei to the hospital?"

Hai Ruo tells her about Zihua and Xu Qi bursts into tears. Hai Ruo decides on a change of plan: she asks Benwen to stay, and tells

Xu Qi to take Xia Lei home. Finally, as Yike leads the old lady away, Hai Ruo instructs her, "Choose one of Zihua's best photos to enlarge as her portrait. And make sure you buy the whole set – the mourning silk, flower wreaths, fruit, joss paper, candles and incense sticks."

"Right," Yike says.

As Qiyu and Yinan are about to set off for the mortuary, Hai Ruo asks Benwen to go instead of Yinan.

Lishui realises that she hasn't any cash on her. "Do you have any money?" she asks Nianchu.

"I've got a card," says Nianchu, before turning to Hai Ruo. "How many pieces of clothing should we buy?"

"A triple set, definitely," says Lishui.

"But what will she look like wearing three sets of clothes?" asks Nianchu.

"It's to make sure she has enough outfits in the afterlife, it's not about being pretty," replies Lishui.

"But it *is* about her looking pretty!" Nianchu protests.

"The dealers of funeral clothing will make sure they match," Lishui says.

"The funeral clothing store?" asks Nianchu. "All they've got are antique Qing dynasty style. Zihua was always chic, and now you want her to wear a long gown with a tunic on top?"

"Go for modern clothes then," Hai Ruo decides. "Get proper underwear and a dress, and an overcoat. Get the smartest and the most expensive."

"What about shoes?" Lishui wants to know. "We can't get her high heels because they'll be made of leather and that means you'll be reborn as a beast of burden."

"Nonsense!" objects Nianchu. "If she's going to have a magnificent outfit, how can she wear flat-heeled cloth shoes!"

"Nianchu does have a point," says Hai Ruo.

Yike takes Mrs Qi by the arm and they go downstairs. Lishui and Nianchu follow behind.

Half an hour later, the teashop assistants arrive. They peer through the crack between the ICU double doors, but can't see anything inside. xiao-Su sinks to the floor and weeps. That starts the others crying too.

Hai Ruo hustles Wenlai along the corridor to the staircase. The young man is still repeating, "I couldn't save her! I couldn't save her!" He beats his chest in anguish.

"You did everything you could," she soothes him. "Zihua was so grateful to you and she still is."

Wenlai finally calms down and stands propped against the wall. When Yi Guang arrives, he is still there, quite silent, looking dazed.

Hai Ruo tells Yi Guang about Zihua and his eyes well with tears. "I didn't believe it was so serious," he says. "I thought she'd recover in no time. So I didn't visit her once in the hospital, and now she's gone. Gone! And far too soon!" And he mutters over and over, "I still had stuff to tell her!"

He is so distressed that Hai Ruo is at a loss how to comfort him. She tells xiao-Zhen, xiao-Su and xiao-Fang to stop crying and relays the doctor's message to Yi Guang. "I've been waiting for you, so we can decide when to take her off life support."

"When was Zihua born?" Yi Guang says, almost to himself.

"This is so painful," says Hai Ruo. "She's forty tomorrow. Just five days ago, her mother was asking me if we could get the hospital to let us take her home for maybe half a day... or let the sisterhood hold a celebration here. It could have given her a big boost. No one ever saw this coming..."

"Tomorrow's her birthday? Do you know the exact hour she was born?"

"I think just after midnight tonight. Zihua once said proudly that she came to this world at twenty-four strokes of the bell."

"Then midnight it is. It will be a complete forty years, not a minute longer or shorter."

Once again, Hai Ruo feels herself trembling all over. Before she can speak, she hears raised voices from the top of the stairs. It sounds like Wenlai is arguing with someone.

Wenlai has been leaning against the wall when two men, both patients' relatives, come over to sneak a few puffs of smoke before resuming their watch outside the ICU. Wenlai feels like stopping them from lighting up. Instead, he swallows his objections and moves a few inches towards the corner.

The two exchange a few remarks about their work, then one exclaims, "Hey, isn't that Yi Guang, that man talking over there?"

"Yup," says the other.

"He looks exactly the same as on TV. What a fantastic opportunity, I must get a selfie with him!"

"Grow up! What do you want a selfie for?"

"He writes good articles and he's a brilliant painter and calligrapher, Xijing's famous thanks to him!"

"If a man writes and paints well, does that make him a good person?"

"What do you mean? Are you saying he's not?"

"I've seen too many like him. They're high-minded posturing bigmouths the lot of them. Until there's a crisis, of course, and then you see they've got no backbone. Inside, they're like jelly. Don't be fooled by them. They might tell everyone they don't want money or power, but just try throwing them a couple of scraps and watch them fight! They bite each other's heads off, and brownnose their betters. They're boozy, lecherous bigots, every one of them."

Wenlai has had enough. "Hey, mind your tongue!" he protests.

"What? This is a private conversation, it's none of your business," retorts the man.

"I'd let it go if I hadn't heard you, but I couldn't help overhearing, so please shut up," says Wenlai.

"So what if I said that about him?"

"If you dare to badmouth him again, I'll rip your tongue out!"

"Wenlai, Wenlai!" Hai Ruo calls. "We have no time for arguments now."

Wenlai approaches and greets Yi Guang with a bow, then stands to one side.

"Go out and buy some joss paper," Yinan tells xiao-Zhen and xiao-Su.

"What paper?" asks xiao-Zhen.

"Joss paper," Yinan repeats. "Underworld banknotes. Lots of them. And not just the usual millions or billions, get some smaller denomination notes too."

"Smaller notes?" xiao-Zhen asks again.

"It's obvious," Wenlai chips in. "You can't spend notes of a hundred million."

"I've already asked Yike to buy some more joss paper," says Lihou.

"That's for the mourning room," says Yinan. "We need to burn joss paper here too, at the moment she passes away."

"There's no way the hospital's going to allow that," says Hai Ruo.

"I know. I don't mean inside," says Yinan. "I'll go down to that big tree by the morgue. The moment her life support is switched off, I'll draw a circle on the ground, burn the joss paper inside it, and call Xiajie's name."

Hai Ruo thinks for a moment, then says, "Fine." She offers xiao-Zhen some cash, but xiao-Zhen refuses, and she and xiao-Su make their way unsteadily down the stairs.

"What shall I do, Hai-jie?" Wenlai asks.

"Stick around. There's plenty needs doing," Hai Ruo tells him.

"I'm off," says Yi Guang. "I owe Zihua a piece of calligraphy. I'll write a couplet for her mourning room."

But before he can leave, Eva and Xin Qi come hurrying up the stairs, their faces gleaming with sweat.

"How did you find out?" Hai Ruo asks them.

"It was me, I called Eva," Wenlai says.

"I was at my landlady's," says Eva. "I called Xin Qi, and she got a taxi and picked me up."

Eva and Xin Qi are desperate to see Zihua and when they are told that the ICU is off limits to visitors, Xin Qi exclaims, "So she'll take her last breath with no one she knows by her side?" This prompts more tears from everyone.

It is the first time Yi Guang has met Xin Qi. "Is this your friend?" he asks Eva in an undertone.

Eva glances at Yi Guang, then looks away. "She's a friend of Xi-jie's. We met not long ago."

"Right," says Yi Guang. Then he asks Eva, "Have you been to Zihua's home?"

"Yes."

Yi Guang turns to Hai Ruo. "Eva can come with me, wait until I've done the couplet, and take it to the mourning room."

"Me?" Eva sounds surprised.

"You don't want to?" asks Yi Guang.

"I'm young, I'll go wherever I'm needed," says Eva.

"I've got everything covered here," Hai Ruo tells her. "You go with Yi-laoshi. Take the couplet to Mrs Qi and stay with her. You can help Yike and Xu Qi there."

Eva looks at Xin Qi, who opens her mouth to speak, but before she can say anything, Yi Guang hustles Eva down the stairs.

"We've been in touch with everyone," says Lihou. "Except for Feng Ying. Her phone's switched off. Is she back in the country yet?"

"She'd have called us the minute she touched down if she was back," says Hai Ruo.

"But if she's not back soon, she might miss the cremation," says Lihou.

"I'll call Mr Fan, he'll know where the delegation is right now," says Hai Ruo.

But Fan Bosheng says, "No, I haven't heard any news either. They're definitely not back yet."

Hai Ruo sighs, and goes to talk to the doctor about switching off Zihua's life support. By the time she returns, xiao-Zhen and xiao-Su have come back with bags of funeral money.

"You've told the doctor?" asks Lihou.

"Yes."

"So once the tubes are removed, that's it?"

Hai Ruo doesn't answer. "What time is it?"

"One minute after ten," says Yinan.

"Even if we can't be with Zihua, we should spend the last two hours of her life repeating 'Amitabha'," says Lihou. "It's a comfort to the dying. Let's say it to ourselves." She sits on the floor, lowers her head and her lips move silently. Wenlai, xiao-Zhen, xiao-Su and Xin Qi follow her example, but they don't know the ritual, so they just keep their heads bent.

"Yes, let's say the 'Amitabha' together," says Hai Ruo.

Loud keening erupts from a ward at the other end of the corridor. A doctor hurries out, stripping the rubber gloves off his hands.

"What happened, Doctor?" asks Yinan.

"Bed Thirty-Four died," is the curt reply.

Yinan glances at the group, then walks down the corridor towards the ward. The door is open. Three nurses are wrapping the body in a bed sheet. An old man leans over the bed, wailing. The body is lifted onto a stretcher and wheeled out. Hai Ruo and the others step aside in silence to let it pass. The stretcher gives a lurch, and the head under the sheet wobbles, a bit like a watermelon. The man's cries are gut-wrenching.

"The ward just turns a person out as soon as they take their last breath?" Lihou is shocked.

No one says anything. Hai Ruo suddenly feels dizzy and rests her head against the wall.

"Are you OK?" asks Lihou.

"Give me a moment."

"You must be exhausted, why don't you sit against the wall and rest, close your eyes for a moment?"

But Hai Ruo says she needs some fresh air. She heads for the window at the head of the stairs. Lihou starts to follow her, but she waves her away. Hai Ruo doesn't stop at the window, she goes all the way down until she reaches the backyard of the hospital. There she slumps to the ground, and the tears pour down.

At this late hour, very few people are coming and going at the hospital and the backyard is deserted. There is a thicket on the right. A path winds around it, leading to a row of single-storey buildings – the morgue. Gazing at its dark windows, Hai Ruo thinks, So *this* is where Zihua will be in two hours' time. Three hundred metres along this path and you're in the Underworld, she muses. She gets to her feet and goes to check there are no pebbles or bits of brick on the path to joggle the stretcher wheels, or low-hanging branches that might catch on the shroud, but there is nothing. As she approaches the morgue, Hai Ruo notices a tall poplar that appears to be covered in funereal white flowers. Do poplars really have such big catkins? she wonders. But they are leaves, not flowers. It is the glare of the distant lights that has bleached the colour from them.

Under the morgue's gable end, a mother and daughter are burning joss paper. They kneel by a small fire, feeding paper into the flames and muttering prayers. The firelight shines on their tear-stained faces. The night is quite still, but the fire flares up all of a sudden in a whoosh that sounds like a gasp. The ashes rise upwards in a column and the flames lick the girl's fringe. She jerks backwards.

"It's all right, don't be afraid, Dad's giving you a kiss," her mother reassures her. She uses a twig to press the burning paper down into the bonfire and scolds, "Why are you in such a hurry! This is all for you, what's the rush?"

Hai Ruo looks up. The column of ash has dispersed, leaving sparks and scraps of paper drifting in the air. The ashes turn from crimson to white to black, and a ghostly presence is almost palpable.

伊
娃

27. EVA • THE CLOUD-GATHERING HALL

AT YI GUANG'S FLAT, Eva follows him upstairs to his studio, the Cloud-Gathering Hall. Before he pushes the door open, Yi Guang hawks and spits to one side. He tells Eva to do the same.

"Why?"

"When you come home at night, ghosts can follow you in. Ghosts eat phlegm and you have to feed them."

Eva is slack-mouthed with alarm, but she obeys, crosses the threshold into the room and bangs the door shut behind her. Yi Guang reaches for the light switch. Eva is still gaping and he takes a step towards her. That makes her shut her mouth and press her lips tightly together until they are hardly visible.

"I haven't seen you since that night," says Yi Guang, with a smile.

"I thought you'd forgotten me. You didn't call or message. Then at the hospital just now, you looked right through me."

"Because Zihua is dying," says Yi Guang, and he reaches for her.

Eva bats his hand away. "And now she's waiting for your couplet!" They fall silent. Yi Guang looks crestfallen. He climbs up to the attic without inviting Eva to accompany him.

The sitting room is brilliantly lit, while the room beyond is in pitch darkness. Eva leans on the door frame, just where light meets darkness, and peers inside. She can just make out the coverlet – the same one that covered her as she lay on the couch that night. The slippers she wore are on the floor beside the bed. She turns back. The curtains are tightly drawn in the sitting room. Between the top of the window and the corner of the ceiling, something glimmers, perhaps a filament of cobweb. But when she tries to get a better look, it disappears. She goes upstairs, too.

In the attic, Yi Guang has prepared the ink and writing brush, and a scroll of paper is spread over the desk. But instead of writing, he is holding a strand of hair he has taken from a small black porcelain pot, and is examining it against the light.

"Did you really keep my hair?" says Eva.

"Yours is in another pot, this is Zihua's hair," says Yi Guang. Inside the glass doors of the cabinet behind the desk is a long row of porcelain pots of varying shapes and colours.

"Eh? You keep their hair, too?"

"Yes."

Eva is indignant. "Have you got a thing with all of them?"

"No."

"Liar! Look at me!"

Yi Guang shrugs and spreads his hands, like a *laowai* does. "Nothing happened."

Eva tosses her hand. "Why am I even asking? Forget it! So when you were looking at Zihua's hair just now, what were you thinking?"

Yi Guang ignores her question. He carefully puts the strand of hair back into the pot, replaces it in the cabinet, and locks it. Then he picks up the brush and begins to write.

The upper line: "The world speeds us post-haste from birth at dawn to death at dusk"

The lower line: "This body, mine for now, evaporates with the morning dew"

Eva reads the archaic language and is none the wiser.

Yi Guang lifts the brush again and writes another couplet.

The upper line: "The birds tweet joyously together"

The lower line: "Fragrant blossoms burst from branches"

"Surely you understand these two lines?" he says.

"But funeral couplets are supposed to be expressions of grief," says Eva, still puzzled.

"The lines describe how the sisterhood feel about each other, and how I feel about them," says Yi Guang. Then he adds, "Did you hear that?"

"What?" Eva is startled.

"It sounds like the wind's getting up."

Eva opens the curtains and the window. The lights are on in countless windows, as far as she can see. The branches of the roadside tree are motionless. "There's no wind," she says.

"It must be Zihua. She likes what I wrote for her." Eva glances around. Anxiety makes her tense and she finds she's holding her breath.

"It's nothing to worry about," says Yi Guang. "She won't harm us."

Eva stares at the couplets, willing the ink to dry. She is still uneasy. "I expect she's come to thank us for our efforts," she says.

Yi Guang lights a cigarette and takes a long, deep drag. He seals his lips and holds the smoke in until the cigarette has burned halfway down, then opens his mouth and the smoke pours out, enveloping the two of them. It reminds Eva of a flock of sheep she once saw on the steppes: a roiling cloud of white wool, carried along by thousands of bony sheep.

"It was Zihua who introduced me to Hai Ruo and the sisterhood," Yi Guang says. "At the time, she was a model. She entered a Xijing model competition that I was judging, and we met there. Zihua already knew Hai Ruo through Xiang Qiyu and took me to the teashop. Through Hai Ruo, I got to meet the whole beehive – Feng Ying, Xi Lishui, Lu Yike, Yu Benwen, Ying Lihou, Si Yinan and Xu Qi."

"The beehive?"

Yi Guang flashes a smile. "The image just popped into my head. You know the beehive on the west wall of the teashop? I pulled strings and got them the permit, so Zihua's mother could treat her arthritic knees with bee stings. When the bees cluster in their hive, I like to think they're united, the same way the sisterhood are united, right?"

"Bees sting," points out Eva.

"Exactly. All small creatures have their own survival skills. I once wrote an essay about it. Hedgehogs have spines. Crabs have shells. Stick insects can change colour. Lizards can regrow their tails. Bees have venom, just like snakes, scorpions, spiders and centipedes do, but they make honey, and that neutralises the venom. With Hai Ruo and the sisterhood, they have tough lives – they're single or divorced, and they have to jump through all kinds of hoops to run their businesses. But they're hard-working, honest and kind, always willing to help. Even with the smallest things, like a joke or a few kind words, or binning a cigarette end lying in the street. Apparently trivial, but meaningful, too."

The conversation flags. When Yi Guang starts pontificating, the best thing is just to listen and nod.

But there is one thing Eva still cannot comprehend: if Hai Ruo and the other women are so honest and upright, how come they have so many business and emotional entanglements? They're each nursing their pain, she can see that. She can almost see them squirming.

Yi Guang folds the couplets and puts them in a bag for Eva. "Give me a hug!" he commands.

Eva looks at Yi Guang, then at the window, then at the trophy pots in the cabinet. Her heart sinks. "You better not kiss me, I might sting you!" she says.

Yi Guang laughs and Eva notices how very white, and very long, his teeth are. Just then, her phone goes off, its ringtone shattering the silence like a ladle of water poured into smoking oil. She pulls it out of her pocket – it's Yike.

She takes the call gratefully and puts it on speakerphone.

"Where are you, Eva?" Yike's voice is very loud.

"At Yi-laoshi's studio, collecting the funeral couplets," Eva replies.

"Oh, so you've heard. If you're with Yi-laoshi, it doesn't matter."

"What's up, Lu-jie? Do you need anything?"

"We need a piece of silk for a wall hanging in the mourning room. Xu Qi bought one, but it's too small. I'm looking for a bigger piece now and I just passed by your landlady's building. I wanted to tell you what had happened, I thought you hadn't heard. Besides, I've spent most of the money I brought, and wanted to borrow some from you. But don't worry, I'm not far from Feng Ying's place. I'll call there and if there's anyone at home, they can give me some cash."

Eva finishes the call and looks down to see Yi Guang lying on the sofa in front of the desk, the same way she sprawled there, the night she got drunk and he made a pass at her. He is looking darkly moody.

"Is something wrong?" Eva asks.

"Bizarre!" he mutters.

"What?"

"I borrowed a hundred and fifty thousand from Feng Ying, and she owes Zihua two hundred thousand. Feng Ying sent word to Hai Ruo, to ask me to give Zihua the hundred and fifty thousand, and Feng Ying would pay Zihua the remaining fifty thousand. I was annoyed at the time that Feng Ying hadn't come to me directly. I've got the money ready, I just haven't had time to get it to Zihua. What's bizarre is that you took this call from Yike, and you put it on speakerphone so I heard it – I feel like it's Zihua asking Feng Ying and me to pay her back!"

Eva's heart skips a beat. She rests her back on the wall and slips down until she is sitting on the floor.

Yi Guang takes wads of one-hundred yuan notes out of the cabinet and puts them in the bag. He has decided to deliver the couplets personally and give the money to Zihua's mother, Mrs Qi. He pulls her to her feet but Eva is still feeling unnerved and weak at the knees, and he has to take her by the arm. They leave the flat and take the lift downstairs.

Outside the front gate, the old gatekeeper is sorting scrap cardboard and empty plastic bottles. "It's nearly midnight, Mr Yi," he says in surprise. "Are you going out?"

"Yup," says Yi Guang, releasing Eva's arm.

"They do work you hard!" says the old man.

They pass the teashop and are about to cross the small square to hail a taxi, when a street-cleaning lorry comes along, spraying the roadway. It stops by some trees to spray them, and the water overflows into the square. Yi Guang and Eva have to stand on the teashop steps and wait.

"Why are they spraying the streets so late?" asks Eva.

"It's best done before dawn," says Yi Guang.

"Does it help to reduce the smog?"

"I don't know about that, but at least it settles the dust."

Eva stretches to ease her stiffness and as she looks over her shoulder, she catches sight of the beehive beneath the upper window on the west wall of the teashop. The bees are asleep. All is silent. She opens her mouth to say something when suddenly a dark shadow darts past and crashes into the hive. It is a pigeon, perhaps part-blind, or startled by the cleaning lorry, or simply trying to end its life. At the impact, the bees explode out of the hive with a deafening buzzing. Yi

Guang and Eva hurriedly duck down and keep quite still, afraid of drawing the bees' ire. For a whole twenty minutes, they freeze, until the water lorry pulls away and the bees calm down.

The two of them hop between the puddles as they cross the square. Eva's eyes are drawn to the darkness beneath the trees. Who knows what beasts might be hiding there? A cat crawls out from under the wire fence and slinks away, unconcerned. Its short legs and long back remind Eva of a tiger. Just then, she jumps in fright and exclaims, "Snakes!" She is looking at earthworms as long as chopsticks all over the pavement, no doubt flooded out from the undergrowth. Meanwhile, a flock of birds are creating a commotion in the branches, like a noisy bunch of gossips.

28. XIAO SU • THE TEASHOP

AFTER XIA ZIHUA'S CREMATION, Hai Ruo sends xiao-Su to stay with Mrs Qi and keep her and Xia Lei company. She and others in the sisterhood take turns dropping in for a chat, taking them out for a meal, and generally keeping them occupied.

The very day of the cremation, the new owner of a flat on the second floor of the housing block began redecorating, meaning that on and off through the day there is hammering and drilling. While Zihua was alive, her mother was in a constant state of agitation. Zihua's cancer was like a bomb suspended over her head that might explode at any moment. Now, Mrs Qi feels the same anxiety about the building works. She cannot relax enough to take her midday siesta. xiao-Su finds her sitting on the sofa and urges her to go to bed but she simply says, "I'll go when they finish." Two hours later, there is still silence. The old lady thinks the workers have taken the day off and goes to lie down. But no sooner has her head touched the pillow than the hammering and drilling start up again. The vibrations shake the building like an earthquake. xiao-Su complains to the owner, but only gets an earful of abuse. A tearful xiao-Su tells Hai Ruo about it. Hai Ruo books a hotel room for them, but Mrs Qi doesn't want to go: it's too much money, and besides, even though Zihua is dead, her spirit will linger in their home. For the first seven weeks, she wants to cook her daughter's favourite dishes and put them in front of her memorial photograph, to help her soul on its journey. Hai Ruo doesn't insist. So when the noise from the building work becomes unbearable, xiao-Su takes the pair downstairs to sit in the courtyard.

A few days later, Lu Yike and Yu Benwen come to the teashop. They have something to discuss with Hai Ruo. The custom among the locals is that if the family has already bought a plot in the cemetery, the casket of ashes is interred on the day of the cremation. The remains of those with nowhere to go yet are stored at the mortuary for the time being. If the family cannot afford a plot, the casket simply stays there and, after ten years, the mortuary can dispose of it. Zihua's ashes have been placed in a casket of top-grade Lantian jade at the mortuary. Now Yike and Benwen have a proposal: how about the sisterhood club together and buy a plot between them? Then they can lay her to rest and the living can have peace of mind too. But where should she go? There are three main cemeteries in Xijing: Whale Gully, Phoenix-Perching Hill and White Deer Slope. Yike and Benwen want Hai Ruo to choose which is best.

But Hai Ruo is undecided. "We want a cemetery with the best feng shui, one that will benefit the family's prospects," she reminds them. So Yike and Benwen agree to visit more places.

The conversation then turns to Zihua's mother and her son, Xia Lei. Mrs Qi is too old and frail to look after such a young kid. How are they going to manage?

"It's a big worry," says Hai Ruo. She raised her concerns with xiao-Tang one day when Zihua was clearly getting worse, and xiao-Tang said, "If Zihua doesn't make it, I'll adopt Xia Lei. If I stay single, I'll have him to keep me company as I get old. And if I do marry one day, he'll come with me."

When her friends hear this, they are impressed that xiao-Tang, the teashop's capable manager, has such a kind heart. They know that xiao-Tang is twenty-nine and has been looking for a partner, but so far without success. "By the way, is there any more news? Is xiao-Tang still under investigation?" they want to know.

"Nothing at all," says Hai Ruo with a sigh. She looks worried.

Yike tries to distract Hai Ruo. "It doesn't feel right to have xiao-Tang shoulder the responsibility while we do nothing," she says. "And what's a kid going to do to her marriage prospects?"

"Do you have any better ideas?" asks Hai Ruo.

"Benwen told me something," says Yike. "Tell Hai-jie what you heard, Benwen."

"Well, last night Yinan and Xu Qi came to eat at my restaurant," Benwen begins. "When they'd finished their meal, Yinan asked about Xia Lei. She says she wants nothing more to do with men, but she still wants a child. She'd like to adopt Xia Lei. But she doesn't know what Mrs Qi would think, or if it's the right thing to do. That's why she hasn't said anything to you."

Hai Ruo's heart skips a beat. She remembers that Xiang Qiyu once commented on how close Yinan and Xu Qi were, and does not know what to say. But then she thinks, If Yinan and Xu Qi are really a couple, and in a long-term relationship, it would be great if Yinan adopted Xia Lei and they brought him up together. So she says, "Yinan is a good woman, the best of all of us. Beneath her rough and ready exterior, she's very focused. She'd take great care of Xia Lei."

"I agree with you," says Benwen. "But will Mrs Qi be willing to give him up?"

"We should talk to Yinan and Mrs Qi," says Hai Ruo.

They discuss the ins and outs of various arrangements, and which is likely to work out best. Finally, they settle on two options. If Mrs Qi agrees to Yinan adopting Xia Lei, she'll still be his grandmother and can visit him often. Ideally, if Yinan and the old lady both agree, she can move in with Yinan too. Of course, there's no reason why Yinan should take on looking after the two of them, so the sisterhood will take care of Mrs Qi. On the other hand, if she doesn't want to give him up for adoption, the sisterhood can find them a *baomu* and will undertake to visit regularly for as long as necessary... be that eight years, ten years or even twenty. When the old lady dies, they'll take care of her funeral, and see Xia Lei through his schooling, all the way to university, so that he grows up a fine young man.

The plans cheer them up. "Why don't we treat ourselves to something special?" says Hai Ruo. She brings out a round flat cake of tea, with "Yunnan Dayi Qizi" printed on the wrapper. She unwraps the paper and prepares to break off small chunks.

"It's just Dayi Qizi," says Yike, pulling a face.

"This is Big Cabbage tea! You must have heard of it!" says Hai Ruo.

"Big Cabbage? You're giving us cabbage leaves!" Benwen exclaims.

Hai Ruo looks scornful. "Is that what you think? Well, I wouldn't expect a lazy nag to appreciate a good saddle!" Then she begins to lecture them, "Do you know where this tea gets its name from? Qizi means Seven Sons, after the seven brothers who picked the best highland tea for their parents: each package is made up of seven flat cakes, *bing*. Each *bing* weighs seven *liang*. That's three hundred and seventy-five grams. The tea cakes are named after the location where these ancient trees grow, so Banzhang tea is made from tea leaves picked at Banzhang, and Manzhuan tea comes from Manzhuan. High-grade tea cakes, aged over ten years, are known by the colour and pattern on their wrappers, so you have Purple, Red and Green Dayi tea. The longest-aged, most fragrant and most expensive kind is called Big Cabbage."

Yike and Benwen are suitably impressed. "You're so knowledgeable, Hai-jie!" "We're so dumb, we don't deserve this refined tea." "You're casting pearls before swine!"

"You two certainly have the gift of the gab!" Hai Ruo retorts, but she's smiling.

By the time they have drunk five infusions of the tea, they are rosy-cheeked and sweating. "It's making me want to pee!" says Benwen and hurries downstairs to the toilet. When she comes out, she sees that it's getting dark. Gao Wenlai, xiao-Zhen, xiao-Fang and Mrs Zhang are pulling down the blinds, setting the chairs and stools around the tables, and getting ready to shut up shop. She suddenly thinks of something. "Is xiao-Su still with Mrs Qi?" she asks xiao-Zhen.

"Yes, would you like me to pass on a message, Yu-jie?" asks xiao-Zhen.

"That's all right, I'll call her."

xiao-Su picks up and Benwen tells her, "We're going to choose a cemetery plot for Zihua tomorrow. Can you get out Yi-laoshi's funeral couplets so we can have them engraved on the tombstone?"

"Couplets?" asks xiao-Su. "I didn't see any. Hai-jie asked me to stay behind at Xia-jie's flat to clean up on the day of the cremation, but Xia-jie was always so nice to me, I wanted to go with the group saying their last goodbyes to her. So Hai-jie asked Mrs Zhang to stay instead. She might have put the couplets away, but I don't know where."

"Mrs Zhang?" Benwen calls. "You stayed at Zihua's on the day of the cremation. Where did you put the calligraphy?"

"Calligraphy? What calligraphy?" asks Mrs Zhang.

"The couplets we hung in the mourning room."

"They were burned with everything else, at the crematorium."

"You sent them to be burned? What were you thinking of?" exclaims Benwen. "Yi-laoshi's funeral couplets are priceless. They should have been put away for her son, to show him what a wonderful woman his mother was. And we need them to do her tombstone engraving. I can't believe you burned them!"

"But that's what we do back home. Everything from the mourning room gets burned after the cremation," Mrs Zhang says.

"This is the city! You do realise that one piece of Yi-laoshi's calligraphy is worth a hundred thousand yuan!" says Benwen furiously.

"But... but no one told me!" stammers Mrs Zhang, and bursts into terrified tears.

Benwen rushes upstairs and tells Hai Ruo and Yike what has happened. The women go pale at the news.

"Ignorant woman! Why did you hire such an ignoramus?" Benwen shouts.

Hai Ruo is equally distressed, but explains, "Mrs Zhang's an illiterate peasant. She came to Xijing with her son, who was sitting in on high school classes. He passed the *gaokao* exams and got a place at university, so she's free to leave but she stayed on because their rent was paid up, and the landlord wouldn't refund it. She got this job at the teashop to tide her over until she goes."

Mrs Zhang comes upstairs, sobbing. "Please forgive me, Mrs Hai," she pleads. "There's no way I can pay back that kind of money." She's so upset that she slaps herself across the face.

"Forget about paying us back," says Hai Ruo kindly. "They're burned and that's all there is to it. Maybe Zihua liked them so much, she got you to send them for burning so she could take them with her. Don't worry." Reassured, Mrs Zhang goes down.

"It's easy for you to say," Benwen says. "But what do we give the engraver to carve on the tombstone?"

"We'll get Yi-laoshi to write another one."

"You think he'll do us the favour? You or Yike had better ask him personally," says Benwen.

"Fine," says Yike. "You carry on checking out cemeteries, and I'll get him to do another couplet."

With her staff gone for the day, Hai Ruo invites Yike and Benwen to dinner, but they both say they're trying to lose weight and are skipping their evening meal. They'd like more tea, though. So Hai Ruo goes without dinner too and makes a fresh pot of Big Cabbage. They sit over their tea until midnight.

Hai Ruo sees them on their way, then comes back upstairs. She is feeling sleepy, and decides to spend the night in the teashop instead of going home. First, she tidies the arhat couch, and lights a stick of incense and places it in front of the Buddha. Then she decides she had better video-call Hai Tong before going to sleep. She's been so preoccupied, she hasn't called him for days, and he hasn't called her either. When he was at primary school and home alone doing his homework, when she had to work late at the teashop, he was forever on the phone to her. He always asked the same question, 'Nana, when are you coming home?' (He couldn't pronounce 'Mama' properly.) And he always ended his calls with smoochy kisses. But now he's a young man, he never calls unless it is to ask for money. Hai Ruo smiles wryly to herself. Her phone rings. She decides it's too late, she's not going to answer it, no matter who it is. Then she thinks, It could be Hai Tong, maybe his ears are burning because I was thinking of him. But she looks at her phone and sees it's xiao-Su. She takes the call anyway. "Yes?"

"Are you asleep, Hai-jie? Did I wake you?"

"No, I'm still at the teashop. Is something up?"

"Yes... I wanted to wait and tell you tomorrow, but I can't cope with it on my own. It's urgent."

"Go ahead then, tell me, and then you can get some sleep."

"Not over the phone. I won't make any sense. I'll come to you."

Hai Ruo sits and waits for xiao-Su, having banished any thoughts of calling Hai Tong. The incense stick has burned halfway down by now and she is increasingly anxious. xiao-Su hardly ever calls me unless it's urgent, she thinks. What can it be? Has Mrs Qi fallen ill with grief? Has Xia Lei been kicking off? Is xiao-Su finding her duties there too onerous? She cannot sit still, and gets up to go downstairs. She unlocks the door and stands on the steps, looking down the road that runs alongside the park.

How quickly the night has passed. It is nearly dawn. The sky is very dark, but the traffic is already getting heavier. The old car park attendant is rummaging through the rubbish bins at the roadside, a large checked carry-bag in his hand. He is conscientious and hard-working, putting in long hours every day in the car park, scrupulously charging every car and issuing the requisite receipt. He would never dream of pocketing a single cent for himself. His only indulgence is collecting scrap whenever he has a free moment. Behind the kiosk is a lean-to for when he's on his break, but he has filled it with bags of rubbish about which the neighbours constantly complain. Hai Ruo is more forgiving. After all, he needs to feed himself somehow. Whenever the teashop has a delivery of fruit, cakes and pastries, or sunflower seeds, she takes him some. Most of the time, the old man is to be found sitting behind his rubbish bags, drinking *baijiu* and dipping into a paper bag of braised pig trotters. He always offers Hai Ruo some of the *baijiu*, and when she refuses, he offers her a bit of trotter.

Hai Ruo frequently tells him he drinks too much. "How do you keep tabs on which cars haven't paid for parking if you are drunk?"

"I never get drunk, I've got a good head for it," the old man always says.

He pauses in his scavenging in the bins and spots Hai Ruo standing by the teashop door. He hobbles over. "Good morning, Mrs Hai. You do work yourself hard! What an early start!"

"You're up even earlier," says Hai Ruo.

The old man chuckles. "Have you got any rubbish? I'll take it out for you."

"Sorry, we put it in the bins last night. How's your haul this morning?"

"Not bad. Six plastic bottles, four pop-top cans, three aluminium tubes, three big staple fasteners and a cast-iron teapot. The teapot must be from your shop. The handle's broken, but you can easily get it mended. You don't need to throw it away."

"Is that so?"

"You need to keep an eye on your staff. They don't own the business so they don't know the value of things. Don't let them throw stuff away."

"Maybe they threw it away for you."

The old man chuckles again. "There are a dozen rubbish bins along this road. I go through them morning and evening and what I sell supplies me with a bottle and trotters at night." And he hobbles off to his lean-to.

Finally xiao-Su turns up in a taxi. She has no make-up on, her hair is a mess, and she is visibly upset. "Didn't you go home last night, Hai-jie? Are the others not here yet?" she asks.

"It's only five o'clock in the morning," says Hai Ruo. "Go and wash your face. Then you can tell me what's up."

xiao-Su obediently goes into the cubicle and Hai Ruo locks the shop door.

xiao-Su's story is a revelation to Hai Ruo. It turns out that Xia Zihua wasn't divorced or widowed. In fact, she never married. She had a lover, a Mr Zeng, who is Xia Lei's father. Zeng is an entrepreneur – he owned some sort of mine – and has another family too. He promised Zihua that he would divorce his wife and marry her, but three years after Xia Lei's birth, his father is still with the other woman. Zihua resigned herself to bringing up her son with her mother. Mr Zeng did buy a flat for Zihua, but was still renovating it when Zihua fell ill. Zeng was generous with his money and met all her needs, and, whenever Zihua's mother and son were at the hospital looking after Zihua, Zeng would visit too. xiao-Su has met him – since Zihua's death, he's been dropping in at Zihua's flat. He has invited Mrs Qi and her grandson to move into the flat he bought for Zihua, but she is not keen. Zeng wants to take on bringing up the boy but Mrs Qi isn't keen on that either. She and Zeng have still not come to an agreement and the old woman is spending all day in her room, crying.

xiao-Su rattles off her story somewhat incoherently. Hai Ruo is silent. "Am I making sense, Hai-jie?" xiao-Su asks.

"You carry on."

"I'm in such a state about it, it's given me cold sores. Why don't you say something?"

"Because it's one thing for Zihua to keep this a secret from everyone else, but why did she never tell me? She shouldn't have kept it from me."

"Are you upset? I was furious when I found out. Mr Zeng treated Xia-jie so badly, maybe that's why she didn't want others to know."

"Yes, it's understandable. But it must have caused Zihua so much pain, and that probably exacerbated her illness."

"Poor thing. How sad for her."

"But she's gone, and all her suffering has ended," says Hai Ruo.

"And now Mr Zeng wants to take over care of Xia Lei," says xiao-Su. "What do you think about that?"

"I was talking to Yike and Benwen about Xia Lei yesterday afternoon. Now we know Xia Lei has a father, it's the natural and the best option for him to go with his dad. The problem is, what will Zeng's wife feel? Could Xia Lei end up getting hurt? I need to meet this man."

"That'd be best. At first he didn't want to meet any of us. He told me he was Xia-jie's cousin. It was Mrs Qi who told me who he was, and then he owned up."

"Is he still with her?"

"He came in the afternoon and left at night. The moment he left, I called you."

"Phone me if he turns up again."

xiao-Su looks up and exclaims, "Thank heavens I've got that off my chest!"

"Let's have breakfast," says Hai Ruo.

However, xiao-Su is eager to get back. "xiao-Zhen and the others will be here any moment. They'll ask about Mrs Qi and Xia Lei. If I start talking, I might let the cat out of the bag." Hai Ruo smiles. xiao-Su continues, "Am I getting too involved in all of this?"

"You're fine."

"No I'm not, but I can't help it."

29. LU YIKE • THE HOTPOT RESTAURANT

THERE HAVE BEEN SULLEN SKIES for days on end. The thick smog seems to be drawing the sky closer to the earth. It's two in the afternoon, and someone has come to the small square in front of the teashop to practise cracking a whip. The whip – four or five metres long – emits a resounding crack as it arcs through the air, seeming to draw a yelp of pain from the sky.

By the books and newspapers stand, a group of peasants looking for day jobs are standing. They have brought their tools – hammers, saws, drills, trowels and paint rollers – which they carry on their backs or keep by their feet. They have been waiting there all morning and no one has taken them on. With nothing better to do, they gossip as they shovel down their lunch. "What's he doing wasting his strength?" says one, mocking the man wielding the whip.

"Are you drinking the oil your *yougao* was fried in?" says another.

"Why not? I can eat any amount of oil, even if it's scalding hot."

Lu Yike and Yu Benwen are back from going around all the cemeteries and come to the teashop for tea. But Hai Ruo is not in and Benwen can't stay long. Yike asks Eva to come with her to ask Yi Guang to compose another couplet for Xia Zihua. Xin Qi tags along with them.

Yi Guang takes a daily nap after lunch. He has just got up when Fan

Bosheng knocks at the door to invite him to the launch of a liquor called Qinjiu. The organisers will offer Yi Guang 200,000 yuan to write a short essay about the *baijiu*, and to do a piece of calligraphy at the event itself. Yi Guang refuses but Bosheng won't take no for an answer. They both end up angry.

So when Yike, Eva and Xin Qi arrive, Yi Guang exclaims in relief, "Aiya! Your timing is impeccable!" He plies them with refreshments, pointedly ignoring Bosheng. Yike turns down the cigarettes and the fruit, and comes straight to the point: they need more funeral couplets for Zihua. Yi Guang is happy to agree and takes them up to the attic.

Eva has taken two bananas and hands one to Xin Qi. She peels hers and takes a bite. "You certainly have clout, Lu-jie," she remarks.

"It's Zihua who's asking, not me," says Yike.

Bosheng gives himself a slap on the cheek.

"What's the matter with you?" says Yike.

"If only I were a woman!" says Bosheng.

Yi Guang is halfway up the stairs but turns to say, "I'm not doing this because they're sexy, I'm standing by my principles."

"All right, forget the essay," says Bosheng. "I can see why a writer like you wouldn't want to write an advertorial. But come and do the calligraphy. It won't take long and a car will pick you up and bring you home."

But Yi Guang says, "No, it's purely commercial. They'll make a big deal of me being there. It will give anyone who doesn't know any better the impression that I've made half a million or even more out of appearing at the event."

"It's true the fee isn't much," admits Bosheng. "But he's a new kid on the block. He's invited all sorts of Xijing bigwigs and is paying each of them fifty to a hundred grand so you're getting by far the biggest fee. How about this, you do several calligraphy pieces to sell to them at the price you name? That'll make you a bit more money."

"I already make enough money from my calligraphy."

"Your calligraphy will be worth no more than the paper it's written on if no one buys it," says Bosheng. Yi Guang turns and goes on up the stairs. "Oh, I almost forgot to tell you, there's an article online, did you see it?" asks Bosheng.

Yi Guang pauses again. "What article?"

"It says you're a writer and by selling your calligraphy, you're stealing food out of the mouths of specialist calligraphers."

"In the old days, all calligraphers were scholars too. There was no such thing as a specialist calligrapher. They're the ones eating *my* dinner!"

"It starts as envy and it finishes as hatred," says Bosheng. "And jealousy unbalances people's minds. Once their feelings turn to hatred, it can lead to serious harm."

"There are no rewards and punishments in this world, only karma," says Yi Guang. "Let them take this karma away from me."

"You should fight back. Why not write an article about that?" suggests Bosheng. Yi Guang comes back down the stairs again.

Up in the attic, Yike is cutting up a large piece of *xuan* paper. "Do you know Mr Fan well, Lu-jie?" asks Eva.

"Not really."

"Do you like him?"

"I have no opinion one way or the other."

"He's always trying to make a quick buck out of Yi-laoshi."

"All big beasts have parasites."

They hear footsteps on the stairs. Yi Guang is declaiming the lines, "A violent gale can uproot a giant tree, but it cannot snap a blade of grass. A hoe may clear away weeds, but it cannot fell a tree. Words of wisdom are not concerned with trivial arguments. The true Way does not limit its horizons."

"Do explain that to us," says Bosheng.

But Yi Guang simply says, "I won't be writing that."

"Then I'll write it."

"Suit yourself."

"Is that a 'Yes' to attending the launch?" asks Bosheng. But they both stop talking as they get to the attic. Yike, Eva and Xin Qi fall silent too.

Yi Guang prepares to write the couplet. He doesn't want to repeat himself, yet cannot think of any new lines. "So, this is for inscribing on the tombstone? Have you chosen the cemetery plot then?" he asks.

"No. Benwen and I went to all three main cemeteries this morning. The Whale Gully has the best scenery so far, but the access is only along a narrow path. Every year on Tomb-Sweeping Day, so many people go there to pay their respects and it gets terribly crowded.

White Deer Slope is quite far from the city, and the setting is not great. Phoenix-Perching Hill is good, but has limited availability. Benwen and I found a nice place, but they wouldn't sell it."

"Why not?" asks Yi Guang. "Mr Fan here knows people at the cemetery."

"Yes, but only in the admin office," Bosheng corrects him and everyone laughs.

"You have connections in the underworld too," Yi Guang needles him. "Several of your friends were buried there with your help, if I remember correctly?"

"True."

"Then could you help us out, Mr Fan?" asks Yike.

"Is it someone close to you?" asks Bosheng.

"One of our sisters," says Yike.

"In your sisterhood? Someone I didn't know? Aiya! I was hoping to get to know all of you and now one's sadly departed! What a shame! I'll certainly do what I can to help. Let me fix it up and I'll be back in touch in a few days."

"Let's not wait," says Yike. "Let's go there now. The sooner we can find a place, the sooner we can lay her to rest."

"But I've got business to discuss with Yi-laoshi," says Bosheng.

"What else is there to say?" says Yi Guang.

"Great, it's a done deal then!" Bosheng turns to Yike. "OK, let's go, we can be there in no time at all."

"Thank you, Mr Fan, allow me to take you to dinner tonight when we get back," says Yike.

"Ah! I already have an invitation. Ying Lihou and Xiang Qiyu are taking me out," says Bosheng.

"Wow, what a social life you have!" says Yike. "Then let's all dine together."

Yi Guang has raised the brush and begins to write:

Oh how brightly she shone, how we sing her praises now she's gone
One of the twin parasol trees withers, one of the double swords falls

Yike reads the couplets and says, "I see what the first one means, but what do the 'twin parasol trees and double swords' mean?"

"Zihua knows," Yi Guang says simply.

Everyone looks at him, confused. But he doesn't explain as he folds the paper and carefully inserts it in an envelope.

"Eva, can you call Yinan please?" says Yike. "Tell her that Benwen's busy in her restaurant, she should join us here as quick as she can. We're all going to Phoenix-Perching Hill to choose a cemetery plot."

"Is Si Yinan coming too?" asks Bosheng.

"You know her?" says Yike.

"No, I've heard of her and I've been wanting to meet her."

They go back down to the sitting room. "You've had plenty of tea at the teashop," says Yi Guang. "Now you can try something different. Could you brew us some coffee, Eva?"

Eva gets the coffee beans out of a drawer and goes to the kitchen. She pours them into a coffee machine. Xin Qi watches her friend in some surprise.

Yi Guang turns to Xin Qi. "You've got classic slanted phoenix eyes," he observes. "That's so rare!"

"Is that so?" says Xin Qi.

"Mind out, Xin Qi," Yike says. "Yi-laoshi is great in so many ways but if he takes a fancy to you, he talks a whole lot of rubbish!"

"But it comes from the heart!" Yi Guang protests, then turns back to Xin Qi. "Come, sit over here and let me take a good look at your hands."

Xin Qi obediently moves over, and displays her hands. "I have small palms, too small to gather riches."

"Such long fingers," Yi Guang is saying. "Phoenix eyes always come with slender fingers."

Eva brings in the first cup of coffee. She heads towards Yi Guang, then hands it to Yike instead. "The first time I saw Xin Qi's hands," she says, "I thought of a bird perched on a power line, gripping it with its long claws."

"You ought to insure your hands for a big sum," Yi Guang says. "Has no one asked you to be a hand model?"

"Yi-laoshi loves beautiful women," says Eva. "Xin Qi's feet are even prettier than her hands. Show them, Xin Qi. Yi-laoshi won't mind the smell!"

Everyone laughs, and Yi Guang rubs his face self-consciously. "I'm just an admirer of beauty," he says.

By the time everyone has had coffee, Yinan and Xu Qi are at the door. Bosheng says to Yike in an undertone, "I see two women. So the other must be Xu Qi, right?"

Yike makes the introductions. Bosheng is eyeing Yinan and Xu Qi, and they smile at him politely. "So that's how it is," Bosheng whispers to Yike.

"What do you mean?" asks Yike.

"Don't keep me in the dark."

"It's true, that *is* Xu Qi."

"You're not being honest with me. You're not like Xiang Qiyu."

So Yike calls over, "Come here, Xu Qi. Apparently, Mr Fan has something to say to you."

Xu Qi comes over. "Hello, Mr Fan. Thank you for helping us to choose the cemetery plot."

But Bosheng looks Xu Qi up and down. "Xiang Qiyu was right."

"Eh?"

"Nothing, no big deal. Everyone should be able to live how they like. It's fine by me," says Bosheng.

Xu Qi looks bemused, but Yinan's smile has vanished. She asks abruptly, "Mr Fan, what exactly did Xiang Qiyu say to you? Has she been gossiping about me and Xu Qi?"

Bosheng looks taken aback. "She didn't say anything."

Yinan glares at him. "If she said nothing, then what was all that nonsense about?"

"What did I say? Xu Qi, did I say anything? I am a very open-minded man," says Bosheng.

It suddenly dawns on Yike what he is referring to. She pulls Yinan aside. "Calm down, will you? That's Mr Fan. He's helping us get the cemetery plot. And he's much older than us. Keep your voice down."

But Yinan is furious. "Age is no excuse for disrespecting us. He's got a filthy mind!"

"But I don't use filthy language!" Bosheng retorts.

Yike tries to appease him. "Yinan's got a quick temper, Mr Fan. Please make allowances. She's only a girl."

"She doesn't look very girlish to me!" Bosheng shoots back.

Yinan lunges at him, but Yike grabs her. "I'm not going to choose Zihua's resting place if he goes." She takes Xu Qi by the hand and marches towards the door. "Let's get out of this place!" The door opens and they're gone.

That evening, Lihou is the first to arrive at Benwen's hotpot restaurant. She calls Bosheng and gives him the address and their room number.

"I'm with Yike, Eva and Xin Qi," answers Bosheng. "They wanted to invite me to dinner, too. Should we come together?"

Lihou readily agrees. She asks Benwen to add another hotpot, and more food and drinks. While she waits for them to arrive, she wanders along the corridors on all three floors, admiring the collection of photographs of old Xijing.

Benwen is an amateur photographer and collects old photos too. When she did up her hotpot restaurant, she had the historical photos scanned and enlarged, and covered the corridor walls with them. The captions explain that some were taken by foreign missionaries in the early twentieth century, others by Chinese across the years since the founding of the People's Republic. The Bell Tower and the Big Wild Goose Pagoda are iconic landmarks of Xijing, and Lihou is fascinated by the changes in their appearance over the decades.

At the end of the Qing dynasty, Xijing's population numbered no more than a few tens of thousands. In the photos, the area around the Bell Tower is completely empty. A few people sit eating in front of some shacks. Some have their nose buried in their bowl, others are licking the last remnants out of it. The Big Wild Goose Pagoda looks lonely and neglected. A raven perches on the branch of an elm that is growing sideways from the roof of the topmost tier. The Grand Mercy Temple by the pagoda has a mere three buildings. A steep flight of stairs leads up to the complex, and a monk can be seen standing at the top. He is dull-eyed and wears a vacant expression.

During the Republican era from 1912 to 1949, the city's population grew to 200,000. Around the Bell Tower, blocks of flats can be seen. In one photo, a man and a woman are being pulled along on a two-wheeled cart. The man wears a skullcap and holds a water pipe. The woman is wrapped in a scarf and her face is invisible. A pair of bound feet peek from the hem of her long gown, pointed like leaf-wrapped sticky rice *zongzi*.

By the early 1950s, the city's population had nearly doubled. On the Bell Tower hangs a giant portrait of Chairman Mao. The streets are lined with shops and filled with cars, bicycles and carts. Even, in one picture, a camel. Armed police march past. The pagoda now sits amid a vast expanse of wheat. At the edge of the field is an execution ground where the prisoners kneel in the dirt, trussed with ropes and carrying wooden boards on their backs inscribed with the words "evil tyrant".

1966. It's the beginning of the Cultural Revolution. By now, Xijing is home to several million inhabitants. Demonstrators throng the area around the pagoda, carrying banners and slogans. On either side of the pagoda, the trees are festooned with children clinging to the branches. They are shouting, hanging on with one arm and holding up slogans written on gigantic sheets of paper with the other. Long strips of white cloth with more slogans hang from the top of the pagoda all the way down to the ground. A group of men who look like monks are earnestly discussing Chairman Mao's Little Red Book.

Lihou is fascinated by the images and gets out her phone to take a few pictures. At the far end of the corridor a man and a woman are talking. "Xijing was a sad sight in the old days," she hears.

"It still is now."

"Nonsense, Xijing has grown huge and the economy is booming."

"True, but don't you find that the more prosperous it gets, the more insignificant and spiritually impoverished we humans become?"

"Well, maybe, but everyone's rolling in money now. We can have anything we want. Cantonese food, hotpot, everything's at our fingertips."

"But we have to wear masks to get it."

"Some people are never satisfied, in any epoch. We all think that over two thousand years ago, the Spring and Autumn period and the Warring States period were a golden age, but Confucius, who lived in the Spring and Autumn period, bemoaned the decline in public morals and wished he could have been born five hundred years earlier when the Western Zhou dynasty was founded. Then again, Prince Boyi and his brother Shuqi chose to starve rather than to accept the Zhou rulers when they took over."

"Don't lecture me!"

Lihou looks in their direction and sees them scrutinising the pictures. She doesn't want to get involved, and anyway her phone rings. It's Zhang Huai.

"Hello," says Lihou.

"Ying-jie, I need to see you," says the debt collector.

"Is something up?"

"I just wanted to tell you how hard our whole company worked on your behalf to recover your debt, Ying-jie. Perhaps you could see your way to paying us a bit more?"

Lihou feels a stab of anxiety. She glances at the two in the corridor. "The signal's poor here, let me find somewhere else." She goes back to the private room reserved for their party and into the adjoining washroom.

"Listen, bruv, I settled up with you, why are you asking for more?"

"It's true you paid our costs, before you stopped us finishing the job. But even so, it was our work that got you your money back, wasn't it?"

"How so? I haven't seen a single cent! Zhang Huai, let me tell you one last time, I've been more than generous with you!"

"It was chicken feed!"

Lihou is furious by now. "You think I'm a cash cow you can carry on milking? That three hundred thousand I gave you, it just dropped into your hands, did it? We signed the contract, you took a copy, I took mine. And you wrote that receipt in your own hand stating that it was in full and final settlement!"

"But, Ying-jie..." Zhang Huai persists.

How dare he try to squeeze more money out of me, Lihou thinks. She almost chokes with anger, and actually drops her phone.

Qiyu opens the door into the room but when she doesn't see Lihou, goes in search of Benwen. "Maybe she's in the washroom," Benwen suggests. Qiyu goes back and pushes open the washroom door, and there is Lihou leaning over the basin, looking whey-faced. "What happened?" she asks, concerned.

"Nothing, just a bit of a tummy upset," says Lihou, picking up her phone.

Lihou and Qiyu sit over cups of tea and crack sunflower seeds until Bosheng, Yike, Eva and Xin Qi arrive.

"How come you spent the afternoon together?" Qiyu asks. Yike tells her about their trip to Phoenix-Perching Hill to choose a plot for Zihua. "Oh, wow, did you choose one?" asks Qiyu.

"We did and we got it, thanks to Mr Fan pulling strings," replies Yike.

"Thank you, Mr Fan," says Qiyu.

"I've been doing my utmost to help out the sisterhood," says Bosheng. "But it's been thrown back in my face!"

"Who threw it back in your face?" asks Qiyu.

"You did!"

"What? Lihou and I invited you to dinner, and I've done something wrong?"

"You told me Si Yinan and Xu Qi are dykes. So this afternoon I took a good look at them and Si Yinan blew up at me."

"You haven't been drinking, have you, Mr Fan? What's all this about?" says Yike.

"But I didn't say anything to you about Yinan and Xu Qi!" Qiyu protests.

"You said they were inseparable," says Bosheng.

"But we're all close in the sisterhood. That doesn't make us all gay!" Yike challenges him.

"Si Yinan's quite masculine, the way she looks and behaves," Bosheng says stubbornly.

"So am I!" says Yike.

"All right, that's enough, let's sit down," Qiyu calls them to order. "We're here for dinner. We shouldn't let anyone spoil our appetite."

"Fine, let's eat," says Yike. "But I'd just like to say that even though being gay is still seen as perverted in China, it's no big deal abroad. As for Yinan and Xu Qi, I never noticed anything going on. And Qiyu, no more from you. We don't want anything to get in the way of our friendship. And we'd be grateful if Mr Fan stopped talking like that too. It's defamatory, and you'll lose our respect."

"I only said it to you. I never mentioned it to Si Yinan and Xu Qi. I don't give a damn whether they're dykes or not!" Bosheng protests.

"You used that word again," Yike points out.

"All right, enough talking. Let's put all this food into our mouths instead," says Bosheng. And gradually the tension eases.

After a few minutes, Yike says, "Qiyu, why don't you call Hai-jie and tell her we've got the cemetery plot, and Yi-laoshi has written new couplets. Ask her if she can join us for dinner."

Qiyu presses Hai Ruo's number and puts it on speaker phone. They hear Hai Ruo say, "I'm so glad that's settled, thank you for all your hard work. Let me pick up the tab for the meal, and you go ahead and order some more dishes from Benwen. But I won't join you this time. I've just bought myself a takeaway."

However, when the call is over, Yike says, "I'll pay today."

"I'll pay," says Qiyu.

"Don't argue, I invited Mr Fan so I'm paying," says Lihou.

"All right, Lihou can pay," says Yike. "And it's all thanks to you, Mr Fan, that we're here!" Then she adds, "Didn't someone say they fancied a drop of Maotai?"

There are cheers of approval round the table, though someone demurs, "Maotai is way too expensive. Let's have bog-standard Erguotou instead."

Lihou smiles. "I'm such a pushover. Maotai it is! I was planning to offer it today anyway. No need for everyone to make such a big deal about it."

Qiyu, Yike, Eva and Xin Qi take their bowls and plates out to the main dining room where an array of seasonings and sauces are laid out on a long table. While they are gone, Lihou tells Bosheng about Zhang Huai's phone call. "This evening was meant to be a celebration, to thank you for your help. But Zhang Huai's such a nasty man, it's spoiling the occasion for me."

"I know you paid him three hundred thousand," says Bosheng. "But he has a lot of people working for him, it might not have been enough."

"But that's not my concern," says Lihou.

"You're better off than anyone else in the sisterhood," says Bosheng. "Rumour has it you're rolling in it."

"There's plenty of money in the bank too, but that's not a reason for robbing it!" retorts Lihou.

Bosheng grunts.

"You'd better warn him I mean business," says Lihou. "If he keeps on like this, I'll sue him. Even if I get nowhere, Yi-laoshi has contacts in government and in gangland. He'll stick his neck out for me!"

"OK, I'll warn him," says Bosheng. Lihou fans her face with both hands and nods. Then Bosheng adds, "It's too bad you haven't got a husband, or you wouldn't be in this mess."

Yike has mixed the seasonings to her liking and is heading back to their room when she bumps into Mr Wu's personal assistant. Yike greets her.

"Hello, Yike!" says the woman.

"You're eating here too? Is your boss with you?" asks Yike.

"No, I'm with some friends from school, we haven't seen each other for years. So we've come for a hotpot," says the woman.

"Isn't hotpot a bit cheapskate if you haven't met for years?" says Yike with a smile.

"It's just us girls, and we love hotpot," says the PA.

They both laugh and Yike asks, "Is Mr Wu still on retreat?"

"No, he finished and came back yesterday."

"I wonder if you know when the Living Buddha's arriving? We've got everything set up for him."

"I did ask my boss, but he doesn't know for sure."

"So you don't know either!"

"We'll just have to be patient."

"Yup, that's all we can do now. Let me pick up the tab for your meal, by the way," Yike offers.

"That's kind of you but I've already paid the bill," says the woman, with a smile.

Back in the room, the waitress has set up the hotpots and pushed in a cart, laden with slices of beef, mutton, fish head, fish fillets, pig trotters, tripe strips, wood ear fungus, tofu, Chinese yam, wide glass noodles, mushrooms and leafy vegetables.

Lihou is sitting there, lost in thought.

"Aren't you getting your seasonings?" Yike asks.

Lihou jumps, then says, "Sure. I'm just going." She gets up – and walks straight into the glass door. The glass is intact but she has given herself a nose bleed.

30. HAI RUO • THE HOUSING ESTATE

THE SMOG STILL HANGS over Xijing, in spite of measures by the authorities to control it. Media reports say that LPG has replaced coal-burning boilers and primitive stoves throughout the city and suburban counties. For petrol and diesel vehicles, a system of no-drive days has been implemented and there are generous discounts if you buy an electric car. Construction sites have been ordered to cover exposed earth in green netting to keep the dust down. Lorries diligently sweep and spray the streets early in the morning and late at night. So why is the smog still there? Does it really have a human cause or is it a sign that the earth itself is corrupted, rotting like an apple?

Everyone hopes the wind will blow the smog away. And today here it comes. It's not much more than a stiff breeze, but the building creaks, and an open window bangs shut, open and shut again. The waitress hurries over to bolt it and looks outside. The trees along the street are blowing this way and that, and passersby are running in every direction, bent double, heads tucked in. The man at the kiosk is frantically trying to gather up the magazines on display outside. The wind whips through their pages as if it is speed-reading. Then newspaper pages break free and fly into the air. A single sheet plasters itself over the restaurant window, completely blocking the view.

Last night, when Xiang Qiyu called Hai Ruo and asked her to join them at dinner, Hai Ruo wasn't eating a takeaway, she was at home, talking to her cousin. Mr Qi had been taken away by the Disciplinary Committee, her cousin told her. They met him off the plane as soon as it landed from Macau. And apparently that very afternoon Mr Ning, the Xijing Party Committee's general secretary, had been taken before the Committee too.

Hai Ruo could have predicted that Mr Qi would face a disciplinary hearing. She hopes he will come clean about the gold, and then xiao-Tang can be cleared of wrong-doing. But if they picked up Mr Ning too, it will not simply be because they want him to assist with their investigations. There must be financial or even political issues involved. Will the developer of the flats where Yi Guang has his studio be implicated too? Hai Ruo has Mr Ning to thank for the low rent she pays on the teashop. He fixed it with the developer.

All night Hai Ruo tosses and turns in bed. The moment she reaches the teashop this morning, she calls Yi Guang and asks him to find out what he can. But Yi Guang is reluctant.

"If it isn't true, it'll only stir up trouble to ask questions. And if it is, all the more reason not to breathe a word to anyone."

So Hai Ruo has had to drop the matter. Yi Guang is right, trying to confirm the rumour is pointless. At this point, xiao-Su calls her to say she's arranged for Hai Ruo to meet Xia Lei's father at noon. She changes into a traditional long gown and takes a taxi, as it is a no-drive day for her car. Halfway there, she feels a craving for the sweet, rich flavour of crab flesh and tells the driver to drop her off at a nearby restaurant serving Jiangsu and Zhejiang cuisine.

As she chooses her crabs, Hai Ruo contemplates the irony that the thick, wet twine binding the crabs' claws would be just another piece of rubbish on its own, but once it's bound around a crab's legs, it suddenly becomes as pricey as the crustacean itself. She chooses three crabs and they are steamed and brought to her. She demolishes two of them, then stops. It strikes her that a crab's lot is a dismal one. They look so fearsome, with their huge pincers and impressive armour, skittering sideways, glaring around and blowing bubbles. And yet their defences are so easily overcome. They are caught, tied up and steamed alive, before being dismembered and chewed into little bits by humans. She feels a twinge of guilt. It's not against Buddhist doctrine for lay Buddhists to eat meat, she thinks, and I didn't personally steam the crabs. But I've been a strict vegetarian for ages. Why did I suddenly crave crabs today? I'm full of shit! She looks around absent-mindedly.

By a table in the corner, there is a man in his seventies. Although he is neatly dressed, his face is wrinkled and weather-beaten. Sucking the flesh from one crab leg seems to require him to drink seven or eight tiny cups of *baijiu*, which he raises to his lips and downs in a single gulp. She imagines the liquor setting his insides aflame.

Hai Ruo tells the waitress to take her third crab away. The bile rises to her throat and she feels nauseous. "Do you have rice porridge?" she asks.

"No, but we do have pancakes."

She doesn't fancy pancakes. "Any salted pickles?"

The waitress brings a saucer of pickles and Hai Ruo shovels half of them into her mouth, settles the bill and leaves, still chewing on them. Outside, she looks for a taxi. When you don't need one, they're everywhere, but now there's not a single one to be seen. She waits for half an hour as the wind tousles her hair and her long white gown billows around her.

She got the gown one day at the Trade and Commerce Plaza with xiao-Tang. She wanted one in a hazy blue but xiao-Tang told her, "The colour of mourning makes a woman look good!" and she had bought it. But white shows up every scrap of dirt, she thinks. It looks dusty already. She is on the point of blaming xiao-Tang for her choice when a distressing thought occurs to her: xiao-Tang still hasn't come back and there's been no news of her since she was taken away. xiao-Tang took nothing with her. And she's such a neat, clean woman, punctilious about showering and wearing fresh clothes every day. She must still be in the clothes they took her away in. It's not likely they'd allow her to go home and change or have her family send some in. A bus pulls up beside Hai Ruo but it is jam-packed. With no taxis in sight, Hai Ruo decides to push her way in anyway, but its double doors snap shut on her.

An hour later, she finally makes it to the housing estate where Xia Zihua's mother lives and meets Mr Zeng. He is tall and strong, square-jawed and fleshy-faced. He should cut an impressive figure, and yet he somehow doesn't carry it off. He slouches, he has droopy eyebrows and, when he walks, is distinctly splay-footed.

At Hai Ruo's request, he tells her briefly about himself. After university, he started his own business, first mounting paintings and calligraphy scrolls, then opening an antique store. Then he moved to the south of Shaanxi Province and took on a contract to run an iron ore mine. The sales of iron ore were enormously profitable and he returned to Xijing to become a property developer, while also running a factory making plastic products on the outskirts of the city. On the day construction began at the housing development, they hired models to put on a performance. Xia Zihua was one of them, and the two fell in love. He always wanted to marry her, but couldn't get a divorce from his wife. Zihua put up with being a mistress, and time passed by. The year before last, his plastics factory was shut down for contravening anti-pollution regulations. That was a heavy blow, but worse was to follow: Zihua's illness and death.

Hai Ruo is surprised to find him pleasantly soft-spoken, though he does have a slightly hangdog air. He is a successful businessman, and must be very determined, because he stuck with Zihua and their child all this time. He clearly knows his own mind. Maybe it's her death that's depressed him. She finds it hard to resent him, in fact she feels sympathy. She decides to trust him and gets straight to the point.

"Things could hardly be worse but we have to find a solution," she begins. "xiao-Su told me you wanted to take over Xia Lei's care."

"That's right. I always wanted to marry her and make Xia Lei legitimate. Who could have imagined she would die so young, before I had time to sort things out? I know I never spent enough time with Xia Lei when Zihua was alive but I'm still his father, and now he's motherless, I want Xia Lei to feel his father's love. If his grandmother were in better health, I'd let him stay here and get them a *baomu*. But she's so old and frail, I can't ask her to look after Xia Lei. It wouldn't be a long-term solution anyway. She'll get older, and Xia Lei needs to go to kindergarten and primary school. I have to do the right thing now. Otherwise, I'd be letting Zihua and Xia Lei down."

"None of us in the sisterhood knew about you," Hai Ruo tells him. "We've been worried about the boy. We even talked about one of us adopting him."

"And that would have been fine if he didn't have a father. But he has me, and I'm not going to wash my hands of him. I'm not a brute!"

"So where are you going to take him? To your home?" asks Hai Ruo.

"I wish I could. If that were possible, I'd have done it a long time ago. But my family doesn't know about him. Imagine how it would look if I suddenly brought a son home!"

"Then where are you taking him?"

"My best friend lives in Guangzhou. He and his wife know about me and Zihua, and they're willing to look after him."

Hai Ruo has a string of questions. "Do your friends have a child of their own? What kind of people are they? Can they be trusted to take good care of Xia Lei? I don't mean just feed and clothe him but bring him up right?"

"They're really good people. When Zihua was alive, we spent a lot of time with them. Their kid's grown up, they have no other family responsibilities, and they'll give him a good home and upbringing. Besides, I'll be there once a month to see Xia Lei."

Hai Ruo says nothing. They hear Xia Lei's wails from the bedroom. It's ear-splitting. Mrs Qi is with him but is having no success at calming him down. His screeches sound like a pig going to slaughter and now she is crying too. xiao-Su stops her dinner preparations and goes in. A long time passes before the boy stops sobbing and xiao-Su comes out.

"What was all that about?" asks Hai Ruo.

"Xia Lei was saying he saw his mum," says xiao-Su. "He said his mum was right there, on the balcony. Obviously, Mrs Qi couldn't see anyone there but she believes that children can see spirits, so that made her cry, too."

Hai Ruo and Zeng are lost for words. Then Zeng gets up and lights fresh incense sticks, which he places before Zihua's portrait on the offerings table. Tears run down his cheeks and he mutters, "Don't worry, Zihua, I'll take good care of Xia Lei."

Hai Ruo goes to the bathroom, where she finds the teddy bear that she asked Gao Wenlai to buy for Xia Lei, sitting by the washbasin. The teddy, by now rather grubby, stares at her with distrustful beady eyes.

She calls Lu Yike and relays her conversation with Zeng. "I'm finding it hard to judge him," she says. "What if we let him take Xia Lei to Guangzhou and something happens to him? Could you come and meet him? I could really use another pair of eyes, and I'd value your opinion."

Yike is there in less than half an hour. She presses the bell and Zeng opens the door. He doesn't know Hai Ruo has asked her friend to come. All he sees is a woman, breathless and sweating, her fringe stuck to her forehead. "And you are...?" he says.

"I've come to see Hai-jie."

"Ms Hai, someone for you," he calls, and retreats to the bedroom.

Hai Ruo is washing the teddy bear. She comes out of the bathroom and greets Yike, "You were quick."

Yike stands stock still in the doorway, one hand over her mouth, eyes wide. She looks like she's been frozen to the spot. "What's wrong?" asks Hai Ruo. "Don't make such a silly face!"

Yike makes an effort to pull herself together. In the bathroom with Hai Ruo, she asks, "Who was that man?"

"That's Xia Lei's father. He looks nice, doesn't he? Cultured. Not how you'd normally expect a big business type to look."

"Fifty-ish? I wonder where he's from," Yike thinks aloud.

"I'm not doing a job performance review on him!"

"Yes, but it freaked me out! The moment he opened the door, I thought I was looking at my own father! He's the spitting image. He asked who I was, and I said I'd come to see you. As he turned away, there was such a melancholic look in his eyes. It was my father to a tee!"

Hai Ruo gives Yike a poke in the face. "Hey, wash your face and pull yourself together. We've got a big decision to make."

Yike obeys, but adds, "If he looks like my father, then he's a good man. Zihua chose him. You should trust her, and my instinct."

Hai Ruo tells her what Zeng has in mind. By now, Yike has calmed down. "Well, he sounds sincere enough, and it's a good plan."

Back in the sitting room, Hai Ruo calls for Zeng and introduces Yike to him. Then they all go to one of the bedrooms for a serious discussion. It is very shabby but on the wall are three studio shots of Zihua from when she was a model. She is strikingly beautiful, with limpid eyes, and gazes down at them as if listening, or on the verge of saying something.

Hai Ruo positions herself under the pictures and begins, "Now we're all three here, let's bring Zihua into this. You have every right to take Xia Lei away, Mr Zeng, and this might indeed be the best solution for him. But Xia Lei is not just yours, he's also the sisterhood's child. No matter where he goes, we'll always be concerned about him. Our only wish is for him to grow up healthy and happy."

"I believe you," says Zeng. "When Zihua was in hospital, it was all of you who looked after her, day in, day out. I never met you in person but I knew how you cared for her. Please allow me to express my gratitude." And he falls to his knees and kowtows three times before Hai Ruo and Yike.

Hai Ruo helps him to his feet and asks, "What about Zihua's mother?"

"That I don't have a satisfactory answer to, I'm afraid," says Zeng. "I did think about letting the pair of them stay here, with you all looking after them and me dropping in now and then. But that isn't a long-term plan. I'm well aware that Mrs Qi will miss him terribly if Xia Lei goes to Guangzhou, but she doesn't want to move to the south. But I'll still look after her like a son-in-law should, get a *baomu* for her, and give her a monthly allowance."

"I asked you because I wanted your opinion," says Hai Ruo. "I've discussed it with Mrs Qi, and you're right, she'll miss him and she's worried he won't settle or the family won't treat him right. And you're all correct that she doesn't want to leave Xijing. So I told her we've got to put Xia Lei's interests first. She's distraught, but she's finally agreed: Xia Lei should go to Guangzhou and she'll stay behind. Don't worry about her, we'll take care of her."

Zeng is about to kowtow again, but Yike stops him. "But do let me pay her allowance and cover the *baomu*'s wages," he persists.

"She has her pension," Yike says, "you don't need to worry."

But Hai Ruo tells her, "Let him pay if he wants, it's his way of doing his duty as a good son-in-law." She turns to Zeng. "There is something that I'd like you to consider. Mrs Qi has just lost her daughter, it would be a heavy blow to part with her grandson so soon. Would it be possible for Xia Lei to stay here a bit longer?"

"I was planning to take him to Guangzhou in seven weeks, after the immediate mourning period is over. By then, I will have chosen a place to bury her ashes and laid her to rest," says Zeng.

"The cemetery plot is sorted, don't worry," Yike says.

"It is?" he says, his tears welling up again. "Then I'll do as you wish.

Let Xia Lei stay here for a while. I know the tradition is that he should stay for three years so he can visit his mother's tomb. But I'm worried about getting him into primary school. He needs to attend a Guangzhou kindergarten first. Otherwise, he'll really have trouble adjusting. Maybe I should wait a year and take him to Guangzhou on the first anniversary of Zihua's death."

"What do you think?" Hai Ruo asks Yike.

"Sounds fine to me."

"Then it's settled."

xiao-Su has laid the table. There are *laobing* pancakes and rice porridge, as well as dishes of shredded potato, scrambled eggs with tomatoes, and celery cooked with lily bulbs. "It's getting late, let's eat," says xiao-Su, who goes to the other bedroom to call Xia Lei and his grandmother.

"Dinner time," says Hai Ruo.

Zeng fetches a bowl from the kitchen, selects morsels from each dish, tops it with a pancake, then rests a pair of chopsticks on the bowl and places it in front of Zihua's portrait.

In the bedroom, Xia Lei is building a tower with wooden blocks. It's already thirteen storeys high and he's laying more blocks. Mrs Qi and xiao-Su both tell him to come out and eat, but the boy is immersed in his own world.

"Why don't you go and get him?" Hai Ruo says to Zeng, and he goes.

"What a good, kind man," she says.

"Look at the way he slouches when he walks. My father used to be like that," says Yike. "It's so weird. Why am I seeing my dad everywhere I go? Are you trying to get me to settle here, Dad? Oh, Dad."

31. XIN QI • THE SHANTY TOWN

IN THE AFTERNOON, xiao-Zhen and Eva are packing up a full set of tea-making equipment: pick, pincer and scoop for breaking up and moving the tea; pots used for storing, brewing and pouring the tea; beautifully-glazed, tiny, shallow bowls in which to savour the prepared liquid; and finally, a special stove that has come with a supply of chrysanthemum charcoal, and a kettle to boil the water.

Eva is curious. "Who's buying this whole set?"

"It's not for sale, it's a gift," xiao-Zhen explains. "The client buys all the tea for his *danwei* work unit from us. His father's come on a visit and the old man is a tea connoisseur."

"But who's the client?" pursues Eva.

"The name wouldn't mean anything to you even if I told you," says xiao-Zhen.

Eva is annoyed and goes to chat with Gao Wenlai. Xin Qi shows up, carrying a large plastic bag that bangs against her legs as she comes in, high heels clicking.

"Ouch, my feet hurt!" she complains. "Does anyone have any plasters?"

"I do," says Eva. But first she reaches for the bag and peeks inside. There is a roast chicken, a bag of braised pork tripe and a box of *jinggao* sticky rice cake. "Amazing! Look at all this food!" she exclaims and begins to lay it out for them all to eat.

"Hai-jie doesn't allow us to eat in the teashop," xiao-Zhen reminds them.

"But none of this is smelly, not like pancakes with chives or stinky tofu or instant noodles. Besides, there aren't any customers now," says Xin Qi.

"She thinks she's taken over from Tang-jie," whispers Eva. "Come on, let's eat!" She pulls the chicken apart, gives one leg to Wenlai and the other to xiao-Fang, muttering, "What a pity a chicken only has two legs." She gives the neck and head to Mrs Zhang. Then she divides up the tripe and the *jinggao* cake. She takes the back of the chicken for herself, and follows it with a portion of the tripe before helping herself to the cake, which is unexpectedly good. She looks at xiao-Zhen. "We've put some aside for you," she says.

"I'm not eating."

So Eva eats xiao-Zhen's share of the *jinggao*, then carefully licks the grains of rice stuck to her fingers.

"Is it good?" asks Xin Qi.

"Delicious!"

"Then if you've finished eating, could you let me have the plasters?"

With a smile, Eva delves into her pocket and brings out a packet of plasters. "Where did you get all this food?" she asks.

"Near where I live. The whole of the street right under my window is lined with snacks stalls."

"Really? I could eat my way down your street."

So Xin Qi takes her there when they knock off work.

It is not exactly a street. It is a huddle of houses thrown up randomly when people needed somewhere to live. When Xijing expanded, high-rise blocks encroached and the houses were turned into street-front stores, most of them selling ready-prepared food, household items and groceries as well as regional specialities. Other trades joined them: hostels, bars, tailors, barbers and hair salons, massage and mahjong parlours and dance halls. Now, you can have your shoes repaired, fingernails polished, ears de-waxed and eyes bathed. You can take a massage, have your back scraped or your body tattooed, and your fortune told. The original sun-dried brick and timber houses have been replaced by single-storey concrete structures which, over time, have had extra floors added, sometimes as many as six. These are all rented out by the owners. They form a labyrinth of narrow lanes, damp and gloomy, in which it is easy to get lost.

Xin Qi leads Eva through the maze of alleys, repeating apologetically, "Mind your feet."

Eva doesn't mind. As she dodges the motorbikes, tricycles, bikes, barrows and carts, and tries unsuccessfully not to bump into the shop displays and rubbish bins, she is having enormous fun. She jumps over dark rivulets that ooze out of nowhere, careful not to trip over the uneven paving stones, taking in all the different noises – the sawing, the banging, the welding, the whirring of electric fans. All around her, she can hear jokes, shouts, swearing and arguments, but has no idea what they are saying. Her eyes follow the buildings upward until she sees a narrow strip of sky crisscrossed by utility power lines. To her eyes, the buildings look worryingly rickety.

But Xin Qi reassures her, "Thousands of migrant workers live here and they don't worry about the buildings collapsing. Unless there's an earthquake or a war, of course."

They have reached a junction where the lane splits into three. There is a butcher's shop in the branch that leads to the west. Pig carcasses, ready gutted and cleaned, hang from a wooden frame. Fish of all kinds swim in a huge tub at the shop entrance. On the right, chickens are crammed into small cages piled right up to the ceiling. The birds stick their heads out through the wire mesh, silent, apparently watching as one of their kind is killed for a customer. There are more wooden tubs, brimming with offal, pigs', cows' or sheep organs all mixed in together, glistening pink or grey-brown, and swarming with bluebottles.

This genuinely upsets Eva. She holds her nose and asks, "Is it much further?"

"Up ahead, turn south, and mine's the door with the roses," says Xin Qi. "Would you like some sour plum soup?" They're just coming to a tiny doorway where the Xijingers' favourite summer drink is on sale.

"No, thanks," says Eva. "You've got roses?" And there they are, as they head into an even smaller back alley, blossoming in three large pots beside the door to a tall building. There is a *jinggao* cake shop opposite and Xin Qi pops over to buy some, while Eva watches a man in shorts and wearing plastic sandals, carrying a braised pig's head and three bottles of liquor, as he talks to someone.

"Blimey, what's the occasion?" his friend exclaims.
"An old comrade-in-arms is visiting."
"This pork smells delicious. Is that really Maotai?"
"Nah, Maotai's not strong enough."
"Right. It's not about what we drink but who we drink it with." They laugh heartily, and the man carries his food indoors.

Xin Qi comes back with a box of cake just in time to catch the end of their conversation. She smiles at Eva, and they too go in.

They are in a small courtyard, with the building constructed around it. They make their way up the winding stairs to the fifth floor. The room is no more than fifteen square metres and is bare, apart from a bed, a table and three cardboard boxes of clothing.

Eva immediately decides that the rice cake is not as good as the one she had at the teashop, but she eats it anyway. "I've never been to a shanty town like this," she says. "What a lot of food outlets in such wretched surroundings."

"Good food is born out of poverty. People can't afford fine wheat and rice, they make do with coarse grains, so they have to try harder to make them taste good. The dirtier the street, the better the snacks on sale."

"But you shouldn't be living in a place like this," Eva says. "If the posh housing estates are too expensive, you can always stay with me."

"I shouldn't have brought you here," says Xin Qi. "What must you think of me living in a place like this?"

"No, I don't mean that, I'm just saying you're too pretty for a place like this."

"You really don't know much about me, do you?" says Xin Qi. She tells Eva everything: where she comes from, her work, her marriage and her present predicament. It's an emotional account, punctuated by bursts that sound like a cough, or perhaps a laugh. She's resentful, angry and fearful. "And now I'm flat broke," she finishes. "I have no way of making money and money certainly doesn't come looking for me. It's a vicious circle. The poorer you are, the harder it is to earn. On top of that, I'm getting a divorce. I've got the furniture, but I can only afford this place. Like a needle dropped into the dirt, no one's ever going to find me here."

"What about the Hongkonger?" asks Eva. "He must care about how you live. We ought to get him to come and see you!"

"No, I've finished with him. It was Hai-jie who brought me to my senses. She and Xi-jie know about the affair and Hai-jie was very sympathetic, but she didn't mince her words. She made me see how badly I was behaving. I won't be going to Hong Kong. As for this place, I haven't told any of my friends about it, not even Xi-jie and Hai-jie. We live in different worlds. They're kind to me, and I see them now and then, but I'm just a tadpole chasing after fish. In the end, they are the fish, I'm only a frog. I could bring you here because you're a foreigner, and somehow I feel drawn to you. I want you to look around the area with me and tell me what you think. Do you reckon I could set up a nail salon, or do eyebrow and lip tattooing? The rents are cheap, I have the skills, and these setups don't need much investment."

It is getting dark and they turn on the light. As she listens to Xin Qi, Eva's thoughts drift back to faraway St Petersburg. Somehow, Xin Qi's story mirrors her own life there. But she keeps her thoughts to herself for now, and concentrates on her friend. Xin Qi is becoming animated. Her eyes shine brightly through her tears and her eyebrows flicker like a moth's antennae.

They hear the urgent wailing of a siren outside, on and on. Maybe someone called an ambulance, or the police have turned up to pick up an addict, a burglar, or to stop a brawl. Engrossed in their conversation, they don't get up to see what's happening. It is almost 10.30 pm.

"Why don't you stay here tonight?" Xin Qi suggests. "Tomorrow morning we can comb the area for premises to let and think about me setting up in business."

Eva calls her landlady and says she's not going home. They lie side by side on the single bed, and decide to talk until they fall asleep. They discuss what it's like living in China and in Russia, the men they've met, and money. Eva is finding it harder and harder to keep her eyes open.

At one point, Xin Qi says something and Eva doesn't reply. "Are you awake? Should I stop talking?" Xin Qi asks.

"Go on, I'm listening," says Eva dreamily, her eyes closed. Finally Xin Qi's eyelids become heavy too, and her voice drops to a murmur.

But before they drop off completely, something startles them awake. They hear strange noises that worm their way deep inside them, and banish every thought of sleep.

"What's that?" asks Eva, jogging Xin Qi's arm.

"Couples having sex," replies Xin Qi.

"Sex?" repeats Eva, startled. She wonders why she is so sensitive to the noises, and feels her cheeks burning. Right, she can hear it now: the panting and moans of love-making. And not just one couple. The noises are coming from half-a-dozen different directions. She looks around the room, the ceiling, the corners, behind the door, under the bed, and outside the window, and imagines the cats and dogs, tigers, geckos, snails, mosquitoes, flies and slugs all frantically copulating.

"The rooms upstairs are rented by young migrant workers," explains Xin Qi. "Mostly couples. It happens every night."

"How do you manage to get to sleep on your own every night?" says Eva with a giggle.

"I couldn't at first, then I got used to it. After all, sex is the only thing that gives them pleasure in this city. And they have to wait till night-time. But I wish they wouldn't make such a racket. I mean, what's the big deal? They don't have to scream blue murder! Oh sorry, you haven't been married, have you?"

"No, but that doesn't mean I haven't tried it."

"No, of course not," Xin Qi apologises, and she leans over Eva and strokes her cheeks. "Tell me, honestly, how many men have you had sex with?"

"How many?" Eva repeats, and they laugh until they're out of breath. Eva raises one finger, then another.

Eventually, silence falls in the building, except for a cat meowing somewhere downstairs. Xin Qi describes the scenes of Russia she has seen on TV – the immense grasslands and forests, the beautiful buildings, churches and streets in St Petersburg. "Why did you come to Xijing to get choked in smog? Which city is bigger? Is it cheaper there? Are there any Chinese people?"

"Of course there are Chinese," Eva says, "and Chinese restaurants, too. You can even get Xijing dishes like *roujiamo* and *liangpi*."

"Are they run by real Xijingers?"

"Yes, you should come and visit."

It's on the tip of her tongue to say she couldn't possibly afford to, but Xin Qi bites back the words. "I haven't got a passport."

"That's easy. It's not like you need a special official passport."

"Xi-jie said you're working at the teashop so you can set one up in St Petersburg when you go back. If you do, I'd love to come and work for you."

"I can't take you on as an assistant! In six months, you'd be running the show and hiring me," Eva laughs.

Xin Qi gives Eva a kiss on the cheek. "You really think I'm that clever? Your smile's so cute. I just love you!"

冯
迎

32. FENG YANG • THE CLOUD-GATHERING HALL

AFTER SHE LEAVES Xia Zihua's mother, Hai Ruo feels a heavy weight lifted from her shoulders. However, she is physically exhausted and her legs almost refuse to obey her. Has the earth's gravitational pull got heavier along with my responsibilities? she thinks wryly to herself. As soon as she gets home, she decides to go to bed. For the last two years, she has been plagued by insomnia, so she helps herself to a nightcap of some wine. When her eyelids start to droop with fatigue, she stretches out on the sofa in the sitting room, in case the trip to the bedroom should make her wakeful again. She falls asleep, and begins to dream.

Her *guqin* master has moved to live on a high mountain peak. Wonderful, she thinks to herself. Yi Guang could write a scroll entitled "A Study Built at the Summit", and mount it in his studio.

She is paying a visit to her *guqin* teacher. She climbs the mountain with her own *guqin* strapped to her back and bags of food in her hands. The path is lined with dense stands of trees covered in red flowers. It isn't August yet, she thinks, so where does the sweet scent of osmanthus come from? Birds are calling to each other in the undergrowth. As she mimics them, they begin to speak to her, in human tongue. Thrilled, she chants some lines from a Ming dynasty essay: "Humans who learn bird songs may sing like birds, but keep their human nature, while birds that mimic human speech will always remain as birds."

Hai Ruo is proud of herself for remembering these lines. She continues up the mountain. Then she realises that she is a vixen, no longer human. And this vixen is carrying the *guqin* and the food uphill. No, wait, the food is a ball of... could it be dung? And the creature pushing it is a dung beetle, straining towards a hole somewhere higher up. She watches this manoeuvre with great interest: the beetle turns around and tries to lift the ball with its hind legs, but the ball rolls down again. Time and again the bug repeats the effort, but it keeps on dropping the ball. It strikes Hai Ruo as both comical and sad.

Then, both beetle and ball thankfully disappear and instead she is looking at a rock rolling up the mountain all by itself, apparently without any means of locomotion. As it moves over the undergrowth, grasshoppers spring out of the way. The rock is wet, not from the crushed grass, but from its own sweat. From the mountain peak, her *guqin* master beckons. But the higher the rock goes, the slower it travels. Then it's not a rock any more, it appears to be a bucket. The bucket notices a well to one side, with a stone tablet bearing these lines: "Along the road a lotus grows in an ancient well. Its flower spans ten *zhang* and its roots are as big as a boat."

How can a lotus grow in a well? The bucket balances itself on the rim for a better look, and tumbles in. A voice reverberates from the depths of the well: "Your bucket was going to fall into my well sooner or later!"

Hai Ruo wakes up in a fright. The light is shining right in her eyes. She must have forgotten to turn it off. She is lying on the carpet, with two sofa cushions on top of her, and she is sweating profusely. Her phone is ringing loudly, the vibrations making it spin in circles on the coffee table.

She reaches for the phone, but it slips out of her grasp. When she finally picks it up, the ringing has stopped, though the caller's name is still visible: Yi Guang.

Back when they first met, Yi Guang was always on the phone to her. Whether she was at work or at home in bed, he phoned whenever he felt like it and she was happy to be at his beck and call. They grew very close. At the end of a day's work, she'd cook for him, and they'd have dinner together. She'd stay until it was almost dawn, and stop off at the morning market for some vegetables on her way home. Sometimes she met her son on his way to the toilet as she opened her front door, and he'd say, "You're up early, Mum." "Go back to bed. I'll wake you up when breakfast's ready." In those days, she always dropped Hai Tong off at school before heading to the teashop. That was a hectic year, but she was always in good spirits and never felt tired. As time passed, however, she got to know the others and the sisterhood grew. Yi Guang called less often. The insomnia started up. But Yi Guang was still a close friend, both to her and the sisterhood. They always shared their problems with him and called on him for help.

"I'm the beating heart of your group," Yi Guang used to say cheerfully. "My heart leaps whether you're happy or sad. Believe me, it can be quite overwhelming!"

So when Yi Guang phones her in the middle of the night, Hai Ruo is delighted. It feels a bit surreal, however, and she wonders if she is dreaming. She calls back, "Was that you?"

"What do you think?"

"What made you call me?"

Yi Guang doesn't answer. Instead he asks, "Is it still dark?"

"It's the middle of the night. Check your watch, it's not quite three. Are you still at the Cloud-Gathering Hall? Can't you sleep?"

"Can you come over? I need you."

Hai Ruo almost laughs, but checks herself. "You need me? What for? What if I don't come?" But he has hung up.

She sits on the sofa, feeling a rush of warmth from her feet to the top of her head. Deep inside her, something stirs. A furry kitten raising its head, a seedling pushing up through the soil. She strips off and goes for a shower. She looks at herself in the misted-up mirror. She's still in good shape. She puts on a pink bra and knickers, then takes them off again. Hurrying into the bedroom stark naked, she rummages through her drawers for some slinky black fishnet underwear. Half an hour later, she is in her car and driving to the Cloud-Gathering Hall.

But Yi Guang is not alone. Fan Bosheng is with him. The ashtray is overflowing with cigarette butts, and the room is wreathed in smoke.

Hai Ruo feels a twinge of disappointment as she stands by the door, the smoke escaping past her.

"You're here so quickly! Sorry to have disturbed your sleep," says Yi Guang.

Hai Ruo sits down opposite him. "I thought you were playing mahjong and needed one more to make up the numbers," she says waspishly. "You shouldn't burn the midnight oil at your age, you look terrible."

Yi Guang smiles sadly. "I'll be grey-haired by morning."

"What's up?"

"There is something we have to tell you. You need to be strong."

"Don't scare me! Who is it? General Secretary Ning? Or Mr Qi? Or is it xiao-Tang?"

Yi Guang shakes his head. "Promise me you won't cry."

"What's wrong? What's happened?" Hai Ruo says anxiously.

"Feng Ying's dead," Yi Guang says. "She died two weeks ago."

Hai Ruo breaks down and sobs loudly.

Bosheng takes up the story. None of the Xijing painters and calligraphers in the delegation had been in touch with their family during their trip abroad, but when relatives called and could not get through, they just assumed they didn't want to use international roaming. Then two weeks ago, a Malaysian flight crashed en route from Kuala Lumpur to Beijing. China Central Television broadcast the news but no one had any idea that the artists were on board. The group included two members from the Xijing Federation of Literary and Art Circles: Wang Ji the painter and group leader, and Feng Ying.

At one point, Wang Ji's wife asked Bosheng when the group would be back. He checked up and wondered what was keeping them so long but simply said jokingly that maybe they'd taken their chance to jump ship!

Bosheng called a Filipino Chinese friend who told him that the visitors had left the Philippines for Thailand. Wang Ji had told him that they might take in Sri Lanka and Singapore as well. Bosheng asked his friend to contact some Thai painters whom Wang Ji may have been in touch with, but the friend drew a blank. The party had not turned up.

Then yesterday, Malaysia Airlines issued a list of passengers presumed to have died on board the doomed flight. Eight Chinese passengers had arrived in Kuala Lumpur from Singapore, all from Xijing – six men and two women. Bosheng had called the families straight away, but as Feng Ying was single, and he knew she was close to Yi Guang, he came here with the news.

Hai Ruo sobs so despairingly that she is physically sick. Yi Guang lets her cry. Then, when she comes back from the toilet and sits down again, he says, "I know this is hard on you, it's hard on all of us. And coming so soon after Zihua's death." He adds philosophically, "Such is the impermanence of life. We have to accept it."

"Could it be a mistake?" says Hai Ruo. "The group went to the Philippines. Even if they went on to Thailand and Singapore, why would they board a plane back home from Malaysia? And there are direct flights between Kuala Lumpur and Xijing, why would they take a plane to Beijing?"

"We don't know, and we may never find out, I'm afraid," says Bosheng. "But Malaysia Airlines have confirmed it. Feng Ying's group was from Xijing, there were eight of them, six men, two women."

Hai Ruo presses both hands to her chest. She is still weeping. "This is so sudden, and so strange. We had time to prepare ourselves when Zihua died. But for Feng Ying to disappear just like that…"

"You're all so close in the sisterhood, did you have no inkling?" asks Yi Guang.

Hai Ruo tells them about her dream.

"It's an odd dream, but it wasn't a nightmare," says Yi Guang. Then something occurs to him. "Didn't you tell me just a few days ago that Zhang Huai said he'd run into Feng Ying and she asked him to instruct me to repay Zihua a hundred and fifty thousand yuan. What was that all about?"

Hai Ruo stares at him, wide-eyed. "You're right. That was ten days after Feng Ying left for the Philippines. I thought he must have been mistaken but he described the woman he met and it sounded exactly like Feng Ying. So I thought Feng Ying might have told him before she left and he just forgot, and then pretended to me that he'd just seen her."

"Is this Zhang Huai the debt-collector?" Bosheng interrupts.

"That's the one," says Hai Ruo.

"He's not devious," says Bosheng. "He's a tough guy but he doesn't lie. And why would he? There's nothing in it for him."

"How bizarre. What day was that?" asks Yi Guang.

"The day Eva arrived. And she's been here now for a fortnight," says Hai Ruo.

"Let me see," says Bosheng. He goes to a corner of the room and thumbs through a pile of newspapers. Eventually he finds one and says, "News about the Malaysian flight's crash came out the previous day."

Hai Ruo feels her legs give way. "So maybe it was Feng Ying's ghost." She begins to cry again.

But Bosheng tells her to pull herself together. Three of the families are planning a trip to Malaysia to find out more details, after which they will arrange the funerals. Wang Ji's wife collapsed when she heard the news and is in hospital, so she has asked Bosheng to go in her stead. Feng Ying has a sister, who might or might not go. Yi Guang is definitely going.

"Are you?" asks Hai Ruo, surprised.

"I had a lot to do with Feng Ying," says Yi Guang. "She lent me the money she had put by for an insurance policy, to tide me over a rough patch. So, yes, I must go."

"Then count me in. Lu Yike and I will both go," says Hai Ruo.

They agree that the four of them will travel together. Hai Ruo remembers that her passport has expired, but Bosheng says he will book the tickets for the day after tomorrow, so that Hai Ruo has time to renew it.

"I know someone at the Border Control Bureau, I can put in a word for you," offers Yi Guang.

"No need," says Hai Ruo. "The year before last, Yike was going to the UK, and her passport had expired but she renewed it without any trouble. Do you have any extra paper, by the way?"

"I'm running low on writing paper, but I have plenty of *xuan* paper," says Yi Guang. "Are you writing an article or doing painting or calligraphy?"

Hai Ruo mutters something inaudible, then goes to the attic and brings down a hundred sheets of *xuan* paper, which she takes away with her.

33. HAI RUO • THE CAR PARK

BACK IN THE TEASHOP, Hai Ruo goes upstairs and turns on the light. Her eyes rest on the murals before moving to the Buddha on the offerings table. She lights an incense stick to the Buddha, then begins to cut up the *xuan* art paper. A full piece of *xuan* paper is two by four chi, 69 by 138 centimetres. She cuts each in half and places the two hundred sheets in a neat pile, a hand span high. On the top sheet, she writes, "To Feng Ying in the Underworld". Dry-eyed and silent, she sets about burning the paper in a large aluminium basin, feeding it into the flames carefully, a sheet at a time.

Normally, you would burn funeral money, she thinks, or at the very least, you would slap a 100-yuan banknote, front and reverse, onto a piece of blank paper to "print" funeral money. But burning the *xuan* paper feels right. Feng Ying never had much money. Of all the sisterhood, she was the least concerned about getting rich. Whenever she had a bit to spare, she'd buy brush, ink, ink slab and paper for her artworks, or else go travelling. Feng Ying would be pleased I'm sending her *xuan* paper instead of funeral money, Hai Ruo tells herself.

The flames grow, as if they are flowers blossoming over the rim of the basin. Hai Ruo notices a curious phenomenon: they are bright red in the basin but turn blue as they rise above it and are reflected against the walls and the floor in flickering waves. Is that Feng Ying's karma? Hai Ruo wonders. Blue was her favourite colour. She dressed in blue and had blue shoes, handbags and a blue car. And now she's vanished into the blue ocean and the blue sky.

By the time all the paper has burnt up, the room is full of smoke. Hai Ruo opens a window. As the smoke drifts outside, a blue river seems to have taken shape in the room, coming from the mural behind the arhat couch. The smoke has thinned out, and the apsaras appear to be hurrying down from the skies. It suddenly strikes Hai Ruo that the topmost apsara looks remarkably like Feng Ying. The figure is particularly slender, and Feng Ying was the slimmest of the sisterhood. Her eyes are half-closed, just as Feng Ying's were often narrowed in a smile. There are other resemblances too. She wonders why she has never noticed. Does this mural hold some secret meaning? The apsara holds a bunch of flowers to her heart, for some reason reminiscent of the way Feng Ying did when she suffered her frequent stomach aches.

Hai Ruo is overwhelmed by another wave of grief. She sniffs and looks up at the ceiling. When she's calmer, she sits at a desk, browsing through some Buddhist sutras. These were borrowed from Mr Wu's shrine and are kept in this room so that anyone in the sisterhood can take one away to read, then return it to her when they have finished with it. She picks up *The Lotus Sutra*. Feng Ying borrowed it once, and returned it on the very day that Wang Ji came to paint the murals. Then she finds a slip of paper, covered with tiny writing, between two of the pages.

> When you read a book, you should find out for yourself what it is about and how it is written. Don't let others tell you.
> We always make excuses for ourselves when we get involved in dirty business.
> What is pain? Is it thwarted desire? You need love. With love, you will clear all obstacles to communication. You will learn to know your desire, and then gradually bring it to an end.
> Acknowledge and accept suffering, then delve into its nature so that you can transform it. To achieve this, practise sitting and walking meditation, focus on breathing and on prostrating, realise complete relaxation.

Pursuing others in the hope of gaining their favour and protection will bring you nothing but darkness and destruction.

You are enriched when you live life in its fullness, whether you are rich or poor, successful or ineffectual, complacent or despairing.

Happiness does not come from status, fame, power or wealth. Happiness is a state completely free of dependence. Fear arises from dependence. Happiness exists in freedom, the freedom to see how things truly are, free of disorder or confusion.

A person free of desire is a god, an angel. Desire makes us unique, it makes us blossom like flowers, but it also keeps us mundane.

If my mind is trivial, narrow and confined, I shall find others much the same.

Life is all about relationships and the process of connecting with people, however many or few they are, and with the society in general. We need to face them together.

Terracotta warriors started off brightly coloured, but the paint fades upon excavation, leaving mere clay statues. This world's colours are also fading, as are those of humans: their capacity for curiosity, passion for endeavour, respect for the elderly, care for the young and romantic love.

Has technology become a god? A religion?

The smog is appalling but hatred, paranoia, greed, jealousy, and the pursuit of power, wealth, status and fame are far more polluting to your spirit.

Keep marching on, keep searching for the truth.

It is a very long time since I heard the cockerel crow, and the rocks around me have grown thick moss.

These must be Feng Ying's notes, Hai Ruo thinks, though she cannot tell which lines have been copied verbatim from the sutras or the classics, and which are Feng Ying's personal thoughts after she finished her reading. The words seem to shine brilliantly and touch Hai Ruo to her innermost being. Hai Ruo is deeply moved. How I underestimated my friend, she says to herself. Feng Ying read far more widely, and deeply, than I ever imagined. I never saw below the surface, and sometimes I got things plain wrong. How did this extraordinary slip of paper end up here? Was I meant to come upon it on this night, of all nights? She rests her head on the desk, moaning softly.

The door bangs open downstairs and Mrs Zhang comes in. It's raining outside. She carries a small bamboo basket full of eggs in one hand, and an umbrella in the other. And the back and sleeves of her coat are soaked. She knows she is the first in this morning and, seeing the light on upstairs, she thinks it must have been left on all night. Without putting down the basket or closing the umbrella, she hurries up the stairs, and finds Hai Ruo trying to move the basin out of the way.

"Aiya! It's you, Mrs Hai," she exclaims. "When did you get here? I thought I was the early bird, but you beat me to it."

Hai Ruo doesn't answer. She looks from Mrs Zhang to her watch, but what she says is, "Is it raining?"

Mrs Zhang puts down the basket and furls the umbrella. "Yes, it is. I knew it would. My legs started hurting yesterday. Whenever my legs play up, it rains, it's more accurate than the weather forecast."

"It wasn't raining during the night. When did it start?"

"I don't know, I was asleep. It was just a shower when I left home, but it was much heavier when I got to the Trade and Commerce Plaza. A woman was sheltering in the pavilion. She had a basket of eggs and I knew she was going to sell them at the market, but she had no umbrella and she was soaked to the skin. So I asked if she'd let me have them cheap. She asked how much I'd give her and I said fifty yuan, and I wanted the basket too. She didn't look happy about that, but I said, 'It's a deal!' I put fifty yuan in her hand, and took the basket of eggs!" Mrs Zhang says gleefully.

Hai Ruo runs her fingers through her hair, rubs her hands over her face and goes downstairs to leave.

"Are you going out for breakfast, Mrs Hai?" asks Mrs Zhang. "Your skin does look dry. Did you have a bad night's sleep? Do you have any moisturiser with you?"

But Hai Ruo simply says, "If you haven't had breakfast, let's go to the Yonghe Soy Milk place together."

"Soy milk and fried *youtiao*? Why don't I poach some eggs here? We have plenty, and they're really good for you. I can boil them in no time."

"OK. You can mop the floor while I poach the eggs," says Hai Ruo, carrying the basket into the cubicle by the stairs.

It's stuffy in the cubicle, so she pushes open the small window on the east wall, letting the rain in. Just then, she sees a man's head hurry by. It must be the car park attendant, she thinks, and wonders if he is still going through the rubbish bins in this rain. But she keeps the remark to herself. Soon the pot of water comes to the boil. She fetches four eggs from the basket, cracks one on the pot's rim and holds it over the water. Nothing comes out. She checks the egg shells. There is a blob of red amid the egg white. The egg must have gone bad, she thinks, cracking another. The same red clot. One more egg, and one more clot.

Startled, she calls out, "Mrs Zhang! Come here, Mrs Zhang!"

Mrs Zhang hurries in and takes a quick look. "That damned woman, she sold me incubating eggs!" She almost rushes out to find the egg seller and get her money back.

But Hai Ruo tells her not to bother. "Maybe the seller didn't know. She might have got the wrong basket. Even if she did try to sell you incubating eggs, she wouldn't wait for you to come back, would she?" Hai Ruo is feeling a bit queasy. It is the first time that she has seen blood clots in an egg. Before life takes form, it is not a pretty sight. She throws the remaining eggs into the bin, scrubs her hands vigorously under the tab, then turns the gas off.

"I must have been blind," Mrs Zhang says remorsefully. "Why didn't I pick one up and hold it against the light, or just shake it? I should be able to tell bad eggs from good ones!"

Hai Ruo leaves her muttering to herself and walks out of the door.

Outside, the rain is coming down in sheets. The wind blows the lines of falling water this way and that, until everywhere looks like a reed pond in winter. Puddles have formed on the small square and empty car park.

Mrs Zhang follows her out. "I'm terribly sorry, Mrs Hai. Are you going out for breakfast?"

"No, I've got some business to do," says Hai Ruo.

"Take my umbrella then," Mrs Zhang offers. "It's old and shabby, but it keeps the wind and rain off."

"I'll be OK thanks, I'm driving."

"Your car's all the way over there, you'll be drenched before you get there. Here, take it."

Hai Ruo accepts the umbrella, opens it and heads for the car park. Her shoes immediately soak up the water.

The attendant emerges from beside the rubbish bins clad in a raincoat. He does not appear to have found any plastic bottles or ring-pull cans today.

"Are you going out, Mrs Hai?" he greets her.

"Yes, what a rainstorm!"

"So it is!"

"If it's not smog, it's a deluge, life's impossible nowadays!" Hai Ruo remarks.

"But we're still alive, aren't we?" the old man says, rather sharply.

Hai Ruo was just trying to be polite, but the old man's reply halts her in mid-stride.

He hurriedly softens his tone. "What I mean is, people can survive anywhere. I come from the Loess Plateau in northern Shaanxi. There are no trees, we can only grow buckwheat and potatoes, and we drink rain water collected in cellars. But all twenty-eight families in our village have sons, and our girls are pretty too. Five of them have jobs greeting guests at big city hotels."

"Of course, you're quite right," says Hai Ruo. Her phone rings. It is tucked into the left pocket of her trousers and she shifts the umbrella from her left hand to the right so she can get the phone out. It's not a number she knows.

"Let me hold the umbrella while you take the call," the old man offers. But the ringing stops and there is no need. The attendant goes back to his bins.

Again the phone rings, showing the same unknown number. She takes the call.

"Why didn't you answer first time around?" says a man in an accusing tone.

Hai Ruo is annoyed. What way is that to start a phone call?

"Who is this?" she demands.

"The Xijing Disciplinary Committee!"

"Discip…" repeats Hai Ruo, confused. "Have you got the wrong number?"

"Do you own the Sojourn Teashop? Your name is Hai Ruo?"

"Er, yes, yes."

"And you have an employee called Tang Yingying?"

"Oh, is this about xiao-Tang? Do you have any news? You can take my word for it, she only knows Mr Qi, there's no way she knows what's going on between Mr Qi and the Xijing Party chief. She was only running errands for Mr Qi."

"This is about you!"

"Me?"

"You'll find out when you come."

Hai Ruo says nothing.

"Hello? Hello!" says the man.

"I'm listening."

"We're calling you on the phone. But we could have come to the teashop. You get my meaning?"

"Yes. I know what you're telling me."

"We'll expect you at the Xiyuan Hotel in an hour."

Hai Ruo turns her phone off. It feels like a hand grenade, she doesn't want to hear anything more from it. From where she's standing to her car is less than a hundred metres, but her legs will barely carry her. She trudges towards it, her trouser legs soaked through, the water running into her shoes and squelching at every step. Finally she reaches her car. Slowly she furls the umbrella and streams of water cascade down along its folds. She has the horrible impression that this is not rainwater, but blood squeezed from her own body.

34. GAO WENLAI • THE TEASHOP

EVA HAS SPENT the night at Xin Qi's place and leaves in the morning for the teashop. A new batch of porcelain teaware has just been delivered from Jingdezhen, while another courier turns up with an online book order. Gao Wenlai, xiao-Zhen, xiao-Fang and Mrs Zhang are busy unpacking the boxes, washing the teaware and putting the items on display. Meantime, Eva's attention is drawn to the books: *Life Codes of Practice*, *The Language of Zen*, *Brief Talks on Records of the Mirror of the Source*, *Gu Zhuo: The Simple Beauty of Ancient Architecture* by Liang Sicheng, *Six Chapters of a Floating Life*, *The Collated and Annotated Pulse Classic* and *The Records of Liu Rushi*.

She is impressed. "Wow, Hai-jie reads about anything and everything!"

She looks up and sees the rain has stopped. They chat about the weather. "What a storm, but it passed so quickly." "It's washed the smog right away and brought us a fine day." "And it hasn't flooded the streets."

Then Wenlai says, "The weather is Heaven's will."

"How so?" asks xiao-Fang.

"The smog's been so bad the past few years, it must be God punishing us for our craziness, don't you think?" replies Wenlai.

"Hey, Wenlai, put our Sojourn Teashop seal on these tags," says xiao-Zhen, as she writes price tags for the teapots and cups on the shelves. "So you reckon the heavens are showing mercy on us by raining?"

"Yup."

"Then why did the rain stop?"

Wenlai says nothing but begins to gather up the wooden crates and protective packaging – plastic foam pads, straw and shredded paper.

"Eva," xiao-Zhen calls, "would you mind sticking the price tags onto the teaware?"

"The other sets are five hundred yuan each, how come these are thirteen hundred?" Eva remarks.

"They bear the seals of master ceramicists," explains xiao-Fang.

"They don't look any different to me, why such a hefty price?" Eva persists.

"Their creators' names are way more valuable than the products."

"But will these ever sell?"

"The more expensive, the faster they sell," says xiao-Zhen. She comes over and jots down "SOLD" on a tag.

"Sold already?" asks Eva, surprised.

"We had a set marked as 'SOLD' not so long ago," recalls xiao-Zhen. "Some business hotshot came in and insisted on buying it. Just wouldn't take no for an answer."

"Who was it? Was it that Mr Wen with the jadeite ring? He has a gold necklace as thick as a dog collar," says Eva.

xiao-Zhen looks askance at Eva but says nothing. She gets a feather duster and passes it over the long table.

"It was Mrs Liu," whispers xiao-Fang to Eva. "The one you said had a wonky jawline."

"Ah, I remember," says Eva. "In her fifties, always dressed to the nines and wears killer high heels, but the plastic surgeon made a terrible mess of her jaw. So what does she do for a living?"

"Nothing in particular," says xiao-Fang. "She knows practically every official in the city. Everyone goes to her to arrange a promotion or transfer, contract big projects, even to get a seat on the CPPCC. She's basically a pimp."

"Hah! But she hasn't shown up for days," says Eva.

"She won't be around for a while yet," says xiao-Zhen, lugging a big jar of tea along the long table.

"She won't? Why's that?" asks Eva.

"Rumour has it that the investigators were heading her way, so she did a runner, went *paolu* last Friday," says xiao-Zhen.

Wenlai is tying the foam pads into bundles on the steps outside. "Give me a hand, Eva," he calls.

Eva comes outside. "Need my help with this tiny bit of work?"

"I haven't had breakfast, I'm out of puff," says Wenlai.

"Let me get you something down in the lane. They've got *jianbing* pancakes made with whole grain."

"I don't eat whole grain," says Wenlai. "I called you so we can work together."

"What do you mean? You want to fondle me?"

"Hey, *laowai*! Mind your tongue!"

Eva gurgles with laughter. "Hey, I've got a question for you, what does *paolu* mean?"

"Why do you ask?"

"I just want to know."

"I'm not telling, you wouldn't get it even if I did."

"You're selfish!" says Eva. "Well, I have something to tell you. You're being watched from across the square."

Wenlai looks up and sees a man standing at the curb on the other side of the square, gazing at the teashop. "He's not looking at me, it's your blond hair he's gawking at," he says.

"Plenty of girls have their hair dyed blonde," says Eva dismissively. "Must be someone you know from back home."

"How do you know?"

"You're both in baggy suits and loafers," Eva points out. Wenlai grunts in annoyance, but Eva says, "Here he comes."

The man comes over and stops by the shop entrance. He looks at Wenlai but says nothing, then turns to Eva and says, "Hey, that hair of yours, it's natural, not dyed, right?"

Wenlai gets to his feet. "What's this about?"

"It must be natural," the man goes on. "The roots are yellow too. Are you a *laowai*?"

Amused, Eva declares, "Sure, I'm a *laowai*."

"Do you know Xi Lishui? She's shorter and plumper than you, she wears scarlet lipstick."

"Xi Lishui? Yes, I know Xi-jie."

The man goes red with fury and grabs Eva by the arm. "Found you at last! I've been looking for you!"

Wenlai pulls Eva away. "Wait a minute, this is a teashop. Get your hands off her!"

Undeterred, the man runs up the steps and kicks the door in. He charges inside, shouting, "Who's the owner? I want to see the owner!"

Everyone freezes. Then xiao-Zhen comes running. "Who are you?" she asks. "You want to see the owner? I've never seen you before!"

Wenlai and Eva follow the man inside.

"I've been searching the city for days," says the man. "Then the heavens had mercy on me and sent me here! Hand over Xi Lishui, now!"

Wenlai and Eva exchange glances and both step forward to stop the man coming any further into the shop.

"And what's your connection to Xi Lishui?" xiao-Zhen asks.

"She put my wife up to it!"

"And your wife is...?"

"Xin Qi! Xin Qi! Xin Qi! The bitch emptied my house while I was away on business!"

Everyone is rooted to the spot, their eyes wide with shock. "Well... that... that's between you and your wife," xiao-Zhen stammers. "Why are you making a big fuss here? Xi Lishui doesn't work here."

Tian Chengbin points at Eva. "You were with them when they robbed me! Old Mrs Wang upstairs saw it all. She said a whole gang came, including a blonde foreigner. Was it you? Was it all of you? Did you all clean my house out?"

"I was there," Eva admits. "Xin Qi is a friend of ours. We were just helping her out. None of us knew the ins and outs of it!"

"She cleaned out all the furniture, even before she sued for divorce!" says Chengbin. "If we'd divorced properly, the court would have given me half."

"Then you should talk to Xin Qi herself," says Eva.

"I can't find her! But I've found you, all of you!"

"Don't try to reason with him, Eva," says Wenlai. "He's nuts."

"Who's nuts?" asks Chengbin.

"You are," says Wenlai, raising his voice. "Nuts!"

"So I'm nuts! Give me back my property, all of it!" Chengbin shouts back, and he kicks a chair so hard that he snaps one of its legs.

xiao-Zhen and xiao-Fang cry out. Furious, Wenlai jumps up and hammers Chengbin with his fists. The man staggers back one step, then another, then he falls and slams the back of his head on the floor. Wenlai is about to throw himself at the man again when xiao-Zhen locks her arms around his waist. Chengbin rubs the back of his head, feels a lump and sees blood on his fingers. He does a nimble kip-up, hefts a large white porcelain jar from a table and hurls it to the floor. Porcelain shards and tea leaves spray everywhere.

Still holding Wenlai, xiao-Zhen yells, "xiao-Fang! Take the tea stove off the table, don't let him touch it!" But Chengbin lunges, grabs the stove and smashes it against the floor.

In the cubicle, Mrs Zhang has just filled the kettle with water and put it on the gas. Hearing the commotion, she rushes out. She looks petrified.

Wenlai is seething. "Let me go!" he shouts and breaks free of xiao-Zhen's grip. He looks around for a weapon, but there is nothing. "Mrs Zhang!" he yells. "Get me the knife in the cubicle, the cleaver!"

Mrs Zhang scurries into the cubicle, and comes back with an iron spatula. Meanwhile, the intruder is sizing up the shelves. xiao-Fang tries to block his way. "No, please!" she begs. "Think of the teaware!"

Chengbin promptly shoves xiao-Fang, sending her careening into the shelves. Teacups, bowls, trays and pots pour onto the ground in a clatter of breaking porcelain. Lying among the shards, xiao-Fang scrabbles forward and bites down desperately on the man's leg. At the same moment, Wenlai throws the spatula at him. Chengbin raises an arm to block the blow but falls over again. Eva, xiao-Zhen and Mrs Zhang, all armed with mop, broom, even the pole for hanging the bamboo screen, shower blows on him. Chengbin tries unsuccessfully to protect his head, belly, back and legs, doubling up like a cut worm. He clutches Mrs Zhang's ankle, and she falls down too. xiao-Fang tries to pull her to her feet, but can't. Eva is hitting his hand with a broom but isn't doing much good, so she takes off one shoe and uses that instead, until the heel breaks off.

"Call one-one-zero, xiao-Fang, call one-one-zero!" shouts xiao-Zhen.

As xiao-Fang gets out her phone, Chengbin struggles up and lunges for it. Wenlai bangs him on the head with an iron bucket, sending the water in it snaking all over the floor. Blood trickles from Chengbin's scalp and he staggers, grabs another shelf and brings it down. Then he turns tail. Wenlai cannot follow him – there is too much on the floor – so he hurls a tea tray. He misses, but sends a chair after it. It hits Chengbin on the back and he falls into the door, which shatters in a cascade of glass. Wenlai reaches him and straddles his prone body. He punches him squarely in the forehead then, as he raises his head, delivers a slap across the face, and another, and another.

"Leave the head, kick his arse!" xiao-Zhen tells Wenlai.

Wenlai gets up and aims a volley of kicks at Chengbin's rear until he stops struggling.

"That's enough," xiao-Zhen warns him.

"You think you can fucking smash up our shop? Well, now see what's coming to you!" Wenlai shouts at him, giving Chengbin a final kick of the boot.

As the melee escalates, the entrance fills with gawpers. Some of them are actually filming the ruckus with their phones.

"Go away, we've dealt with this thug. There's nothing to see here, go," xiao-Zhen tells them.

But Eva whispers in her ear, "Let them stay, he won't be able to escape."

The car park attendant shoulders his way through the onlookers. "I only just went to the toilet and now look what's happened! Did he think he could attack these women, and in broad daylight too?"

"Yes, he did!" says Wenlai.

Chengbin is lying face down on the ground. The old man turns his head to one side and looks but doesn't recognise him. He spits on Chengbin's face then says to Wenlai, "He's taller and stronger than you are."

Eva gives Wenlai a thumbs-up, but xiao-Zhen tells her, "Run upstairs and see if Hai-jie has a spare pair of shoes you can put on." Eva suddenly realises she's missing a shoe.

A police van screeches to a stop in the square, and officers emerge with batons and run over.

"Wow, that was quick," xiao-Fang says.

xiao-Zhen pulls Wenlai behind the door, wipes her fingers on Wenlai's blood-smeared arms and dabs the blood on his cheeks.

"He's the one who's bleeding, I'm fine," Wenlai reassures her.

"You need to show the police."

Wenlai sniffs one arm, then rubs it against his face. He walks out of the shop, his face a gory red, then somehow trips over and lands on the shattered glass.

xiao-Zhen tearfully tells the officers what happened.

"Do you know this man?" asks an officer.

"No, none of us do," says xiao-Zhen.

"So he just showed up to destroy everything for no reason?"

"Some people have a grudge against society and take it out on anyone. We were just in the wrong place at the wrong time."

An officer takes photos of the scene, then asks Chengbin and Wenlai to get up. Chengbin stands up, his lips swollen, forehead and arms covered in cuts, coat torn. He looks for his phone, but it's nowhere to be seen. Wenlai stays sitting. The phone is under him.

"Get up!" the officer orders.

Wenlai makes an effort to stand but sinks to the floor again, pushing the phone underneath a cabinet as he does so. "My back's agony," he complains.

The officer tells xiao-Fang to help him up and with some difficulty, she does. The police then disperse the crowd and order Chengbin and Wenlai to get in their van.

"Why are you taking him?" xiao-Zhen objects. "He works here. He's a victim!"

"He took part in the fight, and they both need to make a statement at our station," explains the officer.

"Then I'm coming, too," says xiao-Zhen.

Eva, xiao-Fang and Mrs Zhang are left in the teashop. They shut the door, but the glass is gone. There's just an empty frame. It is a depressing sight, so they open the door again. Not knowing what to do, they stand outside, keeping people out. Eva calls Hai Ruo, but her phone is turned off. She calls the sisterhood, one by one: Lu Yike, Xiang Qiyu, Yan Nianchu, Yu Benwen, Si Yinan and Xu Qi. Then, before she can contact Xi Lishui and Ying Lihou, they show up anyway. They were out shopping for a new bed for Lishui. After visiting three shopping centres without success, they were on their way to the Trade and Commerce Plaza, but decided to stop by the teashop for tea. They are appalled at the sight that greets them. They take photos with their phones and start to draw up a list of the breakages and damage.

Lihou calls Hai Ruo, but cannot get through either. "Has she been to the teashop today?" she asks Eva.

"I didn't see her when I arrived," Eva says. "Mrs Zhang said when she came to work, Hai-jie was here, but she left in a hurry. Someone from the Tax Bureau came a few days ago, she might have gone to see them."

"But that's no reason to turn off her phone," says Lihou.

In Hai Ruo's absence, they decide to take their list to the police station. It will help back up Wenlai's and xiao-Zhen's statements. So they ask Mrs Zhang to watch the teashop.

Mrs Zhang is not at all sure she is the right person to be left in charge, but the car park attendant offers to stay with her.

As Lishui, Lihou, Eva and xiao-Fang head off across the car park, they spot a woman standing there. It is xiao-Tang.

xiao-Tang is back. Of course they all knew she'd come back eventually, but what a moment to arrive, after all this time!

"xiao-Tang!" Eva gets in first with a big hug. "How I missed you!"

xiao-Tang smiles and teases her, "Really? Or are you just saying so? You don't look very distressed to me!" Eva sucks in her cheeks and sticks out her lips, trying to look haggard.

"You're back!" Lihou exclaims. "When did you get here?"

"Just now," says xiao-Tang.

"Has everything been sorted out?" asks Lihou.

"Sure. I was looking forward to seeing the sun again, but it's wet," says xiao-Tang.

Benwen takes xiao-Tang's hands in hers and checks her wrists for signs of rope marks. Nothing. She flips up xiao-Tang's fringe, but there are no scratches or bruises on her forehead or temples. She smiles and punches xiao-Tang playfully on the shoulder. "Why didn't you come back quicker? You could have stopped the teashop being trashed," she complains.

xiao-Tang looks at the glassless door and the debris inside, and says quietly, "I'm back, Hai-jie…"

But before she can finish speaking, there is a deafening blast. Everyone is knocked sideways, and xiao-Fang bangs her head against the side of a car.

"Earthquake! It's an earthquake!" Lihou cries. She grabs onto the car, but it is rocking wildly. Then debris rains down on them.

Eva is looking at the teashop when the eastern wall, the cubicle wall, suddenly explodes outwards and she sees a body fly out, face skyward, limbs spread-eagled, and then vanish.

The teashop has blown up. First, a spark in the cubicle, then a blinding flash, then a large hole is blasted in the outer wall, and stones, bricks, an iron frame, the cooktop and the cooker, pots and pans, bowls and chopsticks, the rubbish bin, the toilet, clothes and shoes, all spew out, and land all over the car park. It is as if a volcano has erupted. Two kitchen knives go spinning through the air and impale themselves in a tree at the curb, miraculously without causing injury to anyone. But the spout of an iron kettle flies all the way to the newspaper kiosk and hits a fleeing stray cat bang on the head. Without even a whimper, the cat drops dead. A gigantic black mushroom blooms in the air, then takes animal shapes – black bears, an elongated dragon, then a huge whale, before dissipating into wisps of black smoke. All this is accompanied by a cacophony of glass and ceramics falling and breaking.

The blast brings all the traffic to a halt. Passersby freeze momentarily, then there are screams and they sprint in every direction. Drivers brake suddenly and five cars slam into one another. People slowly climb out of the wreckage, some rubbing sprained necks, others checking their cars, unaware that their noses are bleeding. An argument ensues.

In the square, Lihou is the first to get to her feet. She shakes her head, but can't feel any injury and she can still see. She stamps her feet on the muddy ground. "Where on earth did that come from?" Then her eyes alight on a broken chunk of the painted wall, where the remnant of a flying ribbon is still visible. "Lishui! xiao-Tang! Eva! xiao-Fang! Mrs Zhang!" she cries frantically. One by one they stagger to their feet. No one is hurt, but they are all dazed and struck dumb with shock.

35. EVA • XIJING CITY

WHAT CAUSED THE EXPLOSION at the Sojourn Teashop? Rumours are rife. Maybe it had something to do with the current political shenanigans. (The Party chief's fall from grace has been followed by that of a deputy-mayor, then the general secretary of the Xijing Party Committee.) Some people set off firecrackers in celebration, but others are clearly upset – and show it in the oddest ways. The brother-in-law of the Party chief, for example, set his own car on fire in public. A member of the general secretary's staff emptied forty bottles of top-grade Maotai down the toilet. Meanwhile, some business hotshots have turned themselves in for investigation and others have chosen to *paolu*. Of course, everyone knows that Hai Ruo is not related to the disgraced politicos, and never worked for them. But the general secretary did get her a very low rent for her teashop. Rumour has it that she planned the explosion to make people sorry for her and distract attention from her connections.

Others decide there must have been money involved: the Sojourn Teashop was a flourishing business, with a wealthy and powerful clientele, and the owner's friends were all colourful characters. It must have been tempting for a felon. Maybe one sneaked into the teashop pretending to be a customer, planted a bomb underneath the staircase, then made a ransom demand of a million yuan. Probably the owner tried to dissuade the evil-doer by appealing to his better nature and offered a piffling 50,000 yuan, and the bomb went off.

Another theory goes that a fight broke out at the teashop and the kettle on the gas stove boiled over and put the flame out. Gas began to fill the cubicle. Then rubberneckers tried to open its window from the outside so they could get a look in, the front door being blocked. The car park attendant, with a lit cigarette dangling from his lips, went to drive them off but before he could shut the window, the gas caught alight, and BOOM! The old man was sent flying by the blast.

Since no one knows what the truth of the matter is, flocks of busybodies turn up to satisfy their curiosity, taking photos and even livestreaming videos.

The car park attendant regales them with his story, "I was trying to get rid of the crowds. The blast wave sent me flying, all of ten metres! But I never lost consciousness, and I rolled when I landed, so I only had a few cuts and grazes. No broken bones or concussion. And, no, I don't smoke, although I do drink. I did drink half a bottle of *baijiu* before the blast."

The old man must have been convincing because the police do not detain him. In fact, he cordons off the teashop for them. "The investigation's ongoing," he tells anyone who asks.

In Hai Ruo's absence, no one knows what to do with the wrecked premises. The staff still come to work every day, but they just sit around, idle and silent. Only Mrs Zhang is clearly distraught – bursting into tears, pulling at her hair and slapping her cheeks. The sisterhood all show up, at first all together, later on in twos and threes. They don't bother to dress up for their visits these days, though they still wear the jade pendants Hai Ruo gave them.

It is xiao-Fang who first notices something, a small detail. She tells xiao-Tang, and xiao-Tang agrees it is odd. If Lihou arrives and finds Nianchu is at the teashop, she only stays a few moments before leaving. And vice versa. Yike hasn't come since the blast. When they try to call her, her phone is turned off. They have no idea where she is. Then Qiyu gets into an argument with Yinan – something to do with Yike. Yinan gets up and goes, and never shows up again. Xu Qi hasn't come either.

Benwen is indignant. "Fine, let them stay away! People always say husband and wife are like birds, flying off and saving their own skin when disaster strikes. No surprise the sisterhood is breaking up!"

xiao-Tang asks Eva, "Have you asked Yi-laoshi if he knows where Lu-jie is?"

It strikes Eva as strange that Yi Guang hasn't shown up at the teashop. How could he not have heard an explosion so close to his studio? She calls him. His phone is off. He's so close to Hai Ruo, how could he be so callous when she needs him? Is he trying to keep out of trouble? Eva thinks furiously. She keeps calling every few hours, determined to find him. Finally, he picks up.

"I'm in Malaysia with Yike, our plane has just touched down," says Yi Guang.

"What a time to go off on a trip!" Eva yells at him. "And with Lu-jie as well?"

"Feng Ying is dead," Yi Guang says simply.

That afternoon, the teashop is filled with sobs and wails.

Gao Wenlai and Tian Chengbin, Xin Qi's husband, were due to be released after giving their statements but they have to stay another two days because of the blast. They come out at noon on the third day. Chengbin agrees to pay 10,000 yuan in compensation for the damage he caused, but that does not keep him away. He is there every morning, making a spectacle of himself – his face covered in plasters and gentian violet smeared over his swollen lips – hollering at the teashop door, "Xin Qi, Xin Qi! Give me back my belongings!"

They can't chase him away after all that's happened, so they just have to put up with the racket.

Hai Ruo still hasn't come back and there is no news of her whereabouts. She has vanished, like willow catkins gone with the wind, or a sand sculpture washed away by the tide. Surely she is not in real trouble? If her detention is in connection with Mr Qi, so was xiao-Tang's, and she's been released. Of course, Hai Ruo is xiao-Tang's employer and the teashop owner, and she may know more or be more responsible, but all she needs to do is to help them with their enquiries. If the rumours are right and she's being held because of the general secretary, he was no more than a generous patron who fixed up a cheap rent for the premises. The women wonder if they should try to get one of the higher-ups to find out what is happening, but soon relinquish this idea. The only one they can rely on is Yi Guang and he's not around.

One day, Mr Wu drops in, but he can't help either. As he is about to leave, Lishui asks him, "And the Living Buddha, when's he coming?"

But Mr Wu is as non-committal as ever. "I really couldn't say," is all they get.

Mrs Zhang goes into the wrecked cubicle to have another good cry. Benwen and xiao-Tang call to her, "Please come out, it's much too dangerous to sit in there." But Mrs Zhang is slapping herself across the face in despair.

Eva finds it all very upsetting. She goes off in search of Xin Qi.

A few days ago, she visited Xin Qi and warned her to stay away from the teashop for a while. Now she finds her in her rented room, crying. "I feel like a caged animal. I've got to get away!"

"Me too," says Eva.

"Hai-jie is such an amazing woman, she's capable of anything," says Xin Qi. "So how come she hasn't managed to get out?"

"I don't know," says Eva. "Hai-jie has a web of connections, but now she's ended up caught in the web herself."

"But she's so kind, the kindest person I've ever met!"

"She is kind," Eva agrees. "And we all admire her for what she does and who she is. But I'm beginning to doubt if it adds up to anything at all."

"Are you saying she's failed?"

"I can see her, years from now, as just another woman, a mother, someone who once ran a small business and headed up a sisterhood."

"OK, but what should we do?"

"I don't know."

"Why don't we go somewhere nice and take our minds off all this?" asks Xin Qi.

"But where? I came to Xijing to take my mind off things. I should probably leave."

Tears well up in Xin Qi's eyes. "There'll be no one to chat to if you leave! Take me with you? Please!"

"You want to come to St Petersburg with me?"

"Sure, why not? My only trip abroad was South Korea with Xi-jie."

"Then let's go together. I'll take care of your food and lodging," offers Eva.

"Do you mean it?"

"Of course. You've got a passport?"

"Yes, I do."

Eva purchases plane tickets to St Petersburg for them both. She is careful not to breathe a word to anyone else about their plans. Four days go by. Hai Ruo hasn't come back, nor has Yi Guang, or Yike. Eva and Xin Qi catch a taxi to the airport.

That evening, the air quality is horrendous. A few days ago, there were only patches of smog but now it's turned into a pea-souper and has invaded every nook and cranny of the city. It is maddening, choking, deadening... But no matter how panicky and fearful it makes you, you just have to put up with it. Darkness has fallen unusually early. Vehicles turn on their lights and inch forward. It is as if they are driving through a mudflow. Everything outside the taxi windows is a blur. Eva and Xin Qi catch fragmented glimpses of the ancient parapets, buildings, pavement trees, electricity poles, advertising hoardings, and people coming and going, with or without masks. They drive over the old moat, over the Vermilion Bird Flyover, then through the Fengyang Tunnel. They seem to hear cries and moans from outside. But it is not crying and moaning, it is someone singing an aria from Qinqiang Opera. Eva presses her nose against the car window. When she sees a mass of flowers, she knows they're on the Southern Ring Road. The municipal government has made it into a Flower Highway, with rose bushes lining both sides for half a dozen kilometres. The shrubs are no longer as showy in the smog and the gloom, but the car headlights pick out splashes of colour – brilliant white, Buddha yellow and blood-red blooms.

"Is this the Flower Highway?" asks Xin Qi.

"Yes," says Eva, and suddenly she is in floods of tears.

"What's wrong? Why are you crying?"

"Everything! The Living Buddha hasn't arrived, Hai-jie isn't back and Yi-laoshi is away. I never wanted to leave like this."

Xin Qi cannot think of anything to say.

"Xijing never belonged to me. It's time for me to go," sighs Eva.

"I always said you shouldn't have left St Petersburg," Xin Qi says.

"I don't regret coming. You came here from elsewhere too, when you left the countryside."

"You came right when the smog's at its worst. In just two weeks –

three at the most – it'll be windier and warmer, and then it'll be gone."

Xin Qi stops, then asks, "Are you saying that I'm like a fly drawn to Xijing by its smell?"

"No. I mean you can gain a lot by coming here, or so I hoped. But I'm going back home having lost everything."

"Lost? What have you lost?"

Eva says nothing. She puts her arms around Xin Qi and sobs uncontrollably.

Eva has cried herself awake. The apartment is deserted. Outside the window, a plume of smoke rises from a tall chimney and becomes a cloud. A plane passes overhead.

AFTERWORD
JIA PINGWA

THE SOJOURN TEASHOP is probably the last novel I will write before my seventieth birthday. I finished it just as the summer heat abated. It is around 210,000 Chinese characters long, and took me an entire two years to write, longer than any of my previous works. I normally write two drafts of a novel before completing it, but for this one, I wrote four. As I grow older, I find I am getting more demanding, both with other people and, even more so, with myself. I am never satisfied with how my story is shaping up. The less time I have left, the more I seem to waste.

The Sojourn Teashop takes place in Xijing city, a fictionalised version of Xi'an, with Xi'an's street names. I have been living in Xi'an for more than forty years. I'm as at home in the city as I am in my own flat, where I can find my way around – from the sitting room to the kitchen, in and out of rooms, and into every nook and cranny – even on the darkest of nights. For some reason, I have not written much about Xi'an until now. In fact, many readers regard me as a rural, not an urban, writer. But the truth is that there are no such clear-cut distinctions in writing fiction today: in the twenty-first century, life in the city and the countryside are so inextricably linked that you cannot say we come from one or the other. We come from both.

The idea of writing *The Sojourn Teashop* first came to me when the teashop downstairs moved away. Over the years, I used to go there for tea twice a day, before lunch and after dinner. Once you've tasted fine tea, you're hooked. You'll never be satisfied with any brew of lesser quality. But just as I had become a true aficionado of tea, the teashop moved away. It had become part of me by then, like breathing; you take it for granted when you are healthy and only notice how crucial it is to keep drawing breath when you fall sick.

That teashop offered some of the city's finest leaves. The owner was actually a woman. She was good-looking but she wore no make-up and dressed in an entirely neutral fashion. She seemed androgynous – and I realised how people like her can truly stand out from the crowd. She was always surrounded by a large group of women friends, all of whom carried themselves with dignity and appeared at ease with themselves. I used to wonder, why is it that men don't have such close friendship groups but women do, and this one has such a big group of friends? Then I realised that women have so much more on their minds than men do. No matter how remarkable a woman is, there are times when she needs to vent, and that's what friends are for. Sometimes, all of the owner's friends would gather at the teashop, and those were splendid occasions. If one model walks down the street, one or two people might turn around for a better look, but put a dozen models together, and everyone will be gawking. When I saw her and her companions at the teashop, their aura was so bright I was almost afraid to get close to them. Even if I did, I found it impossible to keep up with their brilliant repartee. They were full of vitality, loved fashion, valued their freedom and independence and, above all, put themselves first. They were a world entirely of their own, their ravines as deep as our peaks were high, their waters holding as many fish as our clouds sheltered birds.

But now, the teashop has moved away. I do not know whether it is because of the economic downturn, exacerbated by anti-corruption campaigns, so that the market for the costliest high-end tea is all but gone, or simply that soaring rents and salaries has made it impossible to keep such businesses afloat. And I am left to mourn its departure, gazing at my empty teacup and the guttering candle.

These women have so many stories to tell, but they are not necessarily what *The Sojourn Teashop* is about. The narrative thread follows Xia Zihua's stay in hospital until her death, and along the way, we get to know a dozen women. I explore their relationship to themselves, to each other, and to the community in which they live, as well as how, within the web of these relationships, they find their own identities and position in society. In the words of one ancient text,

> A narrow strip of land to the east of the wall is about two *mu* in size. Chopping away the undergrowth and levelling the rough ground, I encircled it with a low earthen wall, planting elms and willows around the outside, with a few peach trees in among them.

This describes the kind of existence these women have, both physical and spiritual. The trees are draped with dodder vines and threads of old man's beard, and the leaves shimmer, iridescent in the dappled sunlight. In the same way, the narrative of this novel follows qi lines, and the nodes of the story are formed where the energy collects. We also have elements of the uncanny: the appearance of Lu Yike's father, and the mysterious and beautiful manifestation of Feng Ying's ghost. This adds another dimension to this human world: the supernatural. Time and space are constantly transforming, making everything possible in this world of impermanence.

The Sojourn Teashop is still rooted in the details of daily life, just as all my fiction is. What is different this time is that there is more dialogue between the characters. There are meetings and reports, advice and confidences, discussions and arguments, and of course chit-chat and gossip. We humans form our world by talking and listening, although of course we cannot hear as the Avalokiteshvara who discerns every sound within and beyond the universe. To paraphrase *The Lotus Sutra*, although humans do not have the divine faculty of hearing, they will always understand human voices through the ears given by their parents.

Although there is no first-person narrator in *The Sojourn Teashop*, I, the author, am actually somewhere above the teashop – like the swallow that lives not with but alongside us, nesting on the beam, looking down from above. I listen to the women of the sisterhood talking about themselves, about other people around them, and how people talk about them. I see the changing seasons, the sun and the rain, the ice and the snow, the summer heat and the winter chill, the humdrum rhythms of daily life, birth and death, joys and sorrows... and I have come to see life as an unending cycle of suffering, in which we experience the karma generated by past good and evil deeds, in our lives and the environment in which we live. It is evident that the universe is composed of sentient beings, and in literature, writers describe them as they perceive them; they describe their lakṣana. By writing about the attributes of living creatures, we will necessarily form vijñāna, that is, an understanding of this world, and such an understanding finds expression in the meaning, philosophy and poetry of literature.

In writing the dialogue in this novel, I have deliberately made my characters speak just like ordinary people do: a comment here, a sentence there, spoken in straightforward, even awkward words. I have avoided making their language self-consciously literary, or adding absurdist flourishes or embellishments. This might put some readers off. But this is precisely how I want to tell the story.

In this day and age, it is hard to write a novel without having a broad vision or a modernist consciousness. Every writer knows this, and for a very long time, we have been trying to make ourselves more foreign, more modernist. And yet the deeper we delve into realism, the more we understand surrealism, and vice versa. Realism is the grand river of literature, complete with upper, middle and lower reaches, dotted with bends, shoals, pools, gorges and docks. Surrealism is the literary expression of our confusion and doubts, our rebellions and struggles to free ourselves, all of which arise from our environment and society and the age to which we belong, especially when we are young.

I believe that the unpolished, direct and simple language of this novel is something the readers can get a grip on. I believe that the effect is both affirmative and powerful, and gives the novel enduring qualities. I have tried to enrich and strengthen my writing by incorporating surrealist elements that are appropriate to my homeland and my personal circumstances. Your breadth of vision determines how much you will see, and a truly broad vision brings with it tranquillity.

I have written so many novels, and each one is different. My style is not to repeat but to try to grasp and transmit the essence of life in my writing. *The Sojourn Teashop* is my attempt at pole-vaulting, where every extra centimetre counts as success, and every breakthrough is accompanied by failure. Though that never seems to discourage the great Russian pole vaulter Yelena Isinbayeva.

AFTERWORD

When the great painter Qi Baishi turned eighty, he began to inscribe his exact age as part of his signature. Perhaps this was a way of showing he no longer cared, or of showing off. However, the reason that I attempted to focus on a group of women in *The Sojourn Teashop* was precisely because I lacked confidence. Throughout the writing, more often than not, it was not me writing them, but them writing me – and the cracks show through. When I got to the end of the book, what still puzzled me was that women love being in love, and yet these women stayed single, or divorced and never remarried. Why? In this ever-changing world, maybe it is impossible for one's feelings to remain steadfast. Or in the words I read somewhere, "Don't say I love you or you love me, just say we're both hungry."

I remain perplexed. The truth remains enshrouded in mystery just as the smog blankets this city through the months of winter and spring.

September 2019

ABOUT THE AUTHOR
JIA PINGWA

Born in 1952, Jia Pingwa stands with Mo Yan and Yu Hua as one of the biggest names in contemporary Chinese literature. He has a huge following on the Chinese mainland, as well as in Hong Kong and Taiwan. His fiction focuses on the lives of common people, particularly in his home province of Shaanxi, and is well-known for being unafraid to explore the realm of the sexual. His bestseller *Ruined City* was banned for many years for that same reason, and pirated copies sold on the street for several thousand yuan apiece. The novel was finally unbanned in 2009, one year after Jia won the Mao Dun Award for his 2005 novel *Shaanxi Opera*. Over recent years, a steady stream of his works have been published in English translation.

ABOUT THE TRANSLATOR • NICKY HARMAN

Passionate about spreading Chinese literature to English readers, Nicky Harman has translated the works of many renowned Chinese authors into English. They include Anni Baobei's *The Road of Others*, Chan Koon-Chung's *The Unbearable Dreamworld of Champa the Driver*, Chen Xiwo's *Book of Sins*, Han Dong's *A Phone Call from Dalian: Collected Poems*, Dorothy Tse's *Snow and Shadow*, Xinran's *Letter from an Unknown Chinese Mother*, Xu Xiaobin's *Crystal Wedding*, Xu Zhiyuan's *Paper Tiger*, Yan Ge's *The Chili Bean Paste Clan* and Jia Pingwa's *Broken Wings*.

Several of Harman's translations have been recipients of an English PEN Translates award, and she has also won the 2020 Special Book Award of China; the 2015 Mao Tai Cup People's Literature Chinese-English translation prize; and first prize in the 2013 China International Translation Contest. When not translating, she promotes contemporary Chinese fiction to the general English-language reader through the website Paper-Republic.org. She also blogs, gives talks, mentors new translators, teaches summer school and judges translation competitions. She lives in the United Kingdom and tweets as the China Fiction Bookclub @cfbcuk.

ABOUT THE TRANSLATOR • JUN LIU

Currently based in Auckland, New Zealand, Jun Liu is passionate about introducing Chinese literature, arts and culture to the rest of the world. She has translated more than 20 full length books into English since the 1990s. Liu has a keen interest in Jia Pingwa, having read the majority of his works, and she visited the author at his studio in 2010 to discuss his upcoming novel *Ancient Kiln*. In 2016 she helped Nicky Harman with her translation of Jia's *Happy Dreams* by checking against the original, with particular attention to dialect and cultural references. In 2018, she translated an excerpt of Jia's *Tiangou* for *Chinese Arts & Letters*. Liu entered literary translation in 2013 with a collection of essays and stories by 1940's iconic authors Lao She, Feng Zikai and Zhang Tianyi. In 2017, she cotranslated Uyghur author Alat Asem's *Confessions of a Jade Lord* with Bruce Humes. While editing the weekly Reading Page at China Daily in Beijing, Liu interviewed other leading Chinese writers like Mo Yan, Chen Zhongshi, Chi Zijian and A Lai. She also interviewed Zhou Ruchang, a leading expert on *A Dream of Red Mansions*.

About **Sino**ist Books

We hope you enjoyed this tale of love, loss and loyalty in a changing China.

SINOIST BOOKS brings the best of Chinese fiction to English-speaking readers. We aim to create a greater understanding of Chinese culture and society and provide an outlet for the ideas and creativity of the country's most talented authors.

To let us know what you thought of this book, or to learn more about the diverse range of exciting Chinese fiction in translation we publish, find us online. If you're as passionate about Chinese literature as we are, then we'd love to hear your thoughts!

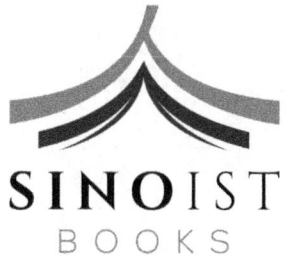

sinoistbooks.com
@sinoistbooks